discover america
american revolution
french indian war
industrial revolution

HOLT
NORTH CAROLINA!

James L. Leloudis

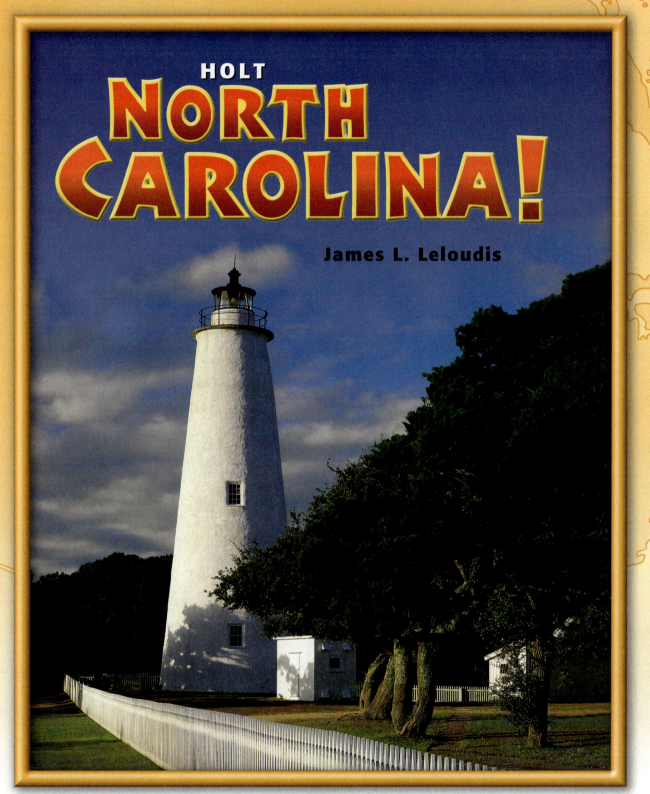

HOLT, RINEHART AND WINSTON

A Harcourt Education Company

Austin • Orlando • Chicago • New York • Toronto • London • San Diego

EDITORIAL

Sue Miller,
Director
Steven Hayes,
Executive Editor
Robert Wehnke,
Managing Editor
Dr. Melissa Langley Biegert,
Project Editor

Technology Resources
Annette Saunders,
Internet Editor

Fact Checking
Bob Fullilove,
Editor
Jenny Rose,
Associate Editor

Support
Gina Tasby-Rogers,
Administrative Assistant
Maricella Edwards,
Assistant Editorial Coordinator

Manuscript Development and Editorial Services
The Quarasan Group, Inc.

EDITORIAL PERMISSIONS

Carrie Jones,
Permissions Supervisor

DESIGN

Book Design
Diane Motz,
Senior Design Director
David Hernandez,
Designer

Image Acquisitions
Curtis Riker,
Director
Tim Taylor,
Photo Research Supervisor
Elaine Tate,
Art Buyer Supervisor

Design New Media
Kimberly Cammerata,
Design Manager
Grant Davidson,
Designer

Graphic Services
Kristen Darby,
Director
Jeff Robinson,
Senior Ancillary Designer

Cover Design
Jason Wilson,
Designer

Ancillary Cover Design
Richard Metzger,
Design Director
Chris Smith,
Senior Designer

Design, Photo Research, and Page Production
The Quarasan Group, Inc.

PRODUCTION

Beth Prevelige,
Senior Production Manager
Gene Rumann,
Production Manager
Vivian Hess,
Administrative Assistant

COVER: *Ocracoke Lighthouse was built in 1823. It is one of the oldest lighthouses still in operation in North Carolina.*

Cover photo: Ocracoke Lighthouse copyright © Laurence Parent

Copyright © 2003 by Holt, Rinehart and Winston

All rights reserved. No part of this publication may be reproduced or transmitted in any form or by any means, electronic or mechanical, including photocopy, recording, or any information storage and retrieval system, without permission in writing from the publisher.

Requests for permission to make copies of any part of the work should be mailed to the following address: Permissions Department, Holt, Rinehart and Winston, 10801 N. Mopac Expressway, Building 3, Austin, Texas 78759.

For acknowledgments, see page 340, which is an extension of the copyright page.

Printed in the United States of America

ISBN 0-03-068248-7

5 6 7 8 9 751 11 10 09 08 07

ABOUT THE GENERAL EDITOR

Dr. James L. Leloudis

Dr. James L. Leloudis is an associate professor of history at the University of North Carolina at Chapel Hill, specializing in the history of North Carolina. Dr. Leloudis also serves as the Associate Dean for Honors, College of Arts and Sciences, and director of the James M. Johnston Center for Undergraduate Excellence at the university. He has written numerous award-winning works on the history of the state, including *Like a Family: The Making of a Southern Cotton Mill World,* co-authored with Jacquelyn Dowd Hall, et al., and *Schooling in the New South: Pedagogy, Self, and Society in North Carolina, 1880–1920.* His most recent research focuses on the history of War on Poverty programs in North Carolina.

EDITORIAL REVIEW BOARD

Dr. David C. Dennard

Dr. David C. Dennard is an associate professor of history at East Carolina University and serves as director of the Institute for Historical and Cultural Research at the university. He specializes in African American history and has had numerous articles published on the topic. He also served as a contributor for the book *African American History in the Press, 1851–1899.* He is currently working on a study of African American North Carolinians during the Civil War, as well as editing a volume of African American preacher tales.

Barbara McAllister

Barbara McAllister is the Language Arts/Social Studies Resource Teacher for middle and high schools in New Hanover County. She has more than 30 years teaching experience in public schools and specializes in reading. She has attended the Reading Master's Program at the University of North Carolina at Wilmington.

Madie M. McDougald

Madie M. McDougald is director of Secondary Education for the Harnett County Schools, and has been teaching since 1973. She is also supervisor for the Scoggins Program for troubled youth in Sanford. Ms. McDougald has served in numerous leadership roles in the county and state, including coordinating the "Closing the Gap" program, the History Bowl, Governors School, and the North Carolina Teaching Fellows Program.

Dr. Sally G. McMillen

Dr. Sally G. McMillen is a professor of history at Davidson College. She specializes in southern women's history. Her publications include the books *Motherhood in the Old South: Pregnancy, Childbirth and Infant Rearing; Southern Women: Black and White in the Old South;* and *'To Raise Up the South': The Sunday School in Black and White Churches, 1865–1915.* Dr. McMillen won the Hamilton-Hunter Excellence in Teaching Award in 2000.

Dr. Myra L. Pennell

Dr. Myra L. Pennell is an associate professor of social studies education in the history department at Appalachian State University. After serving as a classroom history teacher for several years in Caldwell County schools, she now specializes in training social studies teachers. Her publications include "Improving Student Participation in History Lectures: Suggestions for Successful Questioning," in *Teaching History: A Journal of Methods.* She is currently working on a project entitled "Helping Beginning Teachers to Develop a Procedure for Improving Reading Skills in the Social Studies Classroom."

HOLT NORTH CAROLINA! CONTENTS

Atlas x

UNIT 1 Beginnings (Beginnings–1663) xii
Young People in History *Young Native Americans in North Carolina* 1

European weapons of the 1500s

CHAPTER 1
The Land and Its People
(Beginnings–1500) 2

1 The Geography of North Carolina 3
   Connecting to Geography Hurricanes 6
2 The First North Carolinians 9
   That's Interesting! Beringia 9
   That's Interesting! Ancient Peoples 10
3 Native Americans in
   North Carolina by 1500 13
   Global Connections
   Carolina Place Names 17
Chapter Review 18

CHAPTER 2
Europeans Arrive in North Carolina (1400s–1663) 20

1 European Exploration 21
   Connecting to Literature "The Young
   Sailor" by Giovanni da Verrazano 23
2 Exploring North Carolina 25
   That's Interesting!
   Hernando de Soto 26
3 The Effects of Exploration 30
4 English Exploration and Settlement 33
   Historical Document *Barlowe's
   Report to Raleigh* 35
   Biography: *Walter Raleigh* 36
Chapter Review 40

Carolina Charter of 1663 and the Blue Ridge Mountains

UNIT 2 Colonial North Carolina (1663–1815) 42
Young People in History *Growing Up in Colonial North Carolina* 43

CHAPTER 3
A Proprietary Colony
(1663–1729) 44

1 Life under the Lords Proprietors 45
   Historical Document *The Carolina Charter of 1663* 46
2 Conflicts Within the Colony 49
   That's Interesting! *Thomas Eastchurch* 50
   That's Interesting! *The Tuscarora Indians* 54
3 North Carolina on Its Own 55
   Biography *Anne Bonny* 56
4 Becoming a Royal Colony 59
   Biography *John Carteret, Earl Granville* 61
Chapter Review 62

CHAPTER 4
The Culture of Colonial North Carolina
(1663–1770) 64

1 Immigrants and Migrants 65
   Biography *Flora Macdonald* 66
2 The Economy and Social Structure 69
   Connecting to Science and Technology *North Carolina's First Printing Press* 73
3 Internal Conflicts 74
   Biography *William Tryon* 75
Chapter Review 78

CHAPTER 5
The Fight for Independence
(1754–1783) 80

1 Growing Conflicts 81
   Historical Document *The Albany Plan of Union* 82
   That's Interesting! *First in Freedom* 84
2 The Road to Revolution 85
   Biography *Penelope Barker* 86
   Historical Document *The Mecklenburg Resolves* 87
   Historical Document *The Halifax Resolves* 89
3 Fighting the War 91
   Biography *Robert Howe* 92
   Connecting to Economics *Financing the War* 94
4 Establishing Peace 96
Chapter Review 100

CHAPTER 6
Forming a New Nation and State
(1776–1815) 102

1 Ideas about Government 103
   Historical Document *The North Carolina Constitution of 1776* 105
2 Forming a National Government 108
   Biography *James Iredell* 110
3 Forming a State Government 112
   Biography *Nathaniel Macon* 115
4 The War of 1812 116
   Global Connections *Embargoes* 117
   That's Interesting! *The Star-Spangled Banner* 118
Chapter Review 120

Patriot troops at Valley Forge

UNIT 3 Antebellum North Carolina (1790–1860) 122
Young People in History *Life in Antebellum Times* 123

CHAPTER 7
Political Shifts
(1815–1860) 124

1 The "Rip Van Winkle" State 125
   Connecting to Economics *Monoculture* .. 127
2 Reactions to Jackson's Policies 129
   That's Interesting! *Andrew Jackson* 129
   Connecting to Geography
   The Qualla Boundary 131
3 The Constitution of 1835 133
   Biography *Archibald D. Murphey* 134
4 North Carolina Under Whig Control 137
5 The Decline of the Whigs 142
   Biography *David S. Reid* 143
Chapter Review 146

African American slave wedding ceremony

CHAPTER 8
Life and Culture
(1815–1860) 148

1 Religious Movements 149
   Historical Document *Report of
the Great Revival* 151
   That's Interesting! *Camp Meetings* 152
2 Folkways and Customs 153
3 A Literary Movement 156
   That's Interesting! *Reader Sales* 157
   Connecting to Literature *Wood Notes* ... 158
4 The Free Black Community 160
   Connecting to Literature *The Poems
of George Moses Horton* 162
   Biography *John Chavis* 163
Chapter Review 164

CHAPTER 9
Southern Systems in North Carolina
(1790–1860) 166

1 The Economy 167
   Connecting to Economics
Alamance Plaids 168
2 Life under Slavery 173
   Biography *David Walker* 174
   Global Connections
The Demand for Slave Labor 176
   Biography *Lunsford Lane* 177
3 Resistance to Slavery 178
   Connecting to Literature *"The Slave in
the Dismal Swamp" by Henry Wadsworth
Longfellow* 180
   Biography *Levi Coffin* 181
Chapter Review 182

North Carolina governor David L. Swain

UNIT 4 War and Reunification (1800–1877) 184
Young People in History Life during the Civil War 185

CHAPTER 10
North Carolina and National Events
(1800–1861) 186

1. The Industrial Revolution 187
   - **That's Interesting!**
     The Industrial Revolution 188
   - **Connecting to Science and Technology**
     The *Prometheus* 189
2. Westward Migration 191
   - **Biography** James K. Polk 194
3. The Growing Conflict over Slavery 195
4. Secession 199

Chapter Review 202

Steam engine

CHAPTER 11
The Civil War
(1861–1865) 204

1. The War Begins 205
   - **Biography** Daniel Harvey Hill 206
2. Fighting in North Carolina 209
   - **Connecting to Science and Technology**
     The Gatling Gun 211
3. The Home Front 214
   - **Biography** Rose O'Neal Greenhow 216
4. The End of the War 218
   - **That's Interesting!** Gunpowder 220

Chapter Review 222

North Carolina politician John Pool

CHAPTER 12
Reconstruction in North Carolina
(1865–1877) 224

1. Freedpeople after the War 225
   - **Connecting to Geography** James City 227
2. Life during Reconstruction 229
   - **Biography** Albion Tourgée 230
   - **Connecting to Literature**
     A Fool's Errand by Albion Tourgée 231
3. Attacks on Reconstruction 234
   - **That's Interesting!**
     The Freedman's Bank 235
   - **Historical Documents**
     The Kirk-Holden War 237
   - **That's Interesting!**
     Pleading the Fifth 238

Chapter Review 240

Gatling gun

Contents **vii**

UNIT 5 Modern Times (1870–Present) 242
Young People in History *From Farms and Factories to Schoolhouses* 243

CHAPTER 13
North Carolina in the Industrial Age
(1870–1930) 244

1 The Rise of North Carolina Industries 245
   Biography R.J. Reynolds 247
2 Life in the New South 249
   Connecting to Economics The North Carolina Mutual Life Insurance Co. 250
   That's Interesting! Trinity and Duke 251
3 A Changing Society 253
   Connecting to Science and Technology The Wright Brothers' Airplane 254
   That's Interesting! George H. White 255
4 World War I and Its Aftermath 258
   Connecting to Literature Look Homeward Angel by Thomas Wolfe 260
   Biography Harriet Morehead Berry 261
Chapter Review 262

Destroying liquor during Prohibition; children during the Great Depression

CHAPTER 14
Depression and War
(1929–1945) 264

1 The Great Depression 265
   Biography Jane Simpson McKimmon 266
   That's Interesting! Hoover Carts 266
2 World War II 269
   That's Interesting! The Rose Bowl 272
3 Life during Hard Times 274
   Biography Rufus G. Herring 275
Chapter Review 278

CHAPTER 15
A Changing State
(1945–1970) 280

1 A Postwar Economy 281
2 Social Shifts 284
   That's Interesting! Textbooks 285
   Connecting to Literature I Am One of You Forever by Fred Chappell 287
   Biography Edward R. Murrow 288
3 Political Changes 289
   That's Interesting! Jesse Jackson 291
   Historical Documents Account of the Greensboro Sit-in 292
Chapter Review 294

CHAPTER 16
A Modern State
(1970–the Present) 296

1 A Diverse State 297
   Biography Jesse Helms 298
2 The New Economy 301
   Global Connections North Carolina and the Global Economy 302
   That's Interesting! Michael Jordan 303
3 North Carolina Today 305
   Biography Elizabeth Dole 308
Chapter Review 310

North Carolina quarter and Charlotte skyline

ALMANAC 312–323
Glossary 324–328
Index 329–339
Acknowledgments 340

MAPS
North Carolina: Political x
North Carolina: Physical xi
Geographic Regions of North Carolina 5
Native Americans in North Carolina by 1500 14
Explorations of North Carolina 26
The Thirteen Colonies 37
Early Settlements in North Carolina 41
North Carolina Towns by 1740 57
The Great Wagon Road 65
Ethnic Groups in North Carolina (1685–1765) 67
Revolutionary War Battles in North Carolina 93
The State of Franklin 121
North Carolina Roads and Railroads by 1860 139
The Slave Population in North Carolina in 1860 175
The Election of 1860 203
The Civil War in North Carolina 210
Voting Patterns in North Carolina, 1868–1872 241
The Piedmont Crescent 246
Selected Military Installations in North Carolina during World War II 271
Interstate Highways in North Carolina 285
Manufacturing Centers in North Carolina in 2000 303

CHARTS AND GRAPHS
Decline in North Carolina's Native Population after 1500 32
The Eight Lords Proprietors 46
Africans in North Carolina, 1717–1790 68
Naval Stores Exports from Colonial North Carolina 70
North Carolina Tar and Pitch Exports 79
Reform Organizations in North Carolina 147
Occupations in North Carolina Among Free Workers in 1860 171
The Slave and Free Population of North Carolina, 1790–1860 183
North Carolina Deaths in the Civil War 223
North Carolina Farms, 1860–1900 234
Tobacco and Cotton Production in North Carolina, 1870–1900 263
Ethnic Population of North Carolina in 2000 300
North Carolina's Voting Patterns in Presidential Elections 311
Time Line of North Carolina 312–313
State Symbols 314
State Government 315
Governors 316–318
Counties 319–322
North Carolina Population: 1660–2025 323
Population of North Carolina's Ten Largest Cities: 1970–2000 323

INTERNET CONNECTS
The Land and Its People 19
Europeans in North Carolina 41
A Proprietary Colony 63
The Culture of Colonial North Carolina 79
The Fight for Independence 101
Forming a New Nation and State 121
Political Shifts 147
Life and Culture 165
Southern Systems in North Carolina 183
North Carolina and National Events 203
The Civil War 223
Reconstruction in North Carolina 241
North Carolina in the Industrial Age 263
Depression and War 279
A Changing State 295
A Modern State 311

North Carolina Atlas

Political Map

NORTH CAROLINA Atlas
Physical Map

Legend:
- Coastal Plain
- Piedmont
- Mountains

Atlas xi

UNIT 1
Beginnings
(Beginnings–1663)

CHAPTER 1 The Land and Its People (Beginnings–1500)

CHAPTER 2 Europeans Arrive in North Carolina (1400s–1663)

Young People

IN HISTORY

Young Native Americans in North Carolina

The Native Americans who lived in North Carolina were not all the same. However, all Native American groups required children to gain certain skills before they were accepted as adults. Children had to learn basic survival skills. They also learned about their cultural heritage and developed their spiritual lives.

Education did not take place in schools, but through the daily influence of elders in a child's clan, or extended family. For purposes of kinship, children were not considered to be blood relatives of their fathers or grandfathers. In fact, all Native American tribes in North Carolina were matrilineal—meaning that children traced their ancestry through their mother's family.

Boys were trained and educated primarily by their uncles on their mothers' side. Special roles were often passed down through generations within the same family. One Indian priest explained, "I am now [teaching] them [boys who are my near relation] all sorts of doctoring, for when I die they'll be in my place." Other boys might be trained for leadership roles in the war council, or as dancers or singers. Girls received training from their female relatives. They learned how to make meals, baskets, pottery, beadwork, and clothing. Women also taught girls important information about seeds, plants, crops, and the weather.

In the Cherokee Nation baby girls were given names chosen by their maternal grandmothers or oldest female relatives. Girls kept their names for life, unless they experienced some great event. However, boys chose new names for themselves—usually that of an animal—at the age of 16 or 17, when they became warriors. At this age, boys joined war parties—small groups that waged war on other clans. Boys were not considered to have achieved manhood until they received a war rank. This usually did not happen until their late 20s. Some Cherokee women also fought as warriors.

Girls could marry after they reached the age of 12 or 13. Boys usually waited longer, but they often married by the age of 20. Once married, husbands moved in with their wives' families.

Young American Indians used the natural environment to supply the materials they needed for daily life. These beautifully worked moccasins are made mostly of smoked hide.

If You Were There What skills would you have needed to learn as a child in a Native American group?

LEFT PAGE: North Carolina's beautiful landscape was home to ancient civilizations, as well as to the Native American groups that witnessed the arrival of Europeans in the 1500s.

CHAPTER 1
The Land and Its People
(Beginnings–1500)

North Carolina's Chimney Rock

Build on What You Know

Geography has a great effect on our lives. For example, climate and geography influence what foods are available in a certain area or what leisure activities are possible. In this chapter, you will learn about the geography of North Carolina and how it affected the lives of the first North Carolinians.

What's Your Opinion?

Do you **agree** or **disagree** with the following statements? Support your point of view in your journal.

- **Geography** Geography is an important factor in settlement and development.
- **Science, Technology & Society** Geographic resources do not affect quality of life.
- **Economics** Trade is a poor way for people to obtain the things they want or need.

Section 1

The Geography of North Carolina

Read to Discover
1. How do landforms in North Carolina's regions differ?
2. What factors shape the climate of North Carolina?
3. What natural resources are important in North Carolina?
4. How has geography affected North Carolina's settlement and development?

Define
- regions
- terrain
- altitude
- plateau
- barrier islands
- inlets
- groundwater

Identify
- Mountains
- Piedmont
- Coastal Plain
- Blue Ridge
- Tidewater
- Outer Banks

The Story Continues

North Carolina has been greatly shaped by its geography. In fact, much of its history has been the story of people working to adapt to their surroundings. Geography strongly affects how North Carolinians in different parts of the state live even today.

Springtime highlights the natural beauty of the Blue Ridge Mountains.

Did You KNOW?

Mount Mitchell, in Yancey County, reaches an altitude of 6,684 feet. Its peak is the highest point in the eastern half of North America.

The Regions of North Carolina

North Carolina is our nation's twenty-eighth largest state. Geographers divide its more than 52,000 square miles into three **regions** based on their **terrain**, or physical features of the land. A region is an area of land in which places have the same basic characteristics. From west to east, North Carolina's regions are: the **Mountains**, the **Piedmont**, and the **Coastal Plain**. The terrain of each region is different from that of the others.

The Mountains The mountainous region of western North Carolina is part of the Appalachian mountain system. This chain of mountains extends through eastern North America from Canada into central Alabama. The eastern part is called the **Blue Ridge**. The North Carolina portion of the Blue Ridge is about 200 miles long and from 15 to 55 miles wide. It is an area of steep ridges, spectacular waterfalls, and narrow, deep valleys. In all, it covers some 6,000 square miles, or about 10 percent of the state.

At the region's western edge is the Great Smoky Mountains range, which North Carolina shares with Tennessee. The most important range in the eastern part of the region is the Black Mountains. The Blue Ridge contains the most rugged terrain of the entire Appalachian system. Forty-three peaks in North Carolina have an **altitude**, or height above sea level, of more than 6,000 feet. More than 80 others in North Carolina are between 5,000 and 6,000 feet high.

The Piedmont East of the Blue Ridge is a region called the Piedmont. It is part of a broad belt of land that extends from New Jersey to Alabama. The term "piedmont" means "at the base of the mountains." This is a good name for this huge **plateau**. A plateau is a raised, fairly level area of land. Totaling some 22,000 square miles, North Carolina's Piedmont covers about 45 percent of the state. At the foot of the mountains, its altitude is about 1,500 feet. From there, a series of low ridges and hills slope downward and eastward for about 200 miles. Along its eastern edge, the Piedmont is only 300 or 400 feet above sea level.

Cape Hatteras, shown here, forms part of the Outer Banks of North Carolina. The lighthouse here is the tallest in the United States at 208 feet.

4 Chapter 1

The Coastal Plain North Carolina's third major region is the Coastal Plain. It lies between the Piedmont and the Atlantic Ocean. Covering some 21,000 square miles, the Coastal Plain is about the size of the Piedmont. However, the low rolling hills in its western parts quickly give way to level land that extends all the way to the coast.

Tidewater Most of the eastern Coastal Plain is less than 30 feet above sea level. Because ocean tides have had a great effect on this low-lying area, it is sometimes called the **Tidewater**. Salt water flows into rivers with the tides and water levels rise and fall with the tides. Many swamps and natural lakes dot this region. The Tidewater extends inland 30 miles to 80 miles, depending on how close the land is to sea level.

Outer Banks A chain of low, narrow islands called the **Outer Banks** stretches 175 miles south from Virginia and makes up the eastern limit of the Coastal Plain. Some of the islands are more than 20 miles from the coast. Other **barrier islands**—islands that protect a mainland from an ocean—line the southern coast but are closer to shore. Access to the ocean is through **inlets**, or narrow water passages, between the islands.

✔ **READING CHECK** **Finding the Main Idea** What basic difference defines North Carolina's three regions?

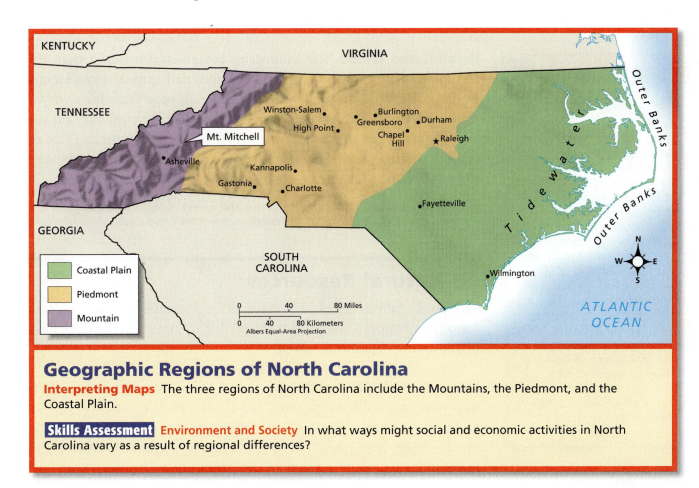

Geographic Regions of North Carolina

Interpreting Maps The three regions of North Carolina include the Mountains, the Piedmont, and the Coastal Plain.

Skills Assessment **Environment and Society** In what ways might social and economic activities in North Carolina vary as a result of regional differences?

The Land and Its People

Fly fishing in the French Broad River, Pisgah National Forest

★ Climate and Weather

North Carolina is known for its pleasant climate. Summers are long and winters are short. Temperatures in Fahrenheit average 62° on the Coastal Plain, 60° in the Piedmont, and 55° in the Mountains.

Location and altitude North Carolina's weather is influenced by its location and by altitude changes within the state. The state is near enough to the equator that the winter sun can warm the air and the surface of the earth. Therefore, not much snow falls except in the cooler, higher altitudes. Any snow that occurs in the Piedmont or Coastal Plain seldom stays on the ground longer than a day or two.

North Carolina's location on the Atlantic Ocean also affects its climate. Due to the ocean's influence, temperatures on the Coastal Plain are milder and temperature differences less extreme than in the Piedmont or Mountains. At the same time, the ocean's moist air makes the Coastal Plain wetter than the Piedmont.

Rainfall and winds The Mountains region is also wetter than the Piedmont because of a combination of winds and altitude. Except along the coast, the winds in North Carolina generally blow from the west. Air masses blown into the state are thus forced to rise when they hit the mountains. As the air rises, it cools and drops large amounts of rain or snow in this region. The ocean's effects do not extend very far inland in the east because of the western winds.

✔ **READING CHECK** Identifying Cause and Effect What three geographic factors influence rainfall differences in the state's regions?

CONNECTING TO Geography

Hurricanes

North Carolina is well known for its terrible hurricanes. Since 1900, more than 25 of these huge and dangerous storms have swept out of the Atlantic and struck the state's coastline. The most powerful was Hurricane Hazel in 1954, which packed winds of over 140 miles per hour. The most destructive, however, was Hurricane Floyd in 1999. The flooding caused by this storm did some $6 billion in damage and destroyed more than 16,000 homes. **What other natural danger besides flooding does a hurricane pose?**

★ Natural Resources

The land's physical features have been a major factor in North Carolina's history and development. But its natural resources have played an important role as well.

Minerals, rocks, and soil More than 70 kinds of rocks and minerals have economic value to the state. The Coastal Plain is a source of sand, clay, and sandstone. The Piedmont also provides clay, as well as slate, granite, mica, and quartz. These last three, in addition to marble and limestone, are also present in the Mountains region. Both the

Mountains and the Piedmont contain deposits of gold, copper, manganese, titanium, and iron ore.

The Piedmont and Mountains regions both have similar clay soils. Piedmont soils are less fertile than those in the Mountains because they are younger and more heavily eroded. The heavy Piedmont clay is also more difficult to farm than is the finer soil of clay and sand in the Coastal Plain.

Water, plants, and wildlife About 70 percent of the fresh water available to North Carolinians is **groundwater**—water that is held within the earth. It comes to the surface in natural springs between cracks in rocks, or through drilling wells. Most of this groundwater is found in the Coastal Plain. The Mountains and Piedmont contain many streams and rivers. In modern times some of these have been dammed to create lakes in which water is stored.

Forests are among the most important plant resources in North Carolina. About two-thirds of the state is still covered in forest. In fact, forests cover 50 percent or more of the land in all but 26 of North Carolina's 100 counties.

In early times, North Carolina was filled with fish and game. Buffalo, elk, and small animals such as foxes and beavers provided both food and clothing for early peoples. Over time, the growth of the human population caused many kinds of animals to be less common or to disappear from the state altogether.

✓ **READING CHECK** **Making Predictions** What role might water and forests have played in the settlement of North Carolina?

Quarries such as this one in Salisbury, North Carolina, have always been important to the state's economy.

The Land and Its People

★ Effects of Geography

Geography had a major effect on North Carolina's settlement and development. This was true for our state's earliest Native American settlers and for its later European settlers. For example, geographic factors discouraged the first European settlers from landing on the Coastal Plain. Wind and storms shifted the sandy barrier islands, making the inlets to the coast shallow and dangerous to navigate. In addition, the coastline generally lacked good natural harbors. This helped to limit the early growth of coastal cities and trade.

The Piedmont's chief rivers—the Catawba, the Yadkin, the Pee Dee, and the Broad—all flow southeast into South Carolina. This lack of westward-flowing water routes discouraged settlers on the Coastal Plain from moving west into the interior. Instead, the Piedmont was settled by people moving north or south from South Carolina, Virginia, and Pennsylvania.

Due in part to the Piedmont's clay soil and colder, drier climate, its farms were smaller than those on the Coastal Plain. However, its rivers and streams provided waterpower, which encouraged the early growth of industry. Thus a different type of life developed in the Piedmont than in the Coastal Plain. Because cities tend to develop where there is industry, most of North Carolina's cities today are in the Piedmont. Geography also explains why the distant, rugged, and heavily forested mountains were the last region settled by Europeans, and why they remain the least populated region of the state today.

North Carolina's mineral resources include mica, shown here.

✓ **READING CHECK** Drawing Inferences and Conclusions Why are most of the state's cities located in the Piedmont?

Section 1 Review

go.hrw.com Homework Practice Online
keyword: SN3 HP1

1 Define and explain:
- regions
- terrain
- altitude
- plateau
- barrier islands
- inlets
- groundwater

2 Identify and explain:
- Mountains
- Piedmont
- Coastal Plain
- Blue Ridge
- Tidewater
- Outer Banks

3 Comparing and Contrasting Copy the chart below. Use it to show similarities and differences in North Carolina's regions.

	Mountains	Piedmont	Coastal Plain
Area (sq. miles)			
Terrain			
Main Land Cover			
Soil Type			

4 Finding the Main Idea
a. What changes in altitude and terrain occur when going from east to west in North Carolina?

b. How have rivers and soil affected North Carolina's development?

5 Writing and Critical Thinking
Analyzing Information Why would the Mountains get more rain than the Piedmont? Consider:
- what happens when air rises
- which holds more moisture, warm or cold air

Section 2

The First North Carolinians

Read to Discover
1. How did the first people in North Carolina live?
2. How and why did life in North Carolina change?
3. Why did some North Carolinians build mounds?

Define
- nomads
- archaeologists
- culture

Identify
- Woodland Period
- Mississippians
- Mississippian Culture

Early illustration of North Carolina plants

The Story Continues

For millions of years no one lived in what is now North Carolina, or in the rest of North and South America. Then, about 2 million years ago, Earth entered an Ice Age, a time when temperatures were much lower than they are now. Because so much water was frozen in ice, ocean levels were greatly reduced. The lower water level exposed a "bridge" of land across the narrow body of water that now separates Alaska and northern Asia. Most historians believe that this land bridge enabled the first people to reach North America.

★ Native American Origins

Perhaps as long as 60,000 years ago, people from Asia began crossing this land bridge into North America. Over many generations, they spread across North America. Because these people and their descendants were the original Americans, they are sometimes called "Native Americans." At least 12,000 years ago they entered what is now North Carolina.

That's Interesting!

Beringia Many scientists believe that a stretch of dry land—a "land bridge"—joined the areas of present-day Siberia and Alaska during the Ice Age. This bridge is thought to have crossed the stretch of open water known today as the Bering Strait. The land bridge that many believe was exposed during the Ice Age provided a means for animals and early people to cross from northern Asia into North America. Today, many scientists refer to the land bridge as "Beringia."

The Land and Its People 9

A team of archaeologists examines the site of the Lost Colony on Roanoke Island.

These first North Carolinians were **nomads**—people who move from place to place. They traveled in small groups, hunting and gathering wild plants to eat. Their tools and weapons were made from stone or bone. For shelter, these early people probably spread brush or skins over small branches cut from trees. Evidence suggests that they seldom stayed long in one place.

As the Ice Age ended, about 10,000 years ago, Earth slowly became warmer. This change in temperature supported a larger variety and greater numbers of plants and animals. People probably did not have to work as hard to find food. They moved less often and began to use their camps as more permanent settlements. Groups did not roam over as large a territory as before. Eventually, some groups probably planted a few of the wild seeds they gathered. This marked the beginning of farming among Native Americans.

✔ **READING CHECK** **Identifying Cause and Effect** How did changes in climate affect early North Carolinians?

That's Interesting!

Ancient Peoples How can we know about peoples who left no written records? Archaeologists carefully dig in places where they once lived. Bones and seeds in the ground can reveal what ancient people ate. The remains of things they owned provide clues about their way of life and technology. Outlines of postholes tell about the size of their houses and villages. Conclusions drawn from this work frequently change, however, as new sites and objects are found.

★ The Woodland Indians

The spread of farming led to what **archaeologists** call the **Woodland Period**. Archaeologists learn about ancient peoples by studying the objects they have left behind. The Woodland Period began about 3,000 years ago and lasted until about A.D. 1200.

Farming required spending more time in the same place. So some base camps, often located along rivers or streams, became permanent villages. Groups still left these places for weeks to hunt and gather, but they generally returned when it was time to harvest their crops. The people who followed this way of life are known today as Woodland Indians. They made tools from shells and animal bones and developed bows and arrows for hunting. They also made large clay pots in which to store and cook their food.

During the Woodland Period, people whose villages were in the same general territory began to develop their own **culture**. A culture is the set of beliefs, material traits, and other practices that a people share. Early cultures were strongly influenced by the geography of their surroundings. As a rule, they followed the basic Woodland way of life. But differences among peoples began to appear.

✔ **READING CHECK** **Finding the Main Idea** What change in Indians' way of life marked the beginning of the Woodland Period?

The Mississippians

By A.D. 1000 a new way of life arose among the Woodland peoples that lasted until Europeans colonized North Carolina in the 1650s. The Indians who practiced this way of life are called the **Mississippians**. They take their name from the culture that they shared with other Indian groups throughout the Lower South and the central regions of North America. **Mississippian Culture** was influenced by the fertile soil of the Mississippi River valley and its connecting river basins.

During this period people relied more on growing than on gathering food. Although hunting continued, people also tended large fields of squash, beans, and corn. A Cherokee legend tells how an old woman taught these Indians to grow corn.

This engraving of Native Americans sowing seeds in Florida illustrates early American agricultural techniques.

> **History Makers Speak**
> "When I have died, clear away a patch of ground . . . where the sun shines longest and brightest. The earth there must be made completely bare. Drag my body over that ground seven times and then bury me in that earth. Keep the ground clear. If you do as I say, . . . you will be able to feed the people."
>
> "The Coming of Corn," a Cherokee story as told by Joseph Bruchac

Analyzing Primary Sources
Identifying Cause and Effect Why would following these instructions have ended early Native Americans' roaming ways?

Farming provided a stable food supply. Systems of government gradually developed so that growing populations could better live and work together. More settled communities also encouraged the development of more detailed artwork and larger buildings. Fine artwork and jewelry made from shell beads, copper, and other materials became common.

✔ **READING CHECK** **Identifying Cause and Effect** In what ways did Mississippian society change with the development of farming?

Mound Building

In North Carolina, the Mississippians were concentrated in the Mountains and southern Piedmont. There, they practiced one of the most distinctive features of Mississippian culture: mound building. They built large, flat-topped earthen mounds with wood buildings on top. The mounds marked the centers of small clusters of towns or villages. People met at the mounds for harvest ceremonies and to bury their dead.

The Land and Its People

Shown here is the Mississippian mound at the Town Creek Historical Site.

The Town Creek Mound This rectangular mound is located in the Pee Dee River valley near Mount Gilead in Montgomery County. Archaeologists believe it was used until probably at least A.D. 1400 as a ceremonial center for several southern Piedmont villages. It faced a large open square that was bordered by several buildings which may have been funeral huts. A ramp led to a temple building on the mound. The area was surrounded by a wooden stockade with guard towers.

Other mounds Nikwasi Mound, in Macon County, was once topped by a large round meeting house called a "townhouse." A similar townhouse atop the Coweeta Creek Mound in Macon County could hold several hundred people. The mound was surrounded by a village. The village around the Garden Creek Mound west of Asheville may have covered five acres. The peoples who built these mounds were the ancestors of the Cherokee.

✔ **READING CHECK** Finding the Main Idea Why did the Mound Builders build their mounds?

Section 2 Review

Homework Practice Online keyword: SN3 HP1

1. Define and explain:
- nomad
- archaeologists
- culture

2. Identify and explain:
- Woodland Period
- Mississippians
- Mississippian Culture

3. Sequencing Copy the flow chart below. Use it to show how early North Carolinians' sources of food changed over time.

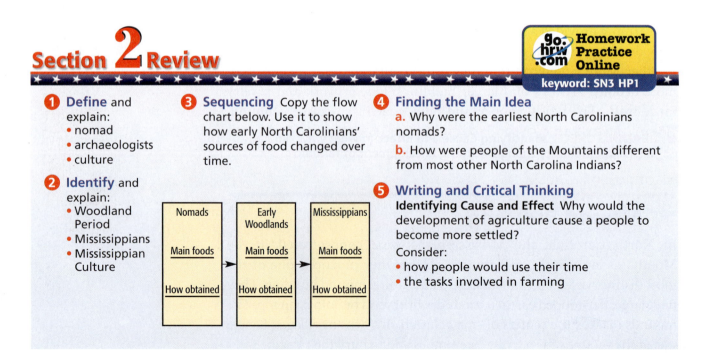

4. Finding the Main Idea
a. Why were the earliest North Carolinians nomads?
b. How were people of the Mountains different from most other North Carolina Indians?

5. Writing and Critical Thinking
Identifying Cause and Effect Why would the development of agriculture cause a people to become more settled?
Consider:
- how people would use their time
- the tasks involved in farming

Section 3

Native Americans in North Carolina by 1500

Read to Discover
1. Which Indian peoples were most important in North Carolina?
2. What were the religious beliefs and practices of North Carolina Indians?
3. How were Indian economies and societies organized?
4. What impact did Indians have on the North Carolina colony?

Define
- anthropologists
- culture area
- rituals
- shaman
- economy
- clan

This engraving, made between 1585 and 1588, shows the Native American town of Secota.

The Story Continues

The Native Americans who inhabited the land that came to be called North Carolina were a diverse group. Yet these early inhabitants shared much in common with each other and with native peoples in other parts of North America. For example, three different "families" of languages existed in North Carolina by the end of the Woodland Period. Peoples who spoke an Algonquian language shared common ancestors with Native Americans in present-day New England and across much of Canada. Groups speaking Iroquoian languages were related to Indians living around Lake Ontario and Lake Erie in what is now western New York. Those who spoke a Siouan language were descended from people who came from west of the Mississippi River.

The Land and Its People 13

⭐ Eastern Woodland Cultures

Early North Carolinians shared many cultural traits with peoples outside North Carolina. In fact, some **anthropologists**—scientists who study human beings and their cultures—view North Carolina as part of the Eastern Woodland Culture Area. A **culture area** is a region in which all peoples share the same basic way of life. The Eastern Woodland Culture Area included large parts of the present-day United States east of the Mississippi River.

The Eastern Woodland region was heavily forested. However, the best natural resources were found in the open areas. As a result the greatest centers of population were near the seacoast, lakes, marshes, and rivers. These locations offered the best opportunities for fishing, hunting, farming, or gathering wild crops.

Other anthropologists do not agree that all Indians in the Eastern Woodland Culture Area were so alike. These scientists divide the culture area into two parts: the Northeast Culture Area and the Southeast Culture Area. The dividing line runs through North Carolina. This view emphasizes the differences between the Algonquian peoples of the northern Coastal Plain and other North Carolina Indians.

✔ **READING CHECK** Categorizing What arguments can be made for and against including North Carolina in one single culture area?

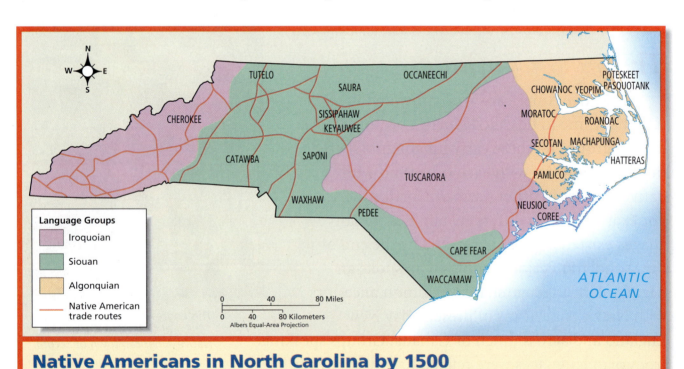

Native Americans in North Carolina by 1500

Interpreting Maps The early Native Americans who settled North Carolina had developed large and complex societies by about 1500.

Skills Assessment Physical Systems In what ways did North Carolina's geography affect patterns of Native American settlement and cultural development?

North Carolina Indians

By 1500, Native American groups in North Carolina had organized themselves into tribes, each with its own territory and government. Anthropologists estimate there were some 30 tribes in North Carolina when the first Europeans arrived. Of these, five played a major role in European efforts to settle North Carolina.

The Hatteras This Algonquian people lived on the Outer Banks. They were the first people encountered by the early European explorers of the North Carolina coast. The Hatteras were fairly new to the region. They had migrated down the coast from Canada, as had other Algonquian peoples in the northern Tidewater and Coastal Plain.

The Chowanoc These Algonquian neighbors of the Hatteras had been in the northern Tidewater for about 500 years by 1500. Most of them lived west of the Chowan River in what are now Bertie and Hertford counties. Like other Algonquians, they spent more time hunting, gathering, and fishing and less time farming than did non-Algonquian peoples.

The Tuscarora This Iroquoian people controlled and hunted over a huge area on the Coastal Plain. The most powerful tribe in the region, they sometimes raided their Algonquian neighbors. They had a well-organized system of government and farmed from permanent villages. In winter they moved to hunting camps, bringing with them the corn they had harvested in the fall.

The Catawba This Siouan people lived in the southern Piedmont. Little is known about their way of life before Europeans first studied them around 1700. Anthropologists believe the first Siouans entered North Carolina from the west around A.D. 1000.

The Cherokee Cherokee groups lived in the mountains and valleys of southwestern North Carolina. Like the Tuscarora, they were related to the Iroquois in the north. Some anthropologists believe they were driven out of that region in early times. The Cherokee were a very large tribe. In the mid-1500s, their population was about 22,000. They controlled more than 40,000 square miles in eight present-day states.

✓ **READING CHECK** Comparing What did the Tuscarora and the Cherokee have in common?

Did You KNOW?
More than 80,000 Native Americans live in North Carolina today. The state has the largest Indian population east of the Mississippi River.

This Native American head vessel was made by Mississippian people between 1300 and 1500.

⭐ Beliefs and Practices

The beliefs and practices of North Carolina Indians in 1500 were shaped by their long history of hunting, gathering, and farming. Like many Native American peoples, nature was a major force in their lives. North Carolina Indians viewed and used its resources in much the same way as the other peoples of the Eastern Woodland Culture Area.

Religion and rituals To many Native Americans, all living things had a spirit. Indians offered sacrifices and prayers so that these spirits would favor them. **Rituals**, or ceremonies, were important. For example, a hunter might offer a valued item to please the spirit of an animal he had killed. A priest or a **shaman**—a healer and holy person—would lead the village in asking for rain or a good harvest. Many peoples believed in life after death and worshipped a "Great Spirit" or supreme being.

Stories that explained the natural world were important to Indian religions. One Cherokee legend describes the sun's origins.

Analyzing Primary Sources
Identifying Points of View
What in this story shows Native Americans' belief in the importance of nature?

"When the earth was dry and the animals came down, it was still dark, so they got the sun and set it in a track to go every day . . . just overhead. It was too hot this way. . . . The conjurers [wizards] put the sun . . . higher in the air, but it was still too hot. They raised it another time, and another, until it was . . . just under the sky arch. Then it was right, and they left it so."

quoted in *Myths of the Cherokee*, by James Mooney

Indians passed on such stories by telling them to their children. These legends are still valued by Native Americans. Today, some continue to follow their traditional beliefs and practices.

Food, shelter, and clothing Many Indians in 1500 wore clothes made from animal skins, just as their ancestors had. However, their diet had changed because of their more settled life. They grew vegetables and boiled them with meat, nuts, and roots in clay pots. Settling down also influenced their shelter. Most lived in houses made from wood poles tied together and covered with tree bark, mats of reeds, or mud.

✔ **READING CHECK** Identifying Cause and Effect How did Indians try to influence the spirits?

⭐ Economy and Government

By 1500, the **economy** of most North Carolina peoples was based on farming. An economy is the way in which a society uses its resources to obtain things that it wants or needs. Crafts and trade were also important. In addition to their pots, tools, and reed mats, these Indians made jewelry and other items from bone, shells, and polished-stone beads.

Early inhabitant of the South, c. 1585–1588

They also used reeds, bark, and vines to make baskets. Other items and materials for crafts were obtained from other peoples, both near and far away. For example, the copper jewelry they wore probably came from Indians who lived near the Great Lakes. To get such things, they traded crops, local materials, and items they had made.

The basic unit of Indian society was the clan. A clan is a group of people descended from a common ancestor. A clan can contain a few families or many. If a clan was fairly small, all its members might live together as a band. Each band usually had its own village. A tribe existed when the people of several bands or villages formed an alliance, usually under a common government. At the head of each tribe was a chief. In some tribes this position passed from father to son. Mississippians tended to be more hierarchical than other North Carolina Indians.

Pipe in the form of a toad, from the Hopewell culture

✔ **READING CHECK** **Finding the Main Idea** What three activities were most important in Indian economies?

★ The Legacy of Native Americans

The first Europeans in North Carolina owed much to the native peoples who were already here when they arrived. From these Indians the colonists learned to grow new crops such as corn, beans, potatoes, and tobacco. Indians showed them the best ways and places to hunt and fish. Some tribes protected the early colonists from other Indians who wanted to drive them away. Very soon, however, the Europeans and the Indians began to view each other as enemies. Europeans generally looked upon Indians as being in the way of European settlement.

✔ **READING CHECK** **Summarizing** In what ways did the relationship between Native Americans and European settlers change over time?

GLOBAL CONNECTIONS

Carolina Place Names

Among the reminders of North Carolina's Native American heritage are the names of many places in the state. The English names for many tribes, like Hatteras and Chowan, survive as names of places. And Roanoke, an Algonquian word for "white-shell place," was probably the first Indian term adopted by the English. **In what ways have Indians shaped North Carolina place names?**

Section 3 Review

keyword: SN3 HP1

1. **Define** and explain:
   • anthropologists
   • culture area
   • rituals
   • shaman
   • economy
   • clan

2. **Comparing and Contrasting** Copy the graphic organizer below. Use it to show how Native American societies were organized.

3. **Finding the Main Idea**
   a. Which Indian peoples had the greatest impact on the settlement of North Carolina?
   b. How did Indians obtain things they wanted or needed?

4. **Writing and Critical Thinking**
   Identifying Points of View Why was Indian religion so closely linked to nature?
   Consider:
   • the way in which Indians lived
   • Indians view of their world

The Land and Its People

Chapter 1 Review

Chapter Summary

Section 1
- North Carolina is a land of widely varying land forms and differing climates.
- Natural resources are plentiful and varied in North Carolina.
- Geography has strongly affected patterns of settlement and development throughout North Carolina's history.

Section 2
- Geographic factors helped to shape early Native American settlements and lifestyles in North Carolina.
- Early Native American lifestyles changed with the development of farming and of new technologies.
- Native American peoples in what is now North Carolina developed distinctive cultural features, such as the building of ceremonial mounds.

Section 3
- Major Indian groups in early North Carolina shared many religious beliefs and practices with Native Americans in other parts of North America.
- Native American groups in North Carolina developed complex and varied social and economic patterns.
- Native American lifestyles and traditions had a strong and lasting impact on European settlers in North Carolina.

Identifying People and Ideas
Use the following terms or people in complete sentences.

1. regions
2. terrain
3. Piedmont
4. Tidewater
5. nomads
6. archaeologists
7. culture
8. anthropologists
9. economy
10. clan

Understanding Main Ideas

Section 1 *Pages 3–8*
1. What is the basic terrain of each of North Carolina's regions?
2. What differences in soil types exist among North Carolina's regions?
3. List three ways in which geography affected the settlement and development of North Carolina.

Section 2 *Pages 9–12*
4. How did North Carolina Indians' way of life change over time?
5. What special ways of life developed among Indians of the Mountains and the southern Piedmont?

Section 3 *Pages 13–17*
6. Why are the Hatteras, Chowanoc, Tuscarora, Catawba, and Cherokee more important in North Carolina's history than were some other Native American groups?
7. Why did North Carolina Indians attach religious importance to things in nature?

What Did You Find Out?
1. **Geography** What advantages did peoples in the Tidewater have over those in the Piedmont?
2. **Science, Technology & Society** How did early peoples in North Carolina use natural resources to improve their lives?
3. **Economics** How did North Carolina's early peoples benefit from trade?

Thinking Critically
1. **Summarizing** How did North Carolina's geography affect Native American cultures?
2. **Supporting a Point of View** Do you believe that North Carolina Indians should be considered part of one culture area or of two? Explain why.
3. **Drawing Inferences and Conclusions** Why would the characteristics of mounds cause archaeologists to believe that they had a role in government?

Building Social Studies Skills

Interpreting Art
Study the engraving below. Then use information from the engraving to answer the questions that follow.

1590 engraving of a John White painting

1. Which statement best describes the people in this image?
   a. In this culture, food preparation was a man's responsibility.
   b. The people of this culture used the forces of nature to improve their technology.
   c. These people made unwise and wasteful use of their natural resources.
   d. This was probably a hunting and gathering culture.
2. In what part of North Carolina did these people probably live? What clues in the artwork suggest this?

Analyzing Primary Sources
Read the excerpt that follows from a Cherokee legend. The story tells what happened when the spirit of the North went out looking for a wife. Then answer the questions.

> "The North went traveling, and after going far and meeting many different tribes he finally fell in love with the daughter of the South. . . . They were married and he took his bride to his own country, ... The next day, when the sun rose, . . . it grew warmer and warmer, until finally the people came to the young husband and told him he must send his wife home again, or the weather would get so warm that the whole settlement would be melted. He loved his wife and so held out as long as he could, but as the sun grew hotter the people were more urgent, and at last he had to send her home."

3. What knowledge about the natural world were the Cherokee passing on in this story?
   a. that the north and south are very far apart geographically
   b. why it is warmer in the south than in the north
   c. that hot weather is unpleasant and can be dangerous
   d. why the seasons change
   e. how to tell direction by looking at the position of the sun in the sky
4. What basic beliefs of Native American religion does this legend illustrate?

Alternative Assessment

Building Your Portfolio

Linking to Community
Archaeologists continue to explore many sites to learn more about early peoples. Much of this work is conducted by colleges and universities. The Office of State Archaeology in the North Carolina Department of Cultural Resources is also involved in this research. Locate a site in your area. Find out what items have been recovered there and what opportunities exist for volunteer workers at the site. Prepare a report of your findings.

internet connect

Internet Activity: go.hrw.com
keyword: SN3 NC1

Choose a topic about the land and its people to:
- Create a poster on North Carolina's geography.
- Research the Mound Builders of North Carolina.
- Write a story about an American Indian from North Carolina.

The Land and Its People

CHAPTER 2
Europeans Arrive in North Carolina
(1400s–1663)

Engraving depicting the arrival of the English in the Chesapeake.

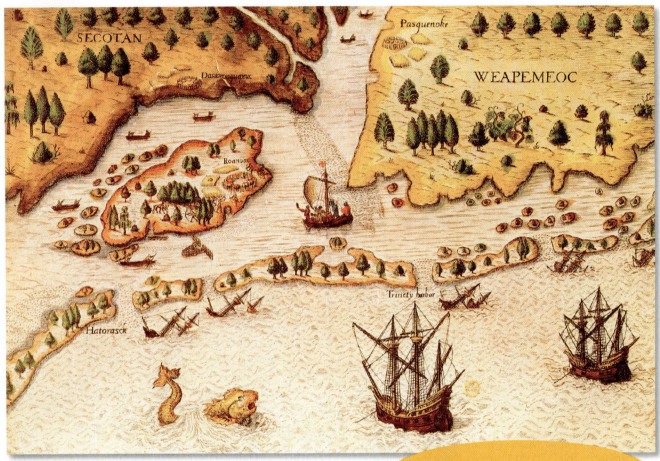

Build on What You Know

The place we know today as North Carolina was entirely different 500 years ago. Around A.D. 1500, North Carolina was peopled by Native Americans living in villages. Their economy was built on farming, hunting, and trade. In this chapter, you will learn how the transformation from past to present began.

What's Your Opinion?

 Themes Journal Do you **agree** or **disagree** with the following statements? Support your point of view in your journal.

- **Economic Development** The arrival of new settlers in a country can change the economies of people already there.
- **Geography** Natural resources and productivity drive exploration.
- **Cultural Diversity** Cultural elements such as religion do not affect the process of exploration.

Section 1

European Exploration

Read to Discover
1. Why did Europeans begin to explore distant places in the 1400s?
2. Why did Columbus travel westward looking for Asia?
3. How did England and France get involved in the race to discover new lands in the west?

Define
- expedition

Identify
- Henry the Navigator
- Vasco da Gama
- Christopher Columbus
- Ferdinand and Isabella
- John Cabot
- Giovanni da Verrazano
- Juan Ponce de León

The Story Continues

Around 1300, people in Europe read of Marco Polo's travels to Cathay (China) and other exciting Asian lands. The adventures Polo wrote about led many Europeans to think about the riches of Asia.

Europeans Branch Out

In the early 1400s, people in Europe began to look to the seas and beyond. Some longed for adventure. Others wanted to spread Christianity far and wide. Most of all, though, people wanted to find riches. The age of exploration and discovery had begun.

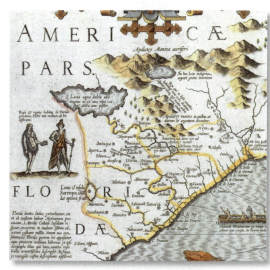

This map from an atlas shows details of the North Carolina coast.

The search for new routes By the late Middle Ages, Europeans had developed a taste for spices in their diets. Most spices came from islands in Asia. Because they had to be shipped halfway around the world on risky voyages, spices were costly. For hundreds of years, the Italian port city of Venice controlled this trade.

Some Europeans began to look for ways to bypass Venice's hold on the spice trade. In Portugal, a prince named **Henry the Navigator** urged

Europeans Arrive in North Carolina   **21**

sea captains to explore southward along the coast of Africa. He wanted someone to find a route around that continent to the Spice Islands, near India. In 1497–1498, Portuguese explorer **Vasco da Gama** found such a route and sailed all the way to India.

Other Europeans had different ideas. **Christopher Columbus** thought Asia could be reached by sailing west from Europe. Columbus persuaded the king and queen of Spain, **Ferdinand and Isabella**, to support an **expedition**, or trip of exploration. Columbus himself gave the king and queen credit for this idea.

Analyzing Primary Sources
Analyzing Information Based on the passage, did Columbus think of himself as a pioneer?

History Makers Speak
"Your Highnesses . . . took thought to send me, Christopher Columbus, to the said parts of India... and ordained that I should not go by land to the eastward, by which way it was the custom to go, but by way of the west, by which down to this day we do not know certainly that anyone has passed . . . ."
—Christopher Columbus, from his journal

In 1492 Columbus led his first expedition westward. He landed in the Bahamas, islands that he believed to be near Asia. On another voyage in 1498, Columbus reached South America. Later, a mapmaker labeled this new continent "America" for another explorer, Amerigo Vespucci. The name stuck.

The Columbian Exchange In the years following Columbus's voyages, a great interaction between the "New World" and "Old World" took place. This interaction is sometimes referred to as the Columbian Exchange. Plants, animals, and even diseases moved between the Western and Eastern Hemispheres. Ways of life changed forever for American Indians in the New World and Europeans and Africans in the Old World. Europeans enjoyed new American foods such as potatoes, tomatoes, beans, and corn. Native Americans made use of horses and cattle, which were introduced into the Americas by the Spanish.

Other exchanges were not as helpful. Smallpox and other European diseases traveled to the Americas and nearly destroyed native populations. Also, a huge slave trade developed as Europeans transported millions of enslaved Africans to the New World to work on plantations.

American fruits and vegetables like the ones in this illustration were familiar to Native Americans but new to Europeans.

✔ **READING CHECK** **Identifying Cause and Effect** How did the Columbian Exchange affect Native American populations?

★ Exploring North America

Even with new lands to explore, some Europeans still clung to dreams of spice riches. They wondered if a passage to Asia existed somewhere in the cluster of lands to the west.

The Northwest Passage One European with such ideas was <u>John Cabot</u>, an Italian living in England. In 1497 King Henry VII sent Cabot on a voyage to the West. The English thought that there might be a water route through the Americas that would lead north and west to Asia. They called this sought-for route the Northwest Passage. Cabot landed on the far northern Atlantic coast of North America—probably the island of Newfoundland. Like other explorers, he failed to find the Northwest Passage. In time, Europeans gave up on their search for the route.

Verrazano's expedition In 1524 King Francis I of France sent Italian navigator <u>Giovanni da Verrazano</u> westward. Verrazano first reached land at North Carolina's Outer Banks. Across those narrow islands he thought he saw the Pacific Ocean. In fact, he was looking at the Pamlico and Albemarle Sounds. Verrazano then explored farther up the coast. Returning to France, Verrazano submitted a glowing report to the king. However, the French king was now occupied with military challenges at home. He did not sponsor any more voyages to the Americas.

✔ **READING CHECK** Finding the Main Idea What did the English hope to gain by finding the Northwest Passage?

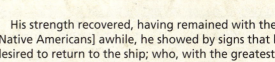

Ceramic portrait believed to be of Verrazano.

"The Young Sailor"
Giovanni da Verrazano

On July 8, 1524, Giovanni da Verrazano wrote a report of his voyage and explorations to King Francis I of France. Verrazano's vivid report detailed the excitement and danger of such a journey, including this story about the experiences of a young sailor.

One of our young sailors . . . was so tossed by the waves that almost half dead he was carried to the edge of the shore. . . . The people of the land ran immediately to him; taking him by the head, legs, and arms, they carried him some distance away. Where, the youth, seeing himself carried in such a way, stricken with terror, uttered very loud cries, which they did similarly in their language, showing him that he should not fear.

After that, having placed him on the ground in the sun at the foot of a little hill, they performed great acts of admiration, regarding the whiteness of his flesh, examining him from head to foot. Taking off his shirt and hose . . . they made a very large fire near him, placing him near the heat. Which having been seen, the sailors who had remained in the small boat, full of fear, as is their custom in every new case, thought that they wanted to roast him for food.

His strength recovered, having remained with the [Native Americans] awhile, he showed by signs that he desired to return to the ship; who, with the greatest kindness, holding him always close with various embraces, accompanied him as far as the sea, and in order to assure him more, extending themselves on a high hill, stood to watch him until he was in the boat.

Understanding Literature

1. How does Verrazano build dramatic tension in his account?
2. A good story presents a conflict and then resolves it. Does "The Young Sailor" fit this definition of a good story? Explain.
3. Did this story surprise you? Tell why or why not.

Europeans Arrive in North Carolina

★ Spanish Exploration

Powerful Spain claimed many of the New World lands. In the early 1500s, Spain was taking control of much of South and Central America and many Caribbean islands, including Cuba and Hispaniola. (That island is now occupied by the nations of Haiti and the Dominican Republic.) Meanwhile, Spanish governors and explorers began to look northward.

Juan Ponce de León was a Spanish official in the New World. In 1508–1509, he explored and settled the island of Puerto Rico. Taking notice back in Spain, King Ferdinand authorized Ponce de León to explore lands north of Cuba.

In early 1513, Ponce de León set out with ships and crew. His expedition landed on the east coast of Florida, a name Ponce de León derived from the Spanish word for "flowers." The ships sailed down the east Florida coast and through the Florida Keys. Then they cruised northward along the west coast of Florida for about 100 miles. Ponce de León's expedition revealed that large tracts of land ripe for exploration lay to the north of the Caribbean islands.

✓ **READING CHECK** Summarizing How did Ponce de León lay claim to Florida for Spain?

This map of the island of Hispaniola was created in 1633.

Section 1 Review

keyword: SN3 HP2

1 **Define** and explain:
- expedition

2 **Identify** and explain:
- Henry the Navigator
- Vasco da Gama
- Christopher Columbus
- Ferdinand and Isabella
- John Cabot
- Giovanni da Verrazano
- Juan Ponce de León

3 **Analyzing Information** Copy the chart below. Use it to identify an explorer associated with each nation.

Nation	Explorer
England	
France	
Portugal	
Spain	

4 **Finding the Main Idea**
a. Why did Europeans begin to look to seas and lands beyond their own borders in the 1400s?
b. What countries got involved in the race for new lands in the 1500s?

5 **Writing and Critical Thinking**
Evaluating Sources If you had lived in Europe in the 1500s, would you have believed every story published by New World explorers? Explain why or why not.

Consider:
- the explorers' motives
- what people in Europe knew about the New World

Section 2

Exploring North Carolina

Read to Discover
1. Why did Spanish officials send expeditions into the present-day southeastern United States?
2. How and when did Spain establish control over Florida?

Define
- mission
- conquistadores

Identify
- Lucas Vázquez de Ayllón
- Hernando de Soto
- Jean Ribault
- Huguenots
- René de Laudonnière
- Pedro Menéndez de Avilés
- Pedro de Coronas
- Juan Pardo
- Hernando Boyano

The Story Continues

In the 1520s, Spain was the most powerful nation in the world. Spanish explorers had claimed huge tracts of land in the New World. They had begun sending gold and silver back to Spain. From their base on Hispaniola in the Caribbean Sea, Spanish officials eyed the North American coast eagerly. Already, Ponce de León had explored and claimed Florida. What rich lands might lie to the north?

Spaniards Come to North Carolina

One Spanish official who had his eyes on the mainland north of Florida was **Lucas Vázquez de Ayllón**. He had seen some of the Atlantic coastline of this region on an expedition in 1520. Ayllón intended to plant a strong colony for Spain along that coast.

Rio Jordán colony In July 1526, Ayllón led a group of over 500 men, women, and children to a river he called "Jordán" (for the Jordan River in ancient Palestine). Historians today believe that it was actually North Carolina's Cape Fear River.

Weapons such as these were carried by Spanish, English, and French explorers and soldiers who helped to open the Americas to European colonization in the 1500s.

Europeans Arrive in North Carolina **25**

The Rio Jordán colony failed due to disease and starvation. Ayllón then took the colonists to a site in present-day South Carolina. However, the colony fared no better there. Disease and starvation overwhelmed the settlers. Ayllón himself died there. In October 1526, the 150 remaining colonists returned to Hispaniola.

De Soto's expedition The Spanish wanted to know more about the interior of North America. Land there might contain gold and silver.

In 1539 **Hernando de Soto** sailed with a military expedition from Havana, Cuba, to the west coast of Florida. From there, de Soto's soldiers marched northward to a site near present-day Tallahassee, Florida. There they spent the winter of 1539–1540. In the spring, de Soto crossed Georgia and South Carolina and passed through the western tip of North Carolina. De Soto and his men were the first Europeans to see these regions. In these mountainous lands they met Cherokee Indians, who treated them with generosity. Members of the expedition then traveled south and west. De Soto died on the trip, but many of his men returned to Mexico.

✔ **READING CHECK** **Comparing and Contrasting** How were the Ayllón and de Soto expeditions similar? How were they different?

That's Interesting!

Hernando de Soto made a relatively brief appearance in the future United States, but his name stuck around. Throughout the southeastern United States of today, streets, towns, and parks bear his name. An American automobile introduced in 1928 was even called the DeSoto. The DeSoto was discontinued in 1961. It is now a popular collector's item!

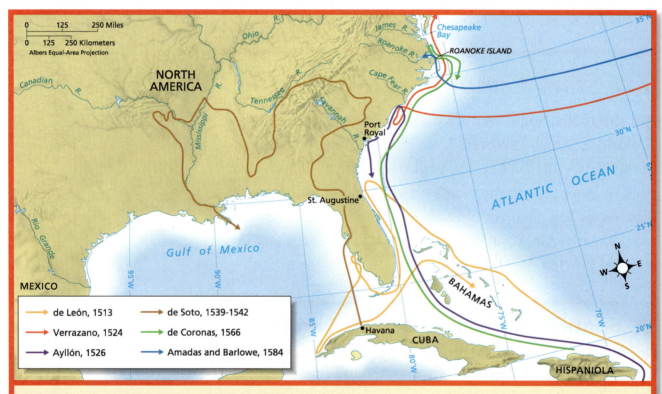

Explorations of North Carolina

Interpreting Maps During the 1500s, much of the European exploration of what is now North Carolina was conducted by the Spanish, in search of wealth and opportunities to colonize and spread Christianity. English explorers became more active toward the end of the 1500s.

Skills Assessment **Environment and Society** What influence might North Carolina's coastal river systems have had on early European efforts to explore and build colonies?

France and Spain Fight for Land

Soon other European nations were challenging Spain. In 1562 France sent a colony under the command of **Jean Ribault** to North America. The colonists were **Huguenots** (HYOO•guh•nahts), or French Protestants. Protestants were sometimes persecuted in Catholic France. As a result, some Huguenots sought religious freedom in the New World.

Port Royal Ribault's Huguenots attempted to settle near present-day Port Royal, South Carolina, in April 1562. In his report to France, Jean Ribault told why the colonists had chosen Port Royal:

> "...[We needed] to harbor our ships, as well for to [repair] them as to get us fresh water, wood, and other necessaries...[and] there was no fairer or fitter place for the purpose than Port Royal...it be one of the goodliest, best, and fruitfullest countries that ever was seen...."

Jean Ribault, *The Whole and True Discovery of Terra Florida*

Analyzing Primary Sources

Drawing Inferences Based on Ribault's comments, was the colonists' passage to North America easy or difficult?

Despite the reportedly favorable conditions at Port Royal, the colonists gave up in 1564 and returned to France. That same year, another band of Huguenots, led by **René de Laudonnière**, settled at Fort Caroline, on the north Florida coast. Jean Ribault brought supply ships to the fort.

St. Augustine To Spanish officials, the French fort seemed a direct threat. In 1565 Spain sent troops under **Pedro Menéndez de Avilés** to Florida. Just south of Fort Caroline, Menéndez built a fort at St. Augustine. Meanwhile, Jean Ribault prepared to attack. A storm wrecked his fleet, however, and Menéndez lost no time in dealing with the unlucky French. He captured Fort Caroline and killed most of the French defenders. In the following years, Menéndez built forts throughout Florida to strengthen Spain's grip. St. Augustine is the oldest permanent European settlement in the present-day United States.

Interpreting the Visual Record

Fortress design This engraving from the 1500s shows the French stronghold of Fort Caroline. How did the design of Fort Caroline utilize the natural environment for protection?

✓ **READING CHECK**
Drawing Inferences and Conclusions How successful was France in trying to compete with Spain for colonies on the North American coast?

Europeans Arrive in North Carolina **27**

Did You KNOW?

The Albemarle Sound, like most of North Carolina's coastal waters, is very shallow. Its depth averages 5 to 10 feet. At its deepest point, the sound is only 25 feet deep.

More Spanish Expeditions

With a secure hold on Florida, the Spaniards looked northward. In 1566 an expedition set out for Chesapeake Bay from the West Indies to set up a Catholic mission. A **mission** is a settlement designed to convert people to a particular religion. Strong winds kept the expedition from reaching Chesapeake Bay. Instead, they entered an inlet in North Carolina's Outer Banks and sailed into Albemarle Sound. Soon they landed at the tip of the Currituck Inlet. There **Pedro de Coronas**, a leader of the expedition, marked their landing by placing a wooden cross on the shore. After a brief exploration of the area, the group returned to their ships. Storms again prevented them from sailing on to Chesapeake Bay, so they returned to the West Indies.

Soon after the victory at Fort Caroline, Spanish officials organized an expedition to explore again the interior country north of Florida. In late 1566, **Juan Pardo** and **Hernando Boyano** led a small group of men to the South Carolina coast. From there, they pushed north and west on nearly the same route that de Soto had taken 25 years earlier. The expedition entered the foothills of the Blue Ridge Mountains, where the soldiers built a fort. Pardo and Boyano explored the surrounding territory. They saw the same mountainous western region of North Carolina that de Soto had visited. The Pardo-Boyano expedition built several forts in the interior. Over the next few years, however, the Spanish abandoned these forts.

Members of the expedition traded with the North Carolina Indians. They may also have tried to convert the Indians to Catholicism. Eventually some of the soldiers returned to the South Carolina coast. Pardo and Boyano, however, returned to the coast of the Gulf of Mexico. Along the way, they explored more new lands.

✔ **READING CHECK** Identifying Cause and Effect What did the Spanish victory at Fort Caroline enable the Spaniards to do?

This illustration shows the Spanish practice of employing Indians to carry equipment on expeditions.

28 Chapter 2

⭐ The Spanish Set Sights Southward

A Spanish conquistador

The Atlantic coastal region that is today part of the southeastern United States had seen a flurry of Spanish activity in the 1560s. At least in part, Spain's concern for this region was motivated by competition with the French.

Spain's rulers, however, had far greater interest in New World lands to the south. **Conquistadores**—military leaders and adventurers—had taken firm control of mineral-rich lands in present-day Mexico and Peru. Gold and silver from Central and South America made Spain a rich country. Spain also held islands in the Caribbean Sea, such as Cuba and Puerto Rico. Rich island soils, tilled by enslaved Africans, produced valuable crops such as sugar and coffee.

Officials in Spain had seen the need to strengthen their hold on Florida. They had responded promptly and firmly to French threats. Now Spanish officials, soldiers, and priests set about tightening Spanish control and converting the Indians to Catholicism. With possession of Florida fairly secure and greater wealth to the south, Spaniards focused their attention southward after the 1560s.

Soon, however, another European nation would compete for a foothold on the North American Atlantic coast. That nation was England.

✔ **READING CHECK** Finding the Main Idea Why did the Spaniards value the lands of Central and South America?

Section 2 Review

❶ **Define** and explain:
- mission
- conquistadores

❷ **Identify** and explain:
- Lucas Vázquez de Ayllón
- Hernando de Soto
- Jean Ribault
- Huguenots
- René de Laudonnière
- Pedro Menéndez de Avilés
- Pedro de Coronas
- Juan Pardo
- Hernando Boyano

❸ **Analyzing Information** Copy the chart below. In each column, list names of two Spanish explorers introduced in this section.

North Carolina Mountain Region	North Carolina Coastal Region

❹ **Finding the Main Idea**
a. Why was Hernando de Soto's expedition important?

b. Why did the Spanish become interested in land north of Florida? Why did they eventually turn their attention southward?

❺ **Writing and Critical Thinking**
Categorizing Write a paragraph describing two explorers who set out to start a colony. In a second paragraph describe two others who scouted new territory but did not settle in one place.

Consider:
- preparations the explorers made
- the type of people on the expeditions

Europeans Arrive in North Carolina

Section 3
The Effects of Exploration

Read to Discover
1. Why did trade spring up between American Indians and Europeans?
2. Why did Europeans in the New World make religious conversion of native peoples a high priority?
3. Why did American Indian populations decline sharply after contact with Europeans began?

Define
- maize

Identify
- Thomas Harriot

The Story Continues

In 1524 Giovanni da Verrazano went ashore on North Carolina's Outer Banks. According to his report, his group made signs of friendship and traded gifts with local Indians. It was the first of many such exchanges to come.

★ Trading with American Indians

Contact between American Indians and Europeans in the New World was certain to affect both groups. From the first, native peoples and European explorers offered each other gifts. Early explorers and colonists often became dependent upon the Indians for food. As time went on, though, Indians grew more dependent upon European goods.

Europeans were delighted by foods the Indians shared or traded. Their delicious vegetables were largely unknown in Europe. These included **maize** (corn), beans, squash, and pumpkins. In time, as colonists learned to produce their own food, European traders came to value the Indians' furs and hides the most. They traded for deerskin and beaver pelts.

This 1628 engraving depicts English explorers trading with Native Americans in the West Indies.

30 Chapter 2

Above all, Indians valued guns, which they did not have. They also wanted European cloth and buttons. These goods quickly spread through Indian trading networks. In the 1500s, before Europeans had direct contact with many tribes in the North America interior, some of those Indians obtained European goods through trade.

 READING CHECK Summarizing What Indian goods did Europeans desire? What European goods did Indians want?

★ Religious Conversion

One issue that came to loom large in relations between American Indians and the Europeans was religion. Europe in the 1500s was aflame with religious conflict as Protestant churches broke away from Catholicism. Religious fervor colored the thinking of many explorers and colonists.

The rulers of Catholic Spain believed that God had given them their New World lands. Their prime duty must therefore be to convert the native peoples. Some explorers and settlers took priests and friars (monks who live among the people) to the New World. Protestant explorers and colonists also hoped to convert native peoples. The English explorer **Thomas Harriot** suggested that the Indians would recognize Europeans' superiority and freely convert to Christianity.

This medallion of the Virgin Mary, found on St. Catherines Island, Georgia, reveals the influence of Spanish missionaries in the region.

 "…. [The Indians will] desire our friendship and love, and have the greater respect for pleasing and obeying us. Whereby may be hoped if means of good government be used, that they may in short time be brought to civilities, and the embracing of true religion."

Thomas Harriot, quoted in *North Carolina through Four Centuries,* by William S. Powell

Analyzing Primary Sources
Analyzing Information
Based on the passage, what was Harriot's attitude toward the Indians?

Native Americans already had their own complex religious beliefs, however. Many believed that everything within the natural world contained a spirit. Some believed in a powerful "Great Spirit." Europeans rejected most of these beliefs.

 READING CHECK Analyzing Information Why did the European settlers feel driven to convert American Indians to Christianity?

★ Diseases

One result of the Columbian Exchange had not been foreseen. Europeans coming to the New World brought viruses and bacteria from their home countries. Native Americans, who had been isolated from other parts of the world for centuries, had never been exposed to these germs. Therefore, they had no resistance to them. New diseases swiftly infected Native Americans and killed huge numbers of them.

Europeans Arrive in North Carolina

Depopulation In the 1500s and 1600s, influenza (flu), smallpox, measles, and other diseases raged among Indian populations. We will never know exactly how many people died. Some scholars think that after 100 years of European contact, the native population in Central America was reduced by 90 percent. Native populations all over the Americas suffered similar declines.

Effects on North Carolina Indians Indians living in North Carolina caught the same deadly mix of diseases as other Native Americans. The chart below shows the decline in North Carolina's native population after arrival of the Europeans.

✔ **READING CHECK** Identifying Cause and Effect Why did Native American populations fall off drastically after the early 1500s?

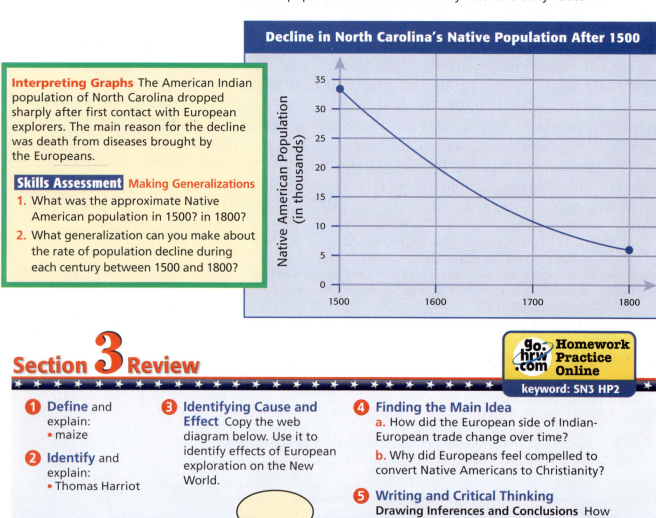

Interpreting Graphs The American Indian population of North Carolina dropped sharply after first contact with European explorers. The main reason for the decline was death from diseases brought by the Europeans.

Skills Assessment Making Generalizations
1. What was the approximate Native American population in 1500? in 1800?
2. What generalization can you make about the rate of population decline during each century between 1500 and 1800?

Section 3 Review

❶ **Define** and explain:
• maize

❷ **Identify** and explain:
• Thomas Harriot

❸ **Identifying Cause and Effect** Copy the web diagram below. Use it to identify effects of European exploration on the New World.

❹ **Finding the Main Idea**
a. How did the European side of Indian-European trade change over time?
b. Why did Europeans feel compelled to convert Native Americans to Christianity?

❺ **Writing and Critical Thinking**
Drawing Inferences and Conclusions How do you know that American Indians regarded European goods as highly desirable?
Consider:
• what kinds of items were traded
• how far trade extended

Section 4

English Exploration and Settlement

Read to Discover
1. Why did England resume exploration of the New World in the late 1500s?
2. What was the result of the first English attempt to set up a colony in North America?
3. What steps led to development of North Carolina as a separate colony?

Define
- sea dogs
- reconnaissance
- patent
- restoration

Identify
- Elizabeth I
- Walter Raleigh
- Richard Grenville
- Amadas-Barlowe expedition
- John White
- Ralph Lane
- John Pory
- Robert Heath
- Charles II

The Story Continues

In the 1570s, Martin Frobisher, sea captain and explorer, guided his ship back to England. The long voyage to lands far across the North Atlantic had cost dearly, but Frobisher was happy. He would report to Queen Elizabeth that he had found what he believed were the riches of the East. Although the ore that Frobisher had found turned out not to be gold, a time of glory was still beginning for England.

Medallion commemorating Queen Elizabeth I of England

 ### England Joins the Quest for Land

After John Cabot's voyage to North America in 1497, England sent no new expeditions westward across the Atlantic for more than 75 years. In 1558, however, a new queen, **Elizabeth I**, came to England's throne. Her imagination and leadership helped launch a new era in English history called the Elizabethan Age.

Europeans Arrive in North Carolina 33

That's Interesting!

Walter Raleigh received his charter for North American exploration from Queen Elizabeth I at a New Year's Day celebration on March 25, 1584. At that time, England used a form of calendar called the Julian calendar, on which March 25 was designated New Year's Day. England switched to the Gregorian calendar, which we still use today, in 1752. Of course, New Year's Day is celebrated on January 1 in the Gregorian calendar.

English sea dog Sir Richard Grenville

During Elizabeth's reign, England underwent many changes. Among the greatest of these was England's shift from Catholic to Protestant religion. Now England faced Catholic rivals such as Spain, which had become rich and powerful from its New World possessions.

The spirited, energetic new queen encouraged adventurous English seafarers to challenge Spain and resume exploration of new lands. A new breed of seafaring explorers and daredevils called **sea dogs** sought the queen's support for their plans.

One of the most famous sea dogs was Sir Francis Drake. Between 1577 and 1580, he sailed around the entire globe, becoming the first English person to do so. In the 1580s, Drake led raids on Spanish New World treasure ships and on the port of Cádiz in Spain. He even succeeded in taking several islands away from the Spanish.

Other sea dogs included **Walter Raleigh** and his older half-brother, Sir Humphrey Gilbert. Raleigh and Gilbert worked to encourage English expansion overseas. In 1577 one of these men wrote to Queen Elizabeth, promising that through overseas exploration the queen would gain "the gold and silver mines and the profit of the soil. You will be monarch of the seas and out of danger from everyone."

Raleigh's cousin, sea dog Sir **Richard Grenville**, was active against the Spanish throughout the 1580s. As a naval officer, Grenville commanded a fleet for the colonization of Virginia. Later, he helped organize English defenses against the powerful Spanish Armada. He also commanded vessels sent to intercept Spanish treasure ships.

Gilbert died at sea in 1583. Raleigh and Grenville, however, were still determined to challenge the Spanish and explore the New World. On March 25, 1584, Raleigh obtained a charter from the queen authorizing an expedition to North America.

✔ **READING CHECK** Finding the Main Idea Why are the late 1500s called the Elizabethan Age in English history?

★ The Amadas and Barlowe Expedition

In the spring of 1584, Walter Raleigh hired sailors for a **reconnaissance**, or fact-finding, expedition to the New World. He chose two experienced captains, Philip Amadas and Arthur Barlowe, to command the expedition. Amadas and Barlowe intended to locate and explore possible sites at which English colonies could be established. In this way, England might be able to compete with Spain and France for the wealth and land of the New World.

On April 27, 1584, the ships of the **Amadas-Barlowe expedition** set sail from Plymouth, England. In early July, the crew sighted North American land. They later found an inlet in the North Carolina Outer

Banks and entered Pamlico Sound. Native Americans in a small boat approached the English ships. One Indian and some English sailors exchanged friendly gestures. A few days later, the English captains arranged to meet with Indian leaders. Expressions of friendship continued, with exchanges of gifts.

The English explored the island and nearby land, making careful observations. When the ships returned to England, they carried samples of plants from Roanoke Island. They also carried two Indians, Manteo and Wanchese.

People all over England were excited about the expedition and its cargoes. For the first time, they had a chance to see Native Americans and some of the natural riches of America. In January 1585, Queen Elizabeth held a ceremony to grant knighthood to Raleigh. After that, he was known as Sir Walter Raleigh. Raleigh named the lands his expedition had explored *Virginia*, in honor of the Virgin (unmarried) Queen.

The two American Indians who went to England in 1584 are remembered and honored today in eastern North Carolina. Manteo and Wanchese are now the two chief towns on Roanoke Island.

✔ **READING CHECK** **Finding the Main Idea** How did the people of England react to the discoveries made by their explorers?

Historical Document

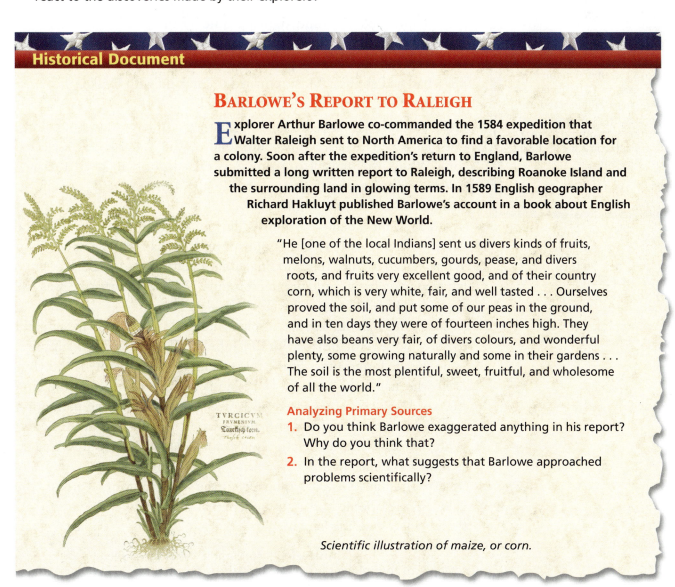

BARLOWE'S REPORT TO RALEIGH

Explorer Arthur Barlowe co-commanded the 1584 expedition that Walter Raleigh sent to North America to find a favorable location for a colony. Soon after the expedition's return to England, Barlowe submitted a long written report to Raleigh, describing Roanoke Island and the surrounding land in glowing terms. In 1589 English geographer Richard Hakluyt published Barlowe's account in a book about English exploration of the New World.

"He [one of the local Indians] sent us divers kinds of fruits, melons, walnuts, cucumbers, gourds, pease, and divers roots, and fruits very excellent good, and of their country corn, which is very white, fair, and well tasted . . . Ourselves proved the soil, and put some of our peas in the ground, and in ten days they were of fourteen inches high. They have also beans very fair, of divers colours, and wonderful plenty, some growing naturally and some in their gardens . . . The soil is the most plentiful, sweet, fruitful, and wholesome of all the world."

Analyzing Primary Sources
1. Do you think Barlowe exaggerated anything in his report? Why do you think that?
2. In the report, what suggests that Barlowe approached problems scientifically?

Scientific illustration of maize, or corn.

BIOGRAPHY

Sir Walter Raleigh
(1554–1618)

As a young man, Walter Raleigh came to the attention of Queen Elizabeth I and soon rose quickly at the royal court. Raleigh's fortunes fell when King James I came to power in 1603. The king imprisoned Raleigh in the Tower of London on charges of treason. Sir Walter Raleigh was executed in 1618. Today Raleigh is remembered as the person most responsible for opening up the North American coast for English colonization. **Why is Walter Raleigh important in the history of North Carolina?**

★ Attempts at Colonization

The English were eager to plant a colony in Virginia. Sir Walter Raleigh made preparations for an expedition.

The Ralph Lane colony A fleet of ships departed from England in April 1585. On board were the homeward-bound Native Americans, Manteo and Wanchese. Also on board were artist **John White**, who would make maps and drawings of the area around Roanoke Island, and writer Thomas Harriot, who kept a journal describing the lands.

The expedition reached Roanoke Island in August. There **Ralph Lane**, an army officer, established a colony with Sir Richard Grenville. When the ships returned to England, a little more than 100 colonists stayed behind.

The military colonists did not plant their own crops. They relied on help from local Indians to survive. But the colony's dependence on the Indians strained relations between the two communities. Uneasiness turned into hostility, and fighting quickly broke out. Lane's forces raided an Indian village, killing many. In 1586, ships led by Sir Francis Drake arrived. By then, Lane and his men, who were very short on supplies, had had enough. Most returned to England with Drake.

The Lost Colony Next the English planned a different kind of colony, one that would include women and children. Sir Walter Raleigh selected John White, the artist from previous expeditions, to head the new colony. White's group departed from England in May 1587, arriving at Roanoke Island in July of that year.

At first, the Roanoke colonists did not plant their own crops. The colony could not survive without more supplies from England. John White agreed to hurry back to England for help. Nine days before White left Roanoke, his granddaughter Virginia Dare was born. She was the first English child born in the New World.

Back in England, war with Spain interfered with plans to send aid to the colony. Not until 1590 did John White return with supplies. However, he found none of the more than 100 men, women, and children who had been on Roanoke Island. White and his men did find the word *CROATOAN* carved on a tree. Croatoan was the name of a local friendly Indian tribe and the place in which they lived. Before White could search further, though, a storm damaged his ships. He had to return to England.

No one knows what happened to the "Lost Colony." Perhaps the colonists died. Some historians believe that the colonists went off to settle elsewhere with the Croatoan Indians.

✔ **READING CHECK Analyzing Information** What factors led to the collapse of the colonies on Roanoke Island?

⭐ Other Colonies Succeed

England failed to establish a permanent colony on Roanoke Island. However, English efforts proved successful elsewhere in North America. A new king, James I, granted a charter to the Virginia Company to colonize lands along the Chesapeake Bay in North America. In 1607, the company established a colony at Jamestown in present-day Virginia. During the first years of its existence, the Jamestown colony struggled to survive. Its initial location proved to be a poor choice, since it was surrounded by unhealthy swamps and disease-bearing water. The first settlers also had great difficulty planting crops and developing reliable sources of food. Many of Jamestown's earliest colonists died of sickness and malnutrition. Troubles with the Native Americans who lived in the area of the colony added to the Jamestown settlers' challenges. In a few years, however, planters discovered that they could raise tobacco in Virginia and sell it to eager customers in England. The growth of trade and commerce between colonial Virginia and England enabled the once-endangered colony to prosper and to attract new settlers.

Far to the north, English Separatists started the colony of Massachusetts. The Separatists refused to participate in the state-sponsored Church of England. They hoped to find religious freedom in the New World. From Massachusetts the colonies of Rhode Island, Connecticut, and New Hampshire were eventually settled. Manhattan Island was settled by the Dutch in 1624. England took control of the area in 1664, renaming it New York. Before the end of the 1600s, successful colonies had also been established in Pennsylvania—centered on the city of Philadelphia—and in New Jersey and Delaware. Maryland was established as a haven for Catholics in the 1630s, but its rich lands soon attracted mostly Protestant settlers. What we now know as South Carolina began when Charles Town (now Charleston) was settled in 1670. James Oglethorpe founded the colony of Georgia, naming it for King George II, in 1733. By then, 13 English colonies clung to the North American coast between Florida and Canada. One of them was North Carolina.

✔ **READING CHECK** Contrasting How were colonists' motivations in Virginia different from those in Massachusetts?

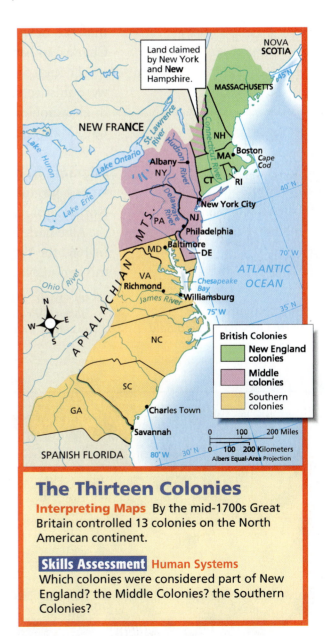

The Thirteen Colonies

Interpreting Maps By the mid-1700s Great Britain controlled 13 colonies on the North American continent.

Skills Assessment Human Systems Which colonies were considered part of New England? the Middle Colonies? the Southern Colonies?

Europeans Arrive in North Carolina **37**

Carolina is Established

As tobacco farming became successful in Virginia, some planters began to look south.

John Pory's search for tobacco land Because tobacco quickly uses up nutrients in the soil, planters needed fresh lands on which to grow tobacco crops. In 1622 a Virginia planter named **John Pory** traveled down into the Albemarle Sound-Chowan River region of present-day North Carolina to scout new tobacco lands. He reported that the land he found there was "very fruitful and pleasant."

Heath's patent In 1629 England's King Charles I granted Sir **Robert Heath** title to a huge tract of land lying roughly between present-day northern Florida and Virginia. The king's **patent**, or land grant, declared that the new province would be called *Carolana*, meaning "land of Charles" in Latin. Over time, the name was changed to *Carolina*.

Though Sir Robert Heath tried to colonize Carolina, all his efforts were unsuccessful. In 1638 he transferred rights of ownership to an English noble, Henry Howard, known as Lord Maltravers. Like Heath, Lord Maltravers had no success starting up a colony in Carolina.

Migrants from Virginia In the end, the need for more land for tobacco among Virginians led to the first permanent settlements in present-day North Carolina. By the early 1660s, hundreds had settled the north side of the Albemarle Sound, an area Virginians called "the Southern Plantation." In 1662 the Virginia Council appointed Samuel Stephens commander of this region. North Carolina was on its way to becoming a colony.

✔ **READING CHECK Making Predictions** Do you think John Pory's report back to Virginians from his travels encouraged settlement in the Albemarle-Chowan region?

North Carolina tobacco field

Unrest in England

In England, the middle 1600s were a time of great upheaval. Political arguments raged between King Charles I and his supporters on the one hand, and most of Parliament and the Puritans on the other. In the end, the situation led to civil war. The king lost the war and was executed on January 30, 1649. England became a republic, or self-governing country without a monarch. A Puritan leader named Oliver Cromwell then became ruler of England. During the 1650s, Cromwell attempted to restore order, but at his death in 1658, the Commonwealth, as the English republic was called, began to come apart.

The former ruling family of England, the Stuarts, still had many supporters. They began to call for a **restoration** of the monarchy—that is, restoring the king to power. As it happened, the dead king's son Charles was available. He had survived the civil war and escaped to France. In 1660 Parliament agreed to the restoration and called **Charles II** to assume the English throne. England quickly returned to familiar patterns. With the problem of government settled, English rulers and leaders again turned their attention to colonizing the New World.

Oliver Cromwell (center, on horseback) suppressed his political and religious opponents through a series of bloody battles like the one depicted in this painting.

✔ **READING CHECK Contrasting** How was the situation in England in 1649 different from that of 1660?

Section 4 Review

1. **Define** and explain:
   - sea dogs
   - reconnaissance
   - patent
   - restoration

2. **Identify** and explain:
   - Elizabeth I
   - Walter Raleigh
   - Richard Grenville
   - Amadas-Barlowe expedition
   - John White
   - Ralph Lane
   - John Pory
   - Robert Heath
   - Charles II

3. **Sequencing** Copy the flowchart below. Use it to list in order the main events of Roanoke Island colonization.

4. **Finding the Main Idea**
   a. What effect did Queen Elizabeth I have on English exploration and colonization?
   b. What was Sir Walter Raleigh's role in colonization of the New World?
   c. Name two important steps in the development of North Carolina as a separate colony.

5. **Writing and Critical Thinking**
   Drawing Inferences and Conclusions Why do you think English citizens of the 1580s were fascinated by Manteo and Wanchese?
   Consider:
   - the kinds of people the average English person would have seen
   - expectations of Europeans of that time about religions and cultures

Europeans Arrive in North Carolina

Chapter 2 Review

Chapter Summary

Section 1
- In the early 1400s, European nations began to explore overseas, searching for new lands and riches.
- Spanish monarchs sent Columbus westward to look for a new water route to Asia.
- The English sent John Cabot to search for what they called the Northwest Passage. The French sent Verrazano to explore North America.

Section 2
- The Spanish began exploring the interior of southeastern North America in hopes that it might hold riches.
- De Soto first explored Florida for the Spanish in 1539-40. In 1565 Spain sent troops to Florida to build more forts there and drive out French settlers.

Section 3
- European settlers traded with American Indians to obtain necessities. Indians valued European goods such as cloth and weapons.
- The Spaniards believed that God had given them control of the New World so that they could spread Catholicism. England competed by converting Indians to Protestantism.
- During the 1500s and 1600s, Native American populations fell by as much as 90 percent as a result of disease.

Section 4
- Queen Elizabeth I sent out sailors to raid Spanish ships and explore the New World.
- In 1587 the English tried to set up a colony on Roanoke Island in Carolina, but the colonists vanished.
- As the Carolina population grew, officials in Virginia appointed a separate commander for the North Carolina region.

On a separate sheet of paper, complete the following activities.

Identifying People and Ideas
Use the following terms or people in complete sentences.
1. expedition
2. Henry the Navigator
3. Hernando de Soto
4. maize
5. Elizabeth I
6. sea dogs
7. Walter Raleigh
8. Richard Grenville
9. John White
10. patent

Understanding Main Ideas

Section 1 *Pages 21–24*
1. How did nations in Europe try to get control of the Asian spice trade? Give two examples.

Section 2 *Pages 25–29*
2. Some Europeans explored New World lands to find riches and then move on. Others explored to plant colonies. Give an example of each type.
3. How did competition between European explorers lead to fighting in the New World?

Section 3 *Pages 30–32*
4. What was the most significant impact of European exploration on Native Americans? State and support your opinion.

Section 4 *Pages 33–39*
5. Why did England lose contact with the "Lost Colony" on Roanoke Island after 1587?

What Did You Find Out?
1. **Economic Development** What impact did trade with Europeans have on American Indian communities?
2. **Geography** What did the earliest English explorers of North Carolina discover about the productivity of the land?
3. **Cultural Diversity** How did religion enter into relations that developed between Native Americans and European explorers?

Thinking Critically
1. **Comparing** Among early explorers who visited today's Carolina coastal regions, what similarities do you note in their reports back home?
2. **Finding the Main Idea** State in your own words the main idea of this chapter.
3. **Supporting a Point of View** Write a paragraph to explain why you agree or disagree with this statement: Sir Walter Raleigh received credit for New World exploration, but others did the work.

Building Social Studies Skills

Interpreting Maps

The map below shows some of colonial North Carolina's earliest permanent settlements. Study the map carefully, and then answer the questions that follow.

1. Based on your analysis of the map, which of the following statements is most accurate?
   a. The area of North Carolina was densely populated during colonial times.
   b. Settlement patterns in North Carolina were heaviest in the northwestern part of the colony.
   c. The earliest settlements in colonial North Carolina were generally located along waterways and coastal areas along the colony's eastern coast.
   d. Patterns of colonial settlement in North Carolina do not appear to have been influenced by geography.

2. Why might North Carolina's earliest colonial settlements have followed the pattern of development shown by the map?

Analyzing Primary Sources

Read the following passage from Jean Ribault's book about the New World. In this excerpt, Ribault describes the appearance and activities of the Native Americans that he encountered in what is now Florida. After reading the passage answer the questions below.

> "One of them [the Indians] had hanging at his neck a little round plate of red copper well polished, with an other lesser of silver in the midst of it . . . and at his ear a little plate of copper. . . . They showed unto us that there was great store of this metal within the country, about five or six jurnaies [days' journey] from thence, both on the south and north side of the same river, and that they went thither in their boats, which boats they make but of one piece of a tree working it hollow so cunningly and fitly, that they put in one of these thus shapen boats or rather great troughs, 15 or 20 persons, and go therwith very swiftly. They that row stand upright having their oars short, made after the fashion of a shovel."

3. Based on this excerpt, the Indians probably made their boats using
   a. saplings or very young trees.
   b. smooth beams of lumber fitted together with great precision.
   c. the hollowed-out trunks of very large standing trees.
   d. planks of wood reinforced with copper.

4. What is Ribault's opinion of the techniques the Indians have developed in order to take advantage of the resources in their environment?

Alternative Assessment

Building Your Portfolio

Cooperative Learning
Build a portfolio about Elizabethan England. Two of the most important people of that era were Queen Elizabeth I and the great writer William Shakespeare. Team members can research and write a short biography of each of these people. Another team member can write a summary of a familiar Shakespearean play. Team members can also gather any other interesting, relevant information about the period.

internet connect

Internet Activity: go.hrw.com
keyword: SN3 NC2

Choose a topic about Europeans in North Carolina to:

- Build a chart describing the motives for European exploration.
- Create a visual image of the Columbian Exchange.
- Write a report on why the American colonies were settled.

Europeans Arrive in North Carolina 41

# UNIT 2
Colonial North Carolina
(1663–1815)

CHAPTER 3 **A Proprietary Colony** (1663–1729)

CHAPTER 4 **The Culture of Colonial North Carolina** (1663–1770)

CHAPTER 5 **The Fight for Independence** (1754–1783)

CHAPTER 6 **Forming a New Nation and State** (1776–1815)

Young People
IN HISTORY

Growing Up in Colonial North Carolina

Children had different experiences growing up in colonial North Carolina, based on their parents' social status. Those in the wealthy class lived in large wooden or brick houses, usually in attractive settings. Children of farmers usually lived in one- or two-room log houses with little furniture and with a single fireplace used for cooking and heat. Most parents needed all their children to work for the family's survival. For this reason, few saw a need to send their children to school. Some wealthy young men went to colleges in other states or in Great Britain. Many people in the colony, however, were self-educated.

Many children worked as apprentices to learn trades. Usually apprentices learned how to read and write. Boys learned trades such as blacksmithing, carpentry, and fishing. At the age of 16, boys were also required to join the militia. Girls learned domestic skills such as weaving, spinning, sewing, cooking, and embroidery. Marriage often took place at a young age. It was relatively easy for a young man to find land, quickly build a house, and begin to make a living for his new family. Girls sometimes married as early as 13 or 14 years of age, and most quickly began having children.

Some colonists paid particular attention to the upbringing of their children. The Moravian religious settlement begun in Wachovia in 1753 put children at the center of family life. One of the first priorities in Moravian communities was the creation of day schools. Even very young children attended these schools and learned by looking at pictures before they could read. Moravian children usually left their parents' homes by the age of 13 or 14. Boys began apprenticeships or full-time work on farms at this time. Young women increased their domestic duties or worked as servants for other families or for local businesses. Childhood ended at about the age of 21. However, most Moravians did not marry until much later. Women usually married in their late 20s and men in their mid-30s.

Many North Carolina boys served as apprentices, learning a trade as they worked. Girls usually learned essential skills from their mothers.

If You Were There How would you have been educated in colonial North Carolina?

LEFT PAGE: Small settlements and isolated homesteads dotted North Carolina's frontiers during the 1700s.

CHAPTER 3
A Proprietary Colony
(1663–1729)

The Moravians who came to North Carolina in the 1700s lived in communities like this restored village.

Build on What You Know

Do you know who heads your government? There are many different kinds of political systems. In early colonial Carolina, eight landowners ruled under the guidance of the British king. These proprietary leaders encountered many difficulties in Carolina. Yet they helped the settlement to become a successful colony.

What's Your Opinion?

Themes Journal Do you **agree** or **disagree** with the following statements? Support your point of view in your journal.

- **Citizenship** If land is plentiful, new settlers and native peoples will have few conflicts.
- **Cultural Diversity** A government must establish an official religion to maintain order.
- **Geography** Leaders must actively protect their towns in order to guarantee stability.

Section 1

Life under the Lords Proprietors

Read to Discover
1. How did the Lords Proprietors come to possess Carolina?
2. What was the organization of the colonial government in Carolina?
3. Why did Carolina grow slowly in the early days of European settlement?

Define
- quitrent
- prerogative party
- popular party

Identify
- Restoration
- Carolina Charter of 1663
- Eight Lords Proprietors
- Carolina Charter of 1665
- Fundamental Constitutions of Carolina

The Story Continues

By 1660 England's attempt to build a commonwealth had failed. Oliver Cromwell, its main leader, had died. England was without strong leadership. The members of England's exiled royal family, together with their supporters, knew exactly how to fill this gap.

Sir William Berkeley, one of the Eight Lords Proprietors

Eight are Chosen

Charles II, the son of Charles I, quickly claimed the throne. The years of his rule were known as the **Restoration** because he restored the monarchy to England. Charles II faced serious problems, however. The new king lacked money and needed political support. He hoped to expand English settlements overseas. Charles II hoped to accomplish these goals by issuing land grants in America to some of his supporters.

On March 24, 1663, Charles II authorized the **Carolina Charter of 1663**. The document used the name "Carolina," which is Latin for "Charles," to honor the new king. The charter gave the old Carolina territory to a group of powerful men known as the **Eight Lords Proprietors**.

A Proprietary Colony 45

The Eight Lords Proprietors		
Proprietor	Background	Reason for Grant
Edward Hyde, Earl of Clarendon	Member of Parliament	Worked as an adviser to Charles I and Charles II
George Monck, Duke of Albemarle	Military general	Changed political sides to help reestablish the monarchy
William Craven, Earl of Craven	Army officer	Served on the permanent council of war
John Lord Berkeley	Strong supporter of the monarchy	Accompanied the royal family when they fled the throne
Anthony Ashley Cooper, Earl of Shaftesbury	Chancellor of the Exchequer	Worked behind the scenes to reinstate the royal family
Sir George Carteret	Naval officer	Housed members of the monarchy on the Isle of Jersey
Sir William Berkeley	Governor of Virginia	Sheltered royal supporters in Virginia
Sir John Colleton	Plantation owner in the West Indies	Possibly suggested the idea of a land grant in Carolina

All of the Lords Proprietors (pruh•PRY•uh•tuhrs) had helped Charles II return to the throne. Two years after the land grant, Charles II issued the **Carolina Charter of 1665**, which expanded the Lords Proprietors' territory even further.

Powers of the proprietors The Carolina Charter of 1663 gave the Lords Proprietors enormous political power in their new colony. According to the document, they could create political offices and courts. They could collect taxes. They could establish forts and towns. However, Charles II demanded full "faith [and] allegiance" from the proprietors. They were in charge of Carolina, but the king was the final authority. The charter also allowed some religious diversity. Perhaps most importantly, the charter included the "freemen," or free male landowning citizens, of Carolina. It granted them the rights of citizens in England.

Creating counties The Lords Proprietors were eager to prove their worth to Charles II. They established three counties, naming all of them after proprietors. Albemarle County was in the northeast part of Carolina. Clarendon County stretched south from the Albemarle area to the Cape Fear Valley. Craven

Historical Document

THE CAROLINA CHARTER OF 1663

Although the Carolina Charter of 1663 granted rights only to free males, it did give the freemen a voice in their colonial government. This feature helped to establish the beginnings of a democratic tradition in Carolina.

"[We hereby] do grant full and absolute power, by virtue of these presents, to them [the Lords Proprietors] … for the good and happy government of the said province, to ordain, make, enact [establish], and under their seals to publish any laws whatsoever, either appertaining [applying] to the [public] state of the said province, or to the private utility [personal matters] of particular persons, according to their best discretion, of and with the advice, assent [agreement] and approbation [approval] of the freemen of the said province, or of the greater part of them, or of their delegates or deputies."

First page of the Carolina Charter of 1663

Understanding Primary Sources
1. According to the Carolina Charter of 1663, what was the political role of the Lords Proprietors?
2. Under the charter, what political role did the freemen have?

County was south of Cape Romaine. The proprietors also imposed a land tax called a quitrent. The establishment of the three counties marked the beginning of proprietary rule in Carolina.

✔ **READING CHECK** **Finding the Main Idea** What did the Carolina Charters of 1663 and 1665 each do?

Creating a Government

The Lords Proprietors saw themselves as long-distance colonial rulers, governing Carolina from England. They established a governor, a council, and an assembly to handle affairs in Carolina.

The governor The Lords Proprietors named William Drummond as the first governor of Albemarle County. At the time, Albemarle was the only county with a significant number of settlers. The proprietors gave the governor important executive, legislative, and judicial powers. As the chief leader in Carolina, the governor had the power to appoint council members and other officials. The governor could discharge these individuals as well—or dissolve the entire assembly. In addition, the governor could veto laws, call military forces, and issue valuable land grants.

The council After choosing a governor, the Lords Proprietors established a colonial council. Six officers formed the council. The proprietors wanted the council to work closely with the governor. Together with the governor, the council could elect civil and military officers. In the beginning years of the colony, the council members could also act as judges.

The assembly The Lords Proprietors also created an elected political assembly. The freemen of the colony could elect delegates to this assembly. These delegates could then help colonial officials create "good and wholesome" laws.

✔ **READING CHECK** **Finding the Main Idea** What three parts did the new Carolina government include?

Early Carolina governor William Drummond

Political Parties

In colonial Carolina, there were two main political parties. The "prerogative party" was made up of colonists who supported the proprietors and the monarchy. This group accepted the idea of a royal prerogative (pri•RAH•guh•tiv), or right to govern. The "popular party" included people who had settled in Carolina before the land was granted to the proprietors. They did not want the Lords Proprietors to interfere in local matters. In addition, these colonists resented the

A Proprietary Colony **47**

Did You KNOW?

Early descriptions of America and Carolina were often based solely on the writer's imagination. The author of one widely read pamphlet about Carolina had never even visited the colony!

governor's enormous political powers. The prerogative party wanted to limit the role of the freemen. The popular party hoped to protect and expand the freemen's involvement in politics. The prerogative party and the popular party clashed on many important colonial issues.

✔ **READING CHECK** Contrasting How did the prerogative party and the popular party differ?

★ Slow Growth

At first, the proprietors had trouble attracting settlers to Carolina. Several factors contributed to this problem. The colonial government seemed unstable. Tax rates were high—two times those in Virginia. Carolina's geography also discouraged settlement. Its stormy coastline and dangerous hurricanes led some settlers to call it the "graveyard of the Atlantic." The land itself was filled with thick forests and tangled swamps, making travel difficult.

The Lords Proprietors changed some of their policies to encourage settlement. They proposed a document called the **Fundamental Constitutions of Carolina**. The Fundamental Constitutions attempted to attract large landowners by guaranteeing their property rights. It described estates with permanent servants—practically a feudal system in America. The Lords Proprietors soon ignored the Fundamental Constitutions, and most of their early efforts to increase settlement were unsuccessful.

✔ **READING CHECK** Identifying Cause and Effect How did Carolina's geography affect settlement in the colony?

A woman draws water from a well outside her log cabin on this Carolina homestead.

Section 1 Review

keyword: SN3 HP3

1 **Define** and explain:
- quitrent
- prerogative party
- popular party

2 **Identify** and explain:
- Restoration
- Carolina Charter of 1663
- Eight Lords Proprietors
- Carolina Charter of 1665
- Fundamental Constitutions of Carolina

3 **Analyzing Information** Copy the web diagram below. Use the web to describe the two main political parties in colonial Carolina.

The proprietary party → Ideas, Policies
The popular party → Ideas, Policies

4 **Finding the Main Idea**
a. What events led to the Carolina Charter of 1663 and the establishment of the Lords Proprietors?

b. What kind of government did the proprietors create in Carolina?

5 **Writing and Critical Thinking**
Problem Solving Imagine that you are a Lord Proprietor. Write a paragraph explaining how you would encourage settlement in Carolina.
Consider:
- the political policies in the settlement
- the geography of the colony

Section 2

Conflicts Within the Colony

Read to Discover
1. What conflicts affected the Carolina colony in the late 1600s?
2. What were the reasons for creating a separate North Carolina colony?
3. Why did the Tuscarora War take place?

Identify
- Plantation Duty Act of 1673
- Thomas Eastchurch
- Thomas Miller
- Culpeper's Rebellion
- Seth Sothel
- Philip Ludwell
- Gibbs's Rebellion
- Vestry Act
- Edward Hyde
- Cary's Rebellion
- Tuscarora War

The Story Continues

By the 1670s the Lords Proprietors were frustrated with their lack of progress in Carolina. Despite all their efforts, they had not found a good governor for the colony. Poor leadership caused many problems in Carolina. The colonial government was unstable. Carolina could not defend itself against local Indians who resented the loss of their lands. In 1675 many colonists were killed when the Chowanoc attacked colonial settlements.

This image shows colonial farmers harvesting tobacco around 1612.

★ Culpeper's Rebellion

The Lords Proprietors became increasingly concerned about events in Carolina. New problems developed shortly after the Chowanoc uprising.

Unrest over taxes In the mid-1600s the English Parliament had passed a series of trade laws called the Navigation Acts. Years later, Parliament issued the **Plantation Duty Act of 1673** to reinforce the

A Proprietary Colony **49**

earlier laws. The act required colonial businesses to pay taxes on certain goods that were shipped within the colonies. The taxed items included tobacco, which directly affected Carolina.

Political groups in Carolina soon took sides on the new trade controversy. Members of the prerogative party generally backed the act of 1673. They wanted to build strong trade ties with England. Followers of the popular party, in contrast, opposed the law. Because many members of the party sold tobacco, the law cost them time and money.

Eastchurch and Miller In 1673 the popular party controlled the executive office under Governor John Jenkins. The governor, together with leading landowners George Durant and John Culpeper, planned to ignore the Plantation Duty Act of 1673. At the time, **Thomas Eastchurch** was Speaker of the Assembly. Eastchurch was a firm member of the prerogative party. He and newcomer **Thomas Miller** went to England to warn the Lords Proprietors about the events in Carolina. In 1676 the proprietors made Eastchurch the governor of Carolina. On the return trip to the colony, however, Eastchurch landed in the West Indies. He sent Miller on to Carolina to assume the duties of governor. Miller was a poor ruler, however. Although he stopped some illegal shipments of tobacco, he interfered with elections and imprisoned his enemies.

Miller's actions angered many colonists in Carolina. In December 1677 a group of settlers led by Durant and Culpeper attacked Miller's house. They kidnapped the colonial ruler and arrested other officials. The event was the beginning of **Culpeper's Rebellion**. Durant and Culpeper soon formed a government and established a free parliament. Culpeper was promptly arrested, however, and the rebellion ended. Culpeper's Rebellion was one of the first revolts in the American colonies.

✓ **READING CHECK** **Identifying Cause and Effect** How did the Plantation Duty Act of 1673 affect colonists?

★ Conflict in Albemarle

The problems in Albemarle did not end with Culpeper's Rebellion. Although the Lords Proprietors wanted to establish peace in their colony, the information they relied on was often confusing. This sometimes led to bad decisions that only caused more conflict.

Seth Sothel After Culpeper's Rebellion, the Lords Proprietors named **Seth Sothel** governor of Carolina. Sothel was one of the Lords Proprietors. Sothel's leadership got off to a bad start, however. On his way to Carolina, he was captured by Turkish pirates. Sothel was imprisoned for five years before he could escape. In the meantime, local officials ran the Carolina colony. Sothel eventually made his way to Carolina and became governor. Like Thomas Miller before him, Sothel

That's Interesting!

Thomas Eastchurch extended his stay in the West Indies because he fell in love with a wealthy widow who lived there. Although the two soon married, Eastchurch died before he could ever take his new bride to Carolina.

Interpreting the Visual Record

This illustration depicts a tax-gatherer being driven away from a North Carolina settlement during Culpeper's Rebellion. *What does the image reflect about settlers' feelings toward public officials?*

abused his power. He accepted bribes and seized land. In 1689 the Assembly put Sothel on trial. It banned him from the colony for a year and barred him from office forever.

Gibbs's Rebellion In 1689 the Lords Proprietors chose **Philip Ludwell** to replace Sothel as governor. Ludwell soon faced a crisis in Carolina. Captain John Gibbs insisted that he was the rightful governor, not Ludwell. Gibbs, a prominent and influential landowner, was also related to one of the Lords Proprietors. According to Gibbs, Sothel had appointed him governor before leaving office. The incident became known as **Gibbs's Rebellion**. Both Ludwell and Gibbs sailed to England to meet with the Lords Proprietors about the matter. The proprietors promptly denied Gibbs's claims to the governorship.

✔ **READING CHECK** **Finding the Main Idea** Why did Gibbs's Rebellion take place?

Growth of the Colony

During his time in office, Governor Philip Ludwell worked to improve the Carolina government. His efforts resulted in a strong and stable system that lasted through the 1690s. For a brief decade, Carolina had an effective government.

During these years of stability, settlers were drawn to Carolina and the colony experienced a period of growth. Many immigrants came from Virginia, including some French Huguenots (HYOO•guh•nahts) in search of good land. In 1706 Carolina officials established the town of Bath on a bluff overlooking the Pamlico River. Bath was the first official town in present-day North Carolina.

This historic house is found on Main Street in Bath, North Carolina.

Meanwhile, settlers continued to build homesteads along the Neuse and Trent Rivers. Around 1710 a large group of Protestant settlers from Switzerland and from southwestern Germany moved into the area. They were led by Baron Christoph von Graffenried and Franz Louis Michel. As their community grew these settlers established the town of New Bern. By 1715 about 11,000 colonists lived in Carolina.

✔ **READING CHECK** **Identifying Cause and Effect** What factors caused the Carolina colony to grow in the late 1600s and early 1700s?

Did You KNOW?
The city of New Bern was designed in the shape of a cross. It was named after the city of Bern in Switzerland.

Conflict over Religion

Charles II wanted the Anglican Church to become the official church in Carolina. Yet the Carolina charters also allowed the Lords Proprietors to permit some religious diversity in the colony.

A Proprietary Colony **51**

Worship in Carolina Despite the king's intentions, the proprietors did not establish official churches in Carolina. On the whole, they let their colonists worship freely. As a result, many non-Anglicans settled in Carolina. Most were Quakers, but others were Presbyterians or Baptists. Some colonists did not follow an organized religion.

The Vestry Act Over time, the Quakers in Albemarle became more powerful than the Anglicans. The new trend contributed to a long-standing conflict between the two groups. Some Anglicans were determined to weaken Quaker influence. In 1701 Anglican Governor Henderson Walker won passage of the **Vestry Act**. The law ordered the creation of official Anglican churches in Carolina. It also established new taxes to support Anglican clergy in Carolina.

Protests Many Quakers and Presbyterians disliked the Vestry (VES•tree) Act. They refused to pay taxes to support Anglicans. At the time, the Quakers had a majority in the Carolina assembly. They planned to overturn the law as soon as they could. The Lords Proprietors also objected to the Vestry Act, but for different reasons. They worried that it gave too much authority to local church leaders, and for that reason they rejected the law before it even went to the Assembly. Yet religious conflicts continued in Carolina. Just two years after the Vestry Act, the governor signed a law requiring that all members of the Assembly be members in good standing of the Anglican church.

The St. Thomas Church in Bath, built in 1734, was the first Anglican church in North Carolina.

✔ **READING CHECK** **Identifying Cause and Effect** Why did many non-Anglicans settle in Carolina?

⭐ Dividing a Colony

The Lords Proprietors named Thomas Cary governor of Carolina in 1705. Cary enforced the parts of Walker's law that hurt Quakers. Cary also created a special government fine that applied mostly to Quaker lawmakers. In response, a Quaker representative went to London to see the Lords Proprietors. The proprietors sent an order overturning some of Cary's policies. William Glover, Cary's replacement while he was away on business, refused to follow the new rules. Glover also claimed the governor's office for himself. Cary regained power only when he joined with a group of Quakers to overturn Glover. Cary continued as governor from 1708 to 1711.

52 Chapter 3

The appointment of Hyde The new political unrest worried the Lords Proprietors. They decided Carolina might be easier to govern as two smaller colonies. In 1710 the proprietors agreed to appoint a new governor of North Carolina who would be independent of the original Carolina governor. The decision effectively divided Carolina into two parts—North Carolina and South Carolina. The proprietors chose **Edward Hyde** as the first governor of North Carolina.

Cary's Rebellion After reaching the colony, Hyde overturned all of Cary's laws. Hyde's actions angered Cary, who considered himself to be the true governor of Carolina. Cary and his followers launched **Cary's Rebellion** to defend that claim. The revolt failed almost instantly. Cary fired cannonballs at Hyde's meeting place, but they rolled off the roof. When a few servants went outside to investigate the noise, Cary mistook them for British forces. He panicked and accidentally crashed his ship on the shore. Cary and his men escaped through the woods, but the rebellion was over.

✔ **READING CHECK** Finding the Main Idea Why did the Lords Proprietors divide Carolina into two parts?

★ The Tuscarora War

The early 1700s were difficult years in North Carolina. Bad weather had resulted in poor crops. Soon a deadly conflict arose between the Tuscarora Indians and the settlers.

Tensions between Indians and settlers There were many long-standing disagreements between the two groups. American Indians resented colonial land practices. Settlers were eager to claim land and establish farms. American Indian groups lost hunting grounds and croplands to these new residents. In 1706 and 1707 a group of settlers attacked the Meherrin Indians near the northern border of the colony. The Meherrin occupied valuable land in the area. The colonists imprisoned the Meherrin for two days and threatened to destroy their crops as well. Other colonists tried to gain Indian lands with deeds, purchase agreements, and treaties.

American Indians also objected to colonial trade policies. Some settlers cheated the Indians by trading inexpensive items such as cloth for expensive products such as furs. The colonial practice of slavery angered Carolina Indians as well. Slave traders raided Indian villages, targeting women and children in particular. They sold these Indian captives into slavery for as little as 10 British pounds.

Fighting breaks out The Tuscarora Indians decided to take action against the settlers. The Corees, the Pamlicos, the Machapunga, and the

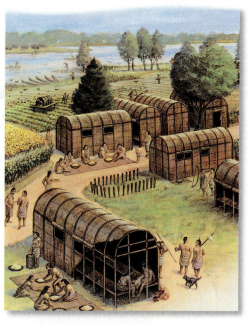

This illustration depicts an Indian village in North Carolina, c. 1600s.

A Proprietary Colony 53

Bear River Indians agreed to join them. Years later, a colonial observer explained their decision.

Analyzing Primary Sources
Identifying Cause and Effect According to Byrd, why did the American Indian groups wage war against the colonists?

"Then it was that all the neighbor Indians, grown weary [tired] of the tyranny [unfair rule] and injustice with which they had been abused for many years, resolved to endure [accept] their bondage no longer but entered into a general confederacy against their oppressors of Carolina."

William Byrd, quoted in *Colonial North Carolina—A History*

That's Interesting!

The Tuscarora Indians and their allies did not attack the Albemarle region. Tom Blunt, the Tuscarora leader in the area, had not taken a side in the conflict. To show their appreciation, the settlers allowed Blunt to use a large piece of their land. The land was later known as Indian Woods.

In early September 1711, the Tuscarora kidnapped Baron Christoph von Graffenried and John Lawson as the two men explored the Neuse River. The **Tuscarora War** had begun. On September 22 Indian forces attacked settlers along the Neuse River and the Pamlico River. They also struck the town of Bath. In one area, about 130 settlers died in two hours.

Governor Hyde called the legislature into session. The group passed laws allowing the government to issue paper money to finance a military campaign and establish a draft to raise troops. A draft is a law that calls citizens into military action. South Carolina also donated money and soldiers.

South Carolina Colonel John Barnwell led an army into North Carolina. Although many Yamasee Indians joined Barnwell's force, the troops were unable to win a decisive victory. In the fall of 1712, Hyde and many other colonists died of yellow fever. Thomas Pollock became the new governor. In December 1712 a new force led by Colonel James Moore defeated the Tuscarora. The war was over.

✔ **READING CHECK** Identifying Cause and Effect Why did the Tuscarora and their allies launch their attack in September 1711?

Section 2 Review

keyword: SN3 HP3

1 Identify and explain:
- Plantation Duty Act of 1673
- Thomas Eastchurch
- Thomas Miller
- Culpeper's Rebellion
- Seth Sothel
- Philip Ludwell
- Gibbs's Rebellion
- Vestry Act
- Edward Hyde
- Cary's Rebellion
- Tuscarora War

2 Analyzing Information Copy the web diagram below. Use it to identify causes of growth in Carolina in the late 1600s.

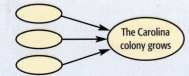

3 Finding the Main Idea
a. What political conflicts occurred in Carolina in the late 1600s and early 1700s?
b. What led the Lords Proprietors to divide the Carolina colony into two parts?

4 Writing and Critical Thinking
Identifying Cause and Effect Imagine that you are a modern-day historian. Explain the causes of the Tuscarora War.
Consider:
- the colonists' treatment of American Indians at the time
- the establishment of colonial settlements

Section 3

North Carolina on Its Own

Read to Discover
1. How did colonial leaders improve their government after the Tuscarora War?
2. Why did piracy take place in North Carolina?
3. What new towns developed in North Carolina in the early 1700s?

Define
- privateer
- borough towns

Identify
- Anne Bonny
- Edward Teach
- Stede Bonnet

The Story Continues

The winter of 1713 was a bitter one for North Carolina. The Tuscarora War had taken a heavy toll on the colony. One observer described how settlers at Neuse and Pamlico had had "most of their houses and household goods burnt, their stock of cattle, hogs, horses, [and so on] killed and carried away and their plantations ruined by the Indians." How would the colony recover from such setbacks?

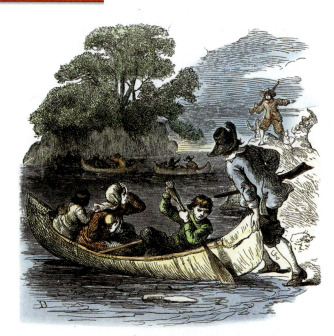

The Tuscarora War drove many settlers to leave their homes, like the women and children fleeing in this canoe.

⭐ Problems for the Colony

The Tuscarora War left North Carolina in shambles. Some colonists thought the damage would be impossible to repair. They fled the colony rather than rebuild.

Effects of the Tuscarora War The Tuscarora War had important social and financial effects on North Carolina. Many settlers had died,

A Proprietary Colony 55

and others had abandoned the area. The colonial economy faced ruin. Bills were high, and the new paper money was almost worthless.

Establishing an effective government The Tuscarora War had been devastating. Yet the aftermath of the conflict brought surprising benefits. To a large degree, the war ended American Indian attacks in the area. The conflict also helped unify the colonists. One leader commented that "the fire of difference and division among the people" had vanished. The new attitude of cooperation was a big change from the political and social divisions of the past.

The colony's government improved in the years after the Tuscarora War. The creation of North Carolina separate from South Carolina allowed leaders to focus their efforts. In 1715 the legislature passed a wide-ranging series of new laws that helped build a stronger government. One established harsh punishments for people who took part in revolts, rebellions, or uprisings. Another new policy guaranteed legal protection for Quakers and other non-Anglicans. Still other laws created plans for new roads, bridges, and channels. These routes would improve transportation and trade.

✔ **READING CHECK** Categorizing List the negative effects of the Tuscarora War.

★ Pirates Raid North Carolina

As the government grew stronger, colonial officials battled piracy. From the late 1600s to the mid-1700s many pirates operated from the Carolina coastline. Some of these pirates saw their attacks as protests against British shipping laws. Others wanted adventure and quick profits. North Carolina's unique geography contributed to piracy. The colony's inlets and islands sheltered pirates. The shallow harbors were perfect for their small ships, while ocean vessels often ran aground in the waters. In addition, the colony was fairly isolated. Pirates could attack and escape before help could arrive. Between 1717 and 1721 pirates captured about 40 ships off the Carolina coast.

Blackbeard and Bonnet One of the best-known Carolina pirates was **Edward Teach**. Teach was known as "Blackbeard" because of his flowing black beard. A captain described the well-known pirate.

> **History Makers Speak**
> "His Beard was black, which he suffered to grow of an extravagant Length; as to Breadth, it came up to his Eyes; he was accustomed to twist it with Ribbons, in small Tails . . . ; he wore a Fur-Cap, and stuck a lighted Match on each Side, under it, which . . . made him altogether such a Figure, that Imagination cannot form an [idea] of a Fury . . . to look more frightful."
>
> —Captain Charles Johnson, quoted in *The General History of the Pirates*

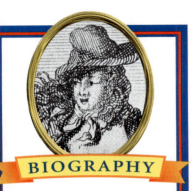

BIOGRAPHY

Anne Bonny
(c. 1700–unknown)

Anne Bonny was a female pirate who was born in Ireland and grew up in Carolina. Bonny teamed with pirate Jack Rackham in raids on the Carolina coast. Observers reported that she had a "fierce and courageous temper."

Rackham and Bonny were eventually captured. Officials executed Rackham. Bonny said of her former partner, "If he had fought like a Man, he need not have been hang'd like a Dog." Meanwhile, she begged for a light punishment. Officials gave her jail time. She eventually disappeared. Her fate remains unknown. **What did Bonny's comment about Rackham reveal about her character?**

Analyzing Primary Sources
Analyzing Information According to the source, what did Blackbeard do to make himself look more frightening to onlookers?

Like other pirates, Teach had begun his career as a **privateer**. Privateers were smugglers who transported goods in times of blockades or harsh shipping laws. Over time, however, Teach became a wholehearted pirate. He operated from the town of Bath.

Stede Bonnet was another pirate. He had served in the British Army and owned an elegant home in Barbados. Some people called him the "gentleman pirate." Bonnet even maintained a library on his pirate ship. Bonnet eventually joined Blackbeard's crew. His headquarters were located along Lower Cape Fear. In his raids Bonnet often targeted the South Carolina coast.

Stopping the pirates Colonial officials took action against the pirates many times. In 1718 they launched a major campaign against Bonnet. Troops cornered him on the Cape Fear River. After a battle lasting five hours, Bonnet was captured, and officials hanged him. Soon after, the Virginia governor sent his men after Blackbeard. Like Bonnet, Teach fought hard, but he and half his crew were killed in the conflict. Later that year, officials executed many other pirates as well. Some piracy continued off the coast of North Carolina, but the worst was over.

✔ **READING CHECK** **Problem Solving** How did colonial officials respond to the pirate attacks?

That's Interesting!

According to legend, Blackbeard was supposed to have left buried treasure somewhere in North Carolina. "Holiday's Island" in the Chowan River, "Teach's Oak" near Oriental, "The Old Brick House" near Elizabeth City, and Ocracoke Island are among the places rumored to contain the pirate's riches. However, no buried treasure has ever been found.

North Carolina Towns by 1740

Interpreting Maps The development of towns was slow in colonial North Carolina. By 1740, however, there were a number of towns in the colony.

Skills Assessment Identify the towns in colonial North Carolina.

1. **Physical Systems** Where was Albemarle Sound located?
2. **Places and Regions** What common factor did all the towns in North Carolina share?

A Proprietary Colony

The Colony Expands

The suppression of piracy allowed new expansion in North Carolina. Several new counties and towns arose.

New counties In the 1720s the colonial government established several new counties in response to growth. Bertie County was created from a portion of Albemarle County. Carteret County was located in parts of Bath County. New Hanover County was in the Lower Cape Fear region.

The Van Der Veer house in Bath was built during the North Carolina growth period of the 1700s.

Cape Fear The Cape Fear area was part of the old Clarendon County. After the Tuscarora War, colonists built homes and farms in the region. The government was eager to collect quitrents from these settlers.

New towns With growth, new towns soon arose in North Carolina. Beaufort and Edenton were located on the northern and central coastal regions of the colony. Brunswick and Wilmington, in New Hanover County, served as the shipping centers for the Lower Cape Fear area. To encourage the establishment of new towns, the legislature passed a law that gave all settlements with 60 families or more the right to have a representative in the Assembly. These were called **borough towns**. The borough town system gave some colonists a new opportunity to participate in the colonial government.

Cape Fear got its name from deadly shallow areas at the southern end of Smith Island.

✓ **READING CHECK** Finding the Main Idea Why did the colonial government create new counties in North Carolina?

Section 3 Review

keyword: SN3 HP3

1. Define and explain:
- privateer
- borough towns

2. Identify and explain:
- Anne Bonny
- Edward Teach
- Stede Bonnet

3. Analyzing Information Copy the web diagram below. Use the web to identify some of the effects of the Tuscarora War.

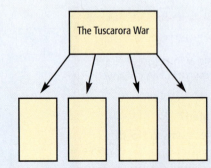

4. Finding the Main Idea
a. How did North Carolina's government seek to strengthen its authority and encourage new settlement and trade?

b. What geographical factors gave rise to piracy in North Carolina?

5. Writing and Critical Thinking
Summarizing Imagine that you are a colonial official. Write a short report on the settlement of the Cape Fear region.
Consider:
- the history of the area in colonial times
- its "rediscovery" after the Tuscarora War

Section 4

Becoming a Royal Colony

Read to Discover
1. Why did the Crown reclaim corporate and proprietary colonies?
2. What was the result of the official land survey for North Carolina?
3. How did the new royal government affect North Carolina?

Define
- survey

Identify
- John Carteret
- Granville District

The Story Continues

The British king and his Board of Trade were frustrated by the slow pace of settlement and commerce in North Carolina. In 1689 the group proposed a controversial plan to make the proprietors far less independent. They also hoped to give more power to the king. Years later, the Board of Trade actually drew up charges against the American proprietors. According to the Board, the proprietors and corporations had neglected their colonial responsibilities. The group proposed "the reuniting to the Crown the Government of all these Colonies." In other words, the English monarchy would take control of the American colonies.

Trade and commerce in colonial North Carolina grew steadily during the early 1700s.

 ### The Move Against Proprietary Colonies

North Carolina was not the only proprietary settlement in America. After the Restoration, the Crown created new proprietary colonies

A Proprietary Colony **59**

In July of 1729, North Carolina became a royal colony under the rule of England's King George II.

in Delaware, New Jersey, New York, and Pennsylvania. Over time, however, the Crown began to regret its decision to establish the proprietary colonies. The monarchy needed a more coordinated colonial empire to defend against the French and Spanish in North America. In addition, the Crown wanted to collect greater profits from colonial trade. For its part, the Board of Trade made several serious charges against the proprietors and companies holding American colonies. The Board argued that these leaders had worked against the best interests of the Crown. The group also insisted that proprietors and companies had neglected colonial defense. In addition, the Board accused them of harboring criminals in their colonies.

Over time, the Crown began to reclaim the proprietary and corporate colonies. In 1684 royal officials canceled the Massachusetts charter. Two years later the monarchy announced the creation of a "Dominion of New England." Royal officials hoped the dominion would allow them to coordinate efforts in the region. Eventually proprietary colonies such as New Jersey and New York came under royal control as well. In 1719 South Carolina became a royal colony. Was North Carolina next?

✔ **READING CHECK** Identifying Points of View Why did the Crown want to reclaim its proprietary and corporate colonies?

Did You KNOW?
William Byrd II bought some property in North Carolina after the survey, calling it the "Land of Eden."

Analyzing Primary Sources
Finding the Main Idea
Why did William Byrd II call North Carolina a "very happy" colony?

★ Land Disputes in Virginia

The Crown considered making North Carolina a royal colony like its neighbor South Carolina. Yet the boundaries of North Carolina were still unclear. Officials in Virginia and North Carolina had quarreled over the northern border area since the Carolina Charter of 1665. Both governments claimed land between 36° N and 36° 30' N.

In 1728 the two colonies began a **survey** of the area. A survey is an official measurement of land. William Byrd II was one of the Virginia surveyors. Like others in his colony, he wanted the North Carolina territory to go to Virginia.

 History Makers Speak
"It must be owned [admitted that] North Carolina is a very happy Country where people may live with the least labour that they can in any part of the world, and if the lower parts are moist and consequently a little unwholesome every where above Chowan, as far as I have seen, people may live both in health and plenty. It is the same I doubt not in all the uplands in that Province."

William Byrd II, quoted in *Colonial North Carolina in the Eighteenth Century*

Despite Byrd's wishes, the survey results favored North Carolina. The colony gained land, settlers, and a permanent border.

✔ **READING CHECK** Finding the Main Idea Which colony did the land survey favor, North Carolina or Virginia?

The Proprietors Leave North Carolina

The Lords Proprietors did not hold their colony long enough to receive the results of the survey. In 1728 seven of the eight proprietors sold their shares in the colony to the Crown. With the sale of these rights to the monarchy, North Carolina acquired the status of a royal province. In some ways, the proprietors were relieved to be free of North Carolina. The colony had been a source of endless trouble—not profit. Only **John Carteret**, the descendant of proprietor Sir George Carteret and later inheritor of the title Earl Granville, decided to keep his interest in North Carolina. The area he owned—a stretch of land along the colony's border with Virginia—became known as the **Granville District**.

At first, the change from proprietors to Crown was not very noticeable. North Carolina still had a governor, a council, and an assembly. There were court offices and land offices, as before. The British king had simply taken the place of the Lords Proprietors. Over time, however, the colonial government became more stable and efficient. The office of the governor was particularly affected by the transition. During the Lords Proprietors period, many Carolina governors had been weak. Political conflicts were common, as demonstrated by Gibbs's Rebellion and Cary's Rebellion. Under royal rule, however, administration of the colony was a direct responsibility of the Crown. The British monarch appointed the colonial governor and gave the office expanded power to set long-term policies. This new authority would serve the Crown well in the coming years.

✓ **READING CHECK** Sequencing When did North Carolina become a royal colony?

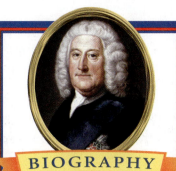

BIOGRAPHY

John Carteret, Earl Granville
(1690–1763)

John Carteret refused to sell his landholdings to the monarchy. In doing so, he gave up all political power in the colonial government. Colonial officials formally surveyed Carteret's territory in 1744. His enormous grant covered at least half of present-day North Carolina. Over time, Carteret donated some of his land to establish new towns in North Carolina. The present-day city of Hillsborough, for example, began on 400 acres of the Carteret land. **Why do you suppose that Sir John Carteret refused to sell his grant?**

Section 4 Review

keyword: SN3 HP3

1. **Define** and explain:
   - survey

2. **Identify** and explain:
   - John Carteret
   - Granville District

3. **Analyzing Information** Copy the web diagram below. Use the web to explain why the Crown wanted to end the system of proprietary and corporate rule in the colonies.

4. **Finding the Main Idea**
   a. How did the land survey affect North Carolina?
   b. What changes did the new colonial government bring to North Carolina?

5. **Writing and Critical Thinking**
   Identifying Points of View Imagine that you are a Lord Proprietor who chose to sell your grant to the Crown. Write a paragraph explaining your feelings about the decision.
   Consider:
   - the original intentions of the Lords Proprietors
   - the actual experience of the Lords Proprietors

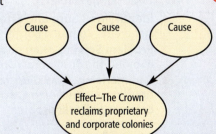

A Proprietary Colony **61**

Chapter 3 Review

Chapter Summary

Section 1
- King Charles II of England granted Carolina—what is now North Carolina and vast surrounding lands—to eight powerful English nobles known as the Lords Proprietors.
- The Lords Proprietors governed the new Carolina colony through a governor, a council, and an assembly.

Section 2
- The Carolina colony saw numerous conflicts among settlers and between European colonists and Native Americans during the late 1600s.
- The Tuscarora War of 1711–1712 caused widespread destruction and death throughout the new North Carolina colony.

Section 3
- In the aftermath of the Tuscarora War, some colonists left the area and the economy suffered, while others united in cooperation.
- Despite piracy and continuing conflict between colonists and Indians, North Carolina slowly developed and grew.

Section 4
- By the late 1720s, most of the Lords Proprietors had sold their shares of North Carolina to the British crown.
- North Carolina's colonial government gradually became more stable and effective under royal supervision.

Identifying People and Ideas
Describe the historical significance of the following.
1. Carolina Charter of 1663
2. prerogative party
3. popular party
4. Vestry Act
5. Edward Hyde
6. Tuscarora War
7. Edward Teach
8. Anne Bonny
9. borough towns
10. John Carteret

Understanding Main Ideas

Section 1 (Pages 45–48)
1. Why did Charles II grant the old Carolina territory to the Eight Lords Proprietors?
2. What were the parts of the new Carolina government?

Section 2 (Pages 49–54)
3. Why did the proprietors establish an independent governor for the colony of North Carolina?
4. Why did the Tuscarora War take place in North Carolina?

Section 3 (Pages 55–58)
5. What factors allowed piracy to exist in North Carolina?

Section 4 (Pages 59–61)
6. Why did the Crown try to reclaim many of its proprietary colonies?

What Did You Find Out?
1. **Citizenship** Why was there so much tension between Indians and colonists?
2. **Cultural Diversity** Why did religious conflicts arise in Carolina?
3. **Geography** How did colonial leaders influence settlement levels in North Carolina?

Thinking Critically
1. **Identifying Cause and Effect** Why did the Vestry Act create so much conflict in Carolina?
2. **Problem Solving** How might the colonists have avoided the Tuscarora War?
3. **Summarizing** How did the new system of royal government in North Carolina solve some of the colony's political problems?

Building Social Studies Skills

Drawing Inferences

Study the image below of the restored church building in Bath, North Carolina's earliest town. Use your analysis of the image to answer the questions that follow.

St. Thomas Church, Bath

1. Choose the response that best describes the image above.
   a. The town plan of Bath was based on the plan of a typical English village.
   b. Bath was a busy commercial center as early as 1710.
   c. Houses in Bath represented a new approach to architecture.
   d. This building probably reflects the traditional architectural styles of the colony's English settlers.
2. In what ways is the building shown above suited to life in the Carolina colony?

Understanding Frames of Reference

Read the following quote about the founding of New Bern. This is how Baron Christoph von Graffenried described the instructions he issued for the plan of the town. Then answer the questions below.

❝Since in America they do not like to live crowded, in order to enjoy a purer air, I accordingly ordered the streets to be very broad and the houses well separated one from the other. I marked three acres of land for each family, for house, barn, garden, orchard, . . . poultry yard and other purposes. I divided the village like a cross and in the middle I intended the church. One of the principle streets extended from the bank of the river Neuse straight on into the forest and the other principle street crossed it, running from the Trent River clear to the Neuse River. After that we planted stakes to mark the houses and to make the first two principle streets along and on the banks of the two rivers.❞

3. Which statement correctly describes what you can infer from the quote?
   a. Religion was important to the residents of New Bern.
   b. Overcrowding was not a problem in western Europe during this period in history.
   c. Land was plentiful in North Carolina.
   d. The people of New Bern were well-fed.
   e. Access to water was not considered important at this stage of the town's development.
4. Based on the excerpt, why did Baron Christoph von Graffenried design the town of New Bern according to this plan?

Alternative Assessment

Building Your Portfolio

Governing the Colony
Imagine that you are a colonial leader in charge of establishing a new settlement in North Carolina. Create a flowchart representing the governments of the original Carolina colony as well as the independent North Carolina colony. Indicate your place in the order of government. Create a text chart listing the strengths and weaknesses of this system of government.

internet connect

Internet Activity: go.hrw.com
keyword: SN3 NC3

Choose a topic on a proprietary colony to:
- Create a political flyer advocating a separate colony called North Carolina.
- Write a newspaper article on piracy in North Carolina.
- Construct a time line around the Tuscarora War.

A Proprietary Colony 63

CHAPTER 4
The Culture of Colonial North Carolina
(1663–1770)

Scottish settlers in North America

Build on What You Know

Under the control of the eight original proprietors, North Carolina grew slowly. Under their rule a government was formed, and the first counties were created, clearing the path for further growth.

What's Your Opinion?

 Do you **agree** or **disagree** with the following statements? Support your point of view in your journal.

- **Culture** People from different parts of the world can successfully coexist when settling the same region.
- **Economics** Economic differences can add to unrest between regions.
- **Citizenship** People who disagree with laws should disobey them.

Section 1

Immigrants and Migrants

Read to Discover
1. Why did many immigrants travel to North Carolina in the mid-1700s?
2. How did the large-scale arrival of immigrants in the 1700s weaken North Carolina's ties with England?
3. How did the slave trade develop in North Carolina?

Define
- backcountry
- immigrate

Identify
- Great Wagon Road
- Scots-Irish
- Highland Scots
- Gabriel Johnston
- Pennsylvania Dutch
- Moravians
- August Spangenberg
- Omar Ibn Said

The Story Continues

Bishop August Spangenberg, a Moravian minister, visited North Carolina in 1752. The Moravians chose to settle in the colony, finding the land similar to a favorite valley in Austria. Thousands of settlers from Scotland, Ireland, and Germany also sought to find a better life than the one they left behind.

★ The Great Wagon Road

By the mid-1700s, most of the good land in Pennsylvania had been claimed. New settlers then headed south. They followed the eastern edge of the Blue Ridge Mountains to the North Carolina Piedmont and beyond. In time, this trail stretched from Philadelphia, Pennsylvania, to Augusta, Georgia—a distance of about 800 miles. It was called the **Great Wagon Road**. After 1744 it grew to become the principle road for the colonial **backcountry** (the Piedmont area). As people traveled the Great Wagon Road, some settled along the way, creating the first settlements in the backcountry.

✔ **READING CHECK** *Finding the Main Idea* What road did people use to travel from Pennsylvania to North Carolina?

The Great Wagon Road
Interpreting Maps
The Great Wagon Road linked colonial towns and villages from Pennsylvania to Georgia.

Skills Assessment
Physical Systems What kinds of terrain influenced the course of the Great Wagon Road?

The Culture of Colonial North Carolina

BIOGRAPHY

Flora Macdonald
(1722–1790)

Flora Macdonald typified the spirit of many Scottish immigrants to North Carolina. In 1746 Macdonald helped Prince Charles Edward Stuart escape from Scotland. After British officials learned of Flora's part in the escape, she became a prisoner in the Tower of London for a short time. Flora married Allan Macdonald, and in 1774 they moved to North Carolina. Allan served in the British Army during the American Revolution. American forces captured him in 1779, and Flora returned to Scotland alone. Allan joined her there after the war. **What characteristic might describe Flora Macdonald?**

 ## New Immigrants

Between 1730 and 1775, thousands of settlers claimed land from the Atlantic to the Blue Ridge Mountains. **Scots-Irish**, **Highland Scots**, Germans, and Africans made up most of this population explosion.

The Scots-Irish Many of the Scots-Irish who moved to North Carolina came from families that had been in America for some time. As good land became harder to find in northern colonies, people looked elsewhere. Scots-Irish had begun moving into the Piedmont by 1735.

The Scots-Irish were descended from Scottish settlers who had been sent to northern Ireland by English monarchs in the early 1600s. The English wanted them to help bring Ireland under English rule and make the country Protestant. Most of the Scots-Irish were Presbyterians. As their presence and success in Ireland grew, they became a threat to the Anglican Church. By the end of the 1600s English monarchs began to encourage the Scots-Irish to leave Ireland for the American colonies.

Highland Scots In 1734 a Scot named **Gabriel Johnston** was appointed royal governor of North Carolina. He promoted Scottish settlement in the new colony by supporting legislative changes to attract Highlanders. The first large band of such settlers arrived from the western highlands of Scotland in 1740.

Meanwhile, Highlanders in Scotland faced food shortages and high rents. In 1746 the English defeated the Highlanders at the Battle of Culloden. Following this battle, the British government took harsh measures against the Highlanders. This prompted more Highland Scots to **immigrate**, or move to a new place from their homeland.

By 1775 there were about 20,000 Highland Scots in North Carolina. They made their homes in the upper Cape Fear River valley—Anson, Bladen, Cumberland, Moore, Richmond, and Robeson counties. Many of the new arrivals spoke only their native Gaelic language. By the end of the 1700s a printer in Fayetteville had begun providing Highlander communities with religious sermons and tracts in Gaelic. Highland Scots in North Carolina remained loyal to Great Britain during the time of the American Revolution.

Germans Other immigrants in the backcountry included the **Pennsylvania Dutch**. The "Dutch" part of their name comes from the word *Deutsch*, which means "German." In Europe, these Germans had experienced war, religious persecution, and poverty. They first arrived in Rowan County in 1747 to find a better life and settled in the Piedmont. Attempting to preserve their culture, the Germans established their own churches and schools. They also kept traditional ways of building and tending their farms.

The **Moravians**, or United Brethren, were a German Protestant group. They held religious beliefs against war and refused to bear arms against others. A Moravian bishop, **August Spangenberg**, explored parts of North Carolina in 1752 with the hope of finding a new home for his group from Pennsylvania and for other immigrants. In what is today Forsyth County, he found a suitable tract of land. The Moravians named this land Wachovia, which means "meadowland." By 1766, they had established the towns of Bethabara and Salem.

Property was held in trust for people in Moravian communities and assigned by the church. Farmers ran their farms with little help from slave labor. Moravians were active traders. Craftsmen produced fine tools and other goods. People in the community were well provided for with medical and dental services. In fact, Moravian teachers and doctors served other back-country communities.

Like the Highland Scots, most German settlers in North Carolina preserved their language until well into the 1800s. This language barrier and their separate cultures kept them from playing a major role in the American Revolution. Instead, most remained neutral.

The couple in this illustration are wearing traditional Moravian dress.

✓ **READING CHECK** **Identifying Cause and Effect** Why did so many immigrants settle in North Carolina?

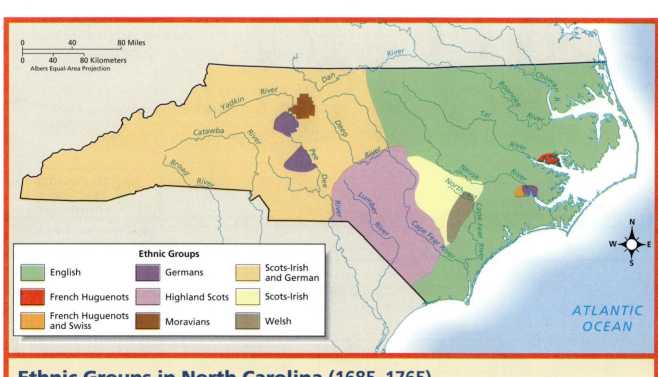

Ethnic Groups in North Carolina (1685–1765)

Interpreting Maps Between 1685 and 1765, diverse groups of Europeans settled across North Carolina. These immigrant groups were distinguished by languages and religions carried over from their home countries.

Skills Assessment The World in Spatial Terms
1. With what other groups did the Welsh share an area of settlement?
2. Who lived further west in North Carolina, the French Huguenots or the Moravians?

The Culture of Colonial North Carolina **67**

Africans in North Carolina, 1717–1790	
Year	Number
1717	1,000+
1720	3,000
1730	6,000
1754	15,000
1765	30,000
1767	39,000
1790	100,572 (slave)
1790	4,975 (free)

Africans Most African settlers in North Carolina were brought to the colony against their will and enslaved. Slavery was made legal in the colony by the Fundamental Constitutions of 1669. Slaves came from Africa and were sold by the Royal African Company.

Some slaves practiced the religion of Islam. One noteworthy Muslim slave in North Carolina was **Omar Ibn Said**, who was an Arabic scholar. He learned English, converted to Christianity, and spent time studying an Arabic translation of the Bible.

Compared with other southern colonies, North Carolina had the smallest population of enslaved Africans and never developed a strong international slave trade. Fewer than 1,000 slaves were in the colony until 1715. One reason for this was a shortage of good ports. Also, the small farmers of the Piedmont generally did not need large numbers of slaves, and the plantations of the Tidewater never grew as large as those in Virginia and South Carolina.

In addition, Quakers living in central North Carolina worked to end slavery. In 1770, the Quakers issued a statement calling for an immediate end to the slave trade and to slavery.

✓ **READING CHECK** Analyzing Information How did the slave trade affect North Carolina?

Many enslaved Africans and their descendants worked in cotton fields like the one in this drawing.

Section 1 Review

keyword: SN3 HP4

1 Define and explain:
- backcountry
- immigrate

2 Identify and explain:
- Great Wagon Road
- Scots-Irish
- Highland Scots
- Gabriel Johnston
- Pennsylvania Dutch
- Moravians
- August Spangenberg
- Omar Ibn Said

3 Categorizing Copy the graphic organizer below. Fill in the missing information about immigrant groups in North Carolina.

Name	Place of origin	Time of arrival
Scots-Irish	Other colonies	
Highland Scots		1740
Pennsylvania Dutch	German-speaking countries	
Moravians		1752
Africans	Africa	

4 Finding the Main Idea
a. Describe ways in which the Moravian settlers in North Carolina were unique.
b. What factors affected the growth of slavery in North Carolina?

5 Writing and Critical Thinking
Supporting a Point of View Imagine that you are a Highland Scot at the time of the American Revolution. Write a letter to a friend defending your decision to stay neutral.
Consider:
- experience of the Highland Scots in Scotland
- possible consequences of losing the war

Section 2

The Economy and Social Structure

Read to Discover
1. What were the main cash crops of North Carolina?
2. What social divisions emerged in North Carolina?
3. Why do you think North Carolinians sharply restricted the activities of enslaved Africans?

Define
- cash crop
- naval stores
- gentry
- artisans
- militia
- yeomen
- indentured servants
- apprentice
- sectionalism

The Story Continues

Early farmers, struggling to survive in a new environment, learned much from their Native American neighbors. They learned to plant seeds in rows and hills, remove weeds with wooden hoes, and use scarecrows to frighten away birds and animals. In North Carolina by the 1700s, agriculture was the way in which about 95 percent of the population made a living.

A 1622 illustration of the tobacco plant

 ## Agriculture

Settlers found that crops such as wheat, oats, and barley flourished in the climate of North Carolina. Native American crops also did well—corn, tobacco, potatoes, squash, beans, peas, sunflowers, and sweet potatoes.

Cash crops Tobacco was the colony's first **cash crop**, which is a crop grown to sell for profit. Farmers in Virginia were the first colonists

The Culture of Colonial North Carolina **69**

Interpreting the Visual Record

Family farm *Most people in colonial North Carolina made their living from agriculture, often on small working farms like the one pictured here. Based on this image, do you think the family living on this farm had much contact with others? Explain.*

to succeed at growing tobacco. They shared their knowledge with the other colonies, and North Carolina farmers caught on quickly. By the mid-1700s, the tobacco industry was thriving. On a smaller scale, rice and indigo were grown with success in the area of the Lower Cape Fear River. England and the West Indies provided a good market for North Carolina farmers. Farm products from the colony were also sold to northern colonies.

Livestock Colonists relied heavily on their livestock. Horses and oxen pulled wagons and plows. Cattle, sheep, chickens, and hogs were raised for sale. North Carolina livestock went to colonial markets including Maryland, New Jersey, and Virginia. North Carolina provided about one eighth of all pork and beef exports from Britain's continental colonies.

Forest products North Carolina's immense forests were also a source of trade goods. By 1768, North Carolina provided about 60 percent of all **naval stores** exported from the colonies to England. Naval stores were non-lumber products that came from trees, such as tar, pitch, rosin, and turpentine. Sailors relied heavily on these products, most of which came from the longleaf pine forests of the lower Cape Fear valley. The nickname Tar Heel State was based on North Carolina's naval stores industry.

Like Great Britain and the northern colonies, the West Indies depended on North Carolina lumber. The West Indies received more than one-half of the colony's wood products.

Trading routes North Carolina, along with other colonies, had few good transportation routes. Roads were often poorly marked paths that were hard to travel. They were also difficult to maintain. Heavy rains caused the roads to turn into mud and the rivers to be difficult routes.

The difficulties of travel hindered trade. Regardless, trading routes formed that ran north to south. Such routes ran between Salem and Salisbury, Edenton, New Bern, and Wilmington. Another went through the towns of Edenton, Bath, Wilmington, and Brunswick on the way from Virginia to South Carolina. The "Great Trading Path" went from Albemarle Sound to the mountains following an east to west direction.

✔ **READING CHECK** Drawing Inferences and Conclusions How did the colony's poor system of roads affect settlers in the backcountry?

★ The Social Classes

By the mid-1700s, a social order similar to the one in England had developed. As a result, structured social classes and distinctions arose in colonial North Carolina.

Naval Stores Exports from Colonial North Carolina		
	Tar and Pitch (bbls)	Turpentine (bbls)	Total
1752–53	73,580	10,429	84,009
1768–69	116,886	10,793	127,679
1769–70	62,386	17,428	79,814
1770–71	84,411	17,955	102,366
1771–72	111,967	15,202	127,169
1772–73	105,581	11,647	117,228
1773–74	84,048	18,891	106,049
1774–75	66,232	30,031	99,703
1775–76	106,086	73,013	179,129
1776–77	3,706	10,704	14,410

The landed gentry The upper class was the gentry. This very small wealthy class included planters, public officials, and professionals such as lawyers and clergy. The gentry enjoyed a comfortable life. They used costly silver to dine off fine china. Paintings adorned their walls, and books lined their shelves. Many gentry entered politics, as they were free from daily physical labor.

Artisans and small farmers The largest social class included artisans and small farmers. Artisans were skilled craftspeople who made products and constructed buildings needed on the farms and in the towns. They also formed the civilian fighting force known as the militia.

Yeomen were small farmers, who raised crops to provide only for their families. These farmers were very independent and not interested in trade. However, they bartered with surplus crops for needed goods.

Down the social ladder from the small farmers were indentured servants. These were poor people who signed indentures, or contracts, to work for others for a certain number of years in exchange for food and shelter. Indentured servants provided an important source of labor.

An apprentice was another type of worker with a contractual relationship. Children were placed in the care of artisans and expected to work. In return, they received instruction in a craft or trade including that of blacksmith, carpenter, or weaver. Food and shelter were also provided.

Slaves and Indians Enslaved Africans were considered to be the lowest social class. As slavery grew, the rights of slaves became more limited. In the 1700s, slaves could not leave the plantation without special passes or gather in social groups. Slaveholders could not free their slaves without county court approval.

Unlike yeomen, slaves such as the ones shown here worked on plantations requiring large numbers of laborers.

The Culture of Colonial North Carolina

Native Americans lived in parts of the colony. For example, the Cherokee Indians had agreed to live in a small area of the southern Appalachians. In time, less and less land was designated as belonging to the Indians. With smaller hunting grounds available, some Indians changed their way of living to that of small farm life.

 READING CHECK Contrasting How did indentured servants differ from slaves?

★ Daily Life

Men and women performed different roles in colonial America, and children were educated differently based on whether they were sons or daughters. For example, sons were taught reading, writing, and arithmetic, and they learned a profession or business. Daughters were also taught to read and write, but much of their education focused on the management of household affairs to make them more attractive as marriage prospects. Women sometimes married at 13 or 14 years of age. The age of 20 was considered old for marriage. Large families were also common. With the challenge of motherhood, the difficult life of a settler, and inadequate medical care, many women died young. Colonial men and women worked together to raise their children. One observer noted the ways in which yeoman families raised their children:

 "The mothers took the care of the girls, they were train'd up under them, ... custom has established it as still necessary for the men to spend their time abroad in the fields; and to be a good marksman is the highest ambition ..."

Janet Schaw, quoted from *Journal of a Lady of Quality* edited by Evangeline Walker Andrews

Analyzing Primary Sources
Finding the Main Idea How did Schaw perceive the roles of men and women in colonial society differently?

Small farmers needed children to keep their farms going. Fathers taught their sons to farm, to care for livestock, and to fish and hunt. They also passed on their knowledge of crafts such as blacksmithing or carpentry. Some women artisans worked from their homes as weavers or seamstresses.

Housing In colonial North Carolina, many houses were not made well. Simple one- or two-room homes were built with clay, stone and wood, which were readily available. There were some log houses with chimneys made from mud and sticks. They typically had wooden shutters, dirt floors, and board roofs. By the time of the American Revolution, some brick houses had been constructed.

This pioneer farmstead, the Ephraim Bales Place, still stands in the Great Smoky Mountains National Park.

Communication Homes were far apart from one another. Isolated farm families enjoyed the opportunity to socialize. Travelers were welcomed with a show of hospitality. Women presented a good meal with their best silver and china. Men gathered at the local inn for conversation and to hear politicians speak. Dances were popular with men and women. People danced whenever someone would play a fiddle or a bagpipe.

Transportation Horses were necessary for travel. Horse-drawn carriages were owned by the wealthy, but most people owned two-wheeled carts. As the population grew, the number of roads connecting north to south and east to west increased. However, for much of the 1700s, rivers remained the main routes of trade.

✔ **READING CHECK** Finding the Main Idea How did people socialize in colonial North Carolina?

★ A Unique Colony

The people of the colony felt strong loyalties for the different regions, or sections, in which they lived. This is called **sectionalism**. It first emerged in conflicts between the northern and southern, and later the western and eastern, regions. Conflicts grew from geographical differences and from cultural differences. Each region was unique in its land and people, who came from various home countries and had different economic interests. Some counties struggled to maintain power as others fought for a greater role in government.

✔ **READING CHECK** Summarizing What factors contributed to sectional differences in North Carolina?

CONNECTING TO SCIENCE AND TECHNOLOGY

North Carolina's First Printing Press

Before the mid-1700s there were no printing presses or bookmakers in the colony, and all publications had to be printed outside of North Carolina. This changed when James Davis arrived in 1749. He set up a print shop in New Bern and was hired by the government to print its paper money. Davis was also appointed the colony's "State Printer."

As state printer, Davis printed legislative journals and proceedings, laws and proclamations, and other official documents. He also printed the first issue of the colony's first newspaper, the *North Carolina Gazette*, in 1751. **What did the first printing press in North Carolina publish?**

keyword: SN3 HP4

① **Define** and explain:
- cash crop
- naval stores
- gentry
- artisans
- militia
- yeomen
- indentured servants
- apprentice
- sectionalism

② **Compare and Contrast** Copy the graphic organizer below. Fill in the circles with information about social classes in North Carolina.

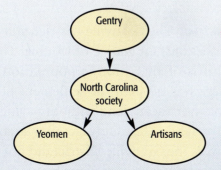

③ **Finding the Main Idea**
a. Identify the main characteristics of the social classes in colonial North Carolina.

b. What is the difference between cash crops and other crops grown by farmers in colonial North Carolina?

④ **Writing and Critical Thinking**
Supporting a Point of View Imagine that you are a woman or an enslaved African living in colonial North Carolina. Write an essay explaining why you think you deserve more status in society.
Consider:
- the contributions of women to society
- the contrast between liberty and slavery

The Culture of Colonial North Carolina 73

Section 3

Internal Conflicts

Read to Discover
1. How did sectional conflicts affect North Carolina?
2. What was the significance of the Battle of Alamance?

Define
- anarchy
- poll tax
- amnesty
- extortion

Identify
- Arthur Dobbs
- William Tryon
- Edmund Fanning
- Regulators
- War on Sugar Creek
- Battle of Alamance

Governor Arthur Dobbs tried to warn the British government about the growing unrest in the colonies.

The Story Continues

North Carolina existed as a royal colony for almost 40 years without a permanent capital. The colony's lawmakers met at various places through the years. Governors Johnston, Dobbs, and Tryon encouraged the colony to agree upon a "fixed seat of government." Many towns throughout the colony were interested in becoming its capital.

★ North Against South

The issue of the capital soon became a source of conflict. The dispute began in the Granville District.

The Granville District The Granville District, still in the possession of John Carteret, was a constant source of trouble. The Granville District contained two-thirds of the colony's population, but it was poorly administered. There was no plan for settlement of the territory. Most settlers simply took over vacant land without paying. Often they refused to pay quitrents, or land taxes. Outrage grew among people in other parts of the colony, as the Granville District did not seem to be carrying its fair share of the colony's economic burden.

74 Chapter 4

Challenges from Cape Fear Unequal representation was a problem in the colonial Assembly. The counties in the Albemarle region had five representatives each. New counties in the Cape Fear region were given two representatives each.

Governor Gabriel Johnston held a personal interest in the Cape Fear region and sided with the southern counties over the matter of representation. In November 1746, the Assembly met without its Albemarle representatives and passed some laws favorable to the southern counties. They agreed on a permanent location for the capital in New Bern and cut Albemarle's representation per county to two. Johnston then had the new laws sent to London for authorization by the king and the colonial authorities.

The Albemarle Revolt The people of Albemarle protested to the authorities. No response came from England for seven years. The Albemarle counties ignored all laws passed by the Assembly between the years 1747 and 1754. During this time **anarchy**, or a complete absence of government, existed in the North.

Governor Johnston died in 1752. King George II replaced him with **Arthur Dobbs**. Dobbs also favored southern interests, but the king ordered that the laws passed by Johnston's Assembly of 1746 not be enforced.

> "The Assembly think themselves entitled to all the Privileges of a British House of Commons and therefore ought not to submit to His Majesty's ... instructions to His Governor and Council here."
>
> Governor Dobbs, reporting to London officials, quoted from *The Colonial Records of North Carolina* edited by William L. Saunders

 READING CHECK **Drawing Inferences and Conclusions** What issues divided the northern and southern counties of North Carolina?

★ West Against East

When Governor Dobbs died in 1765, **William Tryon** became governor. In 1767, he began building a grand residence at New Bern. It was to serve as the capitol building, and it was intended to be the governor's home. However, it resembled a palace. Westerners became angry, fueling an ongoing debate between west and east.

The Assembly created western counties to match the growth of the backcountry's population. At the same time, it created more eastern counties to keep control of the colonial government. In 1770, about one third of the colony's settlers lived in the west. Yet, out of a total of 81 representatives, only 15 served western county interests. Another problem was the **poll tax** enacted to pay for the governor's new building. All adults, rich and poor alike, were taxed at the same rate.

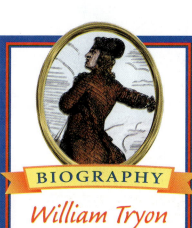

BIOGRAPHY
William Tryon
(1729–1788)

William Tryon served as an English colonial governor in North America. After a distinguished army career, he was appointed lieutenant governor of North Carolina in 1764, and he succeeded Arthur Dobbs as governor in 1765. The colonists were not fond of Tryon, because he defeated the Regulator movement. However, he was an able administrator. In 1771 he was appointed governor of New York. During the American Revolution, he led Tory raids in Connecticut. Tryon returned to England after the war. He died there in 1788. **What were some of William Tryon's political accomplishments?**

The Culture of Colonial North Carolina

Westerners were especially troubled by people they called "foreigners," who rose to power in the colonial government. All English officials were in this category. One such official was **Edmund Fanning**, who was a close friend of Governor Tryon.

In the colony, many public officials obtained their positions as gifts from the king or the governor. They were paid fees fixed by law. Bribery and corruption became a common part of colonial government.

✔ **READING CHECK** Summarizing In what specific ways did eastern and western North Carolina differ?

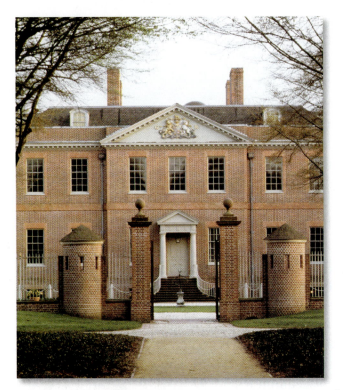

Interpreting the Visual Record

Tryon Palace today *Tryon Palace burned down in 1798. This reconstruction of the palace was built in the 1950s.* **Why might Tryon Palace have angered some colonists?**

The name Regulator came from the settlers, because they wanted to "regulate" their own affairs.

★ The Regulators

In the mid-1760s, a group called the **Regulators** was formed in Orange County to combat what they saw as abuses of power by the colonial government.

In 1765, two landlords decided to sell their land in Mecklenburg County in the backcountry. Surveyors were sent out, but squatters on the land forced them back. This skirmish came to be known as the **War on Sugar Creek**. The governor offered *amnesty*, or a pardon, to anyone volunteering the names of the riot leaders. No names were given.

The Regulators took their first action in 1766, when they called a public meeting to protest what they saw as colonial officials' abuse of power. Leaders included Herman Husband and Rednap Howell, who was a talented writer. His writings criticized royal officials in a humorous way. Howell's favorite target was Edmund Fanning, who lived in Orange County.

In 1768 officials were sent out to collect taxes for the governor's new palace. Many settlers refused to pay and accused government officials of *extortion*, or demands for illegal fees. A sheriff in Hillsborough seized some personal items from a Regulator, which resulted in violent retaliation.

The Regulators suggested a meeting with colonial officials, but Fanning refused. To restore order, Governor Tryon headed for Orange County with a militia of nearly 1,500 men. Arriving in Hillsborough, he found more than 3,700 Regulators and their sympathizers ready to fight.

Some Regulators were convicted of rioting. The king pardoned the settlers based on advice from Tryon. Fanning was convicted of extortion, but the court did not punish him. The Regulators continued to oppose the colonial government.

✔ **READING CHECK** Finding the Main Idea Who were the Regulators and why did they take action?

⭐ The Battle of Alamance

The colonial government realized that changes needed to be made, but the Regulators were not willing to wait. In the fall of 1770 the Hillsborough courthouse was broken into by a group of 150 Regulators. Then they ran through the streets shattering windows and damaging Fanning's house.

In the spring of 1771, a militia of nearly 1,500 faced off against some 2,000 Regulators across the Great Alamance Creek. Tryon called out for the Regulators to lay down their arms or be fired upon, but the Regulators shouted back, "Fire and be damned!" Tryon gave the order to shoot.

The battle raged for nearly two hours with the government forces emerging triumphant. Tryon dealt reasonably with the rebels. Although six were executed for treason, thousands more were spared in exchange for their allegiance to the colonial government.

Although the Regulator movement ended with the **Battle of Alamance**, tensions continued between west and east. Sectional conflicts became less important as protests against British rule took priority.

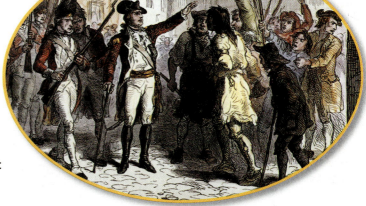
Governor Tryon (center, with an arm raised) confronts the Regulators.

✔ **READING CHECK** Identifying Cause and Effect
How did Governor Tryon treat the Regulators when they rebelled?

Section 3 Review

go.hrw.com Homework Practice Online
keyword: SN3 HP4

1. **Define** and explain:
   - anarchy
   - poll tax
   - amnesty
   - extortion

2. **Identify** and explain:
   - Arthur Dobbs
   - William Tryon
   - Edmund Fanning
   - Regulators
   - War on Sugar Creek
   - Battle of Alamance

3. **Summarize** Copy the graphic organizer below. Fill in the circles with information about the four main sections of North Carolina.

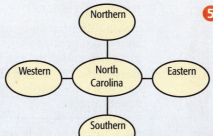

4. **Finding the Main Idea**
   a. Summarize the sequence of events that led up to the Battle of Alamance.
   b. What were some problems in the Granville District?

5. **Writing and Critical Thinking**
   Identifying Points of View Imagine you are a Regulator. Write a newspaper editorial justifying your actions against the colonial government.
   Consider:
   - sectional differences in North Carolina
   - colonial government policies in western North Carolina

The Culture of Colonial North Carolina

Chapter 4 Review

Chapter Summary

Section 1
- During the 1700s, many immigrants from Europe as well as other American colonies came to North Carolina. The Great Wagon Road became one of the busiest routes of colonial times.
- Immigrants to North Carolina included Scots-Irish, Highland Scots, Germans such as the Pennsylvania Dutch and the Moravians, and forced immigrants such as enslaved Africans.

Section 2
- Tobacco became the main cash crop in North Carolina, although rice, indigo, livestock, and lumber were also important to the colony's economy.
- A social order emerged with the landed gentry at the top, followed by artisans, small farmers, indentured workers, and slaves and Indians.

Section 3
- Economic and political rivalry between north and south and east and west led to sectional conflicts within the colony.
- Unrest in the western parts of the colony gave rise to the rebel organization known as the Regulators, who clashed with government forces at the Battle of Alamance.

Identifying People and Ideas

Use the following terms or people in complete sentences.

1. Great Wagon Road
2. Scots-Irish
3. Highland Scots
4. Pennsylvania Dutch
5. Moravians
6. gentry
7. sectionalism
8. William Tryon
9. Regulators

Understanding Main Ideas

Section 1 (Pages 65–68)
1. How did immigration change North Carolina?
2. What effect did the slave trade have on the colony?

Section 2 (Pages 69–73)
3. Why were North Carolina counties unequally represented in the colonial Assembly?
4. Why were people in western North Carolina angry about Governor Tryon's palace?

Section 3 (Pages 74–77)
5. What did Governor Gabriel Johnston do to cause the Albemarle Revolt?
6. What was the War on Sugar Creek?

What Did You Find Out?

1. **Culture** What motives and patterns of living did Highland Scot and Pennsylvania Dutch immigrants to North Carolina share?
2. **Economics** What economic differences contributed to sectional rivalries within North Carolina?
3. **Citizenship** What effects did the Albemarle Revolt have on daily life in the northern counties?

Thinking Critically

1. **Making Comparisons** In what ways were the immigrant groups that settled in North Carolina similar to and different from one another?
2. **Identifying Cause and Effect** How did North Carolina's geography affect the development of slavery there?
3. **Supporting a Point of View** Do you think that the location of trade routes influenced the growth of towns in North Carolina? Use examples to support your answer.

Building Social Studies Skills

Interpreting Graphs

Study the graph, which gives information about tar and pitch exports in North Carolina. Then answer the questions that follow.

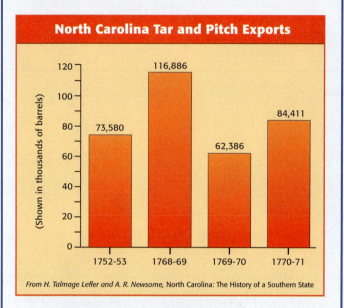

North Carolina Tar and Pitch Exports (Shown in thousands of barrels)

- 1752–53: 73,580
- 1768–69: 116,886
- 1769–70: 62,386
- 1770–71: 84,411

From H. Talmage Lefler and A. R. Newsome, *North Carolina: The History of a Southern State*

1. Which statement correctly describes what you can infer from the graph?
   a. The best year for tar and pitch exports was 1770–71.
   b. The best year for tar and pitch exports was 1768–69.
   c. The worst year for tar and pitch exports was 1752–53.
   d. 1769–70 was a good year for tar and pitch exports.

2. What effects might the level of tar and pitch exports have had on North Carolina?

Understanding Frames of Reference

Read the following verses from a poem by Rednap Howell, the "poet of the Regulation." The poem, entitled *When Fanning First to Orange Came*, refers to colonial official Edmund Fanning. Then answer the questions below.

> "Says Fanning to Frohock [another official]
> 'tis folly to lie;
> I rode an old mare that was blind of an eye.
> Five shillings in money I had in my purse;
> My coat it was patched but not much the worse.
> But now we've got rich and it's very well known
> That we'll do very well if they let us alone. . . .
>
> When Fanning first to Orange came
> He looked both pale and wan,
> An old patched coat upon his back,
> An old mare he rode on.
> Both man and mare warn't worth five pounds
> As I've often been told;
> But by his civil robberies
> He's laced his coat with gold."

3. Which statement describes how the author might feel about the situation he described?
   a. He probably feels kindly toward Fanning.
   b. He probably thinks Fanning needs a new coat and horse.
   c. He probably does not approve of Fanning's actions as an official.
   d. He probably thinks it's the way things should be.

4. How does the author characterize Fanning? Give specific examples.

Alternative Assessment

Building Your Portfolio

Cooperative Learning
Complete the following activity in small groups. Have each person in the group assume the role of a person who is considering immigrating from Scotland, Ireland, or Germany to North Carolina. Some members of the group will support the idea of immigration to find a new home and others will argue against leaving their current home in Europe. Create a journal explaining these differences of opinion.

internet connect

Internet Activity: go.hrw.com
keyword: SN3 NC4

Choose a topic about the culture of colonial North Carolina to:

- Write an essay on slavery in North Carolina.
- Create a chart showing the roles and contributions of North Carolina colonists.
- Draw a map that outlines the sectional differences in North Carolina.

The Culture of Colonial North Carolina

CHAPTER 5
The Fight for Independence
(1754–1783)

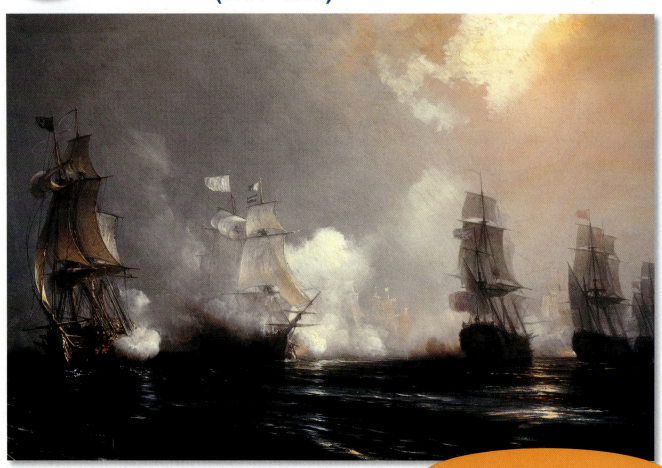

British and French ships face off during the Siege of Yorktown.

Build on What You Know

During the mid-1700s, North Carolina was slowly moving from isolation to greater contact with the other colonies. Standards of living within the colony were slowly improving. These developments encouraged a desire for independence as the colonists came to think of themselves as a people apart from their British rulers.

What's Your Opinion?

Themes Journal Do you **agree** or **disagree** with the following statements? Support your point of view in your journal.

- **Citizenship** Citizens have a right to form a new type of government if they are unhappy with their leaders' policies.
- **Global Relations** Harsh ruling policies can lead a colonial people to revolt.
- **Government** Governments must always represent the views of their people.

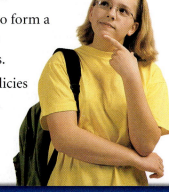

Section 1

Growing Conflicts

Read to Discover
1. How did the French and Indian War affect North Carolina?
2. What British policies concerned colonists after 1763?
3. How did North Carolina react to Britain's new colonial policies?

Identify
- Congress of Augusta
- Stamp Act
- Non-Importation Association
- John Harvey

The Story Continues

In 1754, the president of the North Carolina Assembly read an urgent message from Virginia's governor. The governor wrote that "the French have formed . . . to encroach [trespass] on our settlements to the westward. You know too well gentlemen the importance of the western territory . . . to sit still and tamely see a formidable [strong] foreign power possess themselves of it."

★ The French and Indian War

Hostilities in the French and Indian War began in 1754. The conflict was part of a larger struggle between France and Great Britain for global power. The French claimed a large region of the American interior and allied with Indian groups to prevent British settlers from moving into this western area. The North Carolina Assembly passed a special tax to send troops to help strengthen neighboring Virginia. It also supplied arms and ammunition to North Carolina's frontier counties.

Despite North Carolina's efforts to protect its frontier, the threat grew. Encouraged by the French, Indians killed so many settlers in the next few years that much of the frontier was abandoned. In 1758,

This illustration of the French and Indian War shows George Washington planting the British flag at Fort Duquesne in 1754.

The Fight for Independence 81

however, the French strongpoint of Fort Duquesne in the Ohio River valley was captured by the British. North Carolina troops were involved in this mission.

After the loss of Fort Duquesne, the French strengthened their alliance with the Cherokee. Roaming bands of Cherokee drove colonists off lands along the Catawba River and in Rowan County. Finally a group under the command of James Grant advanced into Cherokee lands. The attack forced the Cherokee to sign a peace treaty in 1761.

After the end of the French and Indian War in 1763, Great Britain sought to make peace with the Indians. At the king's command, North Carolina governor Arthur Dobbs attended the **Congress of Augusta**. He met with other governors, Great Britain's Indian agent, John Stuart, and about 700 Indians. Together they reached a "Treaty of Perpetual Peace and Alliance" with the Chickasaw, Choctaw, upper and lower Creek, Cherokee, and Catawba Indians. The treaty settled all claims and boundaries with Virginia, North and South Carolina, and Georgia.

✔ **READING CHECK** **Identifying Cause and Effect** Why did the Cherokee sign a peace treaty in 1761?

Historical Document

THE ALBANY PLAN OF UNION

Early hostilities in the French and Indian War led many colonial leaders to consider the need for greater cooperation. Delegates from seven colonies—not including North Carolina—met in Albany, New York, in the summer of 1754. At the Albany Congress, Benjamin Franklin helped write a plan calling for a centralized government for all the colonies. The plan influenced later documents that helped build the United States.

It is proposed that humble application be made for an act of Parliament of Great Britain, by virtue [advantage] of which one general government may be formed in America, including all the said colonies . . .

That the said general government be administered by a President-General, to be appointed and supported by the crown; and a Grand Council, to be chosen by the representatives of the people of the several Colonies met in their respective assemblies.

Analyzing Primary Sources
1. What advantages did the Albany Plan offer to the colonies?
2. What was the structure of government suggested in the Albany Plan?

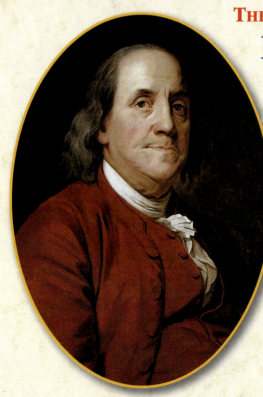

Benjamin Franklin

⭐ Unrest in the Colonies

After the French and Indian War, Great Britain had a huge war debt. To make up some of this debt, Britain sought to make the colonies pay their own administrative and defense costs. This policy increased tensions between many colonists and Britain. The Proclamation of 1763 was the first step. To limit the expense of defending the frontier, this proclamation directed that no colonial settlement would be allowed beyond the crest of the Appalachian Mountains. The Proclamation was of little concern to most colonists at the time because no settlements existed this far west. As colonial expansion continued, however, the Proclamation became a source of conflict between Britain and the colonists.

Many colonists were upset by the Sugar Act of 1764. This act taxed imported goods such as sugar, molasses, indigo, coffee, wine, and silk. The tax was to be used for the military defense of the colonies, but it was to be administered by officials in England. While the act caused outrage in New England, colonists in North Carolina were not as concerned because they imported only small quantities of the taxed items. Another law the American colonists opposed was the Quartering Act. This act required that the colonists house British troops in inns, stables, or other buildings if regular barracks were not available. At the time, however, few British troops were in North Carolina, so the law had little effect on the colony.

As Speaker of the North Carolina Assembly, John Ashe warned Governor Tryon that the colonists would fight to resist the Stamp Act.

✔ **READING CHECK Summarizing** What policies did Great Britain issue after the French and Indian War?

⭐ North Carolina Reacts

North Carolina formally stated its opposition to "new taxes and impositions [burdens] laid on us without our . . . consent" after Parliament passed the Sugar Act. However, the tax acts that followed caused far more unrest in North Carolina.

The Stamp Act protests Parliament passed the **Stamp Act** in 1765. This act required British subjects to pay for a stamp on legal papers and various printed materials. Colonists loudly opposed the Stamp Act, arguing that it violated their rights as British citizens. Public protests took place in Cross Creek, Edenton, New Bern, and Wilmington. Governor Tryon was unable to convince merchants to obey the law. Armed protestors successfully kept stamped paper from entering North Carolina's ports. They also made public officials take an oath that they would not attempt to sell stamped paper in North Carolina. Common opposition to the Stamp Act created growing interest in a union among the colonies.

The Fight for Independence **83**

That's Interesting!

When the United States celebrated the Bicentennial of the American Revolution in 1976, North Carolina used the slogan "First in Freedom" on its automobile license plates. The slogan came from the fact that North Carolina had the first independent representative legislative body in the colonies.

The Townshend Acts In 1767 Parliament passed the Townshend Acts. The acts tried to tax the colonies indirectly by placing new customs duties on items such as wine, glass, and tea. The money raised would pay the salaries of royal officials such as judges and governors. Massachusetts sent a "Circular Letter of 1768" to all the colonies to oppose the act. Some North Carolina officials agreed to support Massachusetts in its opposition to the duties.

Non-importation agreements Parliament responded to the developments in Massachusetts by restricting freedoms guaranteed in its charter. This brought the colonies even closer together, as they feared the same could be done to them. To support Massachusetts, Virginia suggested that the colonies form a **Non-Importation Association** and agree not to buy British goods. When the North Carolina Assembly approved the proposal in 1769, Governor William Tryon dissolved the Assembly. Angered by that action, 64 of the 77 Assembly members reorganized as a convention, to preserve "the true and essential interests of the province," as Speaker **John Harvey** explained. North Carolina had created the colonies' first legislative body to meet independently.

One of the American Patriots killed in the Boston Massacre was Crispus Attucks (center), who may have been a runaway slave.

The Boston Massacre Meanwhile, tensions in Massachusetts continued to increase. Local workers and sailors repeatedly clashed with British soldiers. On March 5, 1770, British troops opened fire on a group of protestors that had been harassing them, killing several colonists. The incident was widely publicized in the colonies and increased the unpopularity of British rule.

✓ **READING CHECK** Sequencing What steps did North Carolina take to protest British policies?

Section 1 Review

Homework Practice Online
keyword: SN3 HP5

1 Identify and explain:
- Congress of Augusta
- Stamp Act
- Non-Importation Association
- John Harvey

2 Analyzing Information Copy the chart below. Use the chart to identify the policies that upset colonists.

Act, date of passage	Description

3 Finding the Main Idea
a. How did the French and Indian War affect North Carolina?
b. How did the French and Indian War contribute to unrest in the colonies?

4 Writing and Critical Thinking
Identifying Cause and Effect How did British policies after the French and Indian War contribute to a desire to unify the colonies?
Consider:
- colonial desires for a voice in government
- economic interests of colonists

Section 2

The Road to Revolution

Read to Discover
1. What events led to the outbreak of the American Revolution?
2. What challenges did North Carolina Patriots face?
3. How did North Carolina break from Great Britain?

Identify
- Penelope Barker
- Josiah Martin
- Provincial Congress
- Richard Caswell
- Mecklenburg Resolves
- Charles Cornwallis
- James Moore
- Battle of Moore's Creek Bridge
- Halifax Resolves

The Story Continues

As the desire to work together against the British grew in the colonies, leaders worked to find ways to increase this unity. One method was through a network of committees that would "obtain the most early and authentic intelligence of all such Acts and resolutions of the British Parliament, or proceedings of Administration as may relate to or affect the British Colonies." These committees marked a new level of cooperation between the colonies.

Resistance to British rule brought colonists together, like the men shown here burning British stamped papers in protest of the Stamp Act.

★ North Carolina's Committee of Correspondence

As the conflict in the colonies heated up, some colonial leaders began organizing a system of committees that would keep each colony informed about the actions of the British Parliament. In December 1773, the North Carolina Assembly named a Committee of Correspondence. The Assembly instructed the Committee to "maintain a correspondence and communication with our sister colonies" to stay informed about British policies and activities.

The Fight for Independence

The committee's first action was to issue a statement in support of the citizens of Boston, who continued to protest British rule. The committee also recommended that a continental congress be formed to promote "conformity and unanimity in the Councils of America."

✔ **READING CHECK** Drawing Inferences and Conclusions How did the committees of correspondence promote unity among the colonies?

Tensions Increase

Parliament passed the Tea Act in 1773. The act removed the taxes on tea shipped from Britain, which made British tea much cheaper than tea sold by colonial merchants. However, many colonists opposed the Act and rebelled against it in several ways.

Tea parties The Boston Tea Party took place in December 1773. North Carolina held a "tea party" of its own the following year. On October 25, 1774, a group of "patriotic ladies" met under the leadership of **Penelope Barker** in Edenton. They made the following statement.

 "We, the Ladys of Edenton, do hereby solemnly engage not to conform to [take part in] the Pernicious [evil] Custom of Drinking Tea . . . [nor] promote ye wear of any manufacturer from England until such time that all acts which tend to enslave our Native country shall be repealed."

Declaration signed at the Edenton Tea Party, October 25, 1774

The North Carolina Assembly dissolves When Parliament passed a series of acts designed to punish Massachusetts, the colonies called for a Continental Congress. Delegates to the Congress were to be chosen by the state assemblies, but North Carolina governor **Josiah Martin** refused to call the Assembly together. In response, North Carolina colonists decided to form a **Provincial Congress**. The congress successfully conducted affairs in North Carolina without a royal governor. This proved to many colonists that they did not need British leadership.

The First Continental Congress met secretly in Philadelphia in the fall of 1774. North Carolina delegate **Richard Caswell** played a leading role in the Congress.

On April 19, 1775, the first live shots of the Revolution were fired at the battles of Lexington and Concord in Massachusetts. It took nearly three weeks for news of the battles to reach North Carolina. The Mecklenburg County Committee of Safety quickly wrote the **Mecklenburg Resolves** to announce that British laws and commissions would no longer be in force.

✔ **READING CHECK** Sequencing What events led to the beginning of the Revolution?

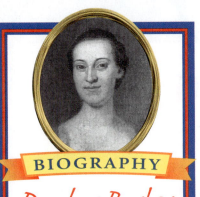

BIOGRAPHY

Penelope Barker
(1728–1796)

Penelope Barker led what later became known as the Edenton Tea Party. In 1774, she invited more than 50 women to her home in Edenton because they could not "be indifferent [uncaring] to whatever affected the peace and happiness of the country." They agreed not to drink British tea or wear clothes made from British cloth. The tea party was so well known that even the London newspapers spread word of it. **How did Penelope Barker contribute to the Revolution?**

The Edenton Tea Party is one of the earliest examples of political organizing by women in colonial America.

Historical Document

1775

THE MECKLENBURG RESOLVES

The Mecklenburg County Committee of Safety met at Charlotte, in May of 1775. The delegates crafted a basic plan of government to replace local British colonial rule.

Whereas by an Address presented to his Majesty by both Houses of Parliament in February last [February 1775], the American Colonies are declared to be in a State of actual Rebellion, we conceive that all Laws and Commissions confirmed by, or derived from the Authority of the King or Parliament, are annulled and vacated, and the former civil Constitution of these Colonies for the present wholly suspended. To provide in some Degree for the Exigencies [needs] of the County in the present alarming Period, we deem it proper and necessary to pass the following Resolves, viz.

- That all Commissions, civil and military, heretofore granted by the Crown, to be exercised in these Colonies, are null and void, and the Constitution of each particular Colony wholly suspended.
- That the Provincial Congress of each Province, under the Direction of the Great Continental Congress, is invested with all legislative and executive Powers within their respective Provinces; and that no other Legislative or Executive does or can exist, at this time, in any of these Colonies.
- As all former Laws are now suspended in this Province, and the Congress have not yet provided others, we judge it necessary, for the better Preservation of good Order, to form certain Rules and Regulations for the internal Government of this County, until Laws shall be provided for us by the Congress. . . .
- That whatever Person shall hereafter receive a Commission from the Crown, or attempt to exercise any such Commission heretofore received, shall be deemed an Enemy to his Country . . .
- That these Resolves be in full Force and Virtue, until Instructions from the General Congress of this Province, regulating the Jurisprudence of this Province, shall provide otherwise, or the legislative Body of Great-Britain resign its unjust and arbitrary Pretentions [claims to rule] with Respect to America.
- That the several Militia Companies in this county do provide themselves with proper Arms and Accoutrements [equipment and uniforms], and hold themselves in Readiness to execute the commands and Directions of the Provincial Congress, and of this committee.
- That this committee do appoint Colonel Thomas Polk, and Doctor Joseph Kennedy, to purchase 300 lb. of Powder, 600 lb. of Lead, and 1,000 Flints, and deposit the same in some safe Place, hereafter to be appointed by the committee.

Signed by Order of the Committee
EPH. BREVARD, Clerk of the Committee

Analyzing Primary Sources

1. Why does the Committee of Safety feel a need to pass the Resolves?
2. What steps did the committee take to ensure Mecklenburg County's defense and safety?

The Fight for Independence

⭐ Choosing Sides

Many North Carolinians supported the independence movement. Some did not, however. People who did not want to break off from Great Britain were called Loyalists or Tories. Highland Scots formed one of the strongest Loyalist groups. Some African Americans chose to fight on the American side. Many hoped that the colonists' battle for liberty and independence might lead to freedom for their own people. For example, John Chavis, a black indentured servant in North Carolina, served as a Revolutionary soldier for three years.

Fears of a slave rebellion White North Carolinians had worried for years about slave insurrections in the South. Now they feared that the Loyalists might arm the slaves and start a slave revolt. To meet this potential threat, North Carolina outlawed the importation of new slaves. Some communities enforced curfews, confiscated guns, and required oaths of allegiance from African Americans.

The Battle of Moore's Creek Bridge Patriots in North Carolina faced several military threats. These included the Loyalists, mostly Scottish Highlanders, organized by royal governor Josiah Martin. Martin planned to join British forces commanded by Major General **Charles Cornwallis**. Major General Henry Clinton was to arrive with troops from Boston to take command of the combined forces. Martin's troops began their move toward the meeting point, Wilmington, on February 18, 1776.

However, Colonel **James Moore**, commander of the First North Carolina regiment, had learned of the British plans. When the Highlanders reached Widow Moore's Creek Bridge, about 20 miles outside of Wilmington, they found that the Patriots had removed the planks and greased the beams. As they struggled across, Moore's men opened fire. At least 50 Highlanders were killed, and 850 were taken prisoner. Only one Patriot died. The Americans' victory at the **Battle of Moore's Creek Bridge** on February 27, 1776, was important. It kept the British from taking over the South at the beginning of the war.

The American victory in the Battle of Moore's Creek Bridge gave many Patriots new enthusiasm for independence.

The Halifax Resolves On April 12, 1776, North Carolina's Fourth Provincial Congress passed the **Halifax Resolves**. This document gave North Carolina delegates the power to join the twelve other colonies in "declaring Independency." When the Halifax Resolves were read at the Continental Congress in Philadelphia, delegates encouraged other colonies to "follow this laudable [admirable] example."

✓ **READING CHECK** Summarizing How did Patriots in North Carolina meet the threats that they faced?

Historical Document

1776

THE HALIFAX RESOLVES

The first official call for independence from Great Britain was made by the 83 delegates to North Carolina's Fourth Provincial Congress, meeting in Halifax in April 1776.

The Select Committee taking into Consideration the usurpations and violences attempted and committed by the King and Parliament of Britain against America, and the further Measures to be taken for frustrating the same, and for the better defence of this province reported as follows, to wit,

It appears to your Committee that pursuant to [as a result of] the Plan concerted by the British Ministry for subjugating America, the King and Parliament of Great Britain have usurped a Power over the Persons and Properties of the People unlimited and uncontrouled and disregarding their humble Petitions for Peace, Liberty and safety, have made divers [various] Legislative Acts, denouncing War Famine and every Species of Calamity daily employed in destroying the People and committing the most horrid devastations on the Country. That Governors in different Colonies have declared Protection to Slaves who should imbrue [soak] their Hands in the Blood of their Masters. That the Ships belonging to America are declared prizes of War and many of them have been violently seized and confiscated in consequence of which multitudes of the people have been destroyed or from easy Circumstances reduced to the most Lamentable distress.

And whereas the moderation hitherto manifested by the United Colonies and their sincere desire to be reconciled to the mother Country on Constitutional Principles, have procured no mitigation of the aforesaid Wrongs and usurpations and no hopes remain of obtaining redress by those Means alone which have been hitherto tried, Your Committee are of Opinion that the house should enter into the following Resolve, to wit

Resolved that the delegates for this Colony in the Continental Congress be impowered to concur with the other delegates of the other Colonies in declaring Independency, and forming foreign Alliances, resolving to this Colony the Sole and Exclusive right of forming a Constitution and Laws for this Colony, and of appointing delegates from time to time (under the direction of a general Representation thereof) to meet the delegates of the other Colonies for such purposes as shall be hereafter pointed out.

A page from the Halifax Resolves

Analyzing Primary Sources

1. According to the Resolves, what was the purpose of the British ministry's colonial plan?
2. Why do the Halifax delegates believe that this declaration of colonial independence is justified?

The Fight for Independence

⭐ Breaking from Britain

On July 4, 1776, delegates to the Continental Congress adopted the Declaration of Independence. William Hooper, Joseph Hewes, and John Penn signed the document for North Carolina. North Carolina received news of the Declaration on July 22. The Council of Safety, which had assumed the duties previously exercised by the royal governor, ordered an election to choose delegates to the Fifth Provincial Congress. It instructed the voters that their chosen delegates would not only "make laws for the good government of, but also . . . form a Constitution for this State." Great debate on how to set up the new government followed. Eventually, a General Assembly was elected and Richard Caswell, former delegate to the Continental Congress, became the first governor of an independent North Carolina in 1777. The government was a weak one, however. The governor in particular had few powers.

Opposition to independence remained in North Carolina. The Council of Safety worked to stop the activities of Loyalists, particularly Highland Scots, in the colony. Some Loyalists were charged with crimes such as corresponding with the British, or speaking out against the Revolution. Those considered most dangerous were imprisoned, and in some cases sent to jails as far away as Philadelphia. Generally, though, Loyalists were left alone as long as they accepted the Revolutionary government. Even prisoners were allowed to be "naturalized" into citizenship if they took an oath of allegiance.

Richard Caswell's signature

✔ **READING CHECK** Sequencing What steps did North Carolina take to break with Great Britain?

Section 2 Review

keyword: SN3 HP5

❶ Identify and explain:
- Penelope Barker
- Josiah Martin
- Provincial Congress
- Richard Caswell
- Mecklenburg Resolves
- Charles Cornwallis
- James Moore
- Battle of Moore's Creek Bridge
- Halifax Resolves

❷ Identifying Cause and Effect Copy the graphic organizer below. Use it to identify the events that helped lead to the Revolutionary War.

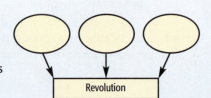

❸ Finding the Main Idea
a. How did North Carolina meet threats to the new government?
b. What documents reflected North Carolina's split from Great Britain?

❹ Writing and Critical Thinking
Supporting a Point of View Imagine you are a member of Britain's Parliament. Do you believe that it is fair or unjust to impose new taxes on the American colonies?
Consider:
- Britain's need for income
- colonial representation in Parliament

Section 3

Fighting the War

Read to Discover

1. How did North Carolina contribute to the war effort in the North?
2. What military events of the Revolutionary War took place in North Carolina and what was the outcome of each event?
3. How did Nathanael Greene contribute to Americans' success in the Revolutionary War?

Identify

- Robert Howe
- Charlotte
- Over-Mountain men
- Kings Mountain
- Nathanael Greene
- Cowpens

The Story Continues

North Carolina Patriots knew that a strong militia would be necessary to defend their state. The new legislature's first law was called "An Act to Establish a Militia in this State." It required all free white males between the ages of 16 and 50 to either volunteer or be drafted into the militia. North Carolina's militia would later fight as part of the Continental Army and make important contributions to American victory in the Revolution.

North Carolina troops spent the bitter winter of 1777–1778 at Valley Forge with revolutionary leader George Washington, shown here at the right talking to French commander Marquis Lafayette.

★ North Carolinians Fight in the North

During the spring of 1776, North Carolina organized several new regiments. These joined the First and Second North Carolina Continentals, commanded by James Moore and **Robert Howe**. In 1775, Howe had led the first troops to see action outside of North Carolina. His Second Regiment helped Virginia remove its royal governor. In January 1777, North Carolina Continentals moved farther north to join General George Washington in Pennsylvania.

The Fight for Independence **91**

They took part in preparations for the Battle of Brandywine, and some fought in the battle. North Carolina troops saw their first action as a unit in October, at the Battle of Germantown. They suffered heavy losses in this battle, including the death of their commander, General Francis Nash. The troops spent the winter at Valley Forge. In the summer of 1778, they served under Washington, pushing General Henry Clinton back through New Jersey. The militia also fought hard in the Battle of Monmouth in New Jersey in June 1778.

 READING CHECK Categorizing In what colonies did North Carolina help fight the Revolution?

The War Comes to North Carolina

Clinton's failures led the British government to turn its focus of the war to the South. In December 1778, the British defeated Major General Robert Howe's forces at Savannah and quickly overtook Georgia. The capital of South Carolina, Charles Town, fell to the British on May 12, 1780.

Cornwallis, who had joined the British troops in Charles Town, turned next to North Carolina. He decided not to move his forces immediately, however. The summer of 1780 was very hot and humid. His soldiers needed a rest and they lacked supplies. Royal governor Josiah Martin, who was with Cornwallis, promised that Loyalists in North Carolina would give British forces all the support they would need. With his victory in South Carolina and Martin's encouragement, Cornwallis became overconfident. While his troops rested, Patriots in North Carolina gathered more men and supplies.

The Patriots remained greatly outnumbered by Cornwallis's men. Their small numbers, however, allowed them to make quick advances and retreats and use other tactics of guerrilla warfare. The Patriots continued their raids on the British throughout the summer of 1780. Aware of the increasing threat in the South, General Washington sent more troops to reinforce the southern army. Many soldiers had little clothing, were barefoot, and suffered from hunger and disease.

Charlotte On September 8, 1780, Cornwallis began his invasion of North Carolina, marching toward **Charlotte**. Raiding bands of rebels slowed his advance, so that he did not reach the city until over two weeks later. While Josiah Martin quickly claimed the restoration of the royal government in Charlotte, Cornwallis was not so confident. He called Charlotte "The Hornet's Nest" of the Revolution; "an agreeable village but in a [very] rebellious country." Rebel bands continued to make British operations difficult. They captured British scouts, stopped their messengers, and kept track of every move the army made.

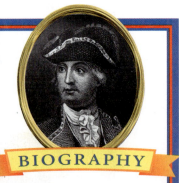

BIOGRAPHY
Robert Howe
(1732–1786)

Robert Howe was born into a wealthy family in the Cape Fear River valley. In 1754 he became captain in the Bladen County militia, and soon moved into politics. Howe served in almost every session of the provincial legislature from 1760 until he took command of the Second North Carolina Regiment in 1775. He first took his troops to Virginia to help remove the royal governor. Promoted to major general, Howe became North Carolina's highest-ranking officer in the Revolution. **What role did Robert Howe play in the Revolutionary War?**

Kings Mountain On his march to Charlotte, Cornwallis had sent one of his best officers, Patrick Ferguson, to create a regiment of Loyalists to protect his left flank. He was concerned about being attacked by bands of "**Over-Mountain men**." These Patriots were organizing in far western North Carolina, over the Appalachians. Eventually this small band of about 500 was joined by hundreds more men from Virginia and more than 1,000 from both Carolinas. After Ferguson organized his force of Loyalists, he positioned his troops on the southern slopes of **Kings Mountain** to await the Over-Mountain men.

On October 7, 1780, the Over-Mountain men attacked Kings Mountain from three directions. In about one hour, Ferguson's forces were demolished, and he lay dead. The Americans had achieved a complete victory, and many saw it as a turning point in the war. Cornwallis began to fear the Americans, and withdrew from Charlotte on October 12 with his troops.

✓ **READING CHECK** Finding the Main Idea What military actions marked the beginning of the Revolution in North Carolina?

Revolutionary War Battles in North Carolina, 1780–1781
Interpreting Maps Despite greatly outnumbering American troops, the British were unable to gain control over North Carolina.

Skills Assessment Places and Regions Who was involved in the battle at Kings Mountain?

The Fight for Independence

CONNECTING TO ECONOMICS

Financing the War

When the war began, North Carolina had an empty treasury and no credit. The Provincial Congress quickly began working to find ways to finance the war. It created new taxes, tried to collect unpaid taxes, received loans, and sold confiscated property. The legislature also issued paper money. A total of $8 million in paper currency was printed between 1775 and 1783. If colonists refused to accept the new money as currency, they faced severe punishment. Altering or counterfeiting the bills was punishable by death. **Why did North Carolina have to issue paper money?**

Battle at Guilford Courthouse

George Washington appointed **Nathanael Greene** to take charge of the southern troops in October 1780. When he arrived in Charlotte in December, Greene found the men in poor physical condition but in high spirits.

Greene's bold move Greene knew his army was too small for a direct attack on the British, so he devised a plan to weaken Cornwallis's troops. General Isaac Huger commanded one half of the southern army, which was sent to the east to threaten forces at Camden. General Daniel Morgan commanded the other half in the western area. This placed Cornwallis and his men in between the two armies. While Greene recognized the danger of this move, he believed Cornwallis would not act to take advantage of the rebels' weakness.

Cornwallis responded by dividing his army as well. He sent Colonel Banastre Tarleton to attack General Morgan in the west. British forces were surprised by the strength of the American forces. Morgan's strategic positioning of his troops at **Cowpens**, South Carolina, allowed the Americans to soundly defeat the British on January 17, 1781.

Cornwallis chases Morgan Tarleton's defeat forced Cornwallis to move his own troops in pursuit of Morgan. General Morgan quickly began a retreat into North Carolina, trying to put the Catawba River between his troops and the British. When Greene learned of Morgan's retreat, he saw an opportunity to attack Cornwallis and quickly began to put a new plan into place. Leading his troops on a masterfully planned retreat from the British, Greene made it possible for the two segments of the American army to unite. The retreat also drew Cornwallis into a trap.

A fierce battle Greene's and Morgan's troops met Cornwallis at Guilford Courthouse on March 15, 1781. Cornwallis had been drawn hundreds of miles from his supplies. In addition, more than 250 men had deserted his army on the march. Meanwhile Greene's success drew many fresh, strong troops into his camp. Greene's goal was simply to damage the enemy, whereas Cornwallis needed a complete victory. After a fierce battle, Greene decided to withdraw his troops, and Cornwallis claimed victory. However, Cornwallis had lost 25 percent of his troops. Furthermore, he could not get many Loyalists to join his cause.

The colonies issued paper money to finance the Revolutionary War.

History Makers Speak

"Many of the inhabitants rode into Camp, shook me by the hand, said they were glad to see us, and to hear that we had beat Greene, and then rode home again; for I could not get 100 men in all the Regulator's Country to stay with us, even as Militia."

Charles Cornwallis, quoted in *North Carolina through Four Centuries* by William S. Powell

Analyzing Primary Sources

Drawing Inferences and Conclusions Why do you think few men were willing to join Cornwallis's troops?

Cornwallis began to march toward Wilmington to repair his army. Greene believed the threat from Cornwallis had all but disappeared. He decided to direct the southern army into South Carolina.

✔ **READING CHECK** **Identifying Cause and Effect** How did Nathanael Greene's skills lead to his army's success in North Carolina?

★ The End of the War

Nathanael Greene continued his brilliant military work in South Carolina. Eventually he forced the British out of every important military post, except for Charles Town and Savannah, Georgia. Cornwallis decided to attempt a move into Virginia. He believed cutting off supplies and reinforcements from Virginia would allow the British to recapture the Carolinas. Finally his weak army took up a position at Yorktown, Virginia. French and American forces surrounded the British on land and sea, leaving Cornwallis no escape. On October 18, 1781, Cornwallis surrendered. The following April, negotiations for peace began. The Treaty of Paris of 1783 officially ended the Revolutionary War and recognized American independence.

This illustration depicts the final British surrender at Yorktown, Virginia.

✔ **READING CHECK** **Finding the Main Idea** Why did Cornwallis move British forces into Virginia, and what happened to him there?

Section 3 Review

go.hrw.com Homework Practice Online
keyword: SN3 HP5

1. **Identify** and explain:
   • Robert Howe
   • Charlotte
   • Over-Mountain men
   • Kings Mountain
   • Nathanael Greene
   • Cowpens

2. **Sequencing** Copy the time line below. Use it to identify the important events and dates related to North Carolina's role in the Revolutionary War.

3. **Finding the Main Idea**
   a. What role did North Carolina play in the Revolution in the North?
   b. What was the outcome of Revolutionary War battles fought in North Carolina?

4. **Writing and Critical Thinking**
   Identifying Cause and Effect Why were the Patriots successful in North Carolina?
   Consider:
   • guerrilla warfare fought by Patriot bands
   • Nathanael Greene's leadership

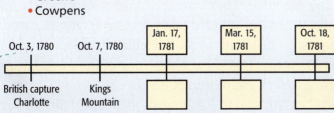

The Fight for Independence 95

Section 4

Establishing Peace

Read to Discover
1. How did the Tory War affect North Carolina?
2. How did the Revolution affect African Americans in North Carolina?
3. How did North Carolina's government respond to problems caused by the Revolution?

Define
- conservatives
- radicals

Identify
- Tory War
- David Fanning
- Quillo
- Raleigh

Loyalist raider David Fanning usually commanded his own independent band of fighters, but sometimes worked with Cornwallis or other British leaders.

The Story Continues

Despite the end of fighting between British and American armies in 1781, life remained unsettled in North Carolina. The state's people suffered continuing destruction and hardship. They also found themselves deeply divided over the Revolution's ideals of liberty and equality. What would those ideals mean for the organization of North Carolina society?

★ The Tory War

North Carolina elected Thomas Burke governor on July 25, 1781. When Burke took office, one of his first challenges was dealing with the so-called **Tory War** that had broken out in the state. Both Loyalists, or Tories, and Patriots were raiding the state. They damaged and stole property and harmed many people. When Burke heard that Loyalists in Orange County were planning an uprising, he left his office in Halifax to plan a campaign against them. Burke knew that **David Fanning**—one of the worst Loyalist raiders—was planning to sack Hillsborough, Burke's hometown.

On September 12, 1781, David Fanning slipped into Hillsborough under cover of darkness. When families awoke to the danger, there was little they could do to defend themselves. Most men stayed in their homes to fight the steady fire from Fanning's band. This prevented the townspeople from joining forces and helping each other. After plundering homes and releasing prisoners from the local jail, the Loyalists began to gather at Burke's house. Although the governor put up a fierce fight, Fanning succeeded in capturing him and about 200 other Patriots.

The events in Hillsborough made it difficult to recruit soldiers for the defense of North Carolina's new independence. Many men did not want to leave their families unprotected. In addition, soldiers were leaving the army camps on a regular basis. Officers grumbled about serving without pay and a continual lack of supplies. To make matters worse, an epidemic broke out.

✔ **READING CHECK** Finding the Main Idea What was the Tory War and how did it affect North Carolina?

Interpreting the Visual Record

North Carolina Loyalists
Pictured here is a button from a uniform worn by a North Carolina Loyalist. It bears an image of the royal crown and the letters "RP," for "Royal Provincials." **How does this button reflect the Loyalists' beliefs?**

★ African Americans after the War

As the British left North Carolina and nearby colonies in the last months of the Revolution, many slaves faced a difficult decision. They could try to escape with the British, or they could remain at home, but in slavery. As many as 5,000 blacks sailed away with the British from Charles Town in 1782. The British also agreed to settle about 1,200 African American Loyalists in Sierra Leone in Africa.

A growing black population and revolutionary ideas increased racial tensions during and after the war. Religious groups such as the Quakers stepped up their efforts to free slaves during this period. Between 1776 and 1800, the threat of slave uprisings deeply concerned many white North Carolinians. In April 1794, **Quillo**, a slave in Granville County, was accused of planning a slave insurrection. Quillo wanted to hold elections for his community's government. Then he and his associates planned to join other insurrectionists marching from Person County. This group was to "force their way where they choosed, and . . . murder all who stood in their way or opposed them," according to the testimony of one slave. The alleged plan was never carried out, but news of the plot spread more fear. By 1800 many slaves were interested in working with each other to gain the freedoms that the Revolution had seemed to promise.

✔ **READING CHECK** Decision Making What decisions did African Americans face as a result of the Revolution?

★ Rebuilding the Economy

The Revolution destroyed most of North Carolina's economy. To support the military during the war, the state had to tax the population heavily. If people did not pay, the state seized their property for military use. Unable to export their products, plantation owners could not make a profit. While paper money continued to decrease in worth, very little commerce took place. Many families fell from comfortable lives into poverty.

The General Assembly opened land offices to distribute the large amounts of land seized from Loyalists. The legislature also sought to improve transportation and commerce by passing laws that encouraged the construction of new roads and bridges. These measures slowly produced results. As the economy began to recover, new towns began to spring up around the state. Twenty-nine were incorporated between 1783 and 1789.

✔ **READING CHECK** Summarizing What economic problems challenged North Carolina and how did the state deal with them?

★ Other Issues for the Government

Members of the General Assembly focused on matters they could agree upon. They first worked to take care of war veterans, granting lands west of the mountains to men who had served. They also arranged for the release of prisoners still held by the British. Finally, the Assembly created a policy for the treatment of Loyalists. The Assembly passed an "Act of Pardon and Oblivion" which forgave most Loyalists. It took several generations before the deep split between Loyalists and Patriots healed, however.

During the Revolution most schools had closed. At that time most schools were supported by the Anglican Church, whose assistance was greatly reduced as colonists cut ties with Britain. As a result, the 1776 state constitution required new schools and universities to be created with some public funding. By 1800 more than 40 academies had been chartered by the legislature.

North Carolinians knew that to meet the democratic ideals of the Revolution, they had to have an educated citizenry. To fill this need, they established institutions of higher education. The first was the former Queen's College in Charlotte, reopened in 1777 as Liberty Hall Academy. In December 1789 the University of North Carolina was chartered, becoming the first state university established in the new nation.

Assembly members argued for years about where to locate the new seat of government. The colonial capital at New Bern was no longer centrally located and could be easily invaded by sea. The legislature considered seven different towns for the honor. Finally, in 1787, the Assembly asked the convention considering the new federal constitution to choose a site. The convention determined that the new capital should be located within ten

Interpreting the Visual Record

State Capitol The Assembly created the city of Raleigh out of wilderness land to serve as the new state capital. The capitol building, shown here, was finished in 1794. It was greatly enlarged between 1820 and 1824 with the addition of a third floor, wings, and a domed rotunda. **Why might the legislature choose an undeveloped site rather than an existing city for the new capital?**

miles of Isaac Hunter's tavern in Wake County. Those who supported other sites, however, stalled acceptance of the recommendation until 1791. The capital was named **Raleigh** in honor of Sir Walter Raleigh and his 1587 colony. The first capitol building was completed in 1794.

✔ **READING CHECK Identifying Cause and Effect** How did the government address problems caused by the Revolution?

★ A Weak Government

North Carolina did face difficult governmental problems. Political conflict was quite intense. Many factions, or small groups, rose as a result. Generally, people who wanted to return to prewar conditions were called **conservatives**. Lawyers, merchants, planters, and other wealthy citizens were in this faction. They wanted to renew trade with England and to restore a strong government. People who opposed the conservatives were known as **radicals**. They wanted few governmental controls, low taxes, and no repayment of prewar debts to British merchants.

The state constitution had created a weak government. It had a governor, a two-house legislature, and courts. However, severe limits were placed on the authority of the new state governor. The governor was elected by the state legislature for a one-year term. He could not veto legislative acts, and had to get agreement from his Council on any important matters.

✔ **READING CHECK Identifying Cause and Effect** Why did North Carolina have a weak government and what problems did it cause?

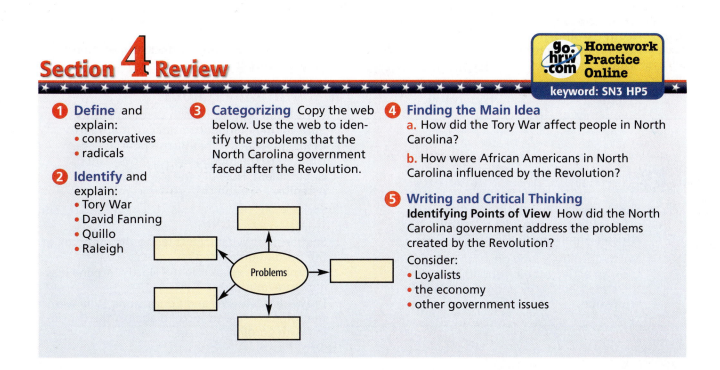

Section 4 Review

1. Define and explain:
- conservatives
- radicals

2. Identify and explain:
- Tory War
- David Fanning
- Quillo
- Raleigh

3. Categorizing Copy the web below. Use the web to identify the problems that the North Carolina government faced after the Revolution.

4. Finding the Main Idea
a. How did the Tory War affect people in North Carolina?
b. How were African Americans in North Carolina influenced by the Revolution?

5. Writing and Critical Thinking
Identifying Points of View How did the North Carolina government address the problems created by the Revolution?
Consider:
- Loyalists
- the economy
- other government issues

Homework Practice Online
keyword: SN3 HP5

The Fight for Independence

Chapter 5 Review

Chapter Summary

Section 1
- The French and Indian War had a powerful impact on North Carolina's development.
- British policies after 1763 caused increasing conflict with the American colonies.

Section 2
- North Carolina was a leader in the struggle for American independence against Great Britain.
- North Carolina Patriots were faced with many challenges throughout the struggle for independence.

Section 3
- North Carolina troops fought for the Continental Army in many of the Revolution's key battles.
- The outcomes of major battles in North Carolina helped to shape the new nation's victory against Great Britain.
- General Nathanael Greene proved to be one of the new nation's most successful military leaders.

Section 4
- The American Revolution had a powerful impact on the lives of many African Americans in North Carolina.
- North Carolina's new government took an active role in rebuilding the state's economy and promoting education.

Identifying People and Ideas

1. Congress of Augusta
2. Non-Importation Association
3. John Harvey
4. Penelope Barker
5. Mecklenburg Resolves
6. Battle of Moore's Creek Bridge
7. Over-Mountain men
8. Nathanael Greene
9. David Fanning
10. Quillo

Understanding Main Ideas

Section 1 *Pages 81–84*
1. How did the French and Indian War contribute to the beginning of the Revolution?
2. What British policies angered colonists after the French and Indian War?

Section 2 *Pages 85–90*
3. What documents demonstrated North Carolina's separation from Great Britain?
4. How did Patriots in North Carolina meet their challenges at the beginning of the Revolutionary War?

Section 3 *Pages 91–95*
5. How did North Carolina help fight the Revolutionary War in the North?
6. What factors most affected the Patriots' military successes in North Carolina?

Section 4 *Pages 96–99*
7. What effect did the Tory War have on North Carolina?
8. How did the Revolution affect African Americans in North Carolina?

What Did You Find Out?

1. **Citizenship** Why did North Carolina Patriots fight for independence from Great Britain?
2. **Global Relations** What British policies contributed to the independence movement?
3. **Government** How did the North Carolina Assembly act upon citizens' concerns?

Thinking Critically

1. **Sequencing** What events led to the outbreak of the Revolutionary War?
2. **Summarizing** What role did North Carolina play in the Revolution?
3. **Drawing Inferences and Conclusions** Why were the colonists able to succeed against the British in North Carolina?

Building Social Studies Skills

Interpreting Political Cartoons

Look closely at this editorial cartoon published in a London magazine. It is a caricature of the Edenton Tea Party. The faces of the ladies are actually well-known politicians in England.

1. Which statement best describes the artists' point of view?
   a. The Edenton Tea Party should be admired and respected.
   b. British politicians are doing a good job.
   c. British politicians contributed to the Tea Party through their unwise policies.
   d. The British should be fearful of Americans' protests.

2. How do you think women in Edenton might have received this cartoon?

Evaluating Sources

Bloody and successful slave revolts in parts of the Caribbean during the late 1700s caused growing concern in many parts of the American South. In the years after the American Revolution, southern slaveholders believed that news of the revolts might encourage similar uprisings at home. They feared, too, that the ideals of the American Revolution—equality, liberty, and freedom from oppression—might cause slaves to rebel against their bondage. Read the report below, written by an observer in New Bern, North Carolina, in 1792. Then answer the questions that follow.

> "The Negroes in this town and neighborhood, have stirred a rumor of their having in contemplation [mind] to rise against their masters and to obtain [gain] themselves their liberty; the inhabitants have been alarmed and keep a strict watch to prevent their procuring [getting] arms; should it become serious, which I don't think, the worst that could befall [happen to] us, would be their setting the town on fire."

3. Which of the following statements accurately represents the evidence in this quote?
   a. Slave uprisings were common during the Revolution.
   b. Whites in North Carolina worried about slave uprisings.
   c. The threat from slave unrest was not serious.
   d. Slaves were allowed to have weapons.

4. How did slaveholders try to prevent slave revolts?

Alternative Assessment

Building Your Portfolio

N.C. History

Connecting to Art
Imagine that you are museum staff members who must put together a presentation about the Revolution in North Carolina. Create a detailed map or diorama of one Revolutionary War battle in North Carolina. Assign group members to research the battle, construct the map or diorama, and write the labels to accompany it.

internet connect

Internet Activity: go.hrw.com
keyword: SN3 NC5

Choose a topic on the fight for independence to:
- Create a time line of events leading up to the Revolutionary War.
- Write an essay on the role of North Carolina in the Revolutionary War.
- Analyze documents that resulted in the formation of a new state government.

The Fight for Independence

CHAPTER 6
Forming a New Nation and State
(1776–1815)

The USS Wasp *fires across the bow of the British ship* Frolic *during the War of 1812.*

Build on What You Know

In 1776, the colony of North Carolina declared its independence from Great Britain. Serious work now faced North Carolinians. They had to develop a system of political leadership for their new state. And they had to join with other former colonists to create a government that could unify the new nation.

What's Your Opinion?

Do you **agree** or **disagree** with the following statements? Support your point of view in your journal.

- **Constitutional Heritage** People must create a plan of government for themselves.
- **Citizenship** Rights of individual citizens must be written down.
- **Government** A strong central government is necessary in a union of states.

Section 1

Ideas about Government

Read to Discover
1. What basic ideals inspired the American Revolution and Americans' views of government?
2. How did North Carolinians state their ideals in the form of a constitution?
3. What were the Articles of Confederation?
4. What happened to the State of Franklin?

Identify
- Richard Caswell
- State of Franklin
- John Sevier

The Story Continues

"The American war is over," Dr. Benjamin Rush noted in 1783, "but this is far from being the case with the American Revolution." Americans fought long and hard to achieve their independence. The actual fighting, however, was only part of their task. They also needed to put the ideals that inspired them to fight into a plan of government.

Ideals of the Revolution

The ideals of the American Revolution—the ideas that Americans fought for—were best expressed in the Declaration of Independence in 1776:

> **Primary Sources**
> "We hold these truths to be self-evident, that all men are created equal, that they are endowed by their Creator with certain unalienable rights, that among these are Life, Liberty, and the pursuit of Happiness. That to secure these rights, Governments are instituted among Men, deriving their just powers from the consent of the governed."

Americans believed that people are born with certain rights that no government can take away. They believed that governments receive their

Colonial-style quill pen

Analyzing Primary Sources
Drawing Inferences and Conclusions What do you think is meant by "the pursuit of Happiness"?

Forming a New Nation and State **103**

authority from the people they govern. And they associated personal happiness with the satisfaction that comes from exercising the rights and responsibilities of citizenship. Equality was restricted mainly to white male property owners, but the idea of who was equal would be widened over time to include more and more people.

Once the colonies had declared their independence, they needed to create a government for the new country that would reflect these ideals. Americans generally agreed that the new country should be a republic. A republic is ruled by elected representatives who are responsible to the people.

Each state within the new country became a republic as well. Like other former colonies, North Carolina also needed to draw up a constitution—a plan for its new state government.

✔ **READING CHECK** Summarizing What basic ideals did Americans hold about government?

Forming a State Government

An election was scheduled for October 15, 1776, to choose delegates for a new provincial congress. North Carolina voters were asked to select these delegates "not only to make Laws for the good Government of, but also to form a Constitution for this State."

North Carolinians agreed that their state should be a republic. Like people in other new states, however, they disagreed on the political nature of that republic. Some were conservatives who wanted very little change from the colonial government. They wanted a strong governor. They also wanted to allow only men who owned property to vote and hold office.

Conservatives were mainly eastern landholders, professionals, and merchants. Opposing the conservatives were the radicals, mainly Piedmont and western farmers. The radicals wanted a strong legislature, a weak governor, and broad voting rights.

Neither side had a clear majority when the delegates met at Halifax on November 12, 1776. For president of the assembly, they elected moderate **Richard Caswell**, whose views were in the middle. The next day a committee was chosen to draw up not only a constitution but also a declaration of rights, which lists the rights of citizens. In drafting its declaration of rights, the committee drew from similar documents already in place in Virginia and Maryland. The committee based parts of the North Carolina constitution on those of Delaware, New Jersey, and Pennsylvania. By mid-December these two documents were ready and adopted. The state of North Carolina now had a plan of government.

✔ **READING CHECK** Contrasting How did the views of conservatives and radicals in North Carolina differ?

Just a few miles west of Kinston, in Lenoir County, lies the gravesite of Richard Caswell, former president of the North Carolina assembly.

Historical Document

THE NORTH CAROLINA CONSTITUTION OF 1776

The Declaration of Rights that was adopted in 1776 consisted of 25 articles listing the rights of people to be protected from a government. It reflected the ideals of the Revolution. The North Carolina Constitution of 1776 itself reflected more radical views than conservative. In 46 articles it established a two-house legislature, the General Assembly, which elected and held power over the governor and other members of the executive branch. The state constitution created a judicial branch in which judges would hold office "during good behavior." It also granted more men the right to vote, though many restrictions still applied.

VII. . . . all freemen, of the age of twenty-one years, who have been inhabitants of any one county within the State twelve months immediately preceding the day of any election and possessed of a freehold within the same county of fifty acres of land for six months next before, and at the day of the election, shall be entitled to vote for a member of the Senate.

VIII. . . . all freemen, of the age of twenty-one years, who have been inhabitants of any one county within this State twelve months immediately preceding the day of any election and shall have paid public taxes shall be entitled to vote for members of the House of Commons for the county in which he resides.

Analyzing Primary Sources
1. What general restrictions were placed on those who could vote for members of the state senate?
2. What requirement was different for those who could vote for members of the House of Commons?

The North Carolina Constitution of 1776

The Articles of Confederation

In addition to forming a government for their state, North Carolinians joined other Americans to form a government for their country. In 1776, the Continental Congress began to develop a plan of government for the United States. The delegates generally agreed that the central government should not be too powerful. One historian has written of Americans of the time that "inbred in their bones was dislike of 'strong government'" because of their experiences with England.

On certain issues, however, the states disagreed. Large states, such as Virginia, wanted the number of representatives to the national legislature to be based on population. North Carolina, with territory stretching all the way to the Mississippi River, was one of these larger states. Small states, such as Rhode Island, feared domination by the larger, more populous states. They wanted all the states to have only one vote each. After a long debate, the small states prevailed. The Continental Congress adopted a plan in 1777. Called the Articles of Confederation, the plan created a league of states. North Carolina ratified, or accepted, the Articles on April 24, 1778. It was not until 1781, however, that Maryland, the last of the states to approve the plan, ratified the Articles.

Forming a New Nation and State

Rights of states The Articles set up a loose confederation of independent, sovereign states. The central government was weak. Its legislature—Congress—was granted very limited powers. Congress could not regulate trade, and it could not tax. There was no executive or judicial branch. These features reflected Americans' suspicion of central authority. They had come to fear the power of kings and royal governors.

The western lands issue Some colonies, including North Carolina, claimed lands west of the mountains all the way to the Mississippi River. Maryland had refused to accept the Articles of Confederation until it was agreed that these lands would be ceded, or given, to the national government. Many North Carolinians east of the mountains opposed cession. They wanted to sell the western lands to help pay state debt. Many westerners favored cession. They felt neglected by the state government in the east.

In April 1784 North Carolina offered to cede the western land, but it set conditions. Among them, a state formed on the land would have the same rights and powers as the other states. Also, Congress must accept North Carolina's offer within a year. Some North Carolina leaders protested, mainly because of the debt issue. Half a year later, in October 1784, North Carolina withdrew its offer. A new state did appear, however.

✔ **READING CHECK Analyzing Information** In what ways did the Articles of Confederation work to set up a loose union of states?

★ The State of Franklin

The cession offer was greeted with much joy in the west. Many western settlers had come across the mountains, led by Daniel Boone, looking for good land. They lived far from the center of the state government and beyond its political control.

Interpreting the Visual Record

Western settlers Those pioneers who ventured west of the Appalachian Mountains lived in isolated circumstances. Based on the picture, what seems to be the main means of transportation for the people living in this settlement?

106 Chapter 6

In August 1784 an election of delegates was called for in the west. In December—after North Carolina had withdrawn its cession offer—a convention met in Jonesboro and decided to seek statehood anyway. It drew up a constitution—one quite similar to North Carolina's—for "the **State of Franklin**," as the territory was called. An election for an assembly was held, and **John Sevier** was chosen governor of the new state.

Trouble lay ahead, however. North Carolina threatened to use force to regain control of the breakaway state. Because North Carolina's offer to cede the land had been withdrawn, Congress could not recognize the new state. This discouraged the westerners. North Carolina then resorted to a shrewder strategy. Governor Richard Caswell appointed Evan Shelby, a friend of Sevier's, as brigadier general of the western district. This move further increased a split that had developed among Franklin's leaders.

In 1787 North Carolina offered to forgive the Franklin rebels. Soon after, Sevier's term as governor expired. Since there was no legislature to elect a new governor, the state of Franklin collapsed. Sevier, however, went on to serve in the North Carolina legislature.

In 1789 North Carolina did cede its western land to the United States—land that would become the state of Tennessee. However, the land was ceded not to the United States under the Articles of Confederation, but to a new form of government.

Before becoming governor of the State of Franklin, John Sevier had led the forces that defeated the British at the Battle of Kings Mountain in 1780.

✔ **READING CHECK** **Identifying Cause and Effect** Why did the state of Franklin cease to exist?

Section 1 Review

① Identify and explain:
- Richard Caswell
- State of Franklin
- John Sevier

② Sequencing Copy the event chain at right. Use it to show the series of events that led to the creation and collapse of the State of Franklin.

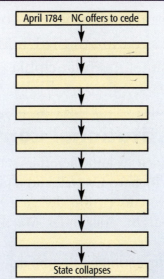

③ Finding the Main Idea
a. What ideals inspired the Revolution and Americans' views of government?

b. How did North Carolinians apply their ideals in their constitution?

c. What type of central government did the Articles of Confederation set up?

④ Writing and Critical Thinking
Comparing and Contrasting How was the North Carolina government set up by the Constitution of 1776 like the government set up by the Articles of Confederation? How was it different?

Consider:
- the makeup of the legislature
- the power of the legislature
- the power of the executive

Section 2

Forming a National Government

Read to Discover
1. What were some of the basic principles and features of the U.S. Constitution created in 1787?
2. How and why did Federalists and Antifederalists clash in North Carolina?

Identify
- William R. Davie
- Richard Dobbs Spaight
- Hugh Williamson
- James Iredell
- Hillsborough Convention

Hugh Williamson was North Carolina's most influential delegate to the Constitutional Convention.

The Story Continues

The weaknesses of the Articles of Confederation caused problems. The most significant were that Congress could not oversee trade or raise money through taxes. In addition, a sense of nationalism arose in the 1780s. Many began calling for a stronger central government. A convention to "take into consideration the situation of the United States" and to revise the Articles met in Philadelphia in May of 1787.

★ The Constitutional Convention

North Carolina decided to join the other states in Philadelphia at the urging of Governor Richard Caswell and a group of eastern conservatives. The state's five convention delegates were **William R. Davie**, **Richard Dobbs Spaight**, Alexander Martin, William Blount, and **Hugh Williamson**.

Soon after the convention began, the delegates scrapped the idea of revising the Articles. Instead, they decided to create an entirely new constitution. The delegates agreed that the new nation would be a federal union—power would be shared between the central government and the states. They also agreed on a separation of powers among the three branches of government—legislative, executive, judicial.

Key questions about the legislature divided the delegates: Should there be one house or two? Should representation in the legislature be determined by state or by population? North Carolina had the fourth largest population, so it voted with the large states to base representation on population. William Davie was a member of the committee that offered a compromise solution: a Senate with states represented equally, and a House with membership based on population. The North Carolina delegates voted with the majority in favor of this "Great Compromise."

North Carolina also supported the "three-fifths" compromise: three fifths of the slave population would be counted when determining population. The state would have gained more representatives if slaves and whites were counted equally, but northern states rejected that idea. Some northern representatives worried that counting slaves and whites equally would give the South, where slavery was concentrated, an unfair advantage in Congress. Slavery itself was not outlawed because the North did not want to lose southern support for the Constitution.

This illustration shows George Washington presiding at the Constitutional Convention. Of the 55 delegates at the convention, more than half were lawyers, and most of the rest were planters and merchants.

The convention agreed on a single executive—a president. North Carolina was alone in calling for a presidential term of more than four years. But Hugh Williamson's demand for the safeguard of presidential impeachment was accepted.

The work of the Constitutional Convention was completed in mid-September. Three North Carolina delegates—William Blount, Richard Dobbs Spaight, and Hugh Williamson—signed the new U.S. Constitution. Now it would be up to nine states to ratify it.

✔ **READING CHECK** Summarizing What were the main features of the Constitution created by the delegates in Philadelphia?

★ Debating the Constitution

Even before the convention was over, the Constitution was being debated by the public. The conservatives, now called Federalists, supported the Constitution. They favored the strong federal government it would establish. The radicals, now called Antifederalists, opposed it. They felt it took too much power away from the states.

Forming a New Nation and State

Antifederalists versus Federalists in North Carolina Antifederalist leaders included Willie Jones, Samuel Spencer, Thomas Person, and Timothy Bloodworth. They maintained that the federal Constitution would make the government too strong and endanger both the rights of North Carolina and the rights of the people.

Federalist leaders in North Carolina included Davie, Spaight, and Williamson. The most effective defender of the Constitution, however, was **James Iredell**. Iredell described the sorry state of the country under the Articles of Confederation and pointed out that the Constitution offered—

> "... popular representation of the people, ... useful checks to guard against possible abuses, ... [and] many provisions calculated to make us as much one people as possible.... Our strength consists in union, and nothing can hurt us but division."

Analyzing Primary Sources
Evaluating How well do you think Iredell answered Antifederalist criticism of the Constitution?

The Hillsborough Convention In late 1787, the North Carolina legislature called for a meeting in Hillsborough in July 1788 to vote on ratification of the U.S. Constitution. An election to choose delegates to the convention was held in March. The campaign between Federalists and Antifederalists to elect delegates was intense and bitter. The Antifederalists swept to victory—184 to 83—and so sent a sizable majority to Hillsborough that summer.

After 11 days of debate, the **Hillsborough Convention** voted to neither ratify nor reject the Constitution. Instead, the Antifederalist-dominated convention declared that a bill of rights should be added and suggested other amendments. The Antifederalists, however, had succeeded at postponing ratification.

✓ **READING CHECK Contrasting** What were the differences between the Federalists and Antifederalists?

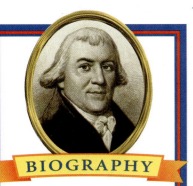

BIOGRAPHY

James Iredell
(1751–1799)

James Iredell was born in England and came to Edenton, North Carolina, when he was in his teens. Iredell had a long record of service to his adopted state: successful lawyer, judge, North Carolina attorney general, and U.S. Supreme Court Justice. In 1793 he dissented in a Supreme Court case, arguing that a citizen of one state did not have the right to sue another state in a federal court. This stand for states' rights was the basis for the 11th Amendment to the Constitution. **In what ways did James Iredell serve North Carolina?**

★ North Carolina Joins the Union

The required nine states had already ratified the Constitution. In fact, only North Carolina and Rhode Island remained outside the new Union. By a close vote in November 1788, the General Assembly called for another convention to consider ratification. This time the Federalists won a commanding majority of delegates.

A Bill of Rights Meanwhile, Congress had passed the Bill of Rights, the first ten amendments to the U.S. Constitution, to guarantee individual liberties. Even before these amendments were ratified by the states in the Union, North Carolina delegates met in Fayetteville. On November 21, 1789, the delegates voted 195 to 77 to ratify the Constitution. North Carolina became a member of the United States of America.

North Carolina in the new government George Washington had already been selected president by the time North Carolina joined the Union. The first North Carolinian he appointed to a government post was James Iredell, who became a U.S. Supreme Court justice.

The state legislature elected Samuel Johnston and Benjamin Hawkins to the U.S. Senate. In the election for the U.S. House of Representatives, the voters chose Hugh Williamson, John Steele, John Sevier, John B. Ashe, and Timothy Bloodworth.

✔ **READING CHECK** Sequencing What events led to North Carolina's ratification of the U.S. Constitution?

★ The Party System

Not long into Washington's presidency, differences of opinion about the government arose again. Alexander Hamilton, secretary of the treasury, believed in a powerful central government. He thought it should be in the hands of "the rich and well-born." Thomas Jefferson, secretary of state, believed in democratic self-government. He felt the people should rule and the central government should guard state and individual rights.

Followers of Hamilton were called Federalists; followers of Jefferson called themselves Republicans. Others, however, called them Democratic-Republicans; later they were called simply Democrats. The two groups developed into political parties. They opposed each other both on the federal level and in the states, including North Carolina.

✔ **READING CHECK** Identifying Cause and Effect How did the party system develop?

Shown here is a letter from President George Washington to the governor and other officials of North Carolina, written shortly after North Carolina voted to ratify the U.S. Constitution. Washington was writing to congratulate North Carolina on becoming part of the United States.

Section 2 Review

Homework Practice Online
keyword: SN3 HP6

1. **Identify** and explain:
   - William R. Davie
   - Richard Dobbs Spaight
   - Hugh Williamson
   - James Iredell
   - Hillsborough Convention

2. **Contrasting** Copy the diagram below. Use it to contrast Federalist and Antifederalist views.

3. **Finding the Main Idea**
   a. What were some of the basic principles and ideas of the U.S. Constitution written in 1787?
   b. How and why did Federalists and Antifederalists clash?

4. **Writing and Critical Thinking**
   Supporting a Point of View Imagine you are a Federalist or an Antifederalist in North Carolina in 1789. Write a letter to the editor stating your view on whether the Constitution should be ratified.
   Consider:
   - your views on states' rights
   - the problems facing the country
   - the need for a Bill of Rights

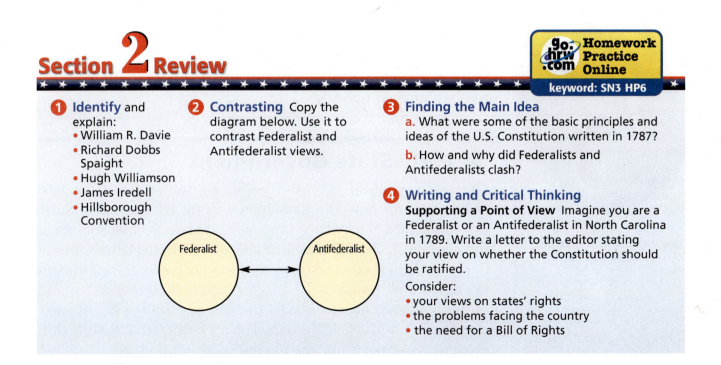

Forming a New Nation and State

Section 3

Forming a State Government

Read to Discover
1. What problems did North Carolina's government have?
2. What was the Whiskey Rebellion?
3. What changing role did political parties play in North Carolina?

Identify
- Nathaniel Macon

Abner Nash found his powers limited as governor of North Carolina.

The Story Continues

Like the Articles of Confederation, the North Carolina Constitution of 1776 led to some problems. Under the state constitution the governor had little authority. And, as Governor Abner Nash would say, "men, not knowing whom to obey, obeyed nobody."

★ Early State Government

The state government of North Carolina was created during the dark, early days of the American Revolution. Like the other colonies, North Carolina needed to send troops and money to help fight the war. Yet its first governor, Richard Caswell, complained "that by the Constitution of this State, nothing can be done by the executive power of itself towards this desirable purpose."

The legislature tried to solve the problem by creating a special three-man board to help defend the state. This act further weakened the chief executive. Governor Nash, who succeeded Caswell, declared:

"You presented me with the Sword of the State as an emblem of the power I was invested with for the protection of the Constitution and the rights of the people ... yet ... deprived me of almost every power, privilege and authority belonging to my office."

Analyzing Primary Sources
Finding the Main Idea What problem did early governors experience?

The constitution also created unequal representation. Property and religious restrictions were placed on voters and officeholders. The east had many more seats in the state legislature than did the west. Many people, especially westerners, felt disappointed and excluded. Support for the constitution—and for the state government—declined.

✔ **READING CHECK** **Identifying Cause and Effect** What weaknesses in the state government were created by the North Carolina constitution?

★ Political Parties in North Carolina

The conservatives and radicals who opposed each other during the making of the state constitution became the Federalists and Antifederalists who opposed each other over ratification of the U.S. Constitution. With few exceptions, those who were Federalists before 1789 supported Hamilton and the Federalist Party in the 1790s. The Antifederalists largely opposed Hamilton, and most, including many North Carolinians, became Republicans. In fact, Republicans were generally strong throughout the state. Federalist strength lay in the towns.

The Federalists controlled the national government in the 1790s. North Carolinians voted mainly Federalists into national office from 1789 to 1793. However, the state's citizens generally distrusted the strong central government. They became dissatisfied with the nationalistic policies of the Federalist administration in Washington. The state legislature often instructed the North Carolina senators to vote against Federalist measures. They particularly opposed many of Alexander Hamilton's policies.

This humorous illustration from 1807 depicts an argument between Federalists and Antifederalists that took place in the U.S. Congress in 1789.

✔ **READING CHECK** **Summarizing** How did North Carolinians view the Federalists and Republicans?

★ The Whiskey Rebellion

One of the challenges the young United States faced was the need to strengthen its economy. This task fell upon the shoulders of Treasury Secretary Alexander Hamilton. His policies included funding the national debt with new federal bonds and having the federal government pay state debts. Most North Carolinians were against both.

Forming a New Nation and State

An angry mob tars and feathers a tax collector in this illustration of the Whiskey Rebellion.

To help raise money, Hamilton proposed a tax on certain goods made and used within the states, most notably whiskey. Farmers deeply resented this whiskey tax. They often converted their surplus grain to whiskey because whiskey was easier to ship and was a popular item of exchange. The tax created an uproar in areas where farmers relied heavily on whiskey production.

Protests in Pennsylvania Efforts to enforce the law in western Pennsylvania caused violent protests. By the summer of 1794, tax agents were being tarred and feathered and run out of town. In July about 500 armed men rioted, burning the home of the local tax inspector. President Washington ordered the men home. When they refused, he sent in some 13,000 troops. The rebels were tried, and two men were convicted of treason. Washington later pardoned them.

Outrage in North Carolina Farmers in North Carolina equally resented the whiskey tax. Protests and threats to defy payment followed its passage in 1791. However, in 1792 the law was revised. The tax itself was reduced, and small distilleries were exempted from paying it. This satisfied many North Carolinians. The violence that later erupted in Pennsylvania did not occur in North Carolina. The whiskey tax and the Whiskey Rebellion, however, further divided the state and the federal government. It also signaled the weakening of Federalist control.

✔ **READING CHECK** Analyzing Information How did the Whiskey Rebellion relate to complaints people had against the government?

Republicans Take Over

The Federalists had been losing ground in North Carolina. In the election of 1794, North Carolina sent nine Republicans and only one Federalist to the House of Representatives. Its once-moderate governor, Alexander Martin, had become a firm Republican and was chosen senator by the legislature. Of the five governors between 1789 and 1802, two were Federalists—Richard Dobbs Spaight and William Davie—but Spaight later became a Republican. From 1802 to 1814 all the governors in the state were Republican. In effect, North Carolina now had a one-party system.

Decline of the Federalists nationally The political mood in North Carolina was echoed throughout the nation. Many people opposed Federalist policies, which placed great power in the central government. The Federalists believed in a loose interpretation of the Constitution—anything that was not directly forbidden by the Constitution was allowed. They were seen by their opponents as elitists, ignoring the common people. In 1801 Republican Thomas Jefferson of Virginia became president. The Federalists were losing national power as well.

Republican beliefs Republicans believed in a strict interpretation of the Constitution—the federal government had only those powers written down in the Constitution. They supported states' rights and favored an agricultural society over industry. As president, Jefferson repealed the tax that had led to the Whiskey Rebellion and reduced the size of the army.

Macon's leadership In North Carolina **Nathaniel Macon** gave the Republicans a strong leader. Macon was elected to the House of Representatives in 1791, became Speaker of the House in 1801, and was elected to the Senate in 1815. Macon furthered the Republican cause by persuading publisher Joseph Gales to start a Republican newspaper in the state's new capital, Raleigh. The *Raleigh Register* was a powerful political tool.

✔ **READING CHECK** Identifying Cause and Effect Why did the Republicans gain power in North Carolina?

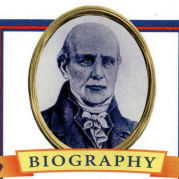

BIOGRAPHY

Nathaniel Macon
(1758–1837)

Nathaniel Macon was born into a family of wealthy North Carolina planters. Despite his aristocratic background, he lived a simple life and supported the rights of the common people. He fought in the Revolutionary War and was elected to the House of Representatives in 1791. He served as Speaker of the House from 1801 to 1807, and in 1815 he was elected to the Senate. Macon served in Congress for more than 30 years. **What were some of Macon's accomplishments as a political leader?**

Section 3 Review

Homework Practice Online
keyword: SN3 HP6

1 Identify and explain:
- Nathaniel Macon

2 Contrasting Copy the chart below. Use it to contrast Federalist and Republican views.

3 Finding the Main Idea
a. What were some problems North Carolina experienced because of its constitution?
b. What was the whiskey tax, and what effect did it have?
c. What happened to the Federalist Party in North Carolina and the nation? Why?

4 Writing and Critical Thinking
Summarizing Imagine you are a historian. Write a paragraph that sums up early North Carolina government.
Consider:
- the power of the governor
- the degree of representation and the feelings of the people
- the strength of each political party by the early 1800s

	Federalist	Republican
View of Constitution		
Central government		
Rule of people		

Forming a New Nation and State **115**

Section 4

The War of 1812

Read to Discover
1. What were the causes of the War of 1812?
2. What role did North Carolina play in the war?
3. How did the war affect the United States?

Define
- impressment
- embargo

Identify
- Johnston Blakeley
- Otway Burns
- Benjamin Forsyth
- Dolley Madison
- Andrew Jackson

The U.S. frigate *United States* is seen here capturing the British frigate *Macedonian* in this scene from the War of 1812.

The Story Continues

Winning its independence from Great Britain was only the first step the United States had to take to establish itself as a new nation. Conflicts in Europe soon led to what has been called "The Second War for Independence."

★ The Outbreak of War

The Revolutionary War did not end the conflict between the United States and Great Britain. The British navy continued to rule the seas, and it began to prey on U.S. trade ships. British-born sailors serving on U.S. ships were considered deserters. They were taken from the ships and forced into military service, a practice called **impressment**.

Great Britain needed experienced seamen to help fight its war against the French. Both Britain and France used naval blockades to disrupt sea trade, and the United States found itself caught in the middle. President Thomas Jefferson tried to show the importance of trade with the United States by imposing restrictions of his own. In 1806 certain British goods were banned. The next year an **embargo** was placed on all international trade to and from U.S. ports. In 1809 trade was resumed with all nations except Britain and France. None of these measures, however, succeeded in forcing Britain or France to honor American rights.

There were also growing conflicts on land. Britain was supporting Shawnee chief Tecumseh and his confederation of several tribes in a series of wars against settlers along the Canadian border. Western settlers, eager to push deeper into Indian territory, found themselves frustrated by the British presence in Canada.

By the fall of 1811, talk of war was in the air. The following summer, on June 18, 1812, the United States declared war on Great Britain.

✓ **READING CHECK** **Summarizing** What actions led to the War of 1812?

GLOBAL CONNECTIONS

Embargoes

An embargo stops shipping between one country and another, usually to force one nation into changing certain policies. The Embargo Act of 1807 is the only time in U.S. history when all U.S. ships were confined to port.

The United States has used embargoes for political reasons. It has placed embargoes against Cuba and Iraq. Because embargoes require the cooperation of third-party nations to succeed, today most embargoes are overseen by the United Nations. **Why would a nation establish an embargo?**

★ North Carolina and the War

Moderates in Congress, led by John Randolph of Virginia and North Carolina's William Gaston, opposed the war. They knew it would take much time and money to win. Public opinion was with the "war hawks" who supported the war, however, and in the end they prevailed.

Political divisions North Carolina itself was divided over the war. Some doubted the wisdom of a second war against Britain. North Carolinians felt no immediate threat. In fact, many thought the actions of Britain and France were no worse than they had ever been. Newspapers both supported and condemned the war, as did the state's elected representatives.

Concerns for security The war was fought on both land and water. North Carolina, with its long shoreline of capes, sounds, and barrier islands, was vulnerable to attack from the sea. British warships were frequently spotted, and in July 1813 several ships landed at Ocracoke. The U.S. Navy was too small to defend the entire coast, so the government asked civilian shipowners and privateers to come to its aid. Privateers were allowed to capture foreign ships and take part of their cargo as reward.

✓ **READING CHECK** **Finding the Main Idea** How did North Carolinians view the war?

★ North Carolina Heroes in the War

Despite doubts about the war, North Carolina did send men into battle. Some North Carolinians even became heroes.

Blakeley, Burns, and Forsyth In June of 1814 the USS *Wasp*, under the command of **Johnston Blakeley** encountered the British ship the HMS *Reindeer*. The battle lasted only 19 minutes. Although outgunned

Soldiers from the USS Wasp *board a British ship.*

That's Interesting!

Our national anthem, "The Star-Spangled Banner," was written by Francis Scott Key during the War of 1812. The flag Key saw had 15 "broad stripes and bright stars." In 1818 an act of Congress reduced the number of stripes to 13, with new stars, not stripes, to be added on the 4th of July following a state's admission to the Union.

Dolley Madison saving important presidential documents

Analyzing Primary Sources

Drawing Inferences and Conclusions Why do you think Dolley Madison became a national hero?

by the British ship, the *Wasp* fought on, and in the end, the captain of the *Reindeer* was killed. In all, the *Wasp* took seven ships and defeated a British man-of-war on its maiden voyage. The news raised spirits at home and alarmed the British public. For his efforts, Congress awarded Blakeley a gold medal. Unfortunately, Blakeley never reached home. On his way back, he defeated the *Atalanta*, a heavily armed British brig, which he sent home with some of his men. The *Wasp* sailed on, however, and was never seen again.

One of the bravest of North Carolina's privateers was **Otway Burns**. In its maiden voyage, Burns's ship, the *Snap Dragon*, captured nine ships, along with several smaller prizes. Within two years, he had captured millions of dollars' worth of goods. The British set a $50,000 price on his head. Following the war Burns went into shipbuilding and built the first steamboat in North Carolina. He later served for 14 years in the state legislature.

Although the war was not fought on North Carolina soil, many of its men saw action against the British. Among the most renowned was Lieutenant Colonel **Benjamin Forsyth**. Forsyth was killed in battle in Canada and was regarded as a hero in his home state. In 1849 the North Carolina legislature created Forsyth County, named in honor of Colonel Forsyth, from a portion of Stokes County.

National heroes Some North Carolinians were heroes to the entire nation. **Dolley Madison** was one. Born Dolley Payne in the Piedmont, she married James Madison in 1794. Madison was elected president in 1808. When the British entered Washington and burned the city in 1814, Dolley kept her head. She refused to flee the White House until she could collect and remove Madison's papers, as well as a famous portrait of George Washington. In a letter to her sister, she wrote:

History Makers Speak

"I insist on waiting until the large picture of General Washington is secured, and it requires to be unscrewed from the wall.... I have ordered the frame to be broken, and the precious portrait placed in the hands of two gentlemen from New York, for safe keeping. And now, dear sister, I must leave this house."

A later president, **Andrew Jackson**, was born in South Carolina, near the border with North Carolina, in 1767. Jackson studied and practiced law in North Carolina, before moving to what became Tennessee. In 1814 he became a major general of the United States army. Jackson earned his greatest military fame at the Battle of New Orleans in

January 1815. A fleet of more than 50 British ships sailed into the Gulf of Mexico, prepared to attack New Orleans and control the Mississippi River. Jackson rushed to defend the city. The battle lasted a mere half hour and ended in victory for Jackson's army. A peace treaty had been signed two weeks earlier, but news had yet to reach forces fighting on the front.

✓ **READING CHECK** *Contrasting* What were the differences between the goals of naval raiders like Blakeley and privateers like Burns?

General Andrew Jackson (at the right, on horseback) achieved a major victory for United States forces at the Battle of New Orleans, shown here.

★ Effects of the War

The war officially ended with the signing of a peace treaty on December 24, 1814. The treaty did not settle impressments, embargoes, or other issues of the war. The Americans' defeat of Tecumseh did, however, open the Northwest to settlements. Federalist opposition to the war greatly weakened the party's support. The war thus signaled the end of the Federalist Party in North Carolina and the nation. Most important, the war helped the United States develop a sense of strength. Americans became confident in their ability to control their destiny. There was a rise in nationalism and a sense of unity in the country.

✓ **READING CHECK** *Drawing Conclusions* How did the United States benefit from the War of 1812?

The official survey of the border between North and South Carolina was delayed by the War of 1812 and was not completed until 1815.

Section 4 Review

keyword: SN3 HP6

❶ Define and explain:
- impressment
- embargo

❷ Identify and explain:
- Johnston Blakeley
- Otway Burns
- Benjamin Forsyth
- Dolley Madison
- Andrew Jackson

❸ Identifying Causes and Effects Copy the diagram below to show the causes and effects of the War of 1812.

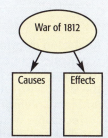

❹ Finding the Main Idea
a. Why did the United States feel it had to go to war against Britain?

b. In what ways did North Carolina help the war effort?

❺ Writing and Critical Thinking
Supporting a Point of View Imagine you are a newspaper editor in North Carolina in 1812. Write an editorial explaining why the country should or should not go to war.
Consider:
- the importance of British offenses to North Carolina citizens
- the security of the state's coast
- what the state has to gain or lose

Forming a New Nation and State **119**

Chapter 6 Review

Chapter Summary

Section 1

- Americans' belief in individual rights and freedoms helped to inspire the Revolution.
- North Carolina's first state constitution reflected the political and social values of its citizens.
- The Articles of Confederation failed to provide a strong framework of government for the new nation.

Section 2

- The U.S. Constitution resolved many of the weaknesses of the earlier Articles.
- In North Carolina, debate over the U.S. Constitution was focused on the issue of federal versus state power.

Section 3

- North Carolina's early state government excluded many citizens from equal representation.
- Among many North Carolinians, the whiskey tax of 1791 symbolized the struggle between federal and state governments.
- Opposition among North Carolina's early political parties was based, in part, on the issue of states' rights and federal powers.

Section 4

- Growing economic and political conflict between the United States and Great Britain led to the War of 1812.
- North Carolinians were divided in their support for the war aims of the United States.
- The War of 1812 helped to establish the United States as a free and independent nation.

Identifying People and Ideas

Use the following terms or people in complete sentences.

1. State of Franklin
2. Richard Caswell
3. James Iredell
4. Hillsborough Convention
5. Nathaniel Macon
6. embargo
7. Johnston Blakeley
8. Otway Burns
9. Dolley Madison
10. Andrew Jackson

Understanding Main Ideas

Section 1 (Pages 103–107)

1. What ideals were reflected in the North Carolina Constitution of 1776?

Section 2 (Pages 108–111)

2. What were key features of the government created by the U.S. Constitution?
3. How did North Carolina Federalists and Antifederalists feel about the U.S. Constitution?

Section 3 (Pages 112–115)

4. What were some weaknesses of the North Carolina constitution?
5. How did Republicans come to take control in North Carolina?

Section 4 (Pages 116–119)

6. What were the causes and effects of the War of 1812?

What Did You Find Out?

1. **Constitutional Heritage** What individuals and groups influenced the writing of the first North Carolina state constitution, and how were they affected by the constitution?
2. **Citizenship** In what ways did changing political and economic conditions affect the development of individual rights in North Carolina?
3. **Government** In what ways did relations with the central United States government affect political parties within North Carolina?

Thinking Critically

1. **Analyzing Information** Explain how the ideals Americans fought for in the Revolution became the basis for the North Carolina constitution and the U.S. Constitution.
2. **Problem Solving** What could have been done to correct some of the weaknesses in the North Carolina constitution?
3. **Sequencing** Explain the rise and fall of the Federalist Party in North Carolina and the nation.

Building Social Studies Skills

Interpreting Maps
Study the map below. Then use the information on the map to answer the questions that follow.

1. Which state besides North Carolina might have felt threatened by the desire of those in Franklin to break away and form their own state?
   a. Kentucky
   b. Tennessee
   c. Virginia
   d. South Carolina

2. What geographic features made the people of Franklin feel removed from North Carolina?

Identifying Bias
Read Articles XXXI and XXXII of the North Carolina Constitution of 1776. These articles established rules regarding who could and could not hold state office in North Carolina. After reading the articles, answer the questions below.

> XXXI. That no clergyman, or preacher of the gospels of any denomination, shall be capable of being a member of either the Senate, House of Commons, or Council of State, while he continues in the exercise of the pastoral function.
>
> XXXII. That no person, who shall deny the being of God or the truth of the Protestant religion, or the divine authority either of the Old or New Testaments, or who shall hold religious principles incompatible with the freedom and safety of the State, shall be capable of holding any office or place of trust or profit in the civil department within this State.

3. Which of the following rights or freedoms does Article XXXII deny to those who might want to hold public office in North Carolina?
   a. the right to be paid for work performed
   b. freedom of speech
   c. freedom of religion
   d. the right to petition the government for change
   e. freedom of assembly

4. What effects might these articles have on government in North Carolina and on citizens' views of government?

Alternative Assessment

Building Your Portfolio

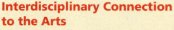

Interdisciplinary Connection to the Arts
Symbols such as flags and seals are important ways to represent ideals and unite people. Both the United States and North Carolina created flags and seals in their early history. Design your own flag or seal to show the ideals that the young nation or state stood for. Include a written explanation of each image you choose to use.

internet connect

Internet Activity: go.hrw.com
keyword: SN3 NC6

Choose a topic about forming a new nation and state to:
- Create a chart showing the Federalist/Antifederalist debate.
- Compare documents that grew out of the Revolutionary War.
- Create a visual and textual time line of the War of 1812.

Forming a New Nation and State

UNIT 3 Antebellum North Carolina
(1790–1860)

CHAPTER 7 Political Shifts (1815–1860)

CHAPTER 8 Life and Culture (1815–1860)

CHAPTER 9 Southern Systems in North Carolina (1790–1860)

Young People

IN HISTORY

Life in Antebellum Times

A typical school day for young, rural North Carolinians in the 1800s usually consisted of sitting on rough benches from early morning until dusk; following strict rules of behavior—or suffering punishment; working in dim light that filtered through the few windows to the room's dirt floor; and studying reading, writing, arithmetic, and spelling. Not all children attended "common," or public, schools, however. Some young people simply had too far to travel to school. Others needed to work on their families' farms. Some parents did not even want their children to attend public school, which they associated with poverty, while others did not want girls and boys to attend the same class.

Girls whose families wanted them to go to an all-girls school—and who could afford to pay—attended one of the few private academies for females. In these schools girls mostly studied household arts, needlework, music, dancing, and art. Boys at private male academies went beyond basic subjects to study classic literature and philosophy.

School was not a part of the lives of African American slave children. They toiled long hours in plantation fields or in the plantation owner's "big house." Only some were taught to read and write. One of these lucky few was Harriet Jacobs, who never even realized she was a slave until she was six years old. Then her mother died, and she went to live with her mother's white mistress. Upon the mistress's death, Harriet was willed to the woman's five-year-old niece.

Other slave children had harsher experiences. Thomas H. Jones, who became free later in life, wrote that he "was made to feel, in my boyhood's first experience, . . . that I must pass through life in a dependent and suffering condition." Thomas worked "early and late" on a plantation. Like many young slaves, he was sold away from his family when he was just nine.

African American young people in antebellum North Carolina rarely had the opportunity to attend school. Instead, most labored on plantations and farms.

If You Were There *How well would you learn if you attended a common school in the mid-1800s?*

LEFT PAGE: *This image shows a romanticized view of a "grand plantation" in the antebellum South. Very few such plantations actually existed in North Carolina, though the ideal is often associated with the era.*

123

CHAPTER 7
Political Shifts
(1815–1860)

Log cabin on a Carolina settlement

Build on What You Know

From the beginning, the War of 1812 had been a divisive issue in North Carolina. Some North Carolinians had agreed that the United States had to combat British aggression. Others had condemned the action as unnecessary. People were proud, however, of North Carolina's war heroes.

What's Your Opinion?

 Do you **agree** or **disagree** with the following statements? Support your point of view in your journal.

- **Economics** The economic system of one region can have a dramatic effect on another region.
- **Culture** All human beings have a right to live where they want to live.
- **Citizenship** Reform movements are necessary in order for change and improvements to take place.

Section 1

The "Rip Van Winkle" State

Read to Discover
1. What caused economic stagnation in North Carolina?
2. What were the effects of North Carolina's stagnation?
3. Why did people move away from North Carolina?

Define
- stagnation
- monoculture
- illiterate

Identify
- Rip Van Winkle state

The Story Continues

During the first half of the 1800s, traveling by roads in North Carolina was difficult. Most roads were no more than paths cutting across fields and through forests. Particularly in the western counties, the going was difficult and costly. In 1842 Governor John Motley Morehead said that it cost half the value of a farmer's crop "to transport the other [half] to market." Transportation in North Carolina needed major improvements.

In the early 1800s there were few roads in the mountains of western North Carolina.

 A Slumbering State

Throughout the United States, the end of the War of 1812 brought a great sense of national pride. A new spirit of democracy and optimism swept the nation. Many citizens turned their attention to making improvements at home.

This was not the case in North Carolina. Citizens seemed unaware of what was happening in the rest of the country or even in their own state. In the early 1800s the state was an economic backwater. It was known to many outsiders as the **Rip Van Winkle state**. (Rip Van Winkle

Political Shifts 125

was a character in a story by Washington Irving. In the story he falls asleep for twenty years.) The wealthy planters who lived mostly along the broad rivers of the Coastal Plain had considerable contact with the outside world. They sold their crops to merchants in the North and in Europe. But a general condition of economic underdevelopment left most North Carolinians living in rural isolation. As a result, the economy of the state went virtually unchanged for years, a condition known as **stagnation**.

During this time, wealthy planters in the eastern part of North Carolina were satisfied with conditions. As a rule of thumb, these were people who farmed 500 or more acres and owned 20 or more slaves. These planters were content to do little or nothing to improve the rest of the state. Citizens in other parts of North Carolina, however, faced serious problems. They were isolated by an absence of good roads and navigable rivers. Most were poor. They lived on small tracts of land where they produced only what they needed for themselves. Markets where people could sell their products were lacking. There were few mills or factories, and there were no public schools. North Carolina was marked by a lack of progress and by political divisions.

✓ **READING CHECK** Summarizing What was North Carolina like during the period after the War of 1812?

Causes of Stagnation

Several factors contributed to North Carolina's lack of economic development. These factors included the general attitude of its people, its lack of democracy in state government, and the effects of slavery.

Isolation and independence Except for a few small towns, North Carolina's citizens were isolated from each other. They lived far apart on farms scattered across the state. As a result, people became very independent. They thought only about their own needs, and they liked things the way they were. They did not want to be told to send their children to school or to pay more taxes. They did not want the state government to interfere in their lives.

Lack of democracy North Carolina's government was democratic in form, but not in practice. Each county elected representatives to the legislature. All the counties, however, had the same number of representatives, regardless of population. Since there were more counties in eastern North Carolina, the east had more representatives. Eastern planters therefore controlled the legislature. They were not interested in increasing their own taxes to improve conditions for what they considered to be "the common people."

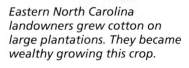

Eastern North Carolina landowners grew cotton on large plantations. They became wealthy growing this crop.

Slavery North Carolina was an agricultural state. Although yeomen with few or no slaves made up the majority of farmers, the state's economy was dominated by eastern planters who used slave labor to grow cotton and tobacco. Because they made good profits this way, planters had little interest in developing industry or improving agriculture. The focus on cotton and tobacco meant there was little manufacturing in North Carolina. People bought few factory-made goods, and those that they did purchase most often came from other states.

Slavery also encouraged wasteful use of land. Planters often grew the same crop year after year on the same field. This growing method is called **monoculture**. This practice quickly depleted the soil's nutrients, which led planters to abandon old fields and clear new ones. The abandoned land eroded and was useless for a long time.

✔ **READING CHECK Finding the Main Idea** What factors contributed to North Carolina's economic stagnation?

Effects of Economic Stagnation

The planter-controlled economy and lack of democracy in North Carolina had widespread effects.

Education In 1840, one third of all white adults in North Carolina were **illiterate**. This means that they could not read or write. Many citizens did not believe education was important. A few sent their children to local academies. Most, however, could not afford to pay tuition for such schools. The academies received no state aid. The eastern landowners in the state legislature were glad to support this situation. They saw no reason why they should be taxed to educate the children of common farmers.

Internal improvements North Carolina had a great need for improved transportation. The state's interior rivers were rocky and shallow, and thus difficult to navigate. There were very few bridges, and many river crossings were dangerous. There were no canals to let travelers bypass the rivers. The roads were no better. They were primitive and poorly maintained. Only the state government could solve these problems. But the eastern planters prevented the legislature from spending state money to make improvements.

✔ **READING CHECK Contrasting** What were the differences between the eastern planters and citizens in the rest of the state?

CONNECTING TO ECONOMICS

Monoculture
Monoculture is the most common way of growing crops in the world today. It was not as successful in the past as it is today. Early farmers did not know that many crops deplete nutrients from the soil. Today farmers can replace those nutrients with special fertilizers. Even so, some scientists worry that monoculture may reduce the genetic diversity of crops and might make them more susceptible to pests and diseases. **How is monoculture today different from North Carolina in the early 1800s?**

A cotton plant, just prior to harvest

★ Migration

Life was hard for many people in North Carolina during the first half of the 1800s. They had to work long hours just to feed themselves. Few saw any chance for improvement. In 1830 a legislative committee said this in a report about North Carolina.

Analyzing Primary Sources
Analyzing Information According to the legislative report, why was there little business or industry in North Carolina in 1830?

"[North Carolina is] a State without . . . internal communication by rivers, roads, or canals; without a cash market for any article or agricultural product; without manufactures; in short without any object to which native industry and active enterprise could be directed."

1830 "Legislative Report," quoted in *North Carolina: The History of a Southern State* by H. T. Lefler and A. R. Newsome

Moving from one state to another in the 1800s was a slow and difficult process.

Many families saw no reason to stay in North Carolina. They moved to other states to find richer land, better transportation, and a chance for advancement. Estimates were that before 1815, some 200,000 North Carolinians had moved to Tennessee, Alabama, and Ohio. Between 1815 and 1850 about one third of all native North Carolinians moved to other states. Of these, thousands who were against slavery moved to states in the Midwest.

✔ **READING CHECK** Making Predictions What effect do you think the mass migration of people out of North Carolina had on the future development of the state?

Section 1 Review

① **Define** and explain:
- stagnation
- monoculture
- illiterate

② **Identify** and explain:
- Rip Van Winkle state

③ **Identifying Cause and Effect** Copy the organizer below. Use it to show the causes and effects of North Carolina's economic stagnation.

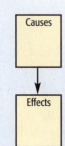

④ **Finding the Main Idea**
a. What conditions caused economic stagnation in North Carolina?

b. What effects did North Carolina's stagnation have on education, transportation, and the economy?

c. What effect did North Carolina's stagnation have on the state's population?

⑤ **Writing and Critical Thinking**
Identifying Points of View Why did planters in eastern North Carolina ignore the problems in the rest of the state?
Consider:
- the economic system in the east
- attitudes of planters
- attitudes of other citizens

Section 2

Reactions to Jackson's Policies

Read to Discover
1. Why did North Carolina support Andrew Jackson for president?
2. Why did some North Carolinians become dissatisfied with President Jackson?
3. What happened when the national policy of removal and resettlement was enacted, and how did North Carolinians react?
4. What was the result when those opposed to Jackson organized?

Identify
- Democratic Party
- Indian Removal Act
- Trail of Tears
- Qualla Boundary
- Whig Party

The campaign of 1824 was the first time candidates appealed directly to voters. They used buttons, flags, and other trinkets to try to gain votes.

The Story Continues

Andrew Jackson was a popular military hero after the War of 1812. His Tennessee friends thought he would make a good president. They convinced the Tennessee legislature to back Jackson as a candidate.

★ North Carolina Supports Jackson

Five candidates—all Democratic-Republicans—competed for the presidency in 1824. Andrew Jackson received more votes than any other candidate. In North Carolina, Jackson won the popular vote. He carried the western counties and several eastern counties. People thought Jackson would favor the internal improvements they needed so badly.

However, no candidate won a majority of the electoral votes. In such situations, the House of Representatives selects the president. John Quincy Adams was selected. Jackson vowed to run again.

In 1828, Jackson easily won the presidential election against Adams. All areas of North Carolina backed him. Yeomen farmers in the western counties and in the coastal regions hoped he would make internal

★★★★★★★★★★★★★
That's Interesting!
★★★★★★★★★★★★★

While he was president, Andrew Jackson relied on his friends to help him make decisions. They were a group of newspaper editors and politicians who had helped elect him. They would meet informally in the White House kitchen. These people came to be known as Jackson's "kitchen cabinet." The phrase is still used today to mean a group of unofficial advisers to a president.

Political Shifts 129

improvements. The eastern planters voted for him because, unlike Adams, Jackson was a southerner. Jackson's supporters later adopted the name Democrats and became the **Democratic Party**.

✓ **READING CHECK** Comparing and Contrasting What were the similarities and differences between the elections of 1824 and 1828?

★ Jackson Raises Controversy

In 1829 Jackson began the first of his two terms as president. It was not long, however, before he began to lose support. By 1830 it was clear that he opposed the idea of federal support for state improvements. Many voters in North Carolina's western counties were disappointed with his position. They withdrew their support.

Another Jackson policy angered many southerners. In 1828 Congress passed a new tariff that doubled taxes on certain imports. These taxes affected the South far more than the North. When South Carolina refused to collect the tariff, Jackson threatened to send in federal troops. His action was not popular in North Carolina, particularly in the counties that bordered South Carolina.

Jackson's long dispute with the Bank of the United States also divided voters. Jackson thought the federal bank was too powerful. He believed it benefited only its rich investors. He wanted to reorganize it. Some of Jackson's supporters agreed with him, but others did not.

At the same time, Jackson was gaining a following among the eastern planters. They agreed with his opposition to internal improvements and the national bank. He won more support when he appointed John Branch of Halifax County as his secretary of the navy. Branch was the first North Carolinian to serve in a cabinet position.

Interpreting the Visual Record

Trail of Tears Thousands of Cherokee were forced to move west after the Indian Removal Act passed. *What indications are there in this painting that this was a forced move?*

✓ **READING CHECK** Summarizing How did the people of North Carolina react to Andrew Jackson's policies?

The Cherokee were the first group of Native Americans to have a written language.

★ Indian Removal

Andrew Jackson's most controversial action was his handling of the **Indian Removal Act** of 1830. The act authorized the relocation of Indian tribes living east of the Mississippi River to Indian Territory in present-day Oklahoma. Their eastern lands would be exchanged

130   Chapter 7

for lands in the west. Under Jackson's direction, the U.S. military removed the tribes by force.

Indians in North Carolina in 1830 There were small tribal groups throughout North Carolina in 1830. The largest group by far was the Cherokee. About 18,000 tribal members lived in northwest Georgia and western North Carolina. In 1838 the Cherokee were forced to march west. The disastrous march has come to be known as the <u>Trail of Tears</u>. About 4,000 Cherokee died from bad weather and food shortages during the 800-mile trek to the Indian Territory.

This basket made on the Qualla Reservation displays traditional Cherokee methods of weaving. The double weave pattern is so tight that some Cherokee baskets can even hold water.

Views of removal Jackson's supporters in North Carolina backed removal. They believed the land exchange was fair and that the Indians would be better off in the west. White settlers and land speculators were also for removal. They wanted access to Indian land. In fact, ever since the late 1780s, North Carolina had been granting land to white settlers that lay within Indian territory, in violation of a 1785 agreement between the Cherokee and the United States government.

Those in North Carolina who were anti-Jackson were against removal. They thought it broke treaties and was unconstitutional. Many church leaders, religious societies, and educators were also against it. To them it was un-Christian and morally wrong. The Cherokee Nation made its views clear in an 1830 newspaper article.

"We wish to remain on the land of our fathers. . . . The treaties with us, and laws of the United States . . . guaranty our residence and our privileges, and secure us against intruders. Our only request is, that these treaties may be fulfilled, and these laws executed."

Nile's Weekly Register, August 21, 1830, quoted in *The Way We Lived*, Vol. 1, edited by F. M. Binder and D. M. Reimers

Analyzing Primary Sources
Finding the Main Idea What main point did the Cherokee Nation make in this passage?

Cherokee escape in the North Carolina mountains When troops began to round up the Cherokee, a leader named Tsali and several hundred followers escaped into hiding in the North Carolina mountains. In return for Tsali's surrender, his followers were allowed to remain. The commander of the federal troops ordered Tsali and his sons shot by other Cherokee captives. Throughout the 1840s U.S. troops searched the mountains to remove Cherokee still in hiding. Finally in 1848, Congress recognized their rights.

The Eastern Band of Cherokee Today, the Cherokee who live in North Carolina are the Eastern Band of Cherokee. They are descended from those who avoided removal. The Cherokee reservation in western North Carolina is known as the <u>Qualla Boundary</u>.

✔ **READING CHECK Identifying Bias** Why did North Carolinians have different opinions of Indian removal?

CONNECTING TO Geography

The Qualla Boundary
The Qualla Boundary is home to over 6,000 members of the Eastern Band of Cherokee. It is an area of over 56,000 acres in western North Carolina.

The economy of the Qualla Boundary is based on tourism and arts and crafts. Some Cherokee artisans are working to revive lost traditions of Cherokee pottery. **Why might Cherokee artisans be interested in reviving craft traditions?**

Political Shifts

Interpreting the Visual Record

Political cartoon of Andrew Jackson *Andrew Jackson's political enemies compared him to the king of England. What points were Jackson's enemies trying to make by comparing him to a king?*

★ Jackson's Enemies Organize

Andrew Jackson's actions as president angered many people. His opponents began calling him "King Andrew." In 1834, the anti-Jackson movement was strong enough to form a national opposition party. It was called the **Whig Party**. The party took the name Whig from a British political party that had opposed the king's power.

The Whig Party quickly attracted followers in North Carolina. Support for the party was strongest in the western counties and in the eastern coastal areas. However, to succeed the Whigs had to do more than simply oppose Jackson. They had to offer ideas that would appeal to voters throughout North Carolina. To this end, the Whigs supported internal improvements and better public schools. These reforms would require changes to the North Carolina constitution, also an idea that many voters supported. On a federal level, the Whigs were in favor of a strong national bank and tariffs on foreign goods. The Whigs believed that these policies would help North Carolina to prosper.

In 1835 the Whigs were able to elect seven of the state's thirteen representatives to Congress. Five of them were from the western counties. Two were from the coastal region. The Whigs were now a serious challenge to the eastern planters. The planters still backed Jackson and the Democratic Party. They opposed a strong federal government. They were also against government spending for improvements. From 1835 until the start of the Civil War, the Whig Party and the Democratic Party contended for control of the state.

✓ **READING CHECK** Identifying Cause and Effect Why did the Whig Party develop, and what effect did it have on North Carolina politics?

Section 2 Review

1. **Identify** and explain:
   - Democratic Party
   - Indian Removal Act
   - Trail of Tears
   - Qualla Boundary
   - Whig Party

2. **Summarizing** Copy the chart below. Use it to show Andrew Jackson's controversial policies and reaction to them in North Carolina.

	Jackson's position	Reaction in North Carolina
Internal improvements		
Tariff on imports		
Bank of U.S.		
Indian Removal Act		

3. **Finding the Main Idea**
   a. Why did North Carolina voters back Andrew Jackson in 1828?
   b. Why did some North Carolinians who had voted for Jackson become dissatisfied?
   c. Why was the Whig Party formed?

4. **Writing and Critical Thinking**
   Supporting a Point of View Imagine you are living in North Carolina in the 1830s. Write a paragraph explaining your position on the Indian Removal Act.
   Consider:
   - whether or not the act was constitutional
   - the religious and moral issues
   - the rights of the Indians

Homework Practice Online
keyword: SN3 HP7

Section 3

The Constitution of 1835

Read to Discover
1. What improvements did Archibald Murphey suggest in his reform plan for North Carolina?
2. What reforms did the western counties demand in the 1830s?
3. What changes were made to North Carolina's constitution in 1835?
4. What were the short- and long-term effects of North Carolina's 1835 Constitution?

Define
- amend
- referendum
- suffrage

Identify
- Archibald D. Murphey
- David L. Swain
- William Gaston

The Story Continues

Between 1815 and 1835, most North Carolinians ignored the lack of development of their state. A few, however, looked ahead. They could imagine a day when conditions in North Carolina would be better.

The reforms begun by Archibald Murphey in the early 1800s provide a tradition that continues to be followed by today's North Carolina General Assembly.

★ Early Calls for Reform

The leading voice of reform in the early 1800s was **Archibald D. Murphey**. Between 1815 and 1818, Murphey wrote a series of reform plans for the General Assembly. His plans called for internal improvements, public education, and constitutional reform.

Murphey's ideas for internal improvements focused on transportation. He proposed a system that would include canals and better roads. He urged the state to drain swamps and marshes in the east to create more farmland. Murphey also proposed public education for white children. He called for state construction of two or more primary schools in each county. Murphey was the first North Carolina leader to outline a plan of publicly supported education.

Murphey also believed that unequal representation in North Carolina's General Assembly had to be changed. He called for a state

Political Shifts 133

convention to change, or **amend**, the constitution. Archibald Murphey died in 1832, before his dreams could become reality. However, he left the state with a blueprint for development.

✓ **READING CHECK** Finding the Main Idea What were the three parts of Murphey's reform plan?

★ The West Demands Change

By 1830, the Whigs had adopted Murphey's program. They saw that the poor conditions in the west were tied to unequal representation. Murphey had mentioned this in a letter to his friend Thomas Ruffin.

"I had no Idea that we had such a poor, ignorant, squalid Population, as I have seen. Who that sees these People, and those of the Centre and the West, can wonder that we wish to have a Convention [to amend the constitution]?"

— Archibald D. Murphey, April 1819, quoted in *North Carolina: A Bicentennial History* by William S. Powell

A westerner, **David L. Swain**, was elected governor of North Carolina in 1832. Swain, only 31 years old, was the first Whig to become governor. He supported amending the constitution. When eastern planters still refused to consider changes, people in the west became very angry. Some actually discussed revolution. Finally in 1834, Governor Swain convinced legislators to hold a constitutional convention.

✓ **READING CHECK** Analyzing Information Why did the Whigs blame conditions in western North Carolina on unequal representation?

★ Meeting in Raleigh

The convention met in Raleigh in June 1835. Delegates included governors, judges, state legislators, and members of Congress.

The two strongest voices at the convention were Governor Swain and **William Gaston**. Governor Swain led the western group. They wanted to make the legislature more democratic. William Gaston was a judge and a Roman Catholic. He led the fight to change the constitution's 32nd article. That article prevented Catholics, Jews, or nonbelievers from holding state office.

The convention lasted more than a month. Finally, delegates agreed on a list of amendments. The changes then had to be approved by voters. The state held a **referendum**, a procedure that allows citizens to directly vote on a proposed public measure. The amendments passed 26,771 to 21,606. The results were sharply divided between the eastern and western counties.

✓ **READING CHECK** Making Generalizations Why do you think the vote on the constitutional amendments was divided by region?

Analyzing Primary Sources
Identifying Points of View
From this passage, what can you tell about Murphey's views on public education?

BIOGRAPHY

Archibald D. Murphey
(c. 1777–1832)

Archibald DeBow Murphey was born in Caswell County. In 1799 he graduated from the University of North Carolina. During his lifetime, Murphey was a teacher, attorney, planter, legislator, and judge. But his greatest contribution to North Carolina came from helping plan the state's future. He imagined good transportation, public schools, productive agriculture, and the elimination of slavery. Murphey died before his dreams came true. **What were some specific reforms that Murphey proposed?**

Changes Due to the 1835 Constitution

The amendments of 1835 made significant changes to the state constitution. The citizens of North Carolina were directly affected by several of these changes.

Religion William Gaston fought hard to change the constitution's 32nd article. Gaston gave a moving speech that lasted for two days. He argued that there should be no religious restrictions at all. In the end, a compromise amendment was passed. The word "Protestant" was changed to "Christian." This removed the restriction against Roman Catholics, but Jews and nonbelievers still could not hold office.

Rights of African Americans and Indians One 1835 amendment actually took rights away from citizens. Suffrage, the right to vote, was taken away from free African American and Indian men. Women were still not allowed to vote.

These new restrictions on the political freedoms of African Americans came about as a result of uneasiness among white North Carolinians. Fear of slave revolts grew during the 1820s and 1830s. In 1831 a slave leader named Nat Turner led a violent uprising in Southampton County, Virginia, located just across the border from Northampton County, North Carolina. The Whigs responded to growing fears by strengthening the code of laws that restricted the activities of slaves. The decision to take suffrage away from free African Americans as well represented an extension of this policy.

The General Assembly Governor David Swain and other Whig reformers from the west succeeded in passing a series of amendments that made the General Assembly more democratic. The Senate would have 50 members. They would be elected by districts and according to the amount of taxes citizens paid. The House of Commons would have 120 members, with the number of representatives from each county to be based on population. By this compromise, the east would control the Senate and the west would control the House of Commons.

Other changes The 1835 amendments changed the way governors would be elected. Now a governor would be elected every two years directly by voters instead of annually by the legislature. General Assembly sessions would now be held every other year. Also, there were now guidelines for how the constitution could be amended in the future.

✓ **READING CHECK** Drawing Inferences Why do you think so many of the 1835 amendments were the result of compromises?

William Gaston was a justice of the North Carolina Supreme Court and a Roman Catholic. He fought hard to remove religious restrictions from the constitution.

Political Shifts

Effects of the New Constitution

The new constitution of 1835 was a turning point in North Carolina history. For the first time, North Carolina voters would elect the governor. The new constitution meant the eastern planters no longer had a monopoly on political power. From now on, the east and west would need to negotiate and compromise.

An important long-term effect of the new constitution was the two-party system of government. The Whig Party and the Democratic Party were evenly matched. Now they would have to campaign for votes. To get elected, their programs would have to appeal to the people. Often, particularly in the western counties, this meant programs for social and economic development. The result was that North Carolina finally awoke from its slumber and the era of stagnation ended.

✔ **READING CHECK** Contrasting In what ways was North Carolina more democratic than it had been before?

Governor David L. Swain was a founder of the Whig Party in North Carolina. He led the movement to reform the state constitution. Later he became president of the University of North Carolina.

Section 3 Review

keyword: SN3 HP7

1. **Define** and explain:
   - amend
   - referendum
   - suffrage

2. **Identify** and explain:
   - Archibald D. Murphey
   - David L. Swain
   - William Gaston

3. **Summarizing** Copy the organizer below. Use it to summarize the changes made to North Carolina's constitution in 1835.

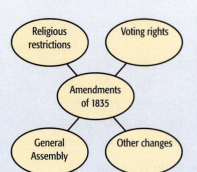

4. **Finding the Main Idea**
   a. What was Archibald Murphey's reform plan and what effect did it have?
   b. Why did the western counties demand reforms?
   c. How did the new constitution of 1835 affect North Carolina?

5. **Writing and Critical Thinking**
   Identifying Cause and Effect Imagine you live in western North Carolina in the 1830s. Write a letter to your newspaper explaining why people in your town are angry enough to revolt.
   Consider:
   - social and economic conditions
   - lack of internal improvements
   - lack of democracy in state government

Section 4
North Carolina under Whig Control

Read to Discover
1. What improvements in transportation were made while the Whigs were in control?
2. What educational reforms occurred under Whig control?
3. What social reforms were made under Whig control?
4. What were the overall effects of Whig reforms on North Carolina?

Identify
- Edward B. Dudley
- John Motley Morehead
- Wilmington and Weldon Railroad
- Raleigh and Gaston Railroad
- North Carolina Railroad Company
- Dorothea Dix

The Story Continues

The constitutional reforms of 1835 opened the door to 25 years of development. It was an age of progress in the history of North Carolina. The first 15 years of this progress were carried out under the leadership of the Whigs.

Interpreting the Visual Record

State capitol building in Raleigh, c. 1840 *The old state capitol building in Raleigh was destroyed by fire in 1831. A new capitol building was completed in 1840.* **What image of the state did the architect of this building want to convey?**

★ The People Choose the Whigs

In 1836 North Carolina had its first direct election for governor. **Edward B. Dudley**, a Whig from New Hanover County, was elected. Voters also elected a Whig-led Senate. There was no real campaigning during this first direct election. However, Dudley's views were well known. He recommended internal improvements, public education, and railroads. As he said in his first inaugural address, he hoped to stop "the torrent of emigration which is desolating our state."

The Whigs controlled state politics in North Carolina from 1836 to 1850. There was an unbroken series of Whig governors. Dudley was

Political Shifts **137**

followed by **John Motley Morehead** for two terms, then by William Graham for two terms, and by Charles Manly. The Whigs also controlled the legislature for more than half of those years. During the years of Whig control, the state government put a number of reform programs in place.

✔ **READING CHECK** **Drawing Conclusions** Why were the Whigs able to gain control in 1836?

★ Improvements in Transportation

The Whigs wanted to meet North Carolina's greatest need—an adequate transportation system. In 1836 the Whig Party started an era of railroad building that changed the state.

The first experimental railroad was built in Fayetteville in 1828. Horses pulled an iron-wheeled wagon carrying commercial goods along rails. Another experimental railroad was built in Raleigh in 1833. It was a mile-long line that ran from a quarry to the site of the new capitol building. During the week it carried stone from the quarry. On Sundays, passengers were taken on pleasure rides.

Some citizens of Wilmington thought the future of their city depended on rail transportation. They decided to build a rail line from Wilmington to Weldon, on the Roanoke River. They formed a private company and sold stock to raise money. Construction began in 1837.

Early trains like this were powered by wood-burning locomotives.

The **Wilmington and Weldon Railroad** ran out of money before the line was completed. The company asked for state aid. Over strong Democratic opposition, the Whigs committed state money to the project. The new railroad was finished in 1840. It was 161 miles long, the longest railroad in the world at the time.

At the same time the Wilmington to Weldon line was being built, Raleigh businessmen organized a railroad company. They built a line from Raleigh to Gaston, also on the Roanoke River. The 86-mile line connected with a Virginia railroad from Petersburg, near Richmond. The **Raleigh and Gaston Railroad** also received state aid.

Before long, farmers near these two railroads began to ship cotton, corn, tobacco, and other goods to market by rail. In 1842 Governor Morehead urged the Assembly to fund a statewide network of rail lines. It would be several years, however, before the Assembly agreed.

In 1849, the General Assembly finally passed the bill that chartered the **North Carolina Railroad Company**. The line would run from Goldsboro through Raleigh to Charlotte. The state agreed to pay

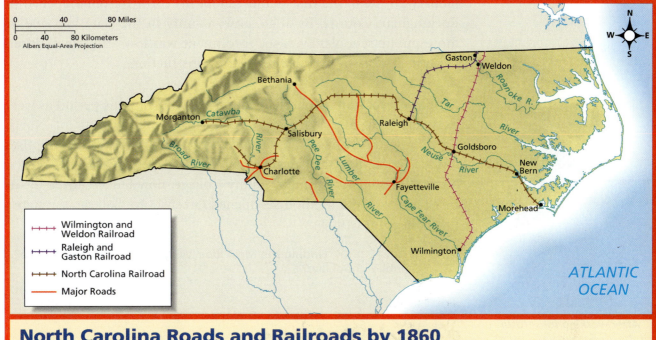

North Carolina Roads and Railroads by 1860

Interpreting Maps By 1860, North Carolina's transportation system was well developed. Railroads and roads crisscrossed the state, connecting west to east and north to south.

Skills Assessment Locate and identify the major east to west and north to south railroads in North Carolina.
1. **The World in Spatial Terms** In 1860, which railroad in North Carolina was the longest?
2. **Human Systems** Which cities had more than one railroad system passing through them?

two thirds of the $3 million necessary for construction. The 223-mile-long railroad was completed in 1856. It opened western North Carolina to the world. Villages and markets sprang up all along its route. Farmers began to prosper.

The railroads brought new prosperity to North Carolina. Farmers began to produce surplus crops for market. Towns and factories grew. There was more travel and a higher standard of living for many people. The railroads created a new sense of pride and helped stop the flow of people out of North Carolina.

✔ **READING CHECK Identifying Cause and Effect** Why were railroads needed in North Carolina, and what effect did they have?

★ Educational Reforms

At the same time the Whigs were promoting railroads, they were also focusing on public education. The plan they followed was modeled on the actions that Archibald Murphey had outlined years before.

Establishing public schools In January 1839 the General Assembly passed North Carolina's first public school law. The law divided the state into school districts. Each district was to create at least one school. On

January 20, 1840, the first public school in North Carolina opened in Rockingham County. By 1846, every county in the state had one or more public schools. Even so, enrollment was low and few children received more than two or three years of instruction.

Higher education Higher education grew during this period as well. Between 1836 and 1860, enrollment at the University of North Carolina grew from 89 to well over 400 students. In 1834, Baptists founded Wake Forest Institute, now Wake Forest University. In 1838, a Methodist minister founded Trinity College, now Duke University. In that same year the Methodists opened Greensboro College, the state's first college for women.

✔ **READING CHECK Finding the Main Idea** What was the purpose of the 1839 public school law?

After working for reform in North Carolina and other states, Dorothea Dix went on to serve as superintendent of women nurses in the U.S. Army during the Civil War.

Analyzing Primary Sources
Identifying Points of View
What can you tell from this passage about Dorothea Dix's opinion of mental illness?

Social Reforms

Under Whig leadership, the state also began a series of reforms to help its less fortunate citizens. In 1848, social reformer **Dorothea Dix** visited North Carolina. Dix's aim was to help people with mental illness. She said in a report to the legislature:

"Could the sighs and moans . . . reach you here and now, how would your sensibilities to the miseries of these unfortunates be quickened: how eager would you be to devise schemes for their relief. . . ."

Dorothea Dix, from a document submitted to the North Carolina General Assembly, November 1848

Legislators agreed with Dix. A state hospital for the mentally disabled opened in 1856. The state also built a school for those who could not hear, speak, or see.

A law passed in 1848 slightly improved the status of married women. A husband now needed his wife's approval to sell or rent real estate that had belonged to her before marriage. In general, however, women continued to receive unequal treatment, even during these years of energetic reform.

In 1831 the General Assembly authorized counties to build "poorhouses" to shelter and provide for the economically disadvantaged. From then on, many of North Carolina's counties built and maintained these public shelters.

Under the Whigs, North Carolina's criminal law remained harsh. Reformers succeeded only in reducing the number of those types of crimes that could be punished by death.

✔ **READING CHECK Drawing Conclusions** In what areas did North Carolina experience social reforms?

The Effects of Whig Reforms on North Carolina

During their 15 years of leadership, the Whigs brought significant change to North Carolina. They supported development of a statewide railroad system and provided for public education. North Carolina built a new capitol as well as hospitals for those with mental and physical disabilities. The state also made some reforms of the criminal code and of the legal status of women.

At the same time, North Carolina's citizens were becoming more prosperous. Factories and mills opened. Farmers began to grow a variety of crops for market. Illiteracy was declining and more newspapers were being published. People were beginning to travel outside the state and return with ideas for change and improvement at home. The state that had been known as the Rip Van Winkle state was clearly wide awake.

✔ **READING CHECK** **Drawing Conclusions** Why were the Whigs able to accomplish so much during their 15 years of leadership?

During the years of Whig Party control, North Carolina saw a large increase in the number of factories and mills.

Section 4 Review

keyword: SN3 HP7

1 **Identify** and explain:
- Edward B. Dudley
- John Motley Morehead
- Wilmington and Weldon Railroad
- Raleigh and Gaston Railroad
- North Carolina Railroad Company
- Dorothea Dix

2 **Problem Solving** Copy the organizer below. Use it to explain the problems the Whigs wanted to solve and how they solved those problems.

Problems
1.
2.
3.

Solutions
1.
2.
3.

3 **Finding the Main Idea**
a. What did the Whigs do to improve transportation in North Carolina?
b. What did the Whigs do to improve education in North Carolina?
c. What social reforms occurred under Whig leadership?
d. How did the Whig Party affect North Carolina?

4 **Writing and Critical Thinking**
Decision Making Decide which improvement or reform made during the Whig years was the most important. Write a paragraph supporting your decision.
Consider:
- short-term and long-term effects
- how many people benefited

Political Shifts **141**

Section 5

The Decline of the Whigs

Read to Discover
1. Why did the Democratic Party develop in North Carolina?
2. Why were the Democrats able to defeat the Whigs?
3. What reforms were made under the Democrats?
4. Why did the Whigs decline nationally?

Define
- free suffrage

Identify
- William W. Holden
- David S. Reid
- Charles Manly
- Calvin H. Wiley

The Story Continues

In the 1830s and 1840s, the Whigs had worked together to solve North Carolina's problems. By 1850, however, the party had lost some of its concern for reform and improvement. Support for the Whigs also began to decline as opponents of slavery grew stronger in the party on a national level.

★ The Democratic Party in North Carolina

While the Whig Party was losing strength, the Democratic Party was growing. A new generation of leaders began to join the party and change it. They were in favor of greater state support for both the railroads and education. They also thought it was time to change the voting requirements in North Carolina.

One of the most active of these new Democrats was **William W. Holden**. Holden was originally a Whig, but he switched parties. At the age of 25 in 1843, Holden became editor of the *North Carolina Standard*, a Raleigh newspaper. An excellent journalist, Holden soon made his newspaper the most influential paper in the state.

William W. Holden was the editor of the most influential Democratic newspaper in North Carolina during the 1840s.

Holden came from very humble origins in Orange County. He stood up for the "common people" and urged the Democratic Party to develop programs that would appeal to a great many voters. Holden saw that the Whig Party was no longer focusing on the needs of most of the state's citizens.

✔ **READING CHECK** **Finding the Main Idea** Why did the Democratic Party attract able young men in the 1840s?

★ Victory for the Democrats

The election of 1848 was a turning point for both the Whig Party and the Democratic Party. Most of the campaign revolved around the issue of voting rights. The futures of both parties were affected by their positions on this issue.

Reid versus Manly In 1848, the Democratic convention nominated **David S. Reid** of Rockingham County to run for governor. Reid was an attorney, a militia officer, and a former member of the General Assembly. Reid had not sought the nomination. Party leaders had to convince him to accept. Reid's opponent was Whig **Charles Manly**.

The Democratic Party's campaign program did not include the issue of voting rights. Reid, however, made it his major campaign topic. He was in favor of giving people more voting rights through **free suffrage**, or voting rights not tied to wealth. Manly was against this change.

Manly managed to win the election by only 854 votes. This was a much smaller majority for the Whigs than in previous elections. The 1848 election was a moral victory for the Democrats. It was also the beginning of the end for the Whig Party in North Carolina.

The issue of voting rights The issue of free suffrage dominated the 1848 campaign. Reid, Holden, and other Democrats supported the reform. They wanted a constitutional amendment that would abolish the requirement that a person own 50 acres of land to vote for state senators. Anyone who voted for a member of the House of Commons would also vote for senators. Holden wrote that there were thousands of people in the state who would gain voting rights. Free suffrage was a popular idea with many people.

The election of 1850 Reid and Manly were again opponents for governor in 1850. Once again, free suffrage was the dividing issue. This time, Reid and the Democrats defeated Manly and the Whigs by a margin of nearly 3,000. The Democrats also won a majority both in the House of Commons and in the Senate.

✔ **READING CHECK** **Summarizing** What was the issue that divided the Whigs and the Democrats, and why were the Democrats able to win?

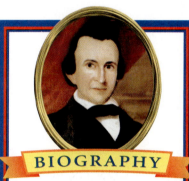

BIOGRAPHY

David S. Reid
(1813–1891)

David Settle Reid was born in Rockingham County. He was a self-educated attorney, militia officer, and legislator.

Reid was the first Democrat elected governor of North Carolina. He served two terms, from 1851 to 1854. He also served in both the U.S. House of Representatives and the Senate.

As a state senator, Reid wrote the law that established the public school system in North Carolina. The first school opened in his home county. **How did Reid shape public education in North Carolina?**

Political Shifts 143

⭐ Democratic Reforms

The Democrats continued the programs the Whigs had started. They supported internal improvements and public education. They used state funds to build more railroads. By 1860, the state had 891 miles of railroad. The lines served every major section of the state except the mountain region.

Voting rights The Democratic legislature passed the free suffrage amendment in 1850. However, the amendment did not take effect immediately. It had to pass two sessions of the Assembly before it would become law. In 1852 those who opposed the bill defeated it. The Democrats had to start all over again. Finally, the bill became law in 1857. Thousands of North Carolinians became eligible to vote for state senators.

Education The Democrats also improved public education. In 1852, the legislature created the office of Superintendent of Common Schools. The first superintendent was <u>Calvin H. Wiley</u>. Wiley was a lawyer, a Presbyterian minister, and an outstanding educational leader. When he took office, Wiley commented that the school system was "obscured in darkness." In his first report, he noted what he thought the system needed.

> "I feel bound to say that money is not our greatest want.... We want more efficient management—a constant embodiment and expression of public opinion—a watchful supervision—a liberal course of legislation, good officers, and patience and energy in all having an official position in the system."
>
> Calvin H. Wiley, from his first annual report to the legislature, quoted in *North Carolina through Four Centuries* by William S. Powell

Wiley worked hard to improve the school system. He drew up a uniform course of study, required annual reports from local school officials,

Analyzing Primary Sources

Drawing Inferences Based on Wiley's comments, what was the school system like when he became superintendent of schools?

The Davidson County School, seen here, was typical of early public schools in North Carolina.

edited the *North Carolina Journal of Education* for teachers, and wrote a textbook called the *North-Carolina Reader*. Even so, Wiley had only limited success. He won little cooperation from the legislature and failed to extend the school term, which was at most only four months long.

✔ **READING CHECK** **Comparing and Contrasting** What were the similarities and differences between North Carolina's accomplishments under the Democrats and under the Whigs?

⭐ The Whigs Decline Nationally

By the mid-1800s, the Whig Party was declining nationally. The party disagreed with President James K. Polk's decision to go to war with Mexico (1846–1848). Polk, a Democrat, had been elected president in 1844.

The Whigs viewed Polk's action as an excuse to acquire territory from Mexico. They were opposed to expanding United States territory in this way. To many people, the Whig position seemed unpatriotic and disloyal.

A North Carolina classroom in the 1800s

At the same time, the Whig Party was deeply divided over the question of slavery. Many of the people in the northern states who opposed slavery were Whigs. These Whigs wanted to exclude slavery from the new western territories, such as Texas. This angered the Whigs in the South. They began to question whether they could count on the party to defend their interests. Many white southerners came to believe that the Democratic Party would be better for the South than the Whig Party.

✔ **READING CHECK** **Summarizing** What two issues caused the decline of the national Whig Party?

Section 5 Review

Homework Practice Online — keyword: SN3 HP7

❶ Define and explain:
- free suffrage

❷ Identify and explain:
- William W. Holden
- David S. Reid
- Charles Manly
- Calvin H. Wiley

❸ Analyzing Information Copy the diagram below. Use it to explain what reforms the Whigs and Democrats proposed and where those reforms overlapped.

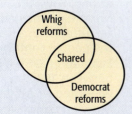

❹ Finding the Main Idea
a. Why did the Democratic Party become stronger in North Carolina?
b. What improvements and reforms were made under the Democrats?
c. What caused the national Whig Party to decline?

❺ Writing and Critical Thinking
Supporting a Point of View Imagine you are a student in North Carolina in 1853. Write a letter to Superintendent Wiley explaining what you think a good school needs most and why.
Consider:
- buildings and equipment
- the material students have to study
- teacher qualifications

Political Shifts 145

Chapter 7 Review

Chapter Summary

Section 1
- The attitudes of the people, lack of democracy in state government, and slavery caused economic stagnation in North Carolina.
- People moved away because they saw no chance for improvement.

Section 2
- North Carolina supported Andrew Jackson for president because people thought he would favor needed internal improvements. Jackson angered North Carolinians when he opposed these improvements. People opposed to Jackson organized the Whig Party.
- After the Indian Removal Act was passed, Indian tribes living east of the Mississippi River were relocated by force to present-day Oklahoma.

Section 3
- Changes to the state constitution in 1835 created more equitable representation in the General Assembly.
- The effects of the 1835 Constitution were that voters became more directly involved in choosing office holders and North Carolina gained a two-party system of government.

Section 4
- The Whigs' social reforms included improved transportation and public education.
- Citizens in North Carolina became more prosperous, business and industry began to grow, and illiteracy declined.

Section 5
- The Democrats were able to defeat the Whigs in 1850 because they backed the popular idea of free suffrage.
- The Democrats continued the Whigs' programs of internal improvements and passed the free suffrage amendment.
- The national Whig Party declined.

Identifying People and Ideas
Use the following terms or people in complete sentences.
1. stagnation
2. Trail of Tears
3. Qualla Boundary
4. Whig Party
5. suffrage
6. William Gaston
7. North Carolina Railroad Company
8. Dorothea Dix
9. William W. Holden
10. Calvin H. Wiley

Understanding Main Ideas

Section 1 (Pages 125–128)
1. What were the causes and effects of North Carolina's economic stagnation in the early 1800s?

Section 2 (Pages 129–132)
2. How did North Carolinians react to President Andrew Jackson's policies?

Section 3 (Pages 133–136)
3. What changes were made to North Carolina's constitution in 1835?

Section 4 (Pages 137–141)
4. What reforms and improvements occurred in North Carolina during the Whig years?

Section 5 (Pages 142–145)
5. Why did the Democratic Party become stronger and replace the Whigs in North Carolina?

What Did You Find Out?
1. **Economics** How did the economic system in eastern North Carolina affect the western counties?
2. **Culture** What were the different perspectives among North Carolinians on the national policy of Indian removal and resettlement?
3. **Citizenship** Why were no improvements made until the Whigs took power?

Thinking Critically
1. **Identifying Points of View** During the first half of the 1800s, the eastern and western regions of North Carolina had social, economic, and political differences. How did the points of view of the people contribute to these differences?
2. **Evaluating** Of the improvements and reforms between 1835 and 1860, which do you think benefited North Carolina the most, and why?
3. **Drawing Conclusions** After 1835, North Carolina had a two-party system of government. The Whig Party and the Democratic Party were evenly matched. Why was this beneficial to the state?

Building Social Studies Skills

Interpreting Charts

As the state government moved toward reform, many individuals began to join reform organizations to help improve society in North Carolina. Study the chart below. Then answer the questions that follow.

Organization	Location	Goal	Services
Seamen's Friend Society	Wilmington	To care for poor sailors	Ran boardinghouse and hospital
Fayetteville Female Society of Industry	Fayetteville	To care for poor women and children	Gave any aid necessary to poor women and children; provided work for women
North Carolina Manumission Society	28 branches throughout the state	To abolish slavery	Encouraged owners to free their slaves; held meetings; assisted emancipated slaves
American Temperance Society	Local groups throughout the state	To persuade others to limit their alcohol consumption	Held meetings; gave speeches and sermons; published books and articles

1. Which statement correctly describes what you can infer from the chart?
   a. Only Fayetteville and Wilmington had local reform organizations.
   b. A large number of poor sailors lived in Wilmington.
   c. The North Carolina Manumission Society did not have many members.
   d. The American Temperance Society was successful in persuading North Carolinians to stop drinking alcohol.

2. Why might groups organized by private citizens care for the poor in North Carolina?

Understanding Frames of Reference

Read this quote from the *Autobiography of Asa Biggs*, written in 1865. Biggs was a North Carolinian who had a long political career. Then answer the questions.

> I have stated that I persistently declined engaging in politics until 1840. But in 1835 I was elected and served as a member from the County of Martin in the State Convention called to amend the Constitution of the State. I was then only 24 years old and I considered myself highly honored by this position of distinction. This body was composed of the most experienced and talented men in the State, 'grave and reverend seignors'; and my association with such a dignified and able convention was an admirable and useful school for me, being nearly the youngest member of the body. I did not participate in the Debates, but was an attentive and careful learner, and always feel gratified that my native county thought me worthy to represent them in such an important assembly.

3. Which statement describes how Biggs might react to a political cartoon that displayed a mocking attitude toward the constitutional convention?
   a. He would probably find it amusing.
   b. He would agree with it.
   c. He would be offended by it.
   d. He would not understand it.

4. What were the results of the constitutional convention of 1835 that Biggs attended? Give specific examples.

Alternative Assessment

Building Your Portfolio

Linking to Community
Both the state government and private citizens helped reform North Carolinian society in the 1800s. The government passed laws and granted funds, while individuals supported causes they considered important. These activities continue in many places today. Find out about groups in your community that are working for change. Write a report about these groups, their goals, and the services they provide.

internet connect

Internet Activity: go.hrw.com
keyword: SN3 NC7

Choose a topic about political shifts to:
- Write an essay about the "Rip Van Winkle" state.
- Debate the Indian Removal Act of 1830.
- Write a newspaper editorial supporting ratification of a new North Carolina state constitution.

Political Shifts 147

CHAPTER

8 Life and Culture
(1815–1860)

Antebellum wedding in a cabin

Build on What You Know

North Carolina was a poor state during much of the early 1800s. Many people had limited contact with the world. In this chapter you will learn how North Carolinians drew on religious faith to guide their lives. You will also learn how they met practical needs and expressed their creativity through folk arts and literature.

What's Your Opinion?

 Do you **agree** or **disagree** with the following statements? Support your point of view in your journal.

- **Geography** The environment in which people live can influence their beliefs.
- **Culture** Oral traditions like folktales are as important as written forms of literature such as novels.
- **Government** People who criticize the government should have some of their rights and freedoms taken away.

Section 1

Religious Movements

Read to Discover
1. How did churches attract North Carolinians to religion?
2. What religious groups were important in North Carolina's early history and development?

Define
- pacifists
- established religion
- evangelism
- camp meetings
- denomination

Identify
- Great Revival

The Story Continues

Through most of North Carolina's colonial history, the official church of Great Britain—the Church of England, or Anglican Church—was the official church of the colony. However, colonial officials usually did not strictly enforce rules about religious beliefs and worship. As Germans, Scots-Irish, and other European immigrants settled in the colony in the 1700s, several faiths became common. By the early 1800s, North Carolina had a long tradition of religious freedom and tolerance.

Religion in the 1700s

Although many faiths were present in North Carolina, most colonists supported no particular organized religion. They cherished freedom in all aspects of their lives. They had resisted efforts to create an official church and were often reluctant to give up practices such as dancing, drinking, and gambling that some others considered sinful. In 1704 an Anglican missionary observed that "a great many . . . have no religion but would be Quakers, if by that they were not obliged to lead a more moral life."

This American print shows the typical dress of a Quaker man in the 1700s.

Life and Culture 149

Interpreting the Visual Record

Camp meeting Religious ceremonies often took place outdoors at camp meetings like the one shown here. *What does this scene reveal about the conditions at some camp meetings?*

The Quakers were the most influential religious group in North Carolina in 1700. During the 1730s, Baptists, Presbyterians, and others began to settle and preach in the colony. At first, however, these groups had few organized churches.

New arrivals from Pennsylvania and New Jersey in the 1750s kept the Quakers' influence strong until the American Revolution. Since Quakers are **pacifists**, they became unpopular during the war. A pacifist is someone who refuses to fight because he or she believes that violence and war are wrong. Quakers refused to fight during the Revolutionary War.

The Anglican Church also declined during the Revolution, because it was the religion of the British and Tories. Also, the first state constitution in 1776 banned any **established religion**—a religion that a government supports as an official church.

✔ **READING CHECK** Identifying Cause and Effect Why did the Quakers' beliefs weaken their influence?

★ The Great Revival

Despite North Carolina's religious changes in the 1700s, only about 1 of every 30 residents was a church member in 1790. The state was thus fertile ground for the **Great Revival**. This is the name given to a wave of **evangelism**, or efforts to convert people to Christianity, that swept the nation after independence. The Great Revival reached its height in North Carolina between about 1800 and 1805. However, evangelism continued to influence American life.

Evangelism was carried out at **camp meetings** where hundreds of people lived in tents and huts for a week or more and listened to long outdoor sermons. Although most of the preachers were uneducated, they were powerful speakers who aroused great excitement as they attacked sin. One Baptist leader described a typical crowd reaction.

Analyzing Primary Sources

Drawing Inferences and Conclusions To whom was Burkitt referring when he wrote of "*backsliders* who had been runaway for many years"?

"Two or three hundred would be in floods of tears, and many crying out loudly *what shall we do to be saved*. . . . Many *backsliders* who had been runaway for many years, returned weeping home."

—Lemuel Burkitt and Jesse Read, *Concise History of the Kehukee Association*

Many educated ministers opposed camp meetings. However, the Great Revival increased the importance of religion in daily life. Church membership increased, and by 1860 about half of North Carolina's adult white population belonged to an organized church.

✔ **READING CHECK** Finding the Main Idea What was the importance of camp meetings?

Historical Document

1802

REPORT OF THE GREAT REVIVAL

Presbyterian minister James Hall took part in a revival in the western Piedmont in 1802. He filed this report on one camp meeting he attended in Iredell County. The report's mention of "exercise" refers to the jerking, trembling, falling down, and other involuntary physical reactions that people often experienced during such meetings.

"From a view of the advantages apparently arising from general [camp] meetings, the members of the Presbytery of Concord, of which I am a member, appointed one on the last week of January, near the center of this county. The number of wagons which came to the ground, besides riding carriages, was about 108. The number of persons who attended on Sabbath, about four thousand. Divine service began on Friday at 2 o'clock. . . . A rain began to fall, which continued until near night. A considerable number were exercised that evening. Next morning a considerable heavy sleet began to fall about 9 o'clock, then snow, which terminated [ended] in a heavy rain. This continued until four in the afternoon. . . . Notwithstanding this, the people collected at ten, in two assemblies, and . . . stood there exposed until sunsetting. Exercises went on rapidly, and large numbers were deeply affected. The work went on gradually increasing, until Tuesday morning, except a few hours before day on Monday morning, when the camp was chiefly silent. At 9 on Tuesday morning the people were assembled in the center of the square, and after some time spent in prayer and exhortation [persuasion], were dismissed. Many who went away unaffected were struck with convictions . . . after they went home. No attempt was made to ascertain [determine] the number of those who were affected with religious exercises, but there must have been during the meeting, several hundreds. There were present eight Presbyterian, one Baptist, and two Methodist ministers."

A circuit-riding preacher, usually traveling on horseback, preached regularly at between 20 and 40 locations.

Analyzing Primary Sources

1. About how long did the camp meeting last?
2. What convinced Reverend Hall of the people's commitment to religion?

Life and Culture 151

That's Interesting!

Camp Meetings Camp meetings originated among Presbyterians, Methodists, and Baptists in western Virginia and North Carolina and on the Kentucky and Ohio frontier. People gathered to pray, sing hymns, confess their sins, and seek salvation. Camp meetings also offered people from far-flung rural communities an opportunity to mingle with each other. The lasting influence of the camp meeting tradition is visible today in the annual revivals held by many churches.

Religious Groups in North Carolina

The Baptists benefited greatly from evangelism. By 1860 there were nearly 800 Baptist churches in North Carolina, with a total of 64,000 members who were mainly small farmers. However, the Methodists gained the most. The Methodist Church was not organized in America until 1784. But by 1860 the revival movement had made it the second-largest **denomination**, or religious group, in North Carolina, with 61,000 members in more than 950 churches. Evangelism also caused the Presbyterian Church to grow, but much more slowly. With 15,000 members, the Presbyterian Church was the third-largest denomination in the state. Most Presbyterians were middle- and upper-class people who lived in towns and in the Piedmont region of North Carolina.

The Disciples of Christ, another church that formed after the Revolution, was also important in the state. So was the Episcopal Church, which had developed from the Anglican Church. The Lutheran, Moravian, and German Reformed churches had a strong influence among the state's German-speaking population in 1860.

✔ **READING CHECK Identifying Cause and Effect** In what ways did evangelism affect religious denominations?

Illustration of a camp meeting

Section 1 Review

1. **Define** and explain:
   - pacifists
   - established religion
   - evangelism
   - camp meetings
   - denomination

2. **Identify** and explain:
   - Great Revival

3. **Comparing and Contrasting** Copy the graphic organizer below. Use it to identify popular denominations in the mid-1700s and the mid-1800s.

mid-1700s	mid-1800s

4. **Finding the Main Idea**
   a. Why did Quakers become unpopular with some people?
   b. How did many churches gain new members in the early 1800s?

5. **Writing and Critical Thinking**
   Drawing Inferences and Conclusions Why did many North Carolinians have little interest in religion before the Great Revival?
   Consider:
   - values, attitudes, and behaviors
   - church organization

152 Chapter 8

Section 2

Folkways and Customs

Read to Discover
1. How did average North Carolinians live in the early and mid-1800s?
2. What common values and beliefs did average North Carolinians hold?
3. What were some common folk arts of North Carolinians?

Define
- tenant farmers

Identify
- Jack Tales

The Story Continues

The oral style and songs of the revivals easily fit into the culture of most North Carolinians at the time. Religion and folk beliefs played an important role in the lives of ordinary North Carolinians. A rich culture of stories and folk wisdom provided an outlet for individual creativity, conveyed important knowledge from one generation to the next, and helped people cope with the challenges of daily life.

This one-room cottage represents the simple living conditions of yeomen farmers.

★ A Hard Way of Life

North Carolina was still a rural state in 1860. Of its nearly one million people, fewer than 25,000 lived in cities and towns. About one third of North Carolinians were enslaved African Americans. Nearly all the rest were of English, Scottish, or German ancestry. The vast majority of these white North Carolinians were small farmers or landless laborers.

Many landless families lived in shacks near towns and villages, where jobs might be available. **Tenant farmers** lived on small plots they rented. Still others lived in isolated rural areas, on unused lands they did not own. These people built log cabins and planted small vegetable gardens. Some raised hogs for meat, but mainly they hunted game in the forest.

Life and Culture 153

Interpreting the Visual Record

North Carolina storyteller *Storytelling is a North Carolina tradition. Throughout history, societies have relied upon storytelling to pass behaviors, values, and ideas from one generation to another.* **In what way does the colonial scene shown here support this idea of the traditional role of the storyteller?**

Tenant farmers and yeomen lived in shacks or small log houses. Their clothes and food were simple. However, their diets were often better than those of the landless poor. Peas, beans, corn, potatoes, hogs, and chickens were the most common foods they produced. Yeomen who owned enough land also grew wheat and oats and raised sheep for their wool and meat. Some families had a few cattle, which added beef, milk, butter, and cheese to their diets. Anything extra that they could produce was sold.

As during colonial times, nature continued to shape the outlook of most North Carolinians. Their lives were structured around the seasonal changes of time. They always knew that their fortunes turned on having good or bad weather. For that reason, their lives always held an element of uncertainty beyond their control.

✔ **READING CHECK** **Identifying Cause and Effect** Why were laborers often worse off than most other free North Carolinians?

★ Folk Beliefs and Stories

Most white North Carolinians in the early and mid-1800s believed in bad luck, spirits, and spells. Many of these beliefs were part of the cultures of their European ancestors. Their dependence on natural forces, many of which they could not control, also explains their belief system. Farmers relied on folk wisdom to know when to plant and fertilize their fields. In a world without modern medicine, in which disease and early death were common, such wisdom also offered comfort and the protection of natural cures. The following saying illustrates some folk wisdom farmers passed down to guide when to fertilize their crops with manure.

Analyzing Primary Sources

Categorizing What part of people's lives did this folk wisdom address?

 ❝When a goose flies east, and walks west, rain is near. Haul out your manure when the little moon turns down, so that it will go into the ground.❞

The Frank C. Brown Collection of North Carolina Folklore, edited by Newman Ivey White

Many folk stories were also related to people's superstitions and their lack of control over their lives. **Jack Tales** are one such set of stories. They all told of a young boy named Jack who used wits and good luck to overcome great difficulties. Jack Tales were part of an oral tradition that provided instruction and entertainment in a time when most people owned few books, and many could not read at all. The tales also offered outlets for creativity and expression. They often contained song and verse, and they changed as individual storytellers adapted them to personal experiences and local concerns.

The fairy tale of "Jack and the Beanstalk" is related to North Carolina's Jack Tales of the 1800s.

✔ **READING CHECK** **Finding the Main Idea** What factors shaped the beliefs of most white North Carolinians?

Folk Arts

The music of the common people was also closely related to their lives. Like their beliefs, much of it came from their European ancestors. Songs expressed dreams of getting rich through hard work or marrying well. Other songs mocked the rich and criticized bad behavior like selfishness or laziness. Religious themes were also popular.

North Carolina folk arts originated out of the everyday necessities of life. People made almost all of their tools and personal items, most out of the natural resources found in the state. Deer antlers were carved into basket handles or knives. Wool and flax were used to make clothing and quilts. Furniture was carved out of the wood from the Appalachian Mountains. Over time, people became quite talented and creative with their crafts. Some skilled artisans passed their secrets down to future generations. Women shared their talents with each other through quilting. Many North Carolina quilts used the "wedding ring" pattern common in southern quilting. Some parents made dolls out of cornhusks for their children.

The quilts, pottery, and other items that common people made for use in their daily lives are today considered to be objects of art. For example, German Moravians produced a type of pottery that is now highly valued and sought-after. They were also well known for their work with tiles, which are very valuable. Regional patterns on the quilts North Carolinians made have carried down to today. They can still be seen in quilts for sale in the many craft fairs that take place across the state.

A Moravian potter named Rudolf Christ made this fish-shaped clay bottle almost 200 years ago.

✔ **READING CHECK** Identifying Cause and Effect How did the folk art of North Carolinians reflect their everyday lives?

Section 2 Review

keyword: SN3 HP8

1. Define and explain:
- tenant farmers

2. Identify and explain:
- Jack Tales

3. Comparing Copy the chart below. Use it to show how many small farmers lived.

4. Finding the Main Idea
a. Why were poor farmers better off than the landless poor?
b. What role did folk wisdom play in the lives of ordinary North Carolinians?

5. Writing and Critical Thinking
Summarizing How would you describe the average North Carolinian in the early 1800s?
Consider:
- how people lived
- people's beliefs

	Yeoman	Tenant Farmer
house	shack/log house	
clothes		simple
food	grew and raised it	
land		rented

Section 3

A Literary Movement

Read to Discover
1. What kind of literature was most popular in the early 1800s?
2. Why did a literary awakening occur and what types of literature developed?
3. How did North Carolina's literary movement affect attitudes about the state?

Define
- almanacs
- literature
- reader
- novels
- fiction

Identify
- *North-Carolina Reader*
- Mary Bayard Clarke
- George Moses Horton

The *Farmers' Almanac* is one of America's oldest continuously published sources of weather, gardening, and other information.

The Story Continues

North Carolina produced few famous writers before the Civil War. North Carolinians were known as "an unreading people." In large part, this reputation was due to the widespread lack of education in the state, especially before the 1830s. Despite this obstacle, an active group of writers developed. Their work helped to increase pride in North Carolina.

A Literary Awakening

The most popular forms of printed matter in the early 1800s were pamphlets and **almanacs**. An almanac is a yearly publication containing information about the weather, farming, and subjects of general interest. One of the most widely read and enduring almanacs was *Gales' North-Carolina Almanack*. It was published in Raleigh from 1815 to 1838. Another was the *Farmer's and Planter's Almanac*, which began publication in Salem in 1829.

Many pamphlets were published in the early years. They generally contained a sermon, a political speech, or a short biography of a

156 Chapter 8

well-known person. Their subject matter and their cheap cost made them among the most popular and common type of early literature, or written works. By 1835 a literary "awakening" was under way in North Carolina. These beginnings were related to the growth of education in the state. The founding of private schools and academies, colleges, and universities—and later, public schools—increased the number of people who could read well, which led to an increased interest in books, learning, and literature.

North Carolina Literary Styles

The growth of education in North Carolina also increased the need for books to use in classrooms. Some of the earliest and best-known books produced in North Carolina were written with this purpose in mind.

State histories The first history of North Carolina appeared in 1812. Its author was Hugh Williamson, one of the three North Carolinians who signed the U.S. Constitution. His *History of North Carolina* ended in 1776, however. François Xavier Martin's two-volume history, published in 1829, also covered only the colonial period. Twenty-two years later, John Wheeler's *Historical Sketches of North Carolina to 1851* provided an up-to-date history of the state. The book did well. About 10,000 copies were sold.

Early textbooks An even more successful book was the *North-Carolina Reader*, by Calvin H. Wiley. It also was published in 1851. A reader is a collection of literary works in one book. Most readers of the time were for a national or regional audience. Wiley believed North Carolina needed a reader of its own. He explained why:

 "Will the North Carolinians continue to patronize [make use of] Readers whose authors have blotted North Carolina from their maps, or who mention it [the state] only to defame [criticize]? Will they send their money to enrich writers whose pens labor to make them infamous [shameful]?"

Calvin H. Wiley, the *North-Carolina Reader*

The *Reader* discussed the state's geography and history. It also included essays with titles such as "The Advantages of State Pride." It "is intended . . . to be used in families and schools," Wiley wrote. "Its object is to sow in the young minds of North-Carolina the seeds of a true, healthy, and vigorous North-Carolina spirit." The *Reader* became North Carolina's first important textbook.

Fiction and poetry North Carolina writers also began to produce plays, novels, and poetry during this period. A novel is a book-length work of fiction, or an imagined story. In 1824, Congressman Lemuel

Calvin H. Wiley

That's Interesting!

Reader Sales Sales of Wiley's book were helped by his appointment in 1853 as the state's first superintendent of public schools. He encouraged county school officials to buy the *Reader* for their classrooms. A copy of the book cost one dollar. Soon after becoming the state's top school official, Wiley gave up his financial interest in the book. Even so, he probably made about $1,000 on it. That was quite a sum in the 1850s.

Analyzing Primary Sources

Identifying Points of View Why did Wiley believe that a state reader was necessary?

Life and Culture 157

CONNECTING TO Literature

Wood Notes

In 1854, **Mary Bayard Clarke** published *Wood Notes,* a two-volume collection of poetry by the state's best-known poets. Among its poems was "The Old North State" by William Gaston. This poem was later put to music and became the state song of North Carolina.

"The Old North State"

Carolina! Carolina! heaven's blessings attend her,
While we live we will cherish, protect and defend her,
Tho' the scorner may sneer at and witlings defame her,
Still our hearts swell with gladness whenever we name her.
Hurrah! Hurrah! the Old North State forever,
Hurrah! Hurrah! the good Old North State.

Tho' she envies not others, their merited glory,
Say whose name stands the foremost, in liberty's story,
Tho' too true to herself e'er to crouch to oppression,
Who can yield to just rule a more loyal submission.
Hurrah! Hurrah! the Old North State forever,
Hurrah! Hurrah! the good Old North State.

Then let all those who love us, love the land that we live in,
As happy a region as on this side of heaven,
Where plenty and peace, love and joy smile before us,
Raise aloud, raise together the heart thrilling chorus.
Hurrah! Hurrah! the Old North State forever,
Hurrah! Hurrah! the good Old North State.

A copy of the sheet music for North Carolina's state song

Understanding Literature

1. Which line honors North Carolina's role in the American Revolution?
2. What recognition does this poem show of North Carolina's reputation as the "Rip Van Winkle" state?

Sawyer wrote *Blackbeard*, a four-act comedy about the famous pirate who operated along the Carolina coast in the 1700s. Calvin H. Wiley's novels *Alamance* and *Roanoke* were published in the 1840s. They are among North Carolina's best examples of historical fiction.

One of the greatest North Carolina poets of the time was <u>George Moses Horton</u>, an enslaved African American from Chatham County who taught himself to read. Horton composed three books of poetry. His first, *The Hope of Liberty*, came out in 1829. It was the first book by an African American author published in the South.

✔ **READING CHECK Finding the Main Idea** How did North Carolina literature in the early 1800s reflect the history of the state?

⭐ Reactions to North Carolina Writers

North Carolina humor writing received the best reviews outside the state. The short stories of Hamilton C. Jones gained national acclaim. One reviewer praised John Bunting's *Life as It Is, or the Writings of Our Mose* as the funniest work in 50 years. *Harper's Monthly Magazine* called H. E. Taliaferro's book *Fisher's River (North Carolina) Scenes and Characters* "one of the half dozen clever books of American character and humor."

A state literature and a growing educational system made reading important in more North Carolinians' lives. Those developments also helped refute North Carolina's reputation as the "Rip Van Winkle" state.

✔ **READING CHECK Identifying Bias** How did the reaction by outside critics to North Carolina humor writers help refute the state's reputation among some outsiders?

Hamilton Chamberlain Jones

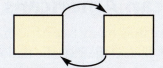 Review

keyword: SN3 HP8

1. **Define** and explain:
   - almanac
   - literature
   - reader
   - novels
   - fiction

2. **Identify** and explain:
   - *North-Carolina Reader*
   - Mary Bayard Clarke
   - George Moses Horton

3. **Sequencing** Copy the graphic organizer below. Use it to show the relationship between the growth of education and the state's literary awakening.

4. **Finding the Main Idea**
   a. What made the literature produced in North Carolina in the early 1800s uniquely North Carolinian?
   b. How did the development of literature affect people's opinions about the state?

5. **Writing and Critical Thinking**
   Identifying Cause and Effect Why would almanacs have been so popular in North Carolina?
   Consider:
   - their contents
   - the state's economy

Life and Culture 159

Section 4
The Free Black Community

Read to Discover
1. Why did the free black community in North Carolina become larger?
2. What was life like for free black North Carolinians?
3. What views did the free black community have toward slavery?

Define
- census
- bond

Identify
- John Chavis
- John Stanly

The Trent River settlement was a free black community located opposite New Bern, North Carolina. This 1866 illustration shows the schoolhouse and chapel.

The Story Continues

In 1860 Louisiana was the only major slaveholding state with a smaller number of African Americans than North Carolina. However, only five states in the entire nation—Maryland, Virginia, Pennsylvania, Ohio, and New York—had a larger free black community. For this reason, free black North Carolinians had an important effect on conditions in the state before 1860, and on its development.

★ Free African Americans before 1830

No one knows for sure how many free African Americans lived in North Carolina before 1790. That is the year the nation's first official **census**, or counting of population, occurred. It found that North Carolina was home to some 289,000 whites and 103,000 enslaved African Americans. In addition, about 5,000 free blacks lived in the state.

For the next 40 years, the free black community was the fastest growing in the state. By 1830 North Carolina was home to nearly 20,000

160 Chapter 8

free blacks, four times more than in 1790. More than two-thirds of these free blacks lived at the eastern edge of the Piedmont and in the Coastal Plain. Most were rural people.

Many free blacks were former slaves who had been freed by their owners or by actions of the state legislature. Some were slaves who bought their freedom or who escaped slavery and "hid out" in the free black community. Others were the children of free black parents. Still others were free African Americans who came to North Carolina from other states. White leaders made this difficult, however. A 1795 law required all free blacks who entered the state to post a **bond** to ensure their "good behavior." A bond is a sum of money that guarantees a promise, and is forfeited if the promise is not kept. In 1827, a law banned any more free blacks from moving to North Carolina. It also provided that any newcomer who failed to leave within 20 days could be fined or sold into slavery for 10 years.

★ Life in the Free Black Community

Attracted by the free black communities of North Carolina, many free African Americans migrated to the state during the early 1800s.

The laws limiting the freedom of free blacks were not rigidly enforced, and some exceptions were allowed. Nevertheless, these laws show how concerned many whites were becoming about the growth of the free black community. They worried that free blacks could have an unwanted influence on slaves in the state. That concern became particularly intense after Denmark Vesey's slave revolt plot in South Carolina in 1822 and Nat Turner's Rebellion in Virginia in 1831. Fearful of such unrest in their own state, North Carolina's leaders tightened restrictions on free blacks.

Rights and freedoms One reason that free blacks moved to North Carolina was that they had more rights here than in most other southern states. In North Carolina, free blacks could not be jailed without being charged with a crime. They had the right to trial by a jury. However, they could not testify against whites, or sue a white person in court. They also lived in constant fear that they might be illegally seized and sold into slavery.

Free black men who owned land could vote until the state constitution of 1835 stripped them of this right. Eventually, free blacks also could not own guns or live in certain places without permission. Limits were placed on their right to engage in trade, as well. They did not, however, lose their right to buy and sell land.

Occupations Most free blacks were involved in farming. About half of this group were yeomen. Many others became tenant farmers on land owned by whites. Still others worked for pay on the farms and plantations of white landowners, or for black yeomen.

Life and Culture **161**

Free black boys and girls sometimes worked as apprentices for white or black skilled laborers. By 1860 some 3,000 free blacks were involved in a variety of trades and crafts. The largest number were laborers and laundry workers. Others worked as blacksmiths, carpenters, painters, seamstresses, and shoemakers. Many had their own businesses.

Education and religion Except for the apprentice system, free blacks had few formal educational opportunities. In addition, after 1838 employers were no longer required to teach black apprentices to read and write. Some continued to do this, however. Methodist, Presbyterian, and Quaker groups worked to educate free African Americans. Free blacks who learned to read and write taught others. By 1850, more than 40 percent of free black adults could read and write. This compared to about 66 percent of the adult white population.

About 30 percent of the state's Methodists and Baptists were free blacks or slaves. Before 1831, when black preachers were deprived of the right to hold services, black churches played an important part in free blacks' lives. After that, they generally attended white churches, where they were usually required to worship in separate services or sit in a

The Poems of George Moses Horton

The enslaved African American George Moses Horton is among North Carolina's most famous poets. Although he could read, Horton never learned to write. Instead, he recited his compositions to others, who wrote them down. The best-known and most touching of his many poems are about the experience of slavery.

"The Slave's Complaint"

Am I sadly cast aside,
On misfortune's rugged tide?
Will the world my pains deride
   Forever?

Must I dwell in Slavery's night,
And all pleasure take its flight,
Far beyond my feeble sight,
   Forever?

Worst of all, must Hope grow dim,
And withhold her cheering beam?
Rather let me sleep and dream
   Forever!

Something still my heart surveys,
Groping through this dreary maze;
Is it Hope? — then burn and blaze
   Forever!

Leave me not a wretch confined,
Altogether lame and blind—
Unto gross despair consigned,
   Forever!

Heaven! in whom can I confide?
Canst thou not for all provide?
Condescend to be my guide
   Forever!

And when this transient life shall end,
Oh, may some kind eternal friend
Bid me from servitude ascend,
   Forever!

George Moses Horton

Understanding Literature

1. What is Horton hoping for in this poem?
2. What is the meaning of the poem's third verse?

separate section of the sanctuary. By 1860, many black churches had disappeared from the state.

✓ **READING CHECK** Identifying Cause and Effect Why did North Carolina leaders limit the rights and freedoms of free blacks?

The Free Black Community and Slavery

Relations between free blacks and slaves also reflected the great concern whites had about the free black community. Nearly every type of connection between free and enslaved African Americans was controlled by law. Social contacts between slaves and free blacks, whether on the plantation or at the free person's home, were restricted. Marriages between free blacks and slaves were even outlawed.

Despite such controls, free blacks did what they could to help slaves. Many provided runaways with a place to hide. Some well-educated free blacks wrote essays and pamphlets that attacked slavery and even urged slaves to revolt. Some free blacks bought slaves and set them free. One wealthy freeman, **John Stanly** of New Bern, purchased and freed 23 slaves between 1805 and 1818.

A few free blacks were themselves slaveholders. About 190 free blacks held 620 slaves in 1830. Many such slaveholders bought slaves who were abused by other masters and gave them better lives. By 1860, however, just eight black slaveholders, with a total of 25 slaves, remained in North Carolina.

✓ **READING CHECK** Summarizing How did free blacks oppose slavery?

BIOGRAPHY

John Chavis
(c. 1763–1838)

John Chavis, a free African American, served as a Continental soldier during the Revolution. He became one of the best-educated blacks in the new nation. Licensed to preach by the Presbyterian Church, Chavis preached throughout Granville, Orange, and Wake counties. A major slave uprising in Virginia in 1831 led to harsh restrictions that forbade free blacks to preach. No longer able to preach, Chavis opened a school in Raleigh (see announcement below) that came to be viewed as one of the state's finest. **Why was John Chavis unable to preach after 1831?**

Section 4 Review

keyword: SN3 HP8

1 **Define** and explain:
• census
• bond

2 **Identify** and explain:
• John Chavis
• John Stanly

3 **Identifying Cause and Effect** Copy the graphic organizer below. Label it to show the relationship between the growth of the free black community and the amount of freedom that free blacks had.

4 **Finding the Main Idea**
a. What rights did free African Americans enjoy, and what limits were put on those rights?

b. Why were relations between slaves and free blacks controlled by law?

5 **Writing and Critical Thinking**
Making Generalizations and Predictions How effective do you think the 1795 law discouraging free blacks from moving to North Carolina was? Why was it replaced with the 1827 law?

Consider:
• the contents of each law
• the purpose of each law

Life and Culture

Chapter 8 Review

Chapter Summary

Section 1
- Quakers were North Carolina's most important religious group before the Revolution, with Baptists, Methodists, and Presbyterians becoming the most important groups later.
- Religious leaders used evangelism and camp meetings to attract thousands of people to God and increase church membership in the 1800s.

Section 2
- Most whites in the early and mid-1800s lived in shacks or log houses and were landless laborers or farmers who produced their own food on small farms.
- People met practical needs and expressed their individual creativity through crafts and folk wisdom.

Section 3
- Almanacs and pamphlets were the first popular literature in North Carolina.
- The growth of education increased people's interest in learning and reading, which encouraged the writing of state histories, readers, fiction, drama, and poetry.

Section 4
- The free black community grew rapidly as some slaves gained freedom and free blacks moved into North Carolina from other states.
- Most free blacks farmed, while others worked as farm and non-farm laborers; many free blacks could read and write and owned land, but most of their other rights and freedoms were limited in some way by state law.
- The free black community worked in a variety of ways to weaken slavery, including helping runaways, writing attacks on slavery, and buying slaves and freeing them.

Identifying People and Ideas
Use the following terms in complete sentences.
1. pacifists
2. Great Revival
3. evangelism
4. tenant farmer
5. literature
6. almanacs
7. George Moses Horton
8. census
9. bond

Understanding Main Ideas

Section 1 *pages 149–152*
1. How did Quakers' pacifism affect their influence in North Carolina?
2. What religious groups benefited the most from the spirit of evangelism?

Section 2 *pages 153–155*
3. How did landless people commonly live?
4. What roles did folk wisdom and crafts play in people's lives?

Section 3 *pages 156–159*
5. Why did the contents of Wiley's *Reader* make it a good textbook for North Carolina schools?
6. What cultural change improved North Carolina's image outside the state?

Section 4 *pages 160–163*
7. What were the different backgrounds of members of the free black community?
8. Why did some free blacks purchase slaves?

What Did You Find Out?
1. **Geography** What characteristics of life in North Carolina during the early 1800s made folk beliefs important to people?
2. **Culture** In what ways did North Carolina's literary awakening benefit the state?
3. **Government** How and why did free blacks lose many of their rights and freedoms?

Thinking Critically
1. **Comparing and Contrasting** In what ways was religion in North Carolina in the mid-1800s similar to religion in the mid-1700s? In what ways had religion changed?
2. **Supporting a Point of View** Do you think that North Carolinians' reputation as an "unreading people" was fair? Explain why or why not.
3. **Identifying Points of View** For what reasons were many white North Carolinians concerned about the state's free black community?

Building Social Studies Skills

Interpreting Artifacts

Puzzle jugs were sometimes given as gifts in the early 1800s. Study the puzzle jug below and answer the questions that follow.

Piedmont puzzle jug

1. Why was this type of pottery called a "puzzle jug"?
   a. It is a container for water or other liquids.
   b. Historians are probably puzzled over its purpose and how it was used.
   c. The user of this jug would not be sure which of its spouts was the working one.
   d. Several people could drink from this jug at the same time.

2. What does this jug suggest about the role of crafts in the lives of North Carolinians during the early 1800s?

Analyzing Primary Sources

Read the following excerpt from a petition to the North Carolina General Assembly in 1831. Then answer the questions.

> "The prayers of your petitioners humbly sheweth that Ralph Freeman, a free man of color, of the county of Anson, has been . . . for many years, a faithful and acceptable preacher of the gospel; that by an act passed at [the last session of the legislature], he was deprived of the exercise of that gift which he and his brethren believe that God had bestowed upon him; and that it is the earnest desire of the undersigned that he be allowed to preach as formerly. We therefore, pray you, that a special act of Assembly be passed granting him that privilege."

3. What is the specific purpose of this petition?
   a. to obtain a permit to hold a camp meeting
   b. to get permission for a freeman to preach again
   c. to demand freedom of religion
   d. to ask for equal rights for black North Carolinians

4. What limitation on free blacks' freedom is the main issue to these petitioners?

5. What does this petition suggest about the importance of religion in the lives of free black North Carolinians in the 1830s?

Alternative Assessment

Building Your Portfolio

Interdisciplinary: Connection to Literature
Research libraries in your area and find a book written by a North Carolina author before 1860. The book might be an almanac, a state or local history, or a novel or book of short stories or poems. Then read and write a review of the book you select. Look at book reviews in a local newspaper before you write your review. This will give you an idea about what information to include.

internet connect

Internet Activity: go.hrw.com
keyword: SN3 NC8

Choose a topic about life and culture to:
- Create a newspaper ad heralding the advent of a camp meeting during the Great Revival.
- Write a biography of one of the literary figures in North Carolina history.
- Research what life was like in a free black community.

Life and Culture

CHAPTER 9
Southern Systems in North Carolina
(1790–1860)

Slaves picking cotton on a southern plantation

Build on What You Know

In the years between 1790 and 1860, life in North Carolina was shaped by powerful religious and social forces. During these years, the state was slowly opened to the nation and the world. In this chapter you will study some of the major elements that characterized North Carolina's economy during the early 1800s.

What's Your Opinion?

Do you **agree** or **disagree** with the following statements? Support your point of view in your journal.

- **Science, Technology & Society** An agricultural society cannot compete against an industrialized society.
- **Economics** An economy built on slavery will not industrialize.
- **Government** All people have basic human rights that should be protected by strong laws.

Section 1

The Economy

Read to Discover
1. How did the North Carolina Gold Rush affect the state?
2. Why was agriculture important to the state?
3. What were the different economic and social classes in the antebellum period?

Define
- antebellum
- cotton fibers
- cotton bolls
- ginning

Identify
- Alamance plaids
- Tar Heel State
- North Carolina Gold Rush
- Charlotte Mint
- Eli Whitney

The Story Continues

The land of North Carolina is rich in natural resources. For example, more than 300 kinds of rocks and minerals are known to exist in the state. There is gold, copper, iron, quartz, granite, and marble, to name a few. The state has also produced farmlands and vast tracts of forest. In the early 1800s, these resources were the basis for economic life.

Interpreting the Visual Record

Improved transportation
This woodcut shows an early passenger train traveling through North Carolina. **What innovation allows the train to get through the mountains?**

North Carolina—a Southern State

North Carolina enjoyed a period of growth and prosperity during the 1840s and 1850s. Transportation improved with the building of roads and railroads. Steamboats traveled on the rivers. It became easier for North Carolina's goods to reach local and national markets. These developments encouraged the growth of new industries. Miners took minerals from the ground, and manufacturers invested in mills to turn North Carolina cotton into yarn and cloth.

Southern Systems in North Carolina **167**

CONNECTING TO ECONOMICS

Alamance Plaids

Edwin M. Holt started the first cotton mill in Alamance County in 1837. Later known as the Alamance Cotton Mill, it was also one of the first in North Carolina. In 1853 Edwin's son, Thomas, learned a technique for coloring cotton thread. Dye works were then added to the cotton mill. Looms were installed and weaving began. The mill produced the first colored cotton fabric in the South, which became famous as Alamance plaids. By the time of the Civil War, the Alamance Cotton Mill had 96 looms and 1,200 spindles. The Holt family business later grew to include several cotton mills in Alamance County. **How do you think the success of Alamance plaids influenced the Holt family's business?**

None of these new activities was as important as farming. North Carolina remained an agricultural society whose economy was centered on the institution of slavery. The vast majority of North Carolinians made their living from the land. By 1860, only 2 percent of the state's population resided in towns and cities. Economic life and the role of slavery in North Carolina were similar to conditions in many southern states. As a result, North Carolina's culture shared many traits with the rest of the South.

✔ **READING CHECK** Summarizing What characteristics of North Carolina were similar to other southern states?

★ Manufacturing

Manufacturing was slow to develop in North Carolina during the early to mid-1800s. More manufactured goods were purchased from outside the state than were produced at home during these years. In some areas, however, North Carolina took the lead over other states.

Textiles By 1860, North Carolina had more textile mills than any other southern state. Michael Schenck built the state's first cotton mill near Lincolnton around 1815. Others followed in Rocky Mount, Leaksville, and Salem. For the most part, these early mills produced rough, inexpensive fabrics, sometimes known as "slave cloth" because they were commonly used to clothe slaves. An important exception to this style was the material produced at the mill that Edwin M. Holt built in Alamance County in 1837. His was the first factory in the South to produce colored cloth. Made on power looms, the cloth was known as **Alamance plaids**.

The Tar Heel State North Carolina led the world in the production of naval stores from about 1720 to 1870. The naval stores industry produced tar, pitch, rosin, and turpentine, all of which were used to build wooden ships. This industry would help to give North Carolina its nickname, the "**Tar Heel State**." Longleaf pine trees, a natural resource of North Carolina, were used to create the industry's products. About one half of the turpentine produced in the United States during these years was manufactured in North Carolina.

✔ **READING CHECK** Comparing In what important way were the textile and naval stores industries alike?

Edwin M. Holt's cotton mill, built in 1837 in Alamance County, produced the distinctive cloth pattern known as Alamance plaids (shown in oval).

⭐ Mining

Mining was an important economic activity in North Carolina following the American Revolution. With its varied deposits of mineral resources, especially in the Piedmont, North Carolina soon built an active and growing mining industry.

The North Carolina Gold Rush Gold was discovered in North Carolina in the 1790s. Conrad Reed, the 12-year-old son of a Cabarrus County farmer, stumbled across a large, glittering rock as he was fishing. Conrad brought the rock home as a colorful souvenir. Several years passed before it was identified as gold. The huge nugget was valued at about $3,600, a sizable fortune at the time. Gold fever quickly spread, bringing thousands of people into North Carolina from all over the world. Within a few years, mines had been built, mining companies had formed, and boomtowns had developed.

The <u>North Carolina Gold Rush</u> of the early 1800s brought new prosperity to the state's economy. North Carolina soon led the nation in gold production and became known as the "golden state." During its busiest years, gold mining was second only to agriculture as North Carolina's most important industry.

The mining industry slowly declined as North Carolina's gold deposits were gradually depleted. New gold and silver strikes in California and other western territories caused much mining activity to move west during the late 1840s and 1850s. Nevertheless, many millions of dollars in gold and other precious metals were mined in North Carolina during the first half of the 1800s.

The Charlotte Mint The easiest and safest way to transport and exchange gold was in the form of coins. Gold miners had a problem converting their raw gold into coins, however, because the closest federal mint was in Philadelphia, Pennsylvania. To solve the problem, a U.S. mint was built in Charlotte, North Carolina, during the 1830s. The <u>Charlotte Mint</u> struck its first gold coins in 1838. Minting stopped in 1861 when the building was turned into a Confederate headquarters and hospital during the Civil War. Today coins from the Charlotte Mint are rare and valuable.

Iron mining Beginning in the colonial period, iron mining in North Carolina grew in importance. By 1860 there were 30 ironworks in the state. Many of these forges and foundries were located in Lincoln County. Some of their products included hinges, locks, pots, pans, ovens, tools, and nails. The industry remained small and declined toward the start of the Civil War.

✔ **READING CHECK** Summarizing What was the relationship between the North Carolina Gold Rush and the Charlotte Mint?

Did You KNOW?

The name "Tar Heel State" most likely started during the Civil War. One story says that during a battle a group of Confederate soldiers backing up North Carolina troops was driven from the field. Afterward, the North Carolinians told the soldiers who had fled that Confederate leaders would use all the tar in the state to brush on their feet and make them stick better in battle. When Confederate general Robert E. Lee heard the tale, he supposedly exclaimed, "God bless the Tar Heel boys."

Gold mining became an important part of North Carolina's growing economy during the early 1800s.

⭐ Agriculture

Agriculture was North Carolina's most important economic activity during the era before 1860, known as the **antebellum** period. The majority of people lived and worked on farms. Tobacco and cotton were North Carolina's major crops.

Tobacco North Carolina has been one of the nation's most successful tobacco-growing states. Customer demand and good soil established tobacco as a major North Carolina farm product. Early tobacco crops were of the dark-leaf variety grown in rich soil. During the early 1800s, customers asked for a more mild-flavored smoking tobacco. In response, tobacco farmers looked for ways to create a new type of tobacco.

Bright-leaf tobacco was discovered in 1839. A young slave named Stephen worked for the Slade family, tobacco farmers who lived in Caswell County. One night, Stephen fell asleep in the barn while watching the curing of leaf tobacco. When he awoke, the wood fire used to cure the tobacco was almost out. He rushed to the charcoal pit, picked up some charred logs, and threw them on the low fire. There was a sudden burst of high heat. The result was a beautiful, yellow leaf. By 1860, there was a large increase in tobacco production due to the demand for the new bright-leaf tobacco.

Cotton Cotton was another important and widely grown crop in antebellum North Carolina. The part of the cotton plant that is used to make cotton fabric is its fiber. **Cotton fibers** are small hairs that grow on the seeds inside the **cotton bolls**, which look like round balls. When fully grown, the cotton bolls burst open to reveal the fibers. Cotton fibers can be fine, medium, or coarse in texture. The fibers are separated from the seeds during a process called **ginning**. Then they are sent to a textile mill to be made into yarn and cloth.

Eli Whitney's original cotton gin, patented in 1794, revolutionized the agricultural economies of North Carolina and other southern states.

Cotton fibers were separated from the seeds by hand until 1793, when <u>**Eli Whitney**</u> invented the first cotton gin. Whitney's new machine mechanically removed the fibers from the seeds, which made cotton processing much faster. Production of cotton in North Carolina rapidly increased. From 1850 to 1860, cotton production in the state nearly doubled, to almost 73 million pounds.

Other crops One of the state's most useful crops during this period was corn. It was an important part of everyone's diet, including farm animals. Rice and wheat were also important crops. North Carolina produced many valuable agricultural products, including buckwheat,

170 Chapter 9

fruit, Irish potatoes, sugarcane, sweet potatoes, and many kinds of vegetables. By 1860 North Carolina produced more honey than any other southern state.

✓ **READING CHECK** Drawing Inferences How did changes in crop production affect the economy?

Did You KNOW?
The first North Carolina state fair was held in 1853. It was sponsored by the State Agricultural Society of North Carolina.

Economic and Social Classes

During the first half of the 1800s, North Carolina's free population was still divided into social and economic classes, just as it had been during colonial times. Although social and economic shifts had caused some changes in the classes, North Carolina's social order remained much like that of other southern states.

Gentry and middle class The highest social and economic class was still the gentry, which mainly included large planters who owned more than 20 slaves. But economic power was expanding a bit by the mid-1800s. At the bottom edge of the gentry there arose a tiny middle and upper class made up of city-dwellers. These were mainly families of professional men, merchants, and manufacturers who identified with planters and aspired to join their ranks. However, the gentry and middle class still accounted for less than 10 percent of the population.

Yeomen The yeomen made up about one fourth of the state population. They owned small amounts of land, usually 50 to 100 acres. Some of these farmers owned two or more slaves, but most owned none. Although few of the white yeomen were slaveholders, they tended to approve of the institution of slavery. Even if they were poor, the yeomen gained a sense of power and superiority from the fact that they were not black, and they were not enslaved.

The landless poor Below the yeomen fell a broad category of landless whites who worked as day laborers or rented land from their more well-to-do neighbors. In most cases they barely eked out a living from one year to the next. Many lived in shacks on the outskirts of towns and villages. Struggles and difficulties filled their lives.

Free blacks Although some free blacks were property owners and skilled craftsmen, legally and socially they were considered beneath even the poorest white person. Even though most free blacks did the same work as yeomen and landless whites, and thus shared many of the same challenges and concerns, racial prejudices usually kept them from uniting together.

✓ **READING CHECK** Summarizing What roles did land ownership and race play in shaping North Carolina's economic and social classes?

Occupations in North Carolina Among Free Workers in 1860	
Occupation	Number
Farmer	87,025
Laborer	63,481
Tradesman	27,263
Professional Worker	7,436
Planter (owning 20+ slaves)	4,065
Merchant	3,479
Teacher	1,936
Clerk	1,626
Manufacturer	1,308

Interpreting Charts
What percentage of free North Carolina workers were manufacturers in 1860?

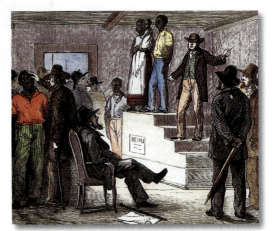

This illustration portrays the dehumanizing process of a slave sale.

Analyzing Primary Sources
Identifying a Point of View What did Mortimer Thomson think of the treatment of slaves in the market?

★ The Slave Trade

Beneath all the free classes was the enslaved population. In general, slaves in North Carolina belonged to one of two groups. One group had been brought into the state directly from Guinea and other slave-trading areas along coastal West Africa. Members of the other group had been born and raised in the colonies, although their ancestors had also been brought to America from Africa.

Although the United States outlawed the importation of slaves beginning in 1808, an active domestic slave trade continued. In 1857 a reporter described the slaves waiting to be sold in a typical slave market.

 ❝On the faces of all was an expression of heavy grief; some appeared to be resigned to the hard stroke of Fortune that had torn them from their homes, and were sadly trying to make the best of it; some sat brooding moodily over their sorrows, their chins resting on their hands, their eyes staring vacantly, and their bodies rocking to and fro, with a restless motion that was never stilled.❞

Mortimer Thomson, "What Became of the Slaves on a Georgia Plantation?" *New York Tribune,* from *Africans in America,* PBS

Such a scene would have been typical in much of North Carolina and across the South. One of North Carolina's slave markets was in Fayetteville, where the market house was sometimes used for slave auctions.

✓ **READING CHECK** **Drawing Conclusions** Why was there a domestic slave trade in North Carolina?

Section 1 Review

keyword: SN3 HP9

1 **Define** and explain:
- antebellum
- cotton fibers
- cotton bolls
- ginning

2 **Identify** and explain:
- Alamance plaids
- Tar Heel State
- North Carolina Gold Rush
- Charlotte Mint
- Eli Whitney

3 **Analyzing Information** Copy the graphic organizer below. Use it to list crops grown in North Carolina.

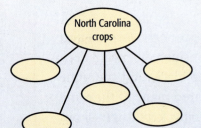

4 **Finding the Main Idea**
a. Why was agriculture important to the people of North Carolina?
b. List at least three of the different economic classes in North Carolina.

5 **Writing and Critical Thinking**
Identifying Cause and Effect Why was there a gold rush in North Carolina, and how did it change the state?
Consider:
- the economic status of individuals
- isolation of the people

172 Chapter 9

Section 2

Life under Slavery

Read to Discover
1. What was the purpose of slave codes?
2. What different types of work existed under slavery?
3. What were the conditions under which slaves lived?
4. How did some slaves gain their freedom?

Define
- overseer
- drivers
- manumission

Identify
- David Walker
- Lunsford Lane

The Story Continues

There was a shortage of labor in America in the 1600s. At that time, the states were still colonies under English rule. To solve the labor problem, people were brought to America from Africa against their will. They were sold as property and forced to work as slaves. After the Revolutionary War, slavery continued in the United States. The slave population increased, and the institution of slavery expanded.

The Slave Population

In the early 1700s most slaves lived and worked in the northeastern part of the colony. This was the tobacco-growing region. By the mid-1700s there was a rapid rise in slavery in rice-growing areas and in the naval stores industry. The heaviest concentration of slaves was in the eastern counties. By 1790 slaves made up more than one fourth of the total state population.

After the invention of the cotton gin, there was an increase in the demand for slave labor by farmers and planters. The institution of slavery had become very important to the state's economy. The concentration of slaves remained heavy in the eastern counties. In addition,

Typically, the life of a slave field hand was characterized by back-breaking work, hopelessness and discomfort, and poverty.

Southern Systems in North Carolina 173

slaveholders moved west toward the central and western counties. Slaves were located throughout the state. By 1860 the number of slaves had increased to more than one third of the total population.

✔ **READING CHECK** **Identifying Cause and Effect** What caused increases in North Carolina's slave population during the early and mid-1800s?

⭐ Slave Codes

Slavery was established in North Carolina during the colonial years. Legally, slaves were viewed as property, not as people. Over the years, slave codes were passed to secure slaveholders' "property" and to prevent slave revolts. These laws existed throughout the South. Under the various states' slave codes, slaves had almost no legal rights.

Colonial codes North Carolina first created a slave code in 1715. It contained 21 articles. The basic purpose of the slave code was to limit slavery to Africans and Native Americans. Another provision of the law was to return runaway slaves to the slaveholder. It was illegal for anyone to protect a runaway slave. By 1741 the slave code had grown to include 58 articles. It was harsher than earlier codes, and punishment for breaking the law was severe. This version of the slave code was used throughout the later colonial period.

Codes of the 1830s In general, slaves were not allowed to own property or firearms, read or write, marry, vote, or leave a slaveholder's land without permission. Fear of slave insurrections grew in North Carolina in the 1820s and 1830s. The slave code was revised again in the 1830s to further restrict the lives of slaves. In addition to the restrictions slaves already faced, they were not allowed to gather in large groups, teach, preach, or be set free easily.

Enforcement Punishment for violation of the slave codes was severe and could include whipping and hanging. To enforce the codes, slave patrols were created. The patrols were usually made up of the landless poor. Slave patrols had the authority to punish anyone who violated a slave code.

✔ **READING CHECK** **Identifying Points of View** Who benefitted from the slave codes?

⭐ Work under Slavery

Slaves worked in many different roles. Some worked in the slaveholder's house, most worked in the fields, and a few were trained to perform specific tasks. Each work role had its own routine. Field work, however, was strongly affected by changes in the seasons.

BIOGRAPHY

David Walker

(1785–1830)

David Walker was born a free African American in Wilmington, North Carolina. He settled in Boston and became active in the abolitionist movement. Walker wrote articles for the nation's first African American newspaper, called *Freedom's Journal*. In September of 1829 Walker published a pamphlet called *Appeal to the Colored Citizens of the World*. In his pamphlet, which came to be known as *Walker's Appeal*, he wrote that slaves must fight if necessary to obtain their freedom. Slaveholders were angered by his pamphlet. To slaves, Walker's words were inspiring and a source of hope. **What was David Walker's contribution to the abolitionist movement?**

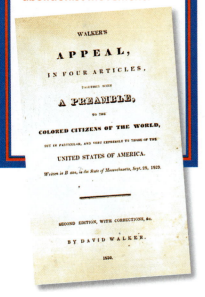

Domestic servants Also known as household servants, domestic servants worked in the slaveholder's house. Some wealthy planters in North Carolina owned more than one home. Their servants traveled with them between homes. Servants worked as cooks, maids, butlers, seamstresses, and nurses. Their work included contact with the slaveholder's family, and sometimes slaves and masters formed close relationships. Black and white children often played together and genuinely cared for one another, but as they grew older, they confronted the reality that masters and slaves were never going to be equal under a slave economy.

Interpreting the Visual Record

Household slavery Domestic slaves on southern plantations often performed menial tasks and services for the slaveholder's family and guests. *What is the servant in this image doing?*

Working crops The majority of the slaves worked as field hands under the supervision of an **overseer**, who was often a relative of the plantation owner. Some slaves, known as **drivers**, assisted the overseer. Drivers and overseers made sure that the slaves worked hard all day. The work usually started at sunrise and ended at sunset, depending on the crop. The most difficult crop to tend was rice. Concentrated in the lower Cape Fear region of North Carolina, rice crops required constant care and back breaking labor.

Other work Some slaves were trained with special skills to work as blacksmiths, carpenters, millers, shoemakers, weavers, and in other crafts. Others labored on riverboats to transport products along waterways.

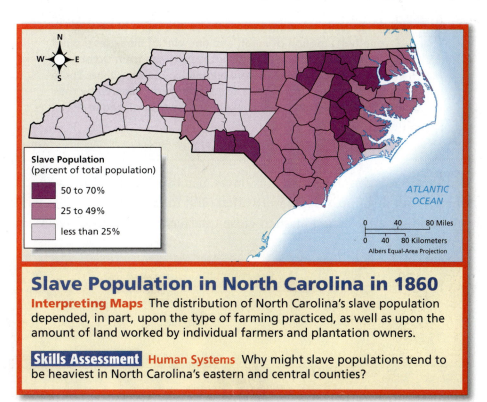

Slave Population in North Carolina in 1860
Interpreting Maps The distribution of North Carolina's slave population depended, in part, upon the type of farming practiced, as well as upon the amount of land worked by individual farmers and plantation owners.

Skills Assessment **Human Systems** Why might slave populations tend to be heaviest in North Carolina's eastern and central counties?

Southern Systems in North Carolina

Since this type of work was seasonal, many of these slaves worked in the fields when crops were being harvested. Some slaveholders also leased their slaves to other farmers or merchants in towns and cities.

✓ **READING CHECK** Categorizing What types of work did slaves do?

Conditions under Slavery

Slaves lived under difficult conditions. Poor nutrition led to sickness, which was only made worse by the demands of hard labor. In the lowlands of eastern North Carolina, malaria was commonplace and often led to death. Slaves were often harshly disciplined with whipping.

Clothing Slave clothing differed depending on the individual slave's role. Domestic servants typically wore better clothing than did field hands. Their attire was meant to reflect their owners' wealth and high social status. Slaves usually received a yearly clothing allowance. For most, this included two outfits (one for winter, one for summer), a pair of shoes, a coat, and a hat.

Food Most slaves were given a daily food allowance, which varied in quality. On many plantations, slaves were also allowed to tend small gardens in which they grew vegetables for their own tables and sometimes for sale. In 1899 a planter's son, who had worked as the family's overseer, recalled the rations given to slaves on their rice plantation near Wilmington.

" The daily allowance of food was one quart of meal, . . . one-half a pound of meat, and one pint of molasses a week for each adult. Sweet potatoes were given from October to March instead of meal, and peas were allowed in planting time. There was a regular allowance of tobacco. The meals were prepared by the cooks and sent to the field ready cooked. Milk was furnished at the cook's place. "

A former overseer, quoted in *Slavery in the State of North Carolina* by John Spencer Bassett

Housing Accommodations for slaves usually consisted of wooden shacks with dirt floors. They were often built to house two families with no dividing wall. Living at such close quarters meant that privacy for

GLOBAL CONNECTIONS

The Demand for Slave Labor

One of North Carolina's largest plantations was Somerset Place, located in Washington County. Somerset was established in the 1780s by Josiah Collins and other investors from Halifax and Edenton. Collins and his partners chartered a ship to travel to the Guinea coast. They brought back enslaved Africans to clear the land and drain the swamps for farming. Today, Somerset is a state historic site. Every few years, descendants of the slaves who once worked on the plantation gather from around the country for a family reunion.

From what area were most of the slaves on Somerset Place descended?

Analyzing Primary Sources

Drawing Inferences Do you think the slaves were given adequate food allowances to meet the demands of their workload?

Many slave cabins offered little more than primitive shelter and the barest necessities of life.

slaves was an unknown luxury. Beds were collections of straw and old rags thrown down in the corners and boxed in with boards.

✓ **READING CHECK** **Drawing Conclusions** How well did slaveholders care for their slaves?

⭐ Gaining Freedom

Before 1830 some slaveholders freed their slaves for reasons of good work and good conduct. The act of legally freeing someone from servitude is called **manumission**. Once freed, slaves were usually expected to leave the state.

Harsh slave codes were passed throughout the South in the early 1830s in response to uprisings such as Nat Turner's Rebellion. These codes often placed strict limits on a slaveholder's ability to free slaves. Such codes made it illegal to free a slave without special permission from the court system. Under special circumstances, a few slaves were allowed to buy their freedom. Others were given the gift of freedom upon the death of the slaveholder. Even when some owners were willing to set slaves free, state laws made it difficult to do so. For example, Lunsford Lane, born in 1803, grew up as a slave on a plantation near Raleigh. He was a domestic servant, and he cut wood at night to earn money. With his father, Lane later sold pipes and special smoking tobacco. He eventually earned enough money to purchase his own freedom, but that was illegal. In 1835 Lane's owner took him to New York and set him free.

✓ **READING CHECK** **Summarizing** How did some slaves legally gain their freedom?

BIOGRAPHY

Lunsford Lane
(1803–c. 1863)

Lunsford Lane worked in his spare time to earn money to buy his freedom. Eventually, Lane was taken to New York and freed. He twice returned to North Carolina to buy his family's freedom. Each time he was charged with breaking a law limiting the actions of free blacks, and was forced to leave. Finally, white friends smuggled him and his family north to freedom. **Why could Lane not buy his freedom in North Carolina?**

Section 2 Review

Homework Practice Online
keyword: SN3 HP9

❶ Define and explain:
- overseer
- driver
- manumission

❷ Identify and explain:
- David Walker
- Lunsford Lane

❸ Analyzing Information Copy the graphic organizer below. Use it to list different types of slave labor.

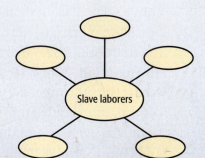

Slave laborers

❹ Finding the Main Idea
a. What rights were slaves denied?
b. Under what conditions did slaves live and work?
c. What methods did slaves use to gain their freedom?

❺ Writing and Critical Thinking
Identifying Points of View Imagine you are a slave in the 1800s in North Carolina. Write a brief narrative describing one day in your life.
Consider:
- different types of slave work
- slaves' typical housing, food, and clothing

Section 3
Resistance to Slavery

Read to Discover
1. What were important elements of slave culture in North Carolina?
2. How did slaves resist slavery?
3. How was the antislavery movement supported?

Define
- extended family
- maroons

Identify
- Harriet Jacobs
- Great Dismal Swamp
- Judith Mendenhall
- Levi Coffin

The Story Continues

Slaves clung to their own traditions and beliefs apart from those of their masters. Slaves developed a culture that reaffirmed their humanity within a system that defined them as mere property. Thus, slave culture not only bound the community together, but also offered another form of resistance against slavery.

Slave weddings, like the one pictured in this image (c. 1820), were often informal, but they were culturally important events that strengthened social ties among participants.

★ Slave Culture

Families were an important part of slave culture. The slave system often tore apart families. Slave marriages were not even protected by the state. Still, slaves married and had children. To maintain family ties even in the face of separation through sale, slaves embraced the concept of **extended family**. This could include friends as well as grandparents, aunts, uncles, and cousins. For example, a slave who was not a relative might act as a separated child's parent.

178 Chapter 9

Many slaves turned to religion for inspiration and comfort. Some practiced religions common in Africa, including Islam, but most practiced Christianity. Some churches in North Carolina received African Americans as members. However, slaves were only allowed to sit in the balcony or in the back of the church during services. Most slaves in antebellum North Carolina were Methodists or Baptists. Evangelists from these churches often visited the large plantations. Through their religion, slaves focused on the hope for justice in this world and for a better life after death.

In the evenings, slaves gathered to tell stories, sing, and dream of a better life. Singing and storytelling were parts of an oral tradition that slaves preserved from West African cultures. Slave songs and stories were seldom written down. They were instead memorized and handed down from generation to generation by word of mouth.

✔ **READING CHECK** **Identifying Cause and Effect** How was slave culture a form of resistance to slavery?

Quilts made by slaves were sometimes coded with symbols that gave instructions for escape.

⭐ Slave Rebellions

Slaves resisted their captivity in many ways. Among slaveholders, the most dreaded form of resistance was the rare slave rebellion, during which slaves banded together to fight for their freedom.

Bertie County In 1800 the majority of the population of Bertie County was African American. In 1802 reports circulated about a slave rebellion in the county and surrounding areas. The *Raleigh Register* reported that there had been a plan to start a general slave uprising, to begin on June 10. The suspected leaders of the rebellion were arrested and punished.

Nat Turner One rebellion that had a great effect on North Carolina actually took place in Virginia. A slave named Nat Turner led an armed rebellion in Southhampton County, Virginia, in 1831. The violence began in the village of Cross Keys, near the Virginia–North Carolina border. The governor of North Carolina sent a state militia to the border for protection. Officials eventually captured the rebels. Turner was tried and executed. Some slaves in North Carolina were accused of being connected with the revolt. They were also tried and executed. In response to this slave revolt, North Carolina officials strengthened the state slave codes.

✔ **READING CHECK** **Drawing Conclusions** How did the rebellions in Bertie County and in Virginia affect North Carolina?

This handwritten note, written by a slave in 1802, discussed a planned slave rebellion in Bertie County.

Southern Systems in North Carolina

Other Forms of Resistance

Escape by running away was another form of resistance to slavery. To gain freedom, some slaves resorted to running away to the North. One of the most famous runaways from North Carolina was **Harriet Jacobs**. She was born a slave in Edenton, North Carolina, in 1813. She escaped to the North by boat and worked at several different jobs to support herself and her children. In 1861 she wrote a book about her life called *Incidents in the Life of a Slave Girl*, which brought great attention to the treatment of female slaves.

Runaway slaves were at great risk of being caught and returned to their slaveholders. They needed safe places to hide on their journey to freedom. The **Great Dismal Swamp**, between North Carolina and Virginia, was a favorite hiding place. In fact, runaway slaves established a number of free communities, or **maroons**, in the swamp's dense woodlands. Although most maroon communities tried to remain isolated, in 1856 members of maroon communities in Bladen and Robeson counties staged an uprising that renewed white fears of a slave rebellion.

Connecting to Literature

"The Slave in the Dismal Swamp"
Henry Wadsworth Longfellow

The Great Dismal Swamp was so well known as a hideaway for runaway slaves that it inspired northern writer Henry Wadsworth Longfellow to write an antislavery poem about it in 1842.

View of the Great Dismal Swamp

In dark fens [watery lowlands] of the Dismal Swamp
  The hunted Negro lay;
He saw the fire of the midnight camp,
And heard at times a horse's tramp
  And a bloodhound's distant bay.

Where will-o'-the-wisps [marsh light]* and glow-worms shine,
  In bulrush and in brake;
Where waving mosses shroud the pine,
And the cedar grows, and the poisonous vine
  Is spotted like the snake;

Where hardly a human foot could pass,
  Or a human heart would dare,
On the quaking turf of the green morass [swamp]
He crouched in the rank and tangled grass,
  Like a wild beast in his lair.

A poor old slave, infirm and lame;
  Great scars deformed his face;
On his forehead he bore the brand of shame,
And the rags, that hid his mangled frame,
  Were the livery of disgrace.

All things above were bright and fair,
  All things were glad and free;
Lithe [graceful] squirrels darted here and there,
And wild birds filled the echoing air
  With songs of Liberty! . . .

*The term "will-o'-the-wisps" can also mean "an elusive goal."

Understanding Literature

1. What is the general mood that Longfellow's poem conveys?
2. Do you think the runaway slave thought of the swamp as "dismal"? Explain.

Slaves also resisted slavery in other ways. For example, they might slow down their work pace, break farm equipment, or destroy crops. As another form of resistance, some slaves learned to read and write in defiance of efforts to keep them illiterate.

✓ **READING CHECK** **Making Predictions** How might secretly learning to read help slaves?

★ The Antislavery Movement in North Carolina

Slavery was a violation of human rights. By the late 1700s, some antislavery groups were calling for an end to slavery in the United States. Despite the strong presence of the slave system in North Carolina, there was antislavery sentiment in the state. The Quakers were one of the leading religious groups that struggled against slavery in North Carolina.

One function of the antislavery movement in North Carolina was support of the Underground Railroad. At great risk to themselves, many Quakers helped slaves escape from southern plantations. Other Quakers served as "conductors," performing the dangerous work of guiding escaping slaves along the Railroad's secret routes. Some allowed escaping slaves to hide in their homes. One Quaker, **Judith Mendenhall**, contributed in a different way to the antislavery movement. She educated slave children in a school near Greensboro.

✓ **READING CHECK** **Summarizing** How did some people in North Carolina work against slavery?

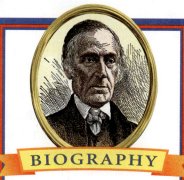

BIOGRAPHY

Levi Coffin
(1798–1877)

Levi Coffin was raised on a farm in New Garden, now Greensboro, North Carolina. Coffin was a devout Quaker and strongly opposed slavery. He moved to Indiana in 1826 and worked with the Underground Railroad. Fugitive slaves escaped to the North and Canada using Underground Railroad routes. Coffin opened his home, which was on one of the routes, to help fugitive slaves. More than 3,000 escaping slaves passed through his home. Coffin became known as the President of the Underground Railroad. **Why was Levi Coffin important to fugitive slaves?**

Section 3 Review

1 Define and explain:
- extended family
- maroons

2 Identify and explain:
- Harriet Jacobs
- Great Dismal Swamp
- Judith Mendenhall
- Levi Coffin

3 Analyzing Information Copy the graphic organizer below. Use it to list different forms of resistance to slavery.

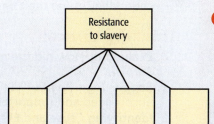

4 Finding the Main Idea
a. Why was the development of a slave culture important to the slave community?
b. What were some ways that slaves resisted slavery?

5 Writing and Critical Thinking
Identifying Points of View Imagine you are involved in the antislavery movement in North Carolina in 1850. Write a brief narrative describing how you might help slaves.
Consider:
- forms of resisting slavery
- the Underground Railroad

Southern Systems in North Carolina **181**

Chapter 9 Review

Chapter Summary

Section 1
- Cotton textiles and turpentine manufacturing were important to the state's economy.
- The North Carolina Gold Rush affected population growth and the development of towns.
- Agriculture was the most important industry, led by tobacco and cotton.
- North Carolina's population was divided into economic and social classes.
- The domestic slave trade existed in North Carolina.

Section 2
- African Americans lived and worked against their will as slaves in difficult conditions.
- The slave population increased as the cotton gin led to an increased demand for cotton.
- Slave codes were harsh and denied the slave population their basic human rights.
- It was extremely difficult for a slave to gain freedom legally.

Section 3
- Slaves developed their own culture as a way to survive and resist the institution of slavery.
- There were many forms of resistance to slavery among the slaves and among organizations that opposed slavery.

Identifying People and Ideas
Use the following terms or people in complete sentences.
1. Alamance plaids
2. North Carolina Gold Rush
3. Charlotte Mint
4. David Walker
5. manumission
6. Lunsford Lane
7. extended family
8. Harriet Jacobs
9. maroons
10. Judith Mendenhall

Understanding Main Ideas

Section 1 (Pages 167–172)
1. What was the most important industry in North Carolina in the years between 1790 and about 1860?
2. What group formed the largest economic class in North Carolina in the years between 1790 and 1860?

Section 2 (Pages 173–177)
3. Why did slaves have few rights?
4. What were some of the ways in which a slave could gain freedom?

Section 3 (Pages 178–181)
5. What were some of the typical forms of resisting slavery?
6. What were some activities of abolitionists in North Carolina?

What Did You Find Out?
1. **Science, Technology & Society** How did North Carolina make use of its resources?
2. **Economics** What were the economic motives that influenced North Carolina planters' reliance on slave labor?
3. **Government** How did slavery and the slave codes deny slaves their basic human rights?

Thinking Critically
1. **Evaluating** How did the gold rush change North Carolina?
2. **Supporting a Point of View** Why was slavery encouraged and supported?
3. **Identifying Cause and Effect** How did the antislavery movement in North Carolina start? What was its result?

Building Social Studies Skills

Interpreting Graphs

Study the graph below on the growth of the slave population. Use the information on the graph to answer the questions that follow.

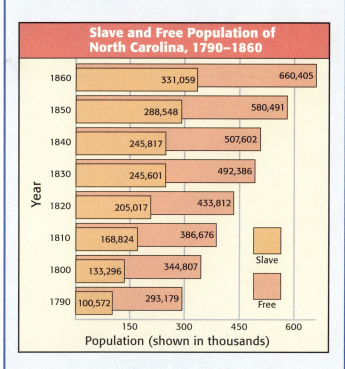

Slave and Free Population of North Carolina, 1790–1860

Year	Free	Slave
1860	331,059	660,405
1850	288,548	580,491
1840	245,817	507,602
1830	245,601	492,386
1820	205,017	433,812
1810	168,824	386,676
1800	133,296	344,807
1790	100,572	293,179

Population (shown in thousands)

1. Which decade represents the largest increase in the slave population?
   a. 1790–1800
   b. 1820–1830
   c. 1850–1860

2. Based on what you know about the slave population, what do you think accounts for the increase represented by your answer in question 1?

Analyzing Primary Sources

Read this quote from Peter Randolph, a former slave, and then answer the questions that follow.

"Not being allowed to hold [religious] meetings on the plantation, the slaves assemble in the swamps, out of reach of the patrols. They have an understanding among themselves as to the time and place of getting together. This is often done by the first one arriving breaking boughs from the trees, and bending them in the direction of the selected spot. Arrangements are then made [for conducting religious services among themselves]. . . . The male members then select a certain space, in separate groups, for their division of the meeting. Preaching in order, by the brethren; then praying and singing all round, until they generally feel quite happy. . . . The slave forgets all his sufferings, except to remind others of the trials during the past week, exclaiming: 'Thank God, I shall not live here always!' . . . As they separate, they sing a parting hymn of praise."

3. Which of the following statements best describes Randolph's point of view?
   a. Slaves do not need to hide their plans.
   b. Slaves are sometimes able to forget their suffering.
   c. Slaves are not afraid of their slaveholders.
   d. Slaves prefer to meet in public.

4. How did the institution of slavery contribute to the type of meeting portrayed in the quote? Give specific examples.

Alternative Assessment

Building Your Portfolio

Cooperative Learning
Complete the following activity in small groups. Have each person in the group assume the role of a slave. Some members of the group will support the viewpoint of slaves who want to risk escape and others will support the viewpoint of slaves who do not want to risk escape. Create a journal describing the differences of opinion and the rationale behind those opinions.

internet connect

Internet Activity: go.hrw.com
keyword: SN3 NC9

Choose a topic on southern systems in North Carolina to:

- Create a museum display about the North Carolina Gold Rush.
- Write a report on the institution of slavery in North Carolina.
- Research North Carolina's role in the Underground Railroad.

Southern Systems in North Carolina

UNIT 4
War and Reunification
(1800–1877)

CHAPTER 10 **North Carolina and National Events** (1800–1861)

CHAPTER 11 **The Civil War** (1861–1865)

CHAPTER 12 **Reconstruction in North Carolina** (1865–1877)

Young People
IN HISTORY
Life during the Civil War

For young people as well as adults, the Civil War brought drastic changes. Some young boys lied about their ages in order to join the troops and fight. Many joined the army as drummers. Because drumming was a way to communicate orders to troops, drummers were often the target of enemy fire.

Many young people kept diaries or later wrote memoirs about the war years. These writings have become important primary sources for historians. For example, Eliza Tillinghast Stinson wrote about the war in Fayetteville:

> "I was a very young miss in my teens, then, but I remember as well as yesterday my impressions on seeing the first real soldiers I had ever beheld. . . . The morning they arrived we were wending our way down the hill to school, and met them marching up to the Arsenal."

Later Stinson wrote about girls' contributions to the war effort:

> "The schoolgirls were wild; no use was it to mention books to them; it was their plain duty to sew for the soldiers, and sew they did. . . . There were dress parade suits and fatigue suits to be made, as well as underclothing suitable to camp life. . . . us girls were proud to feel that we had done our part as well as school-girls could be expected to."

In her memoirs Josephine Bryan Worth described General Sherman's raid on Fayetteville:

> "I was then a schoolgirl, with ardent love for the South. . . . A blue line now appeared behind the breast-works which formed the outer defense of the Arsenal. . . . It was undoubtedly the Yankees. . . . For the space of perhaps a quarter of an hour there was silence, during which we *waited*. . . . The main body of Sherman's army now began to pass by in martial array, with flags flying, the field officers on horseback . . . the soldiers proudly keeping step to the music of the band!"

Young people like this "powder monkey" aboard the Union warship New Hampshire *served and fought on both sides in the Civil War.*

If You Were There How would you have felt about the Civil War?

LEFT PAGE: North Carolina saw much fighting during the Civil War, including the Battle of Fort Fisher, near Wilmington, in December 1864.

CHAPTER 10
North Carolina and National Events
(1800–1861)

New Bern in the mid-1800s

Build on What You Know

North Carolina made great social and economic progress between 1800 and 1861. At the same time, however, Americans became divided by sectional interests. Regional differences pushed the nation closer to conflict, and North Carolinians felt threatened by the changing national scene.

What's Your Opinion?

Do you **agree** or **disagree** with the following statements? Support your point of view in your journal.

- **Constitutional Heritage** Laws in one area of a nation should not contradict laws in a different area.
- **Citizenship** Different regions of a country should have equal political power.
- **Government** Governments should try to compromise instead of going to war, regardless of the issues.

Section 1

The Industrial Revolution

Read to Discover
1. What major innovations were made during the Industrial Revolution?
2. How did technological advances affect North Carolina's economy?
3. What was the impact of the Industrial Revolution on daily life in North Carolina?

Identify
- *Prometheus*

The Story Continues

During the early 1800s North Carolina's economy was dominated by agriculture and slave labor. There was very little manufacturing in the state. However, the spread of the Industrial Revolution throughout the country would lay the foundations for later industrial development in North Carolina.

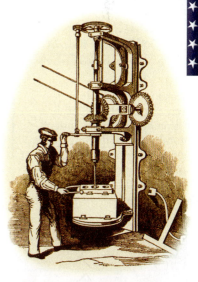

Interpreting the Visual Record

Coming of the machine age Machines developed during the Industrial Revolution were in use in North Carolina metalworking factories during the mid-1800s. *What does it look like this man is doing?*

 ### The Impact of the Industrial Revolution

Between the late 1700s and the mid-1800s, industrialization began to transform life in the United States. The Industrial Revolution was marked by rapid growth in the use of machines in manufacturing. It was characterized, too, by strong economic and urban growth, new inventions and technologies, and widespread social change.

Three innovations especially helped spur the Industrial Revolution. The invention of new steam engines led to the creation of powerful machines and locomotives. The development of furnaces enabled the production of metal products used for machinery and for steamboats, railways, and other forms of transportation. And the creation of

North Carolina and National Events **187**

steam-driven spinning machines helped foster the textile industry in North Carolina.

The Industrial Revolution greatly changed life and work in the United States. Major changes, such as the rise of the factory system, increased city development, and new forms of transportation, were seen first in the North. By the 1830s and the 1840s, however, industrialization was slowly beginning to affect North Carolina and other southern states as well. A few southern leaders, like North Carolina governor David Reid, welcomed the economic and social changes that would result from industrialization.

Analyzing Primary Sources

Making Generalizations and Predictions How might the ability to "carry property with safety" have affected North Carolina's economy?

 "The farmer and other classes [of people] need cheap transportation and convenient markets where they can carry their property with safety. They need commercial and manufacturing towns and cities at home, with shipping to do their own importing and exporting, without continuing to pay tribute [taxes or payments] to the North."

David Reid, quoted in *North Carolina: The History of a Southern State*

During the first half of the 1800s, many of the changes that Reid and others encouraged began to take place in North Carolina. By the second half of the century, industrialization would transform the state and its ways of life.

✓ **READING CHECK** **Finding the Main Idea** What were three major innovations of the Industrial Revolution?

★ The Effects of Inventions

Although North Carolina remained almost entirely dependent on agriculture, the Industrial Revolution still affected manufacturing, farming, and transportation in the state.

Industry Innovations such as spinning machines and new steel- and iron-making processes gave rise to new industries in North Carolina. Businesspeople built 32 new cotton mills in the 1840s alone. More mills followed in the 1850s. As a region, the South produced 25 percent of the nation's textiles by 1860. Other industries grew in North Carolina as well. Businesspeople opened ironworks in the Piedmont area, especially in Lincoln County. These forges and furnaces helped supply the state with the iron products it needed to grow and develop. Still, industrialization remained limited in the state.

★★★★★★★★★★★★★★★
That's Interesting!
★★★★★★★★★★★★★★★

The Industrial Revolution Despite the Industrial Revolution, North Carolina remained a largely agricultural state. In the late 1820s one observer said, "Our habits and prejudices are against manufacturing."

During the mid-1800s, improved agricultural techniques helped tobacco growers and other farmers in North Carolina to greatly increase production.

Farming New technologies and practices also affected farming in North Carolina. New processes for curing and preparing tobacco also helped to open new markets for North Carolina products. During the Industrial Revolution, some farmers began to use improved plows with stronger metal blades. These plows cut deeply into the soil and increased

188 Chapter 10

productivity by making it easier to plant more crops. As a result, crop yields rose sharply in North Carolina. Cotton production quadrupled from 1840 to 1860. However, not as many North Carolina farmers used these new technologies as farmers in other states. For some crops, increased production had the negative effect of driving down prices.

Transportation Industrial growth brought a revolution in transportation as well as in manufacturing. The development of steam engines and iron-making processes led to major advances in transportation. The steamboats of the Industrial Revolution, for example, allowed captains to navigate the difficult rivers of northeastern North Carolina. Not every advance in transportation relied on new technology, however. In the mid-1800s, North Carolinians built wood-plank roads. The country's longest plank road was between Fayetteville and Bethania, North Carolina. These new roads helped to speed economic growth and activity. Road and railroad construction enabled farmers and manufacturers to move their goods to distant markets.

✔ **READING CHECK Identifying Cause and Effect** How did the development of new inventions affect North Carolina?

CONNECTING TO SCIENCE AND TECHNOLOGY

The *Prometheus*

The *Prometheus* was the first steamboat in North Carolina. The ship helped mark the state's move into the industrial age. The *Prometheus* was built by Otway Burns, a well-known North Carolina privateer during the War of 1812.

Burns completed the *Prometheus* in 1818. The ship was a paddle-wheeled steamboat designed to navigate North Carolina's winding, sometimes dangerous river courses. The *Prometheus* operated on the Cape Fear River, making regular runs between Fayetteville and Southport. These trips helped to spur the region's settlement and to build its economy.

Understanding Science and Technology
1. What was the significance of the *Prometheus*?
2. How did Otway Burns's background contribute to the development of the *Prometheus*?

The development of steam-powered engines greatly improved transportation in North Carolina during the Industrial Revolution.

★ Technology and Daily Life

Industrial changes affected daily life in North Carolina. In some cases, the economic growth that accompanied industrialization led to new jobs, higher average incomes, and higher standards of living. The Industrial Revolution also helped link North Carolina to the rest of the nation. In the late 1700s and early 1800s, North Carolinians produced most of their goods for themselves. New economic developments and transportation methods, however, allowed industries to specialize in the production of items such as cotton cloth. As more states specialized in the manufacture of certain goods, they became increasingly tied to one another.

Labor-saving inventions also improved life for many North Carolinians. Technical advances in the textile industry, for example, transformed everyday life. As sturdy, inexpensive fabrics became increasingly available, many women were able to abandon the time-consuming chore of spinning and weaving their own cloth. Some women even bought clothing rather than making it themselves. The introduction of new plows and farming techniques helped farm families do more in less time. Road and railroad construction helped people travel more easily than before, strengthening ties between communities.

✔ **READING CHECK** Summarizing How did the Industrial Revolution affect daily life in North Carolina?

Small foundries such as the one pictured here produced the iron needed by North Carolina's early manufacturers.

Section 1 Review

keyword: SN3 HP10

① Identify and explain:
• Prometheus

② Analyzing Information Copy the web diagram below. Use it to identify the main innovations that sparked the Industrial Revolution.

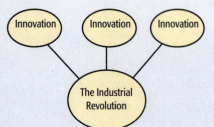

③ Finding the Main Idea
a. How did the Industrial Revolution alter North Carolina's industries?
b. How did the Industrial Revolution change North Carolina's agricultural processes?

④ Writing and Critical Thinking
Drawing Inferences and Conclusions Imagine that your family lives in North Carolina during the Industrial Revolution. Write at least two short diary entries describing how the Industrial Revolution has changed your daily life.
Consider:
• new ties with the rest of the nation
• improved farming and other tools
• the development of labor-saving machines

Section 2

Westward Migration

Read to Discover

1. How did the Louisiana Purchase and the Lewis and Clark expedition affect North Carolina?
2. How did the Walton War reflect growing cooperation between southern states?
3. How did the war with Mexico affect political conditions in North Carolina?
4. In what ways was North Carolina affected by the California Gold Rush?

Identify

- Walton War
- Nathaniel Alexander
- James K. Polk

The Story Continues

North Carolinians, like other Americans, were on the move in the early and mid-1800s. During these years, many people in North Carolina migrated westward in search of better lives. Some moved beyond North Carolina to follow the nation's shifting boundaries.

This old map shows the huge increase in size experienced by the young United States as a result of the Louisiana Purchase of 1803.

★ The Nation Grows

The United States grew rapidly during the first half of the 1800s. This growth was a result of purchase, exploration, and settlement, as well as of conquest.

In 1803, the United States purchased Louisiana from the French. The new territory more than doubled the size of the young nation. On the whole, North Carolinians supported the Louisiana Purchase, and the state's senators and representatives called it an "honorable acquisition

North Carolina and National Events **191**

[purchase]." Louisiana did not border North Carolina, of course. Even so, the Purchase had important effects on the state.

In 1804, President Jefferson asked Meriwether Lewis and William Clark to explore and map the Louisiana Purchase. Lewis and Clark had two main objectives. They wanted to find an overland route to the Pacific Ocean. They also sought to learn about the new land itself and about the Native American tribes that peopled it. Over the course of two years, the Lewis and Clark expedition gathered much information about America's new western frontiers. Their descriptions of the wealth and possibilities of the new lands created much excitement in North Carolina. Many North Carolinians left their state during the early 1800s, heading west in search of opportunity and open land.

The Purchase was also important to North Carolina because of the growing debate over slavery. Throughout the first decades of the 1800s, Congress worked to create a balance between free and slave states. Many southerners, including North Carolinians, wanted to migrate to the new lands of the Purchase, bringing their slaves with them. A growing number of people in the North, however, worked to ban slavery in the new territories. The Missouri Compromise of 1820 was an attempt to end this debate. Missouri was admitted to the Union as a slave state, while the area of Maine was declared a free state. The Compromise also banned slavery in the Louisiana Purchase territories north of 36° 30' latitude. For a time, North Carolinians and other Americans thought that the bitter issue of slavery would be settled.

✓ **READING CHECK** **Identifying Cause and Effect** How did the Louisiana Purchase and the Lewis and Clark expedition affect North Carolina?

Meriwether Lewis and William Clark, with their American Indian guide, Sacagawea, led the first organized exploration of the vast new frontiers of the Louisiana Territory.

⭐ The Walton War

Soon after the Louisiana Purchase took place, a bitter conflict over land broke out between North Carolina and Georgia. Both states claimed a 12-mile piece of land in the Blue Ridge Mountains. Some people called the land the "Orphan Strip." Officials in Georgia insisted that the strip belonged to their state. In 1803 they incorporated the land as part of Walton County. North Carolina objected. Soon the two states entered into the **Walton War**. Residents of both states fought over the land.

After years of conflict, North Carolina governor **Nathaniel Alexander** took action. He proposed a meeting between North Carolina officials and Georgia's leaders. In 1807 a group of representatives met in Asheville. These delegates knew that the solution to the land conflict would be based upon the exact placement of the 35th parallel. In those days, the location of the parallel was still uncertain. Experts from the University of North Carolina and the University of South Carolina decided that Georgia should not claim land to the north or the west of the Blue Ridge. They also determined an eastern and southern boundary. The temporary solution held until 1819. In that year, the Georgia legislature accepted a survey of the 35th parallel. From that point on, the parallel served as the border between North Carolina and Georgia.

✔ **READING CHECK** **Problem Solving** How did officials end the Walton War?

★ James K. Polk and the Texas Debate

Mexico won its independence from Spain in 1821. As a means of settling lands north of the Rio Grande, Mexico's government encouraged Americans to migrate to the Mexican province of Texas.

Texas and slavery The Mexican government banned slavery, but many immigrants from the American South wanted to bring their slaves into the Mexican land they planned to settle. In 1835 a group of Texans revolted against Mexico's government. In 1836 Texas won its independence. Many Texans wanted to join the United States as a new state, but the move to admit Texas to the Union failed in the U.S. Senate. In part, this was because northern senators feared that the admission of Texas would destroy the balance between slave and free states.

In 1844 North Carolina native **James K. Polk** won the presidential election. Polk supported western expansion and lobbied effectively for Texan statehood. In the year after Polk's election, the U.S. Congress annexed Texas. The Union had a new state.

The war with Mexico The Texas annexation sparked a war between Mexico and the United States. In 1846 the two countries clashed along the Rio Grande. The Mexican War had begun. By late 1847 the U.S. Army occupied Mexico's capital of Mexico City. In the peace agreement that resulted, the United States forced Mexico to sell a huge area of land that came to be known as the Mexican Cession. The land made up much of today's American Southwest, as well as California.

Many Whigs in North Carolina opposed the war with Mexico and the Mexican Cession. Many citizens supported the effort, however. Over time, the Whigs' position on Texas led to the party's decline in North Carolina and across the nation.

✔ **READING CHECK** **Finding the Main Idea** Why was the annexation of Texas a political issue?

Mexico's major fort of Chapultepec, located on high ground near Mexico City, was stormed by U.S. troops in September 1847, ending the Mexican War with an American victory.

North Carolina and National Events 193

BIOGRAPHY
James K. Polk
(1795–1849)

James K. Polk was born in Mecklenburg County. Polk's family moved to Tennessee when he was eleven. Polk later attended the University of North Carolina and began a career as a lawyer. Between 1825 and 1839, Polk served as a U.S. Representative for Tennessee. The Democrats chose Polk as their presidential candidate in 1844, and he won the national election. President Polk supported westward expansion, open trade policies, and banking reform. **Why might Polk have supported westward expansion?**

★ California and the Compromise of 1850

The Mexican Cession of 1848 sparked more debate over slavery. Would southerners be able to hold slaves in the new territory? New developments in California affected the issue as well. In the late 1840s, a settler discovered gold in California. The California Gold Rush soon followed, leading to a massive population boom in the territory. Many North Carolinians and other Americans migrated to California to strike it rich. The new residents quickly pushed for California statehood. Many northerners wanted California to be free, while southerners hoped to protect slavery in the cession lands. The Missouri Compromise of 1820 began the custom that new states would be admitted to the Union only if the balance between free and slave states was maintained. Yet no slave territory was ready to be admitted into the Union. Many southerners accused northerners of trying to grab political power and force an end to slavery. The U.S. Congress soon became deadlocked over the issue.

Congress managed to resolve the situation with the Compromise of 1850. The compromise admitted California as a free state. It also banned the slave trade in the District of Columbia. These moves pleased northerners. To satisfy southerners, Congress passed a new fugitive slave law. In addition, it created the New Mexico Territory and the Utah Territory out of the Mexican Cession lands. Congress neither permitted nor banned slavery in these areas. The move raised the possibility that settlers or local courts would eventually allow slavery in the new territories.

✔ **READING CHECK** Identifying Cause and Effect How did the California Gold Rush affect North Carolina?

Section 2 Review

keyword: SN3 HP10

1 Identify and explain:
- Walton War
- Nathaniel Alexander
- James K. Polk

2 Drawing Inferences Copy the web diagram below. Use it to show what political changes took place in North Carolina during the Mexican War.

3 Finding the Main Idea
a. How did the Louisiana Purchase and the Lewis and Clark expedition change North Carolina?
b. How did the California Gold Rush affect North Carolina?

4 Writing and Critical Thinking
Drawing Inferences Imagine that you are Nathaniel Alexander. Prepare a letter to the governor of Georgia explaining why the two states should strive to find a peaceful solution to their border dispute.
Consider:
- the states' common interests
- how the fighting might affect the South as a whole

194 Chapter 10

Section 3

The Growing Conflict over Slavery

Read to Discover
1. What was the significance of the Kansas-Nebraska Act for North Carolina?
2. What role did *The Impending Crisis of the South* play in widening regional tensions?
3. Why was John Brown's raid significant to North Carolinians?

Identify
- Nashville Convention
- Hinton Rowan Helper
- *The Impending Crisis of the South*

The Story Continues

Not all Americans were happy with the Compromise of 1850. Some southerners regarded it as a defeat for slavery and for the South. They organized the **Nashville Convention** to address "southern interests" in the wake of the compromise. North Carolina Democrats were particularly hopeful that North Carolinians would attend the meeting. A newspaper of the day wrote that the convention was "of first importance to the South…and North Carolina ought, by all means, to be represented in it." To the disappointment of conference leaders, however, North Carolina did not send delegates to the meeting. North Carolinians were far too busy with their own concerns—their farms, schools, and businesses.

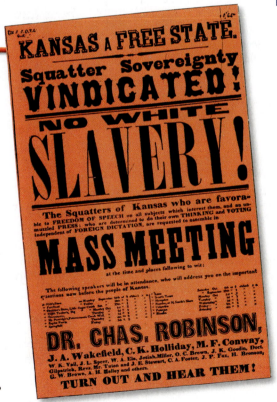

The issue of slavery became increasingly explosive during the 1850s, leading to new and more dangerous sectional clashes between southerners and northerners.

The Kansas-Nebraska Act

In 1854 U.S. Senator Stephen A. Douglas helped pass the Kansas-Nebraska Act. Douglas was a Democrat from Illinois. The new act essentially overturned the Missouri Compromise. It divided the remaining lands of the old Louisiana Purchase into two separate territories. These were known as Kansas and Nebraska. The Kansas-Nebraska Act allowed the settlers of the territories to decide the slavery issue for themselves. In a system known as popular sovereignty, they would vote to either allow or ban slavery in their territory.

The new law caused a crisis in Kansas. Many settlers in the territory came from Missouri, a slaveholding state. These new residents hoped to establish slavery in Kansas as well. Many other southerners, including some North Carolinians, supported this goal. Northern abolitionists, on the other hand, wanted Kansas to be a free territory. Abolitionist leaders urged their followers to move to Kansas and work for "free soil." Before long, pro-slavery and anti-slavery settlers in Kansas became involved in violent, often deadly conflicts. The new territory soon became known as "Bleeding Kansas." North Carolinians, like many in the South, watched the events in Kansas closely. To many North Carolina supporters of slavery, it was a sign that the slave debate was taking a dangerous turn.

✔ **READING CHECK** Identifying Cause and Effect How did the issue of slavery affect North Carolinians?

Interpreting the Visual Record

Bleeding Kansas *The Kansas Territory of the mid-1800s was a scene of growing conflict between well-armed groups of "free soilers" and pro-slavery forces.* **How might the possession of a cannon by this pro-slavery group be considered confrontational?**

Divisions Increase

Conflict over slavery was not limited to Kansas. During the 1850s, social and political tensions between the regions of the United States continued to worsen.

A new party The Kansas-Nebraska Act outraged northerners who opposed the spread of slavery. They viewed the act as a federal surrender to southern slaveholders. In 1854 these people formed the Republican Party. Members included northern Whigs, free-soil supporters, and abolitionists. The Republicans wanted to end the expansion of slavery into the territories. Some also opposed slavery in general and demanded that it be outlawed throughout the United States.

Many Republicans, however, insisted that they did not seek an end to slavery in the South. Their aim was to prevent slavery's expansion

196 Chapter 10

into new territories. Even so, many southerners believed that Republicans wanted to abolish slavery completely. Republican leader Abraham Lincoln later said that the nation could not exist as "a house divided" between slave and free states. As the party gathered more support, white southerners began to fear even more for their political power and way of life.

The *Dred Scott* case

In the late 1850s a Supreme Court decision widened the gap between Republicans and southerners. Dred Scott was a slave who sued for his freedom. Scott had once lived with his slaveholder above the Missouri slaveholding line. He argued that his residence in a free territory entitled him to freedom. The case finally went to the U.S. Supreme Court.

In 1857 the Court ruled against Dred Scott. The Supreme Court declared that African Americans were not citizens at all. As noncitizens, they could not sue others in court. The justices also insisted that Congress could not ban slavery in the territories, because it interfered with the slaveholders' right to control their property—slaves. The Court's decision overturned the Missouri Compromise by allowing slavery in all territories. The *Dred Scott* case inflamed American politics. Southerners applauded the verdict, while Republicans despised it. Even nonabolitionist northerners disliked the decision because it overturned the doctrine of popular sovereignty.

The Supreme Court's decision against Dred Scott (pictured above) in 1857 inflamed abolitionists throughout the North and moved the nation closer to sectional conflict.

The Impending Crisis

A controversial book by a North Carolinian contributed to the uproar over slavery. **Hinton Rowan Helper** was from Davie County. Unlike most southerners, Helper was an abolitionist. He believed that slavery had ruined the South and its white workers by limiting workers' ability to move up economically through a wage-labor system. In 1857 Helper published **The Impending Crisis of the South**. The book called for an immediate end to slavery.

Did You KNOW?

The North Carolina legislature passed a law that punished with imprisonment anyone found guilty of distributing *The Impending Crisis of the South*.

> **History Makers Speak**
>
> " . . . [S]lavery is a shame, a crime, and a curse—a great moral, social, civil, and political evil—an oppressive burden to the blacks, and an incalculable injury to the whites—a stumbling-block to the nation, an impediment [barrier] to progress, a damper on all the nobler instincts, principles, . . . and enterprises of man, and a dire enemy to every true interest."
>
> —Hinton Rowan Helper, *The Impending Crisis of the South*

Many northerners praised Helper's work. *The Impending Crisis* was seen by many as an attack on slavery from within the slaveholders' own ranks. The new Republican Party gave away 100,000 copies of the book. Most southerners, on the other hand, rejected Helper and his book. They accused him of being a traitor to his region and his culture.

✔ **READING CHECK** **Finding the Main Idea** What was Hinton Rowan Helper's main argument against slavery?

The federal arsenal at Harpers Ferry, Virginia, became a sectional battleground in 1859 as a result of John Brown's raid. Brown is pictured in the right center of this interior scene of the deadly fighting.

Analyzing Primary Sources
Summarizing According to the *Mercury*, what was the significance of John Brown's raid?

★ Violence Breaks Out

The conflict over slavery soon moved closer to North Carolina. Neighboring Virginia, like North Carolina, was a slaveholding state. In 1859 the abolitionist John Brown tried to end slavery in Virginia. Brown was a well-known anti-slavery crusader. He had fought alongside other abolitionists in "Bleeding Kansas." Brown and his soldiers attacked the federal arsenal at Harpers Ferry, Virginia. They hoped to steal the firearms stored there, arm slaves throughout the South, and then lead a slave revolt. Brown was quickly captured, tried, and executed.

The nation quickly responded to John Brown's raid. Many northerners supported Brown's effort. Author and abolitionist Ralph Waldo Emerson even called him "that new saint." Most white southerners, on the other hand, condemned Brown and his mission. They saw Brown's attack as a northern plot against slavery and the entire South. The *Charleston Mercury* expressed the views of many people in the South.

 ❝[John Brown's raid] fully establishes the fact that there are at the North men ready to engage in adventures upon the peace and security of the southern people...and capable of planning and keeping secret their infernal [wicked] designs. It is a warning profoundly symptomatic [showing the symptoms] of the future of the Union with our sectional enemies.❞

— An editorial from the *Charleston Mercury*

For many people observing from North Carolina, the violence that started with "Bleeding Kansas" was now coming very close to home.

✔ **READING CHECK** **Identifying Cause and Effect** Why would John Brown's raid have concerned North Carolinians?

Section 3 Review

keyword: SN3 HP10

1 Identify and explain:
- Nashville Convention
- Hinton Rowan Helper
- *The Impending Crisis of the South*

2 Analyzing Information Copy the diagram below. Use it to complete the information about *The Impending Crisis of the South*.

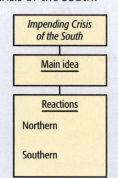

3 Finding the Main Idea
a. How did the Kansas-Nebraska Act affect North Carolina?
b. Why might reaction to John Brown's raid have been strong in North Carolina?

4 Writing and Critical Thinking
Drawing Inferences and Conclusions Imagine that you are a modern-day historian. Write a short report describing the impact of the slave debate on North Carolina during the 1850s.
Consider:
- the effects of "Bleeding Kansas" and John Brown's raid
- effects of *The Impending Crisis of the South*

198 Chapter 10

Section 4

Secession

Read to Discover
1. How did North Carolina vote in the 1860 election?
2. What were North Carolina's reactions to the idea of secession?
3. What were the main causes for North Carolina's secession from the Union?

Define
- secessionists

Identify
- Unionists

The Story Continues

Daniel Worth was a minister who lived in Guilford County, North Carolina. Unlike many white North Carolinians, Worth opposed slavery. He preached his beliefs at the Wesleyan Methodist Church. In 1859 authorities arrested Worth for distributing an abolitionist book. His punishment was harsh: a public whipping and a year in prison. Worth escaped before the sentence could be carried out, but his story came to symbolize the debate over slavery in North Carolina.

★ The Election of 1860

The conflict over slavery reached a boiling point during the presidential election of 1860. Not surprisingly, slavery was a major issue in the campaign. The controversy fractured the Democratic Party, splitting it into Northern and Southern branches. The northern Democrats nominated Stephen Douglas of Illinois for president. The southern Democrats chose John C. Breckinridge of Kentucky as their candidate. The Republican Party nominated Abraham Lincoln. Lincoln opposed the

John C. Breckinridge, a southern Democrat from Kentucky and a powerful spokesperson for states' rights, was a popular political leader throughout North Carolina and the South in 1860.

expansion of slavery and supported internal improvements. A fourth party participated in the election as well. The former Whigs established the Constitutional Union Party. They selected John Bell as their candidate on a platform that supported both slavery and the Union.

The results of the election deepened the nation's regional conflicts. Breckinridge won in North Carolina, but by a small margin. Other southern states also voted for Breckinridge. In the North, however, Lincoln won every state but New Jersey. In the end, he won a majority of the national electoral votes and became president. The split in the Democratic Party, along with Lincoln's platform, swung the election to the Republicans. Lincoln's victory angered and scared most white southerners. They felt certain that the new president planned to ban slavery completely. Some southern states quickly moved toward secession, or withdrawal from the Union.

✔ **READING CHECK** Identifying Cause and Effect What were the results of the presidential election of 1860 in North Carolina?

The Secession Debate in North Carolina

Many people in North Carolina believed firmly in the United States of America. These **Unionists** pointed out that North Carolina was one of the original 13 states. They argued that North Carolina had a responsibility to work for the Union, not against it. Some Unionists believed in a state's right to secede but thought it unwise. On the whole, however, the Unionists in North Carolina were divided and disorganized.

Secessionists supported withdrawal from the Union. These people argued that the new Republican government was planning to abolish slavery in the South. The secessionists believed that a ban on slavery would destroy the regional economy. They also feared for their way of life, one supported by the labor of enslaved African Americans. In addition, most secessionists argued that states had the right to secede from the Union if their sovereignty was endangered by federal actions. Unlike the Unionists, North Carolina's secessionists were well organized.

In December 1860 the South Carolina legislature voted to secede from the United States. Mississippi, Florida, Alabama, Georgia, Louisiana, and Texas all voted to leave the Union as well. In February 1861 these states formed a new nation called the Confederate States of America. They elected Jefferson Davis as their president.

✔ **READING CHECK** Contrasting How did Unionists and secessionists in North Carolina differ?

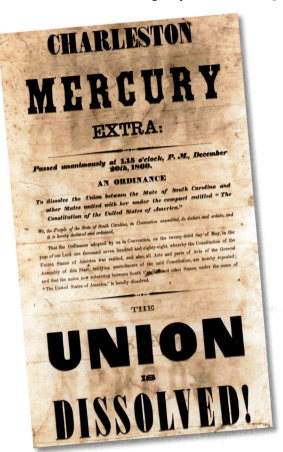

The front page of the Charleston Mercury, December 20, 1860, announced South Carolina's secession from the Union. North Carolina joined the rebellion the following May.

The Vote to Secede

In April 1861 President Lincoln decided to reinforce Fort Sumter, a military base in Charleston Harbor, South Carolina. The Confederacy, on the other hand, considered the fort southern property. On April 12, 1861, Confederate forces attacked Fort Sumter. The fort fell after two days of heavy bombardment. On April 15, President Lincoln called for 75,000 volunteers to put down the Confederate rebellion.

For most North Carolinians, the northern call to arms ended the secession debate. North Carolina would not fight against other southern states. On May 20, 1861, state leaders voted to secede from the Union.

The bombardment of Fort Sumter, April 1861

Analyzing Primary Sources

Critical Thinking According to the primary source, what action made North Carolina a free and independent state?

History Makers Speak

"The ordinance adopted by the State of North Carolina in the convention of 1789, whereby the Constitution of the United States was ratified and adopted . . . [is] hereby repealed . . . We do further declare and ordain, That the union now subsisting [existing] between the State of North Carolina and the other States, under the title of the United States of America, is hereby dissolved . . ."

— The North Carolina Ordinance of Secession

North Carolina was one of 11 southern states that joined to form the Confederacy. The seceding states also included South Carolina, Mississippi, Florida, Alabama, Georgia, Louisiana, Texas, Virginia, Arkansas, and Tennessee. During the next four years, these states battled the North in the course of the bloody struggle known as the American Civil War.

✔ **READING CHECK** **Identifying Points of View** Why did the North Carolina legislature vote to secede from the Union?

Section 4 Review

1. **Define** and explain:
   • secessionists

2. **Identify** and explain:
   • Unionists

3. **Analyzing Information** Copy the web diagram below. Use it to identify effects of the election of 1860 on the North and the South.

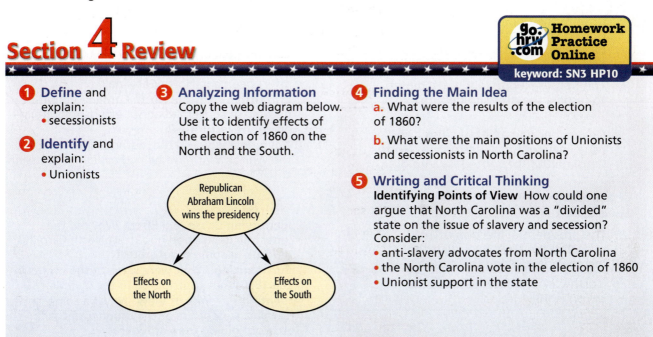

4. **Finding the Main Idea**
   a. What were the results of the election of 1860?
   b. What were the main positions of Unionists and secessionists in North Carolina?

5. **Writing and Critical Thinking**
   Identifying Points of View How could one argue that North Carolina was a "divided" state on the issue of slavery and secession? Consider:
   • anti-slavery advocates from North Carolina
   • the North Carolina vote in the election of 1860
   • Unionist support in the state

Chapter 10 Review

Chapter Summary

Section 1
- The Industrial Revolution of the early and mid-1800s was an era of rapid change that would later affect life in North Carolina.
- Technological advances began to change some ways of life in North Carolina between 1800 and 1861.
- Industrialization in North Carolina led to advances in areas such as transportation.

Section 2
- The early 1800s were years of major exploration and expansion in the new United States.
- North Carolinians were affected by the Missouri Compromise, the Walton War, and the Mexican War.
- The California Gold Rush affected North Carolina by encouraging westward migration.

Section 3
- Despite the Compromise of 1850, the United States was increasingly divided by sectional conflict between 1850 and 1861.
- The Kansas-Nebraska Act attempted to resolve the growing debate over slavery.
- Slavery became a bitterly disputed issue even within states such as North Carolina that permitted slaveholding.

Section 4
- The presidential election of 1860 reflected the strong conflicts that increasingly divided the nation.
- North Carolina seceded from the Union in 1861.

Identifying People and Ideas
1. *Prometheus*
2. Walton War
3. Nathaniel Alexander
4. James K. Polk
5. Nashville Convention
6. Hinton Rowan Helper
7. *The Impending Crisis of the South*
8. Unionists
9. secessionists

Understanding Main Ideas

Section 1 (Pages 187–190)
1. How did the Industrial Revolution affect North Carolina?

Section 2 (Pages 191–194)
2. How did the Louisiana Purchase affect political conditions in the United States and North Carolina?
3. Why did many North Carolinians move to California in the late 1840s?

Section 3 (Pages 195–198)
4. Why did the Republican Party develop?

Section 4 (Pages 199–201)
5. What was the outcome of the presidential election of 1860 in North Carolina?
6. What two groups represented the opposing sides of the secession debate in North Carolina in 1860?

What Did You Find Out?
1. **Constitutional Heritage** How did the difference in values between the North and the South affect people in North Carolina?
2. **Citizenship** Why did North Carolina politicians become so concerned about efforts to ban slavery in the territories?
3. **Government** Could the methods used to end the Walton War have helped avoid the secession crisis?

Thinking Critically
1. **Identifying Cause and Effect** Why did the Industrial Revolution not affect North Carolina as much as some other states?
2. **Summarizing** What were some of the events in the 1850s that contributed to the Civil War?
3. **Identifying Points of View** Why did some North Carolina supporters of the Union eventually support joining the Confederacy?

Building Social Studies Skills

Interpreting Maps

Study the map below, showing the results of the election of 1860 in North Carolina. Then use the information on the map to answer the questions that follow.

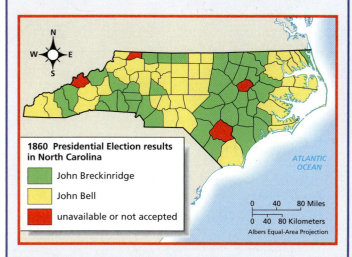

1860 Presidential Election results in North Carolina
- John Breckinridge
- John Bell
- unavailable or not accepted

1. Which statement is most accurate based on the map's information?
   a. Southern Democrat John C. Breckinridge won all but ten of North Carolina's counties.
   b. The Constitutional Union candidate in 1860 was Abraham Lincoln.
   c. John Bell, the Constitutional Union candidate, won most North Carolina counties.
   d. Neither Bell nor Breckinridge won a clear victory in North Carolina.

2. Why might the candidate who won more counties in North Carolina still fail to win the state's electoral votes?

Analyzing Information

John Brown's raid on the arsenal at Harpers Ferry, Virginia, helped to further divide opinion in the United States concerning slavery. This editorial in the November 2, 1859, issue of the Raleigh *Register* describes attitudes in many parts of the South regarding northern responses to Brown's raid. Read the excerpt carefully and answer the questions that follow.

> We are told that the people of the North by a vast majority hold the late invasion of the South [Brown's raid] in unmitigated abhorrence [strong opposition]. We hope they do.... Why have not public meetings in the cities and towns of the North, been held to give expression to [northern opposition toward actions that interfere] with the rights and property of the South?

3. According to this editorial, which of the following statements is most accurate?
   a. John Brown was a popular figure throughout much of the South.
   b. The writer wanted to see more visible northern reaction against Brown's raid.
   c. The writer claimed that few northerners supported Brown's raid.
   d. The writer believed that most northerners felt the slave issue should be decided by the individual states.

4. Why might the writer of the editorial above have used the phrase, "invasion of the South" to describe John Brown's raid on Harpers Ferry?

Alternative Assessment

Building Your Portfolio

Connecting to Science
Imagine that you are an American inventor during the Industrial Revolution of the early to mid-1800s. Develop a design for a labor-saving device that could be used in North Carolina homes, farms, or businesses. Then create an advertisement that will encourage people to buy your device. Describe the ways your invention will improve daily life.

internet connect

Internet Activity: go.hrw.com
keyword: SN3 NC10

Choose a topic on North Carolina and national events to:
- Write a magazine article detailing the impact of the Industrial Revolution on North Carolina.
- Create a poster of the Lewis and Clark expedition.
- Draw a series of maps highlighting the growing conflict over slavery.

CHAPTER 11
The Civil War
(1861–1865)

A lonely Confederate sentry looks across Charleston Harbor to the ruins of Fort Sumter. Warships of the Union naval blockade appear along the horizon.

Build on What You Know

By 1861, the conflict over slavery and states' rights had become open warfare. During the next four years, North Carolinians and other Americans waged a bloody and tragic civil war to decide the issues. In this chapter you will learn how the war affected North Carolina.

What's Your Opinion?

 Do you **agree** or **disagree** with the following statements? Support your point of view in your journal.

- **Citizenship** North Carolinians who fought against the Union were wrong to do so.
- **Government** A draft is usually necessary to fight a war.
- **Economics** An area dependent on trade for goods will face greater economic hardships during war than a self-sufficient area.

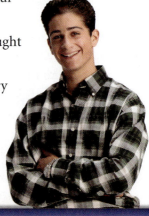

Section 1

The War Begins

Read to Discover
1. What was the first major victory for Confederate troops from North Carolina?
2. How did its coastline affect North Carolina during the war?
3. What did blockade-runners do?

Define
- arsenal
- blockade-runners

Identify
- John W. Ellis
- Daniel Harvey Hill
- Walter Gwynn
- Fort Fisher
- William Lamb
- Benjamin F. Butler
- Ambrose E. Burnside

The Story Continues

In April 1861, South Carolina soldiers attacked federal troops stationed at Fort Sumter in Charleston Harbor. The sudden strike shocked many people in North Carolina, but they were even more surprised by President Lincoln's response. The president called up troops to stop the rebellion. The Civil War had begun. On May 20, 1861, North Carolina left the Union to join the Confederacy.

North Carolina Mobilizes

In many ways, North Carolina was unique among Confederate states. It provided more troops than any other state, but it was also the only Confederate state with an outspoken peace movement. North Carolina troops made up more than one sixth of the entire Confederate force. However, North Carolinians were very divided over the war. Several units were organized to fight for the Union during the war. In all, North Carolina lost more than 40,000 men in the war, either in battle or to disease. This loss was the greatest of any southern state.

Even before secession, North Carolina's governor, **John W. Ellis,** prepared for war by ordering state troops to take over three federal forts. All

President Abraham Lincoln delivered his Gettysburg Address on November 19, 1863. The Address, only ten sentences in length, is considered by many to be one of the great expressions of our democratic ideals.

The Civil War **205**

BIOGRAPHY

Daniel Harvey Hill
(1821–1889)

Daniel Harvey Hill was born in South Carolina, but played a key role in North Carolina's history. After graduating from West Point in 1842, and fighting in the Mexican War, he left the military to teach. He later taught at Davidson College in North Carolina and was serving as superintendent of the North Carolina Military Institute when the Civil War broke out. He quickly volunteered for service to the Confederacy and was assigned as a colonel over the 1st North Carolina Volunteers. He was largely responsible for the success of the North Carolina volunteers at Big Bethel. He rose to the rank of general and played a key role in numerous southern battles. After the war he served as president of two colleges. **In what areas did Daniel Harvey Hill contribute to North Carolina's history?**

---

three surrendered peacefully. The state also took control of the U.S. Mint at Charlotte and the federal <mark>arsenal</mark> at Fayetteville. An arsenal is a place where weapons and ammunition are stored.

Training camps Once the war began, North Carolina's first order of business was to recruit, train, and arm troops. Thirteen training camps were established, including facilities at Raleigh, Southport, and Asheville.

> "We are busily engaged in getting up volunteers all over the state. Gov. Ellis has called for 30,000 volunteers. He can get at least 50,000 if he wants them. I was among the first to volunteer my services in the company at Kinston which will march next week."
>
> — A young North Carolinian writing to his mother, quoted in *The Civil War in North Carolina* by John G. Barrett

North Carolinians fight at Big Bethel In June 1861, the first North Carolina troops saw battle at Big Bethel in Virginia. Although outnumbered by three to one, the troops, led by J. B. Magruder and **Daniel Harvey Hill**, were victorious. The victory aroused great enthusiasm in the South and was taken as proof that Confederate soldiers were the finest in the world. North Carolina's Confederates were proud of their troops.

✓ **READING CHECK** Summarizing How did North Carolina prepare for the Civil War?

⭐ Protecting the Coast

The coast of North Carolina was open to Union attack, so Confederate general **Walter Gwynn** established forts on the Outer Banks. Fort Clark and Fort Hatteras were built at Hatteras Inlet. These forts were armed with 32-pound cannons obtained from the Norfolk Navy Yard. They provided protection while Confederate ships sailed out to harass Union merchant vessels. Construction of **Fort Fisher** in Wilmington Harbor began in 1861. It consisted of a huge L-shaped earthwork near the mouth of the Cape Fear River. Commanded by Colonel **William Lamb**, it protected shipping and helped make Wilmington the last Confederate port to remain open.

Butler's attack The Union Navy knew the importance of capturing these forts. In August 1861, Union general **Benjamin F. Butler** brought in troops with that goal in mind. The Union forces were successful in taking Fort Clark but could not capture Fort Hatteras. So Butler had his ships bombard the fort. As a result of the bombardment, part of the fort caught on fire. The defenders quickly surrendered and the Union had a foothold on the Outer Banks. This gave them a great advantage in the war.

McClellan's plan Butler's success inspired Union army commander George B. McClellan to continue the action in North Carolina. He planned to attack and take control of Roanoke Island and New Bern. The Wilmington and Weldon Railroad would be destroyed. This railroad was the main line connecting the Confederate capital of Richmond, Virginia, with the South. McClellan reasoned that if Union troops could cut the railroad lines there, then they could stop supplies from reaching General Lee's Virginia-based army.

Burnside's attacks In the fall of 1861, McClellan began plans to assign General <u>Ambrose E. Burnside</u> an army of 12,000 to 15,000 troops and a number of ships with which to seize Roanoke Island and New Bern. In February 1862 Burnside made quick work of the nearly 1,500 Confederate troops that opposed him, and also sank some Confederate gunboats.

Burnside's victory cleared the way to move against the North Carolina mainland. Union troops made the most of it by occupying Elizabeth City, and burning and sacking Columbia and Winton.

Burnside captures the coast Albemarle Sound was under Union control now, allowing Burnside to attack New Bern the next month. The Confederates were no match for the Union troops, but they managed to set fire to the town before retreating. Burnside then headed south, down the Atlantic coast, taking Beaufort and Morehead City. By April, Burnside's forces controlled the coast of North Carolina from Morehead City to the Virginia border.

✔ **READING CHECK** **Summarizing** What was the Union's strategy in attacking the North Carolina coast?

The Union victory in the Battle of New Bern enabled the federal army to win control of coastal North Carolina.

⭐ Blockade-Runners

The Union naval blockade also affected North Carolina, which relied heavily on foreign trade for manufactured goods. The blockade prevented foreign ships from entering southern ports. European manufacturers tried to avoid the blockade by shipping goods to the West Indies, where Confederate ships picked them up. In exchange, Confederate ships carried cotton, and sold it to the Europeans.

It was a profitable system, but an inconvenient one. Confederate captains soon found ways around the Union blockade. Known as **blockade-runners,** these ships set out in the dead of night to slip past the Union ships. The vessels were painted gray to help them avoid discovery. By sailing close to the coast, the ships were hard to see. When approaching Union ships, they put on speed, and usually managed to avoid capture.

Blockade-running was successful. In 1864, the Confederacy began requiring blockade-runners to rent one half of their cargo space to the government. The intent was to help provide the Confederacy with supplies. North Carolina officials criticized these regulations, because they made blockade-running too expensive.

The Union made use of ironclad warships, such as the Monitor, shown on the right engaging the Confederate ironclad Merrimac, to strengthen its blockade of Confederate ports along the Atlantic coast and the Gulf of Mexico.

✓ **READING CHECK** Making Predictions
How might North Carolina's textile mills have helped the state during the blockade?

Section 1 Review

go.hrw.com Homework Practice Online
keyword: SN3 HP11

1 **Define** and explain:
- arsenal
- blockade-runners

2 **Identify** and explain:
- John W. Ellis
- Daniel Harvey Hill
- Walter Gwynn
- Fort Fisher
- William Lamb
- Benjamin F. Butler
- Ambrose E. Burnside

3 **Sequencing** Copy the graphic organizer below. Use it to outline the major events that took place in the coastal war from the building of Fort Fisher to the taking of Beaufort and Morehead City.

Fort Fisher is built
Burnside takes Beaufort and Morehead City

4 **Finding the Main Idea**
a. How did North Carolinians contribute to the Confederate cause? the Union cause?
b. How did the Union blockade affect North Carolina?

5 **Writing and Critical Thinking**
Supporting a Point of View Imagine that you are a young man from North Carolina at the outbreak of the Civil War. Write a letter to a northern friend defending your decision to fight for the Confederacy or the Union.
Consider:
- secessionist beliefs and values
- Unionist beliefs and values
- possible consequences of fighting in a war

Section 2

Fighting in North Carolina

Read to Discover
1. How did Union forces take over eastern North Carolina?
2. Why did deserters and draft resisters hide in the mountains?
3. What role did black North Carolinians play in fighting the war?

Define
- cavalry
- deserter
- draft resister

Identify
- James Longstreet
- *Albemarle*
- Robert F. Hoke
- Camp Vance
- Frank Roberts

The Story Continues

North Carolina supported the war effort in many ways. Factories made Confederate uniforms, shoes, and rifles. Foundries formed scrap iron into cannons. In 1862, the state bought four steamships. Privately owned ships joined them in running the Union blockade to bring in medicines, farm tools, and military supplies. Still, as the war progressed farther onto North Carolina soil, life became more dangerous and difficult for both soldiers and civilians.

Fast and powerful steamships, such as the Confederate steamer Nashville *(shown here running the Union blockade at Beaufort, North Carolina), were sometimes able to outrun or outgun their federal opponents.*

★ The War in Eastern North Carolina

After a large force of Union troops took Roanoke in February 1862, the island became a stronghold from which they could attack the rest of eastern North Carolina. Union troops then raided eastern towns and cities causing great destruction. Railroad tracks, bridges, mills, houses, and barns were destroyed. Confederate forces lost control of the region.

The Civil War **209**

Confederate general
James Longstreet

Longstreet's offensive Almost a year passed before the Confederacy made a serious effort to retake eastern North Carolina. General **James Longstreet** assigned General Daniel Harvey Hill to distract Union forces stationed at New Bern while Longstreet attacked Suffolk, Virginia. At New Bern, Hill tried a four-part attack, but two of his commanders failed to capture their objectives. Hill was forced to withdraw. He also tried surrounding Union troops at Washington, North Carolina, but Union ships filled with reinforcements managed to get through. He had to withdraw once again. By early 1864, Confederate general Robert E. Lee was warning that New Bern had to be retaken soon.

Analyzing Primary Sources
Drawing Inferences and Conclusions What was Lee indicating about the timing of an attempt to retake New Bern?

 "The time is at hand when, if an attempt can be made to capture the enemy's forces at New Bern, it should be done. I can now spare the troops for the purpose, which will not be the case as spring approaches."

Robert E. Lee, quoted in *The Civil War in North Carolina* by John G. Barrett

Pickett's attack on New Bern Confederate general George Pickett used 13,000 men in an attempt to regain New Bern once more in February 1864. First, he sent sailors and marines down the Neuse River in small boats to destroy Union ships. They managed to set fire to one ship, but the Union positions north and south of New Bern drove them back. Pickett had to abandon the attack. Meanwhile, General James G. Martin was more successful. He attacked Newport Barracks at Beaufort

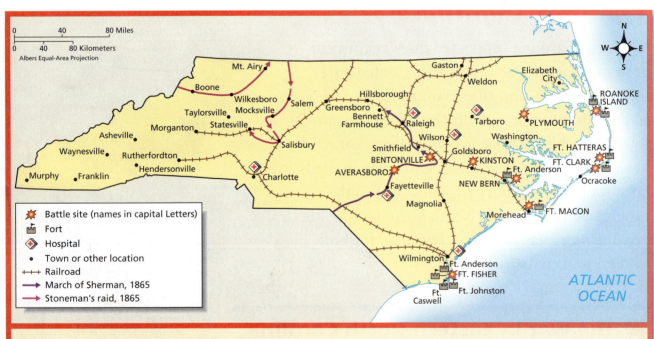

The Civil War in North Carolina
Interpreting Maps North Carolina was the scene of several major battles during the Civil War, as Union forces sought to win control of the state's transportation and shipping hubs.

Skills Assessment **Human Systems** Why was so much of the fighting in North Carolina located along the state's eastern coastal region?

to prevent Union reinforcements from reaching New Bern. He kept the Union troops pinned down and captured many needed supplies.

Plymouth Next, Confederate forces focused on the town of Plymouth along the Roanoke River. Plymouth was an important access point to Albemarle Sound and was heavily fortified with Union troops. In the early months of 1863, the Confederate navy started construction of an ironclad battering ram named the *Albemarle* near Plymouth. The ram was designed to destroy other ships by ramming holes in their sides. According to the plan, the *Albemarle* would head downriver and destroy the Union ships holding Plymouth. At the same time, army forces would attack the Union troops on land. In April 1864, the *Albemarle* set out on its mission.

Confederate general **Robert F. Hoke** had surrounded Plymouth and taken one of its Union forts. He needed the *Albemarle* to sink two Union ships that were defending the town. When the *Albemarle* arrived, it almost fell into a trap. The two Union ships were facing upriver with huge chains stretched between them blocking the way. They intended to snag the *Albemarle* between them like a fish in a net and use their guns to sink it. The *Albemarle*'s commander, James W. Cooke of Beaufort, avoided the trap. He sank one ship with a head-on collision and chased the other one downstream. This allowed General Hoke to capture the Union troops defending Plymouth. With Plymouth again under Confederate control, Union forces in Washington, North Carolina, fled to avoid a similar fate.

Hoke's attack on New Bern With these victories behind them, Confederate leaders hoped to drive Union forces completely out of the state by retaking New Bern. General Hoke decided to use the *Albemarle* in a combined land and water attack. When Commander Cooke approached New Bern in May 1864, he found seven Union ships lying in wait. The Union ships opened fire, but their cannonballs merely bounced off the *Albemarle*'s two-inch-thick iron shield. Then a Union ship rammed the *Albemarle*, causing severe damage. Commander Cooke was forced to retreat. General Hoke intended to carry out the land attack even without the *Albemarle*'s support. Then he received orders to join General Lee, who was under attack in Virginia. In October, a Union raiding party managed to sink the *Albemarle* while it was anchored at Plymouth. After that, Union troops continued to occupy eastern North Carolina, and the Confederacy turned its attention to defending the mountains in the west.

✓ **READING CHECK** Summarizing
What role did the *Albemarle* play in the Battle of New Bern?

CONNECTING TO SCIENCE AND TECHNOLOGY

The Gatling Gun

One of the most important new weapons of the Civil War was the Gatling gun. It was invented by Richard Jordan Gatling, a native of Hertford County.

Introduced in 1862, Gatling's crank-operated, multibarreled gun could fire up to about 400 shots per minute, an incredible rate of fire at the time. Although it saw only limited use during the war, the Gatling gun's destructive power made it a much-feared weapon.

Gatling developed the gun to decrease casualties during battle. He reasoned that greater firepower would reduce the number of soldiers needed and the number of deaths. He also believed that his gun's destructive power would discourage warfare. By the late 1800s, the Gatling gun was being used by armies all over the world. **Was Gatling correct in assuming that more powerful weapons would decrease casualties?**

The War in Western North Carolina

As the war raged along the coast, the western mountains remained peaceful until 1863. That year, Union forces took up positions across the border at Chattanooga and Knoxville in eastern Tennessee. The Confederacy worried that these troops might make their way across the mountains to cut railroad lines in North Carolina. Troops were then positioned to block key mountain gaps. Included among this mountain force were Cherokee fighters under the command of Colonel William Holland Thomas.

At the same time, General James Longstreet tried to drive the Union forces back with an attack at Knoxville. He asked for reinforcements from North Carolina, and General Robert B. Vance hurried to join the fray. However, Vance and his troops were captured near Newport, leaving western North Carolina almost completely exposed. Union troops took advantage of the situation by staging a series of raids in the mountains. **Cavalry**—troops mounted on horseback—successfully raided Cherokee County and Quallatown early in 1864. Soon after, Union colonel George W. Kirk led infantry through the Linville and Toe river valleys and captured an important Confederate training camp near Morganton named **Camp Vance**. Then Kirk and his forces set fire to the Morganton railroad facilities and fled back to Tennessee, taking many prisoners.

The destruction of railroads was a special priority for Union troops as they moved through the Deep South.

✔ **READING CHECK** Making Generalizations and Predictions Why did Confederate leaders in North Carolina fear attacks from Tennessee?

Unionist Support in the Mountains

One reason Confederate troops feared a Union attack through the mountains was the strong Union support in that area, which housed few slaveholders. Many of North Carolina's mountain dwellers remained faithful to the Union during the war. This, along with the rough terrain, made the region a safe haven for Union soldiers, as well as army deserters and draft resisters. A **deserter** is a soldier who leaves military service without permission. A **draft resister** is one who refuses to be forced to serve in the army. Union supporters in western North Carolina hid these people and helped escaping Union prisoners find their way to Union lines in Tennessee. At times, deserters and draft resisters banded together to harass Confederate forces. Complete control of the western mountains remained beyond the Confederacy's grasp.

✔ **READING CHECK** Identifying Cause and Effect Why was Unionist support in the mountains a problem for the Confederacy?

By about 1864, African Americans composed several effective fighting units in the Union army.

African American Soldiers Fight for the Union

Another group of North Carolinians who supported the Union were African Americans, both free and slave. The Union army began hiring African American laborers in July 1862. Soon after, some African American Union regiments were formed. As Union troops gained victories in the South, they helped organize local African Americans who wanted to fight against the Confederacy. In all, five African American regiments were formed for the Union army in North Carolina. About 1,000 more black North Carolinians served as Union sailors during the war. White officers led these units, but some black North Carolinians, like Sergeant **Frank Roberts** of Elizabeth City, became noncommissioned officers. As in other areas of the South, the presence of African American soldiers among the Union troops changed the tone of the war. Black North Carolinians were now fighting to end slavery for all African Americans.

✔ **READING CHECK** **Identifying Points of View** Why might some African Americans in North Carolina have volunteered to fight for the Union?

Section 2 Review

keyword: SN3 HP11

1. **Define** and explain:
   - cavalry
   - deserter
   - draft resister

2. **Identify** and explain:
   - James Longstreet
   - *Albemarle*
   - Robert F. Hoke
   - Camp Vance
   - Frank Roberts

3. **Summarize** Copy the graphic organizer below. Use it to list the Civil War events in this section and their outcomes.

Battle	Result
Longstreet's offensive	
Pickett's attack on New Bern	
Plymouth	
Hoke's attack on New Bern	
Raid on Cherokee County and Quallatown	

4. **Finding the Main Idea**
   a. Why were Union troops in Tennessee a threat to North Carolina?
   b. Why did draft resisters and deserters hide in the mountains?

5. **Writing and Critical Thinking**
   Supporting a Point of View Imagine that you are a free black man in North Carolina. Explain why you want to join the Union forces.
   Consider:
   - the situation of African Americans in North Carolina
   - the focus of the war by 1863

The Civil War 213

Section 3

The Home Front

Read to Discover
1. Why was the election of 1862 significant in North Carolina?
2. How did conflicts with the Confederate government influence North Carolina during the war?
3. What role did North Carolina women play in the war?
4. How did the peace movement affect North Carolina?

Define
- conscripts

Identify
- William Johnston
- Conservative Party
- Zebulon B. Vance
- Conscription Act
- Sarah Pritchard Blalock
- Rose O'Neal Greenhow

William Johnston was North Carolina's Democratic candidate for governor in the election of 1862.

The Story Continues

By the election of 1862 the secessionists, who controlled the state government, found themselves in trouble. Many North Carolinians blamed them and the Confederate government for the Union conquest of eastern North Carolina. People particularly blamed Governor John W. Ellis for the wartime problems facing the state.

★ The Election of 1862

Throughout the 1850s, William W. Holden, editor of the *North Carolina Standard*, had helped lead the state's Democratic Party to victory. In 1860, the party split over the issue of secession. Governor Ellis proposed that North Carolina join the secession movement. Holden remained steadfast to the Union. The Democratic candidate for governor in 1862 was a secessionist named **William Johnston**. Holden wanted a Unionist candidate for the new **Conservative Party**. Conservatives nominated a young man named **Zebulon B. Vance**.

Each candidate relied on popular newspapers to express and support their views. The *Raleigh Register* backed Vance while the *Raleigh State Journal* rallied behind Johnston. In a surprising outcome, Vance

214   Chapter 11

was elected by more than a two-to-one margin. Conservative candidates also won a majority of the seats in the state legislature.

This election reflected the lack of strong support for the Confederacy in many parts of the state. North Carolina became the only Confederate state in which Unionists led the state government.

✔ **READING CHECK** **Drawing Inferences and Conclusions** Why did William W. Holden break with the Democratic Party?

★ Conflicts with the Confederacy

Although a tough critic of Confederate president Jefferson Davis, Governor Vance always encouraged the state to give support and loyalty to the Confederacy. Davis, on the other hand, felt that Vance was a rebellious governor. They disagreed on several issues including conscription, taxes, appointment of Unionists to government office, and promotion of North Carolina officers.

Compromise over the Conscription Act The **Conscription Act** of 1862 called for men between the ages of 18 and 35 to be drafted into the Confederate army. It also permitted the wealthy wanting to avoid the draft to hire substitutes. Many people in the Conservative Party considered the Conscription Act to be unconstitutional. Many North Carolina **conscripts**—those forced to join the army—refused to report for duty. Despite his opposition to the law, Vance arranged for state militia officers to round up the conscripts.

The Conscription Act allowed exemptions to planters. The Davis administration, moreover, had promised to allow conscripts to choose the regiments they would join, but that policy was changed. Despite these difficulties, North Carolina supplied more conscripts than any other state.

Governor Vance also objected to Confederate policies concerning the appointment of officers. Few North Carolinians were appointed as officers in the Confederacy. The state's tradition of strong Unionist sentiment was probably a factor. In addition, the Confederate War Department appointed officers from other states to command North Carolina's regiments. Governor Vance expressed outrage at this policy.

Abuse of Confederate military power An 1863 incident involving the rights of prisoners stirred up controversy in North Carolina. A group of Unionist civilians in Madison County raided Marshall, taking salt and other supplies. They fled to the mountains near the Tennessee line. Confederate lieutenant colonel James A. Keith

Interpreting the Visual Record

Confederate flag *This battle-scarred Confederate flag belonged to the 26th North Carolina Infantry Regiment.* **What does this flag reflect about the fighting during the Civil War?**

captured 13 boys and old men, declared them guilty, and had them executed. By law these mountaineers should have been tried in a civilian court. An investigation into the incident was launched, leading to Keith's resignation from his position.

✓ **READING CHECK** **Summarizing** What issues caused conflict between Vance and Davis?

★ Women and the War

During the war, everyday life grew very hard. There were food shortages. Meat became a luxury, because salt used to preserve it was scarce. The army took all the cloth from the textile mills, leaving none for civilian clothing. Medicines also became scarce for civilians. Things were at their worst for women whose husbands, sons, and fathers had gone off to war. They were left behind to tend the children and keep the farms producing. Many of them worked hard in the fields to raise food. Those with slaves relied more than ever on their slave laborers.

City women fared a bit better. Many of them worked as nurses or sewed uniforms for troops. Some women voluntarily knitted socks and caps for soldiers. A charitable organization in Wilmington was formed, called the Ladies' Soldiers' Aid Society, to help soldiers traveling through town.

Prices rose as goods became scarce. A barrel of flour costing $18 in 1862 cost $500 in 1865. In the same period, salt rose to $70 a bushel, and one pound of coffee sold for $100. High food prices and scarcity drove some women to violence. On March 18, 1863, a group of women marched on shopkeepers in Salisbury, North Carolina, demanding to be able to buy flour and salt at half the price the merchants wanted. When the storeowners refused, the women broke down the doors of one store with hatchets and took supplies of flour, salt, molasses, and some cash. Many of the women were wives of soldiers fighting in the war.

A few women actually helped fight the war. Unionist **Sarah Pritchard Blalock** disguised herself as a man and joined Confederate troops with her husband in March 1862. The Blalocks intended to desert and join Union forces as soon as they got the chance. They eventually joined a group of deserters in the mountains and carried out guerrilla raids on Confederate troops. Mrs. Blalock was wounded in the shoulder during one fight. She is the only known female soldier from North Carolina.

Other women aided their cause by serving as spies. One of the most famous female spies for the Confederacy was **Rose O'Neal Greenhow**. In 1862 Confederate president Jefferson Davis assigned her to Europe, where she gathered information from diplomatic sources. In the fall of 1864 she headed back home with important information and a supply of gold. She was aboard the Confederate blockade-runner *Condor* when

BIOGRAPHY

Rose O'Neal Greenhow
(1817–1864)

Rose O'Neal Greenhow was born in Port Tobbaco, Maryland. A wealthy socialite, she had many important friends in the nation's capital. When war broke out she quickly organized a spy ring to get messages to Confederate leaders. Jefferson Davis credited her with the southern victory at the First Battle of Bull Run because of the secret messages she was able to get to the Confederate general in charge.

Greenhow was arrested twice for her activities. Even while jailed, though, she continued to gather and send out secret messages. She used such creative methods as hiding notes in the bun of a woman's hair. After the Union exiled her to the Confederacy, Davis sent her to Europe. While there, she wrote a best-selling memoir that described her Confederate views. **How did Rose O'Neal Greenhow help the Confederacy?**

a Union ship ran it aground on a sandbar near Wilmington, North Carolina. Greenhow was allowed to escape in a lifeboat, but the small craft capsized and she drowned. She was buried with honors at Wilmington. Her tombstone at Oakdale Cemetery reads, "Mrs. Rose O'N. Greenhow, a bearer of dispatchs to the Confederate Government."

✔ **READING CHECK** **Finding the Main Idea** How did North Carolina women react to scarcity during the war?

★ The Peace Movement

Depressed by Union victories and eager to bring the war to an end, by 1863 many Confederate North Carolinians wanted peace. A growing peace movement proved to be the driving force of the 1864 state election. William W. Holden led the peace movement using his newspaper as a platform. He criticized the Confederacy and its leadership. Holden echoed the cry that the war was "a rich man's war and a poor man's fight." He insisted on peace talks to end the war.

Holden's opinions reflected political divisions within the state. President Davis strongly suggested to Vance that Holden be charged with treason. Vance refused. He believed in freedom of the press. However, he did issue a statement discouraging peace meetings and pleading with North Carolinians to obey Confederate laws.

The 1864 campaign for governor was a race between Vance and Holden. Vance argued that the way to peace was to support the Confederacy and win the war. Vance was elected by a large majority, and North Carolina remained faithful to the Confederacy through the war.

✔ **READING CHECK** **Identifying Cause and Effect** Why did Confederate president Davis want to charge William W. Holden with treason?

Many American women played active and important roles in the war effort, including serving in hospitals.

Section 3 Review

keyword: SN3 HP11

1. **Define** and explain:
   • conscripts

2. **Identify** and explain:
   • William Johnston
   • Conservative Party
   • Zebulon B. Vance
   • Conscription Act
   • Sarah Pritchard Blalock
   • Rose O'Neal Greenhow

3. **Summarize** Copy the Venn diagram below. Fill in the circles with information about Zebulon Vance and William Holden.

   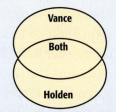

4. **Finding the Main Idea**
   a. Summarize the events that caused conflict between Governor Vance and President Davis.
   b. How did high prices affect life in wartime North Carolina?

5. **Writing and Critical Thinking**
   Identifying Points of View Imagine you are either Sarah Pritchard Blalock or Rose O'Neal Greenhow. Write a letter explaining why you are risking your life for your cause.
   Consider:
   • the roles most women played during the war
   • what happened to Blalock and Greenhow

The Civil War

Section 4

The End of the War

Read to Discover
1. Why was Fort Fisher important to the Confederacy?
2. What were General Sherman's objectives in North Carolina?
3. What were the effects of the war on North Carolina?

Identify
- Braxton Bragg
- Joseph E. Johnston
- Battle of Bentonville
- Wade Hampton
- George H. Stoneman

This lithograph shows a stylized view of the capture of Fort Fisher in January 1865. A month later, the Confederacy's last major port of Wilmington fell to Union forces.

The Story Continues

The end of the war drew near as Union forces tightened their grip on North Carolina. A large Union force was preparing to attack Wilmington and shut down the last important blockade-running port in the Confederacy. Several miles downriver lay Fort Fisher, which was the key to Wilmington's defense.

★ Fort Fisher

Fort Fisher, with its 48 big guns guarding the entrance to the Cape Fear River, was the only remaining obstacle to Union domination of North Carolina. Its walls of sand were two stories high and 25 feet thick. They stretched more than half a mile across the peninsula.

On Christmas Eve 1864, Union general Benjamin F. Butler blew up an old ship loaded with gunpowder only 200 yards from the fort, but it did little damage. Union admiral David D. Porter drew his nearly 60 ships up to the fort. They fired their 600 guns until it was said that their ammunition "fell like rain." The shells exploded harmlessly into the soft sand walls. Butler attacked with several thousand men on Christmas Day. He withdrew his troops due to bad weather and approaching darkness.

218   Chapter 11

Union forces attacked the fort again in January 1865, just three months before the end of the war. Union ships bombarded the fort for three days. Then General Alfred H. Terry charged in with 8,000 men. Within two and one-half miles north were 6,000 Confederate soldiers, under the command of General **Braxton Bragg**, trying to join the battle. Two brigades of African American Union troops held them back. Inside the fort, 1,500 Confederate troops fought the Union troops for six hours before finally surrendering. Then Wilmington fell in February.

 READING CHECK Drawing Inferences and Conclusions Why was Fort Fisher so hard to destroy?

⭐ Sherman's Invasion

Union general William T. Sherman was headed north from Savannah, Georgia, with an army of 60,000 men. His two main objectives were to cause as much destruction as possible and to unite with General Grant's army in Virginia. While moving through North Carolina, Sherman intended to occupy towns and overtake the rear of Lee's army.

Sherman entered North Carolina in early March. He knew that there was strong Unionist sentiment in the state, and he ordered his men to stop their raids on private property. Unfortunately, his troops entered North Carolina's pine forests, and they saw where bark had been stripped from trees to collect rosin and make turpentine. Touched with a flame, the rosin flared up. Union soldiers ran through the woods setting the forest on fire. Many acres of longleaf pine trees were destroyed.

Sherman's troops took Monroe, Wadesboro, Rockingham, and Fayetteville. They picked up supplies and set out for Goldsboro. Sherman left orders to destroy public property that the troops could not take with them.

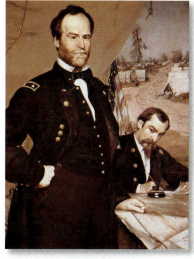

Union general William T. Sherman was one of the first military leaders to practice the concept of "total war."

 "Destroy . . . all arsenals and public property not needed for our own use, as well as all railroads, depots, and machinery . . . spare all dwellings, colleges, schools, asylums, and harmless private property."

— William T. Sherman, quoted in *Report of General William T. Sherman on the Campaign of the Carolinas*

Analyzing Primary Sources
Drawing Inferences and Conclusions Why would Sherman order the destruction of most public, but not private, property?

Lee's counterattack in North Carolina Sherman was taken by surprise when, on a Sunday morning in March 1865, he met up with Confederate troops under the command of General **Joseph E. Johnston**. The Confederates confronted an advance party of Sherman's troops and drove them back. The **Battle of Bentonville** had begun. It would be North Carolina's bloodiest battle of the war.

The Battle of Bentonville occurred because Confederate General Lee had hoped to gather an army in North Carolina to stop Sherman. He had ordered General Johnston to organize and lead these troops.

The Civil War

That's Interesting!

Gunpowder Gunpowder was the first real explosive. It is believed to have originated in China, where explosive grenades and bombs were used as early as A.D. 1000. The Arabs and the English had learned of it by the 1200s. By the early 1300s, gunpowder and guns were being manufactured in Europe.

General Johnston had sent most of his men to Smithfield and placed General **Wade Hampton**'s cavalry ahead of Sherman's troops to report on their movements.

In mid-March, Hampton attacked Sherman's left wing near Averasboro on the Cape Fear River. In the skirmish, Sherman lost about 700 troops. More importantly, the battle delayed the advance of the left wing. With Sherman's forces thus separated, Hampton advised Johnston to attack Sherman's left wing at Bentonville. Johnston's men surprised Sherman's left wing on March 19. Vastly outnumbered, the Confederates retreated when the rest of Sherman's army appeared.

✔ **READING CHECK** Sequencing What was the sequence of events that led to Sherman's victory in the Battle of Bentonville?

Stoneman's Raid and Johnston's Surrender

Next came Union general **George H. Stoneman** and his 7,000 men. His orders were to tear up the railroad tracks west of Lynchburg, Virginia, to prevent General Lee from escaping into the mountains. He also intended to destroy the railroads south of Danville and to free Union prisoners believed to be held in a Salisbury prison. Stoneman met his objectives. His men destroyed sixty miles of railroad as they moved through Boone, Wilkesboro, and Mount Airy, southwest of Lynchburg. Turning south, they cut the railroad near Greensboro and smashed a cotton mill at Salem. They set fire to a Confederate storehouse in Salisbury, but the military prison they had hoped to liberate was already empty. They moved on to sever railroad lines surrounding Charlotte. By the end of April, they occupied several towns, including Asheville, Greensboro, and Morganton.

General Johnston knew that further resistance was useless. General Lee had already surrendered at Appomattox Courthouse, Virginia, on April 9. Grant's army was heading south. Sherman was moving on Raleigh with a force of 80,000 men. The railroads to the west were ruined, and the supply base at Salisbury was destroyed. On April 13, Johnston called for a truce. He and Sherman met at a farmhouse near Durham, and on April 26, Johnston surrendered. Except for a small skirmish near Waynesville the following month, the Civil War was over.

Interpreting the Visual Record

End of the fighting
Confederate general Joseph E. Johnston surrendered the last major Confederate force to Union general William T. Sherman on April 26, 1865, near Durham, North Carolina. The long and terrible American Civil War was over at last. **What does this image suggest about the feelings and attitudes of both sides at the end of the war?**

✔ **READING CHECK** Identifying Points of View Why did General Johnston surrender?

The Effects of the War on North Carolina

The state took heavy losses, with nearly 20,000 men falling in battle and almost 21,000 perishing from disease. North Carolina's total loss exceeded that of any other southern state. The survivors took pride in being "First at Bethel, farthest at Gettysburg, . . . and last at Appomattox." At the war's end, the people of North Carolina found themselves in dire straits. With necessities lacking, hunger was never far away. With little cloth available for new clothing, they wore the clothes they had until they hung in tatters. Agriculture had suffered since broken tools could not be replaced, and many of the men who worked the farms had been killed or wounded in battle. Rail fences, barns, and other structures had fallen to ruin. Bridges, buildings, and public works had been destroyed. Railroad tracks had been torn up. Worst of all was the death of thousands of young men. There was barely a family in the state that did not feel the loss of one or more loved ones.

✔ **READING CHECK** Identifying Cause and Effect How did the war cause a decline in agriculture in North Carolina?

This lone cannon standing before a restored Civil War–era cabin in the Chickamauga and Chattanooga National Military Park is a reminder of the loss and suffering experienced throughout the war-torn nation.

Section 4 Review

1. **Identify** and explain:
   - Braxton Bragg
   - Joseph E. Johnston
   - Battle of Bentonville
   - Wade Hampton
   - George H. Stoneman

2. **Summarize** Copy the graphic organizer below. Fill in the circles with information describing the effects of the war on North Carolina.

3. **Finding the Main Idea**
   a. What was the strategic importance of Fort Fisher?
   b. Summarize the sequence of events that led up to General Johnston's surrender.

4. **Writing and Critical Thinking**
   Identifying Points of View Imagine you are a defeated Confederate soldier. Write a plan of action telling what you will do to return your life to normal.
   Consider:
   - emotional consequences of war
   - changes to home life caused by the war

keyword: SN3 HP11

Chapter 11 Review

Chapter Summary

Section 1
- North Carolina seceded from the Union and joined the Confederacy.
- A significant number of Confederate troops were from North Carolina.
- North Carolina troops first fought at Big Bethel in Virginia.

Section 2
- The Union army gained control of eastern North Carolina.
- Ironclad ships became important during the war.
- The Confederacy lost control of western North Carolina to the Union.
- Many African Americans from North Carolina fought for the Union.

Section 3
- With the election of 1862, North Carolina became the only Confederate state with a Unionist-led government.
- Governor Vance and President Davis experienced many political conflicts.
- The war caused hardships for women.
- A peace movement began in North Carolina by 1863.

Section 4
- Fort Fisher was an important strategic stronghold for North Carolina.
- As Sherman invaded North Carolina, the Confederacy began to fall.
- Confederate general Johnston surrendered to Union general Sherman near Durham, North Carolina.
- The effects of the war were devastating in North Carolina.

Identifying People and Ideas
Use the following terms or people in complete sentences.

1. arsenal
2. blockade-runners
3. Daniel Harvey Hill
4. Fort Fisher
5. Zebulon B. Vance
6. Sarah Pritchard Blalock
7. Rose O'Neal Greenhow
8. *Albemarle*
9. Joseph E. Johnston
10. Battle of Bentonville

Understanding Main Ideas

Section 1 (Pages 205–208)
1. How did North Carolinians help the Confederacy? the Union?
2. What role did North Carolina's blockade-runners play in the Civil War?

Section 2 (Pages 209–213)
3. What important battles were fought in eastern North Carolina?
4. What role did African American soldiers in North Carolina play in the war?

Section 3 (Pages 214–217)
5. What was the significance of the 1862 governor's election?
6. How did North Carolina women react to the hardships of war?

Section 4 (Pages 218–221)
7. What events led up to General Johnston's surrender?
8. How did the results of the war affect North Carolina?

What Did You Find Out?
1. **Citizenship** Why did North Carolinians choose to fight for the South? for the North?
2. **Government** Why did Conservatives oppose the Conscription Act?
3. **Economics** How did North Carolina's prewar economy affect the state during the war?

Thinking Critically
1. **Making Comparisons** In what ways were Sarah Pritchard Blalock and Rose O'Neal Greenhow similar to and different from one another?
2. **Identifying Cause and Effect** How did the presence of African American soldiers change the war in North Carolina?
3. **Supporting a Point of View** Was William W. Holden right in calling the war "a rich man's war and a poor man's fight"? Why or why not?

Building Social Studies Skills

Interpreting Graphs

Study the graph below on North Carolina casualties in the Civil War. Use the information in the graph to answer the questions that follow.

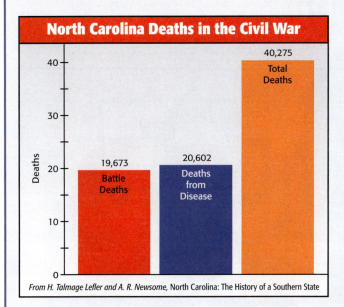

North Carolina Deaths in the Civil War
- Battle Deaths: 19,673
- Deaths from Disease: 20,602
- Total Deaths: 40,275

From H. Talmage Lefler and A. R. Newsome, *North Carolina: The History of a Southern State*

1. For North Carolina soldiers in the Civil War, what were the chances of dying in battle compared with dying from disease?
   a. There was a better chance of dying in battle.
   b. There was a better chance of dying from disease.
   c. The chances of dying in battle or dying from disease were about the same.

2. Based on what you know about medicine at the time of the Civil War, what do you think accounts for the numerous nonbattle deaths?

Analyzing Primary Sources

Read this excerpt from the *Report of General William T. Sherman on the Campaign in the Carolinas.* Then answer the questions that follow.

> "In anticipation of the occupation of the city, I had made written orders to General Howard [a Union commander and one of Sherman's subordinates] touching the conduct of the troops. These were to destroy, absolutely, all arsenals [places where weapons were manufactured and stored] and public property not needed for our own use, as well as all railroads, depots, and machinery useful in war to an enemy, but to spare all dwellings, colleges, schools, asylums, and harmless private property."

3. Which of the statements below best describes the intent of General Sherman's orders?
   a. Sherman probably wanted to destroy everything in the path of his invading army.
   b. Sherman wanted to ensure that his soldiers did not cause damage to any property—public or private.
   c. Sherman probably believed that the destruction of public and military property would speed the war's end.
   d. Sherman probably wanted North Carolinians to feel comfortable with his troops.

4. How did Sherman decide what to destroy and what to leave alone?

Alternative Assessment

Building Your Portfolio

N.C. History

Cooperative Learning
Work with a small group of three or four classmates to conduct research on any of the historical figures discussed in Chapter 11. The subject of your research might be a government official, a military leader, or another public or private individual who lived during the Civil War and who is described in this chapter. As a group, create a biography of the person and illustrate it with a picture or drawing.

internet connect

Internet Activity: go.hrw.com
keyword: SN3 NC11

Choose a topic on the Civil War to:
- Create an annotated time line of the Civil War in North Carolina.
- Write a political advertisement arguing for peace in North Carolina.
- Build a model of Fort Fisher.

The Civil War

CHAPTER 12
Reconstruction in North Carolina
(1865–1877)

The city of Charlotte after the Civil War

Build on What You Know

More than 40,000 men from North Carolina died in the Civil War. The war destroyed North Carolina's economy as railroads, bridges, homes, schools, and businesses lay in ruin. By 1865, North Carolina families and their government faced the enormous task of rebuilding their state.

What's Your Opinion?

 Do you **agree** or **disagree** with the following statements? Support your point of view in your journal.

- **Constitutional Heritage** Rebellious states should write new constitutions to rejoin the Union.
- **Culture** Reconstruction changed the lives of blacks and whites in North Carolina.
- **Citizenship** People should form secret societies as a means of changing government.

Section 1

Freedpeople after the War

Read to Discover
1. What was the presidential plan for Reconstruction?
2. What was the social, economic, and political impact of Reconstruction on freedpeople?
3. What was the Congressional plan for Reconstruction?

Define
- repudiate
- freedmen's convention

Identify
- Conservatives
- Jonathan Worth
- A.H. Galloway
- James City

The Story Continues

When the Union first gained control of eastern North Carolina in early 1862, President Lincoln believed the state needed a plan for rejoining the Union. His first step was to name Edward Stanly governor in 1862. Most North Carolinians opposed Stanly, however, and he resigned in January 1863. No further steps toward Reconstruction in the state were taken until after the war.

★ Differing Views on Reconstruction

President Lincoln believed the states in rebellion should repeal their acts of secession and free the slaves before rejoining the nation. He planned for all former Confederates—except top leaders—to be pardoned after they promised to obey the Constitution and the laws of the United States. When at least 10 percent of the population had taken this oath and peace had been established, the state could return to the Union. The military would be withdrawn and the states would work on solving their problems without federal interference.

Starting with his home state of North Carolina, President Andrew Johnson began putting Lincoln's plan into effect after Lincoln's

Governor Edward Stanly proved to be unpopular with North Carolina voters shortly after he was appointed by Abraham Lincoln.

Reconstruction in North Carolina **225**

assassination. Johnson addressed Reconstruction basically the same way as Lincoln, but differed in that he required harsher treatment of Confederate leaders. He appointed William W. Holden as the provisional, or temporary, governor in May 1865. Johnson gave Holden the use of military forces to restore order, enforce laws, and stop any guerrilla warfare. He also instructed Holden to call a convention to revise the state constitution. Elections also had to be held for state officials and congressmen. Most former Confederates were allowed to vote and hold office if they simply took an oath of loyalty. However, some people with larger roles in the war were required to get a presidential pardon to qualify to vote.

✔ **READING CHECK** **Comparing** How did Presidents Lincoln and Johnson plan to readmit states to the Union?

★ Holden's Plan

Holden began Reconstruction in North Carolina by appointing more than three thousand people to political offices in the state. Many were yeomen or Unionists who had been excluded from government during the Civil War. He also decided which Confederate officials should or should not be pardoned.

The Convention of 1865 As President Johnson instructed, Holden called a state convention in October 1865. Only white men who had taken oaths of loyalty to the Union could vote or be chosen as delegates. Delegates to the convention repealed the Ordinance of Secession. They also formally outlawed slavery and voted to **repudiate**, or reject, the Confederate war debt. While many delegates had opposed repudiation, President Johnson had issued a strong statement demanding it. Rejecting the debt seriously damaged the state's banks, colleges, and universities. It also hurt hundreds of citizens who had bought state bonds during the war.

The election of 1865 More than 50 convention members asked William Holden to run for governor in the 1865 election. Meanwhile, the Conservative Democrats, or **Conservatives**—native whites who were mostly prewar Democrats—asked **Jonathan Worth** to run. Worth had disapproved of secession but had also opposed President Lincoln's actions leading up to the Civil War. After the war, Worth strongly opposed repudiation of the war debt. Holden's supporters argued that his election would allow North Carolina to return quickly to the Union. Worth won the election, however. Northern newspaper editors wrote that the election showed that North Carolina was not yet ready for statehood.

With the support of the conservative white community, Jonathan Worth became governor in North Carolina's first post-Civil War election.

✔ **READING CHECK** **Sequencing** How did Reconstruction proceed under Governor William Holden?

★ The Black Codes

Throughout the period of Reconstruction, African Americans worked for political and social equality in North Carolina. While they called for cooperation with whites, African Americans argued that they deserved the same equal citizenship as anyone else born in America.

Freedpeople meet in Raleigh In 1865 black delegates from about half of the counties in North Carolina met in Raleigh. Most had been slaves, although a few had been free before the war. Many of the 117 delegates were former members of the Union army, including **A. H. Galloway** of Fayetteville. Galloway was a former slave who had escaped to Ohio and returned to North Carolina after the war. Galloway organized a **freedmen's convention**. The convention wrote an address that was sent to the state convention being held at the same time. It called for justice and equal rights for North Carolina's freedpeople, including education of black children and legal protection for black families and orphans.

> **History Makers Speak**
> "We most earnestly [deeply] desire to have the disabilities under which we formerly labored removed, and to have all the oppressive [unfair] laws which make unjust discriminations [distinctions] on account of race or color wiped from the statutes of the State."
>
> Address of freedmen's convention delegates, as quoted in *A History of African Americans in North Carolina*, by Jeffrey J. Crow, Paul D. Escott, and Flora Hatley.

The legislature draws up its own code Many whites reacted negatively to African American desires for equality. Most leaders did not want black North Carolinians to have rights such as giving testimony in court or sitting on juries. In addition, African Americans continued to be subjected to violent attacks, often by white leaders. In 1866 the General Assembly passed a group of laws called "Black Codes." Similar laws had been passed in other southern states. The Black Codes defined the rights and responsibilities of freedpeople. The marriages of former slaves were declared legal, and African Americans were given limited protection against fraud in contracts with whites. At the same time, the Black Codes sought to enforce black subordination. In some parts of the South, freedpeople were forbidden to speak or act in ways that might be seen as threatening to the established government. Unemployment was treated as a crime. Freedpeople without jobs or labor contracts with white employers could be forced by local courts to work without pay.

✔ **READING CHECK** Finding the Main Idea How did Reconstruction affect freedpeople?

CONNECTING TO Geography

James City
In 1862 hundreds, and later thousands, of slaves left plantations to find freedom in New Bern. The Freedmen's Bureau created **James City** as a temporary site to meet their needs. Freedpeople were allowed to live on the property well into the 1880s. Then the landowner began legal action to remove the city's inhabitants. The residents agreed to pay rent. However, people slowly began leaving the property. By the mid-1900s, the settlement had been largely abandoned. **Why do you think people moved away from James City?**

Interpreting the Visual Record

Uncovering James City *This contemporary map shows the location of a current archaeological project in James City.* **What do you think historians might want to learn about freedpeople in this city?**

Congress Takes Over

When the U.S. Congress met in early 1867, it rejected President Johnson's plan to readmit southern states to the Union. Many northerners were concerned that the South had not made significant changes, despite losing the war. With a majority in Congress, Republicans who held this belief developed their own plan for Reconstruction.

When all southern states except Tennessee refused to ratify the Fourteenth Amendment, which granted citizenship to African Americans, Congress began its new Reconstruction plans. Overriding President Johnson's veto, Congress approved An Act to Provide for the More Efficient Government of the Rebel States in March 1867. This law and three additional acts deeply affected the southern states. Congress divided the South into five military districts each under the command of an army officer. It declared that state governments were only temporary and could be changed or brought to an end.

The Reconstruction Acts called for each state to write a constitution that complied with the U.S. Constitution. African Americans could participate as delegates in this process. However, many former Confederate leaders—about 10 percent of North Carolina's white population—could not vote or serve as delegates, because they had not yet been pardoned. In addition, states had to ratify the Fourteenth Amendment to return to the Union. Some Conservatives believed that they had to cooperate with the acts in order to gain control of the constitutional convention. Others felt it would be dishonorable and humiliating to cooperate with Congress.

✔ **READING CHECK** Summarizing What requirements did states have to meet in order to return to the Union?

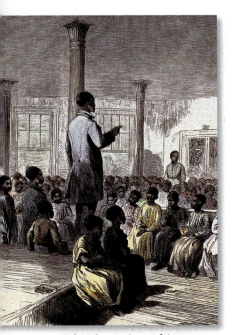

Schools serving African American communities, such as the one shown here, sprang up throughout the South during Reconstruction.

Section 1 Review

Homework Practice Online keyword: SN3 HP12

1. **Define** and explain:
   - repudiate
   - freedmen's convention

2. **Identify** and explain:
   - Conservatives
   - Jonathan Worth
   - A.H. Galloway
   - James City

3. **Summarizing** Copy the graphic organizer below. Use it to identify the main points of Presidential Reconstruction.

4. **Finding the Main Idea**
   a. What changes did Governor Holden make under Reconstruction?
   b. What effects did Reconstruction have on freedpeople?

5. **Writing and Critical Thinking**
   Comparing and Contrasting What were the similarities and differences between Presidential and Congressional Reconstruction?
   Consider:
   - requirements for states to rejoin the Union
   - involvement of the federal government in solving southern states' problems

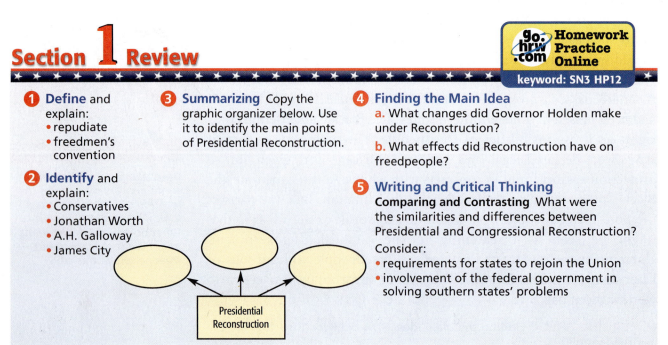

Section 2

Life during Reconstruction

Read to Discover
1. How did North Carolinians react to military rule in their state?
2. How did the Republican Party develop in North Carolina, and who made up its membership?
3. What were the provisions of North Carolina's 1868 Constitution and how was it received by political groups?

Identify
- Daniel Sickles
- E.R.S. Canby
- Union League
- Wyatt Outlaw
- Albion Tourgée

The Story Continues

President Johnson visited Chapel Hill in the spring of 1867 to attend graduation ceremonies at the University of North Carolina. Johnson was joined by other officials, including Major General Daniel Sickles, commander of North Carolina's military district. University students recognized Johnson and his colleagues with honorary memberships in campus literary societies. Johnson became a member of the Dialectic Society and all the others except Daniel Sickles were accepted in the Philanthropic Society. The students rejected Sickles "by a small minority . . . to emphasize their hostility to the Reconstruction Acts."

Union general and politician Daniel Sickles in Civil War uniform

Military Rule

Major General **Daniel Sickles** commanded the Second Military District, which was made up of North and South Carolina. Sickles was a lawyer from New York who had served in that state's legislature. His appointment came as no surprise, because he had recently served as military

Reconstruction in North Carolina **229**

commander of South Carolina. Sickles held beliefs that made Conservatives hopeful that he would serve them well. He argued that the South should be treated with "justice and conciliation [peaceful actions]." He also urged African Americans to find work and avoid people who might want to create racial tension.

Many people in North Carolina began to dislike Sickles, however, when he issued a series of "General Orders." Under these orders, Sickles placed the military in control of the courts and took control over local elections. Many critics, including Governor Worth, thought Sickles had gone beyond his authority by issuing orders that were not directly stated by Congress. President Johnson agreed. However, Congress passed an additional act over the president's veto reaffirming that all provisional governments were under the complete control of the district commanders. Congress clearly gave commanders the right to remove and appoint government officials, including governors.

President Johnson expressed his disagreement by replacing Sickles with General **E. R. S. Canby** in August 1867. However, Canby continued Sickles's policy of carrying out the terms of the Reconstruction Acts. In fact, he interfered in state and local government more often than Sickles had.

✔ **READING CHECK** Drawing Inferences and Conclusions What effect did military rule have on North Carolina?

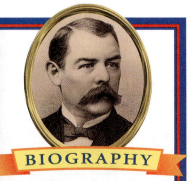

BIOGRAPHY

Albion Tourgée
(1838–1905)

Albion Tourgée was born in Ohio. During the Civil War, Tourgée fought many battles for the Union Army, suffering two serious spinal injuries. In 1865 he and his wife moved to Greensboro, North Carolina. He supported freedmen's voting rights and was influential in writing the new 1868 constitution. Tourgée served for six years as a judge on the Superior Court. Tourgée decided to move back to Ohio in 1879. He continued to work for racial equality, however. In 1896 he argued against racial segregation in the Supreme Court case *Plessy v. Ferguson*. **How did Tourgée work to change North Carolina?**

★ Republicans in North Carolina

William Holden began formally organizing the Republican Party in North Carolina in the spring of 1867. Loyal Unionist white men as well as any interested blacks were invited to attend a party convention. The convention agreed to support the Reconstruction Acts and civil and political equality for African Americans. Northern newspapers expressed satisfaction with the formation of the new party. The *Nation* wrote, "In North Carolina we suppose nearly half of the vote of the State can be controlled by it [the Republican party]." In contrast, a North Carolina paper wrote that "part of its members were honest, genuine men, who were bamboozled [tricked] into the affair to give it éclat [respectability]. The remainder were shams, perfect political mushrooms."

The Union League The Republican Party in North Carolina received a lot of support from the **Union League**. Founded in Illinois in 1862, this organization worked to maintain northern morale in the Union during the war. Later, the Union League promoted the plans of Congressional Reconstruction and encouraged freedpeople to support the Republican Party. William Holden was the first president of the Union League in North Carolina. Other leaders included a black Republican named **Wyatt Outlaw** and Mayor William R. Albright of Graham.

Carpetbaggers and scalawags In addition to freedmen and Unionists, so-called "carpetbaggers" and "scalawags" made up the Republican party. Northerners who came to the South after the war were called "carpetbaggers," after the bags in which many carried their possessions. Some came to help blacks gain full citizenship. Others were trying to improve their economic fortunes. One of the most influential northern migrants to North Carolina was **Albion Tourgée**. "Scalawags" were native whites—mostly small farmers—who opposed the landowning gentry and joined with freedpeople in hopes of winning economic opportunity and political equality.

The election of 1867 Most native whites opposed Reconstruction and the Republicans. This group supported the Conservatives. However, they were not organized and many chose not to participate in the 1867 election. As a result, a majority of voters called for a new constitution. Only 13 Conservatives attended the constitutional convention held the following spring.

✔ **READING CHECK** Summarizing Who were the members of the Republican Party, and how did it develop in North Carolina?

CONNECTING TO Literature

A Fool's Errand: By One of the Fools

The book cover of A Fool's Errand by Albion Tourgée

Albion Tourgée wrote A Fool's Errand in 1879, after recognizing the failure of Reconstruction. In the excerpts below, Tourgée expresses his views on Reconstruction and how problems in the South should have been solved.

"Reconstruction was a failure so far as it attempted to unify the nation, to make one people in fact of what had been one only in name before the convulsion of civil war. It was a failure, too, so far as it attempted to fix and secure the position and rights of the colored race. . . .

"I have given the years of my manhood to the consideration of these questions, and am accounted [considered] a fool in consequence [as a result]. . . .

"The Nation nourished and protected slavery. The fruitage [product] of slavery has been the ignorant freedman, the ignorant poor-white man, and the arrogant master. . . . Now, let the Nation undo the evil it has permitted and encouraged. Let it educate those whom it made ignorant, and protect those whom it made weak. It is not a matter of favor to the black, but of safety to the Nation. Make the spelling-book the scepter [symbol] of national power. Let the Nation educate the colored man and the poor-white man *because* the Nation held them in bondage, and is responsible for their education; educate the voter *because* the Nation can not afford that he should be ignorant . . . Honest ignorance [lack of knowledge] in the masses is more to be dreaded than malevolent [wicked] intelligence in the few . . . Poor-Whites, Freedmen, Ku-Klux, and Bulldozers are all alike the harvest of ignorance. The Nation can not afford to grow such a crop."

Understanding Literature

1. Why does the narrator believe that many people considered him a fool?
2. What is the key to successful Reconstruction, in Tourgée's view?

The State Constitutional Convention of 1868

More than 100 Republicans attended the 1868 state convention in Raleigh to write a new constitution. Of these, 18 were white northerners, 15 were African Americans, and 74 were native whites. James H. Harris, A. H. Galloway, and James W. Hood led the black delegates. Albion Tourgée played a leading role at the convention. While delegates worked hard to create the new constitution, many newspapers pointed out that they had little or no experience. However, the delegates produced a document that was democratic and effective. Much of this constitution has stood the test of time and is still in effect today.

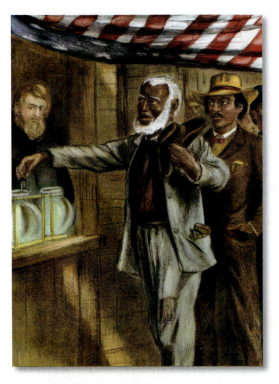

This illustration from Harper's Weekly shows African Americans casting their first votes.

Voting rights The new constitution granted suffrage, or voting rights, to all men, including African Americans. Previous restrictions based on religious affiliation and the ownership of property were removed.

Officials State officials were now to be elected by popular vote—not by the legislature. All men qualified to vote could hold public office, except for atheists—people who do not believe in God. The constitution created four new elected offices—lieutenant governor, auditor, superintendent of public works, and superintendent of public instruction. In addition, the two-year term for governor was lengthened to four years.

Conservatives did not approve of the new constitution. Some did not want African Americans to be able to vote. Some did not like the fact that men did not have to own property to vote or hold office. This significantly reduced wealthy landowners' political power. Many people feared that black voters who could not read and write would not vote wisely.

The ratification campaign The vote to ratify the constitution and to elect new state and county officers and representatives to Congress was set for April 1868. The Union League actively campaigned for ratification of the constitution, while Conservatives fiercely opposed ratification.

In addition to the support of the Union League, Republicans were backed by the federal troops in the state. They also attracted votes from some white yeomen who had long opposed the landowning gentry and believed that political reform would give them a larger voice in government. Black students from Howard University in the U.S. capital traveled through North Carolina, making speeches in support of Republicans and the new constitution. As a result, Republicans won a big victory. The constitution was accepted and William Holden was elected governor. The Republicans won 58 of North Carolina's

89 counties. Conservatives elected only one judge, one solicitor, and one representative to Congress.

✓ **READING CHECK** **Contrasting** What groups supported and opposed the 1868 constitution and why?

⭐ North Carolina Rejoins the Union

The Republican-controlled legislature quickly ratified the Fourteenth Amendment. It also elected Republicans John Pool and Joseph C. Abbott to be United States senators. General Canby ordered Governor Worth to leave office on July 1, and William Holden became governor the next day. General Canby gave all his powers to the elected government, but military forces remained in the state. Soon afterward, Congress approved the state constitution and admitted North Carolina's representatives and senators. The state had rejoined the Union. However, the majority of native whites in the state held great dislike for the people who controlled state government. One Conservative newspaper expressed the disrespect many people had for the Republicans.

Republican politician John Pool was one of those chosen to represent North Carolina in the U.S. Senate as the state rejoined the Union.

 ❝These representatives of the people—these public servants 'so called'—these incapable and indifferent [uncaring] legislators . . . lend themselves to the wildest schemes . . . wink at corruption . . . indulge in vice and immorality, and conspire [plan] to paralyze the best interests of the State . . . .❞

Raleigh *Daily Sentinel*, as quoted in *The North Carolina Experience: An Interpretive and Documentary History*, edited by Lindley S. Butler and Alan D. Watson

Analyzing Primary Sources
Identifying Bias What evidence of bias does this excerpt show?

✓ **READING CHECK** **Sequencing** What sequence of events allowed North Carolina to rejoin the Union?

Section 2 Review

Homework Practice Online
keyword: SN3 HP12

1 Identify and explain:
- Daniel Sickles
- E.R.S. Canby
- Union League
- Wyatt Outlaw
- Albion Tourgée

2 Contrasting Copy the chart below. Then use it to identify support and opposition to the 1868 Constitution.

Supported by	1868 Constitution	Opposed by
	Fewer voting restrictions	

3 Finding the Main Idea
a. Describe the members of the Republican Party in North Carolina.
b. How did North Carolinians react to military occupation?

4 Writing and Critical Thinking
Identifying Points of View Why were Republicans able to gain control of the state government?
Consider:
- the effect of Congressional Reconstruction
- the political concerns that many white yeomen shared with former slaves

Section 3

Attacks on Reconstruction

Read to Discover
1. What social and economic changes did Reconstruction bring to North Carolina?
2. How did Conservative Democrats gain control of the government?
3. Why did Reconstruction come to an end?

Identify
- Freedmen's Bank
- Milton Littlefield
- Josiah Turner, Jr.
- Shoffner Act
- Kirk-Holden War

The Story Continues

Mary Neeley was one of many northerners who moved to the South to teach school after the war. Like most Americans at the time, she believed African American and white students should not attend the same schools. In a letter to James A. Garfield, she expressed her beliefs, "For my part I protest against an attempt to compel [make] black and white to mingle more together. I would not consent to our children attending a mixed school." Such northern beliefs about racial issues eventually helped weaken Reconstruction.

★ Changes under Reconstruction

Freeing the slaves brought enormous social and economic changes to North Carolina. Many people worried about the ability of whites and African Americans to live and work alongside each other.

Freedpeople While a few slaves had run away to join Union camps, most had remained on their plantations during the war. Once free, many stayed on the same land and worked for wages or crop shares.

North Carolina Farms after the Civil War, 1860–1900

	Number	Average Size
1860	72,203	316 acres
1870	93,565	212 acres
1880	157,609	142 acres
1890	178,359	127 acres
1900	225,000	101 acres

Interpreting Charts Under the sharecropping system, the number of farms increased significantly while the average size of farms decreased. **By what number did farms increase between 1860 and 1880? What was their decrease in size during the same period?**

Early hopes of receiving 40-acre homesteads had quickly faded when President Johnson ordered confiscated lands to be returned to their owners. By 1866, the government was encouraging all freedpeople to sign annual contracts to work on plantations. Sharecropping soon replaced the old plantation system.

In March of 1865, the U.S. Congress created the Freedmen's Bureau to help African Americans make the adjustment from slavery to freedom. Each southern state had local units and officials to help freedpeople find work, buy or rent land, and make fair labor contracts. The Bureau also helped African Americans fight disease, build schools, settle problems with each other and with whites, and learn citizenship skills. The Freedmen's Savings and Trust Company, called the **Freedmen's Bank**, was created to help African Americans save money and achieve some measure of financial independence. The Bureau spent about $1.5 million on food, clothing, hospital care, and education for freedpeople in North Carolina.

The Freedmen's Bureau experienced some difficulties, however. Many white North Carolinians did not like the organization interfering in problems they thought southerners should solve themselves. In addition, some of the bureau's agents treated freedpeople poorly. They sometimes favored white landowners in negotiating labor contracts.

That's Interesting!

The Freedmen's Bank The Freedmen's Bank was created to help freedpeople save money to purchase land or businesses of their own. Deposits from freedpeople in New Bern, Raleigh, and Wilmington totaled more than $57,000. However, the bank failed in 1874. Investors from the same three cities lost nearly $20,000 of their savings.

Education The public school system in North Carolina collapsed during the Civil War. After the war, Governor Worth—who had supported public education before the conflict—asked the legislature to abolish the state school system. He worried that if the state paid for white children's education, it would be "required to educate the Negroes in like manner."

In the absence of public schools, the Freedmen's Bureau and many northern churches helped rebuild schools in North Carolina. They sent teachers and also provided books and supplies. Some schools were for whites only and some were for blacks. A few had both races attending. The new state constitution in 1868 created a system of free public schools, with separate facilities for whites and blacks. However, only about one fifth of school-aged children attended school in North Carolina in 1870.

Funding for education did not improve when Conservatives returned to power in 1871. Eager to deny freedpeople access to education, they made schools a low priority for whites as well. By 1880 only about one third of school-aged children attended school for the nine weeks offered by most schools. Fewer people could read and write in 1880 than in 1860.

Students and teachers pose outside a Freedmen's Bureau school in the Reconstruction era.

✔ **READING CHECK** Summarizing How did Reconstruction affect social and economic life in North Carolina?

⭐ Railroad Bond Scandal

After the Civil War many of North Carolina's railroads lay in ruins. The General Assembly issued $28 million in bonds to improve and rebuild the railroads. Many people criticized the legislature for overspending on these bonds. Bond purchasers began to worry that the state would not be able to pay such large sums, and bond prices fell. In addition, some politicians and businessmen found ways to personally profit from bond sales. Legislators broke the law by starting new railroads without public elections. Some also sold their votes to businessmen for large amounts of money or personal favors.

A northern migrant named **Milton Littlefield** was connected to much of the dishonest activity in the legislature. George Swepson, president of the Western Division of the Western North Carolina Railroad, hired Littlefield to get the legislature to vote for railroad bonds. Littlefield gave food, tobacco, drinks, money, loans, and other favors to legislators in exchange for their votes. The railroad scandals were widely publicized in Conservative newspapers. **Josiah Turner, Jr.**, editor of the Raleigh *Daily Sentinel*, was one of the most vocal critics of the Republican legislature.

✔ **READING CHECK** Making Generalizations and Predictions Why was the railroad bond scandal significant?

⭐ The Rise of Conservatives

Publicity about the railroad bond scandals led to public criticism of the Republican administration. The scandals also energized Conservatives to organize against the Republicans.

Conservative whites believed they had to find a way to oppose the political activities of the Union League and Freedmen's Bureau. They began organizing secret political groups to regain power.

The role of the Klan The Ku Klux Klan first appeared in North Carolina in 1867. As many as 40,000 white men may have been members of the secret organization. Members usually wore white sheets, tall cone-shaped hats, and masks. Their purpose was to terrorize African Americans and the whites who associated with them. The Klan used warnings, threats, whippings, and murder to frighten Republicans away from voting. In an effort to stop Klan activities, the Republican legislature passed a law making it illegal to go masked, painted, or disguised on the highways. In 1869 the General Assembly passed the **Shoffner Act** "for the better protection of life and property." It gave the governor authority to use military force to restore order where Klan activity was out of control.

In February 1870 the Klan captured black Republican leader Wyatt Outlaw. They took Outlaw to the town square in Graham, the Alamance

Ku Klux Klan members in North Carolina prepare to execute African American John Campbell in this 1871 illustration. Law enforcement arrived to prevent the murder.

236 Chapter 12

County seat, and hanged him from a large oak tree near the courthouse. In May, Klansmen murdered a white Republican leader named John Stephens in Caswell County. Using his authority under the Shoffner Act, Governor Holden placed the two counties under martial law. Colonel George Kirk took command of the troops in the counties.

The Kirk-Holden War Colonel Kirk arrested suspects in Alamance County and Caswell County and put them in jail. Governor Holden denied their release. Holden argued that he was "satisfied that the public interest requires that these military prisoners shall not be delivered up to the civil power." Conservatives called this incident the **Kirk-Holden War**. Eventually, President Grant ordered Holden to obey a federal writ of habeas corpus, which prevents people from being jailed without being charged with a crime. Meanwhile, the Ku Klux Klan had accomplished its goals in the county. The Conservatives won a clear victory in the 1870 election. Without the president's or the public's support, Holden disbanded Kirk's troops and ordered the prisoners to appear before a judge.

✔ **READING CHECK** Finding the Main Idea How did Conservatives gain power in North Carolina?

Historical Document

THE KIRK-HOLDEN WAR

On November 22, 1870, in his annual address to the state legislature, Governor Holden described the actions of the Ku Klux Klan. Then he explained his decision to place some counties under martial law.

"I have information of not less than 25 murders committed by members of this Klan, in various counties of the State, and of hundreds of cases of scourging and whipping. Very few, if any, convictions have followed in these cases. . . . There was no remedy for these evils through the civil law, and but for the use of the military arm, to which I was compelled to resort, the whole fabric of society in the State would have been undermined and destroyed, and a reign of lawlessness and anarchy would have been established. The present State government would thus have failed in . . . the protection of life and property under equal laws; and, necessarily the national government would have interfered, and, in all probability would have placed us again and for an indefinite period under military rule. . . .

"In July, of the present year, I deemed it my duty to embody a portion of the militia, and to make a number of arrests of suspected persons in the Counties of Alamance and Caswell. . . .

"The result of this action . . . has been in the highest degree fortunate and beneficial. The power of the State government to protect, maintain, and perpetuate itself has been tested and demonstrated. The secret organization which disturbed the peace of society . . . has been exposed and broken up. . . . The poor and the humble now sleep unmolested in their houses, and are no longer scourged or murdered on account of their political opinions."

Banner of the Raleigh Daily Sentinel *from shortly before the election of 1870*

Analyzing Primary Sources
1. Why did Governor Holden mention the national government and the possibility of military rule?
2. Why did Governor Holden believe it was necessary to impose martial law in some counties?

Reconstruction in North Carolina

That's Interesting!

Pleading the Fifth During the federal investigation of the Ku Klux Klan's activities, the man thought to be the head of the organization was questioned as a witness. William L. Saunders answered every question with the phrase, "I decline to answer." He became one of the first prominent people to use the Fifth Amendment, which protects witnesses from incriminating themselves. Recently, "pleading the Fifth" has become a common practice.

Republican governor Tod Caldwell had little real power in Conservative-dominated North Carolina.

Analyzing Primary Sources

Making Generalizations and Predictions Why did the General Assembly believe the Constitution should be revised?

★ The Impeachment of Holden

Conservatives argued that Governor Holden should be impeached for placing Alamance and Caswell counties under martial law. In December 1870 a house committee approved a resolution introduced by a former Klan member. Then it drew up eight articles of impeachment, charging Holden with high crimes and misdemeanors. These included declaring martial law, unlawfully raising troops, and illegally declaring counties to be in a state of insurrection. Holden was also charged with unlawfully arresting 18 citizens and with refusing to obey a writ of habeas corpus.

During his trial, Holden was found guilty of six charges. He became the first American governor to be impeached and convicted. The senate voted to remove him and prevented him from holding public office in the future. Holden's lieutenant governor, Tod Caldwell, succeeded him. However, as a Republican, Caldwell held little power. The General Assembly repealed the Shoffner Act. It also made membership in secret political and military societies illegal (a move aimed more at the Union League than the Klan). Once Conservatives held political control, the Klan's activities greatly decreased. It remained active only in a few western counties. Federal investigations later determined that the Klan's actions were violent and unlawful. Eventually, federal laws were passed to outlaw such activities.

✔ **READING CHECK** Drawing Inferences and Conclusions Why was Governor Holden impeached?

★ The Conservatives Take Charge

In the election of 1872, Republicans managed to keep the governorship in Tod Caldwell's hands. However, they lost control of the General Assembly to the Conservatives. Conservatives turned their attention to calling for a constitutional convention that would revise the 1868 constitution. In 1875 the General Assembly wrote the following resolution.

> **History Makers Speak**
>
> ❝The present Constitution is unsuited to the wants of the people of the State, is a check upon their energy, and impedes [blocks] their welfare, and . . . the people demand that the burdens contained in the same shall be removed from their shoulders.❞
>
> North Carolina General Assembly, as quoted in *North Carolina: The History of a Southern State* by Hugh Lefler and Albert Newsome

At a constitutional convention held in 1875 delegates decided to keep the 1868 document. However, they added 30 amendments. The changes to the constitution included declaring secret political societies illegal, keeping white and black schools separate, and outlawing marriages between blacks and whites. The constitution also reversed Republican political reforms by giving the legislature the authority to abolish elected county governments and to put power back into the hands of appointed officials. This change was to ensure white Conservative control over eastern counties with large black populations.

✓ **READING CHECK** **Summarizing** What changes did Conservative Democrats make to North Carolina's government?

★ Reconstruction Ends

Political Reconstruction came to an end in North Carolina with the Republicans' loss of power. The reform ideas of native-born citizens as well as outsiders had been rejected. The expansion of public education had failed. Plans to give freedpeople full citizenship were left behind as they met with great resistance from native whites. The new Republican Party had lost control of the government. Many northerners had returned home. In 1876 Conservative Democrats successfully elected Zebulon Vance as governor of North Carolina. Many members of the party believed Vance's election proved the state had been saved from the "evils" of Reconstruction.

When Rutherford B. Hayes became president in 1877, he ordered the withdrawal of federal troops from the South. This marked the end of the Reconstruction era. The traditional white ruling class had returned to power. Without the support of federal troops or carpetbaggers, fewer and fewer blacks participated in the political process. They could not risk offending dominant whites by doing so.

✓ **READING CHECK** **Sequencing** What factors led to the end of Reconstruction in North Carolina?

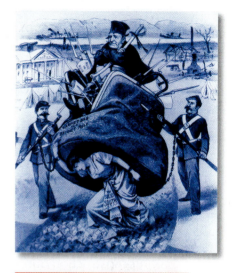

Interpreting the Visual Record

Resistance to Reconstruction This political cartoon from the 1870s shows a woman representing the South being crushed beneath U.S. President Ulysses S. Grant, flanked by federal soldiers. **In what way does this cartoon express a southern point of view about Reconstruction?**

Section 3 Review

keyword: SN3 HP12

1 Identify and explain:
• Freedmen's Bank
• Milton Littlefield
• Josiah Turner, Jr.
• Shoffner Act
• Kirk-Holden War

2 Identifying Cause and Effect Copy the graphic organizer below. Use it to identify the factors that led to the end of Reconstruction.

3 Finding the Main Idea
a. How did Conservative Democrats rise to power in North Carolina?
b. Why was Governor Holden impeached?

4 Writing and Critical Thinking
Analyzing Information How did Reconstruction change life in North Carolina?
Consider:
• economics
• social life
• political life

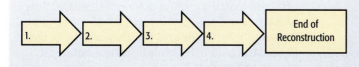

Reconstruction in North Carolina **239**

Chapter 12 Review

Chapter Summary

Section 1
- The southern states that had composed the Confederacy in 1861 were subjected to federal policies of Reconstruction following the Civil War.
- Freed slaves in North Carolina experienced new liberties and new challenges in the years following the Civil War.
- Policies became harsher and more restrictive as Congress took control of Reconstruction during the late 1860s.

Section 2
- Reconstruction brought military rule to North Carolina.
- Republicans won control of North Carolina and other southern state governments during Reconstruction.
- North Carolina drew up a new state constitution in 1868 as a means of rejoining the Union.

Section 3
- Reconstruction brought major social and economic changes to North Carolina.
- Political conflict over some Reconstruction policies and Conservatives' use of violence eventually led to the collapse of Republican power in North Carolina's government.
- Reconstruction in North Carolina ended as Conservatives reversed Republican reforms and the federal government ended military occupation.

Identifying People and Ideas

1. Conservatives
2. Jonathan Worth
3. A.H. Galloway
4. Daniel Sickles
5. Wyatt Outlaw
6. Albion Tourgée
7. Milton Littlefield
8. Freedmen's Bank
9. Josiah Turner, Jr.
10. Kirk-Holden War

Understanding Main Ideas

Section 1 (Pages 225–228)
1. What role did William Holden play in early efforts at Reconstruction in North Carolina?
2. What was the Congressional plan for Reconstruction?
3. How did Reconstruction affect the lives of freedpeople?

Section 2 (Pages 229–233)
4. How did military rule affect political conditions in North Carolina?
5. Describe the development of the Republican Party in North Carolina.
6. What changes did the State Constitutional Convention of 1868 help bring about?

Section 3 (Pages 234–239)
7. How did Reconstruction affect economic and social life in North Carolina?
8. What factors allowed Conservative Democrats to gain power in North Carolina?
9. How did the activities of the Ku Klux Klan in North Carolina help create the conditions that led to the Kirk-Holden War?

What Did You Find Out?

1. **Constitutional Heritage** What major changes did the 1868 constitution bring to North Carolina's government?
2. **Culture** How did Reconstruction affect freedpeople in North Carolina?
3. **Citizenship** What effect did the Ku Klux Klan have on North Carolina?

Thinking Critically

1. **Summarizing** What political changes came about in North Carolina as a result of Reconstruction?
2. **Analyzing Information** Which leaders most affected North Carolina during Reconstruction and why?
3. **Drawing Inferences and Conclusions** How did Reconstruction affect relationships between blacks and whites?

Building Social Studies Skills

Interpreting Maps

Study the map below. It shows the distribution of African American political power in North Carolina in the elections following the Civil War. Then answer the questions that follow.

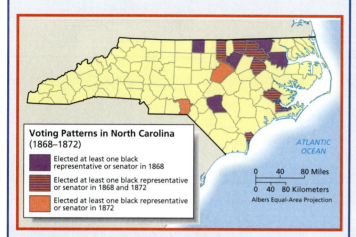

1. Based on the map, which statement best describes voting patterns in North Carolina between 1868 and 1872?
   a. More North Carolina counties elected blacks in 1868 than in 1872.
   b. More blacks were elected in North Carolina in 1868 than in 1872.
   c. Most North Carolina counties elected blacks in 1868.
   d. More North Carolina counties elected blacks in 1872 than in 1868.
   e. Black representatives were elected in 1872 only in counties where they had won in the past.

2. In what region were most of the counties that elected black representatives or senators located?

Evaluating Sources

Read the following report published in the *Raleigh Daily Standard* in April of 1869. It describes the activities of the Republican legislature. Then answer the questions that follow.

> "Altogether, we think the General Assembly did well. Day by day its good works, which live after it, will become more apparent and more appreciated. Its revilers [those who insult it] will be hushed by the hum of wheels that its laws have called into motion, and the entire people will yet applaud its liberality [kindness] and independence. In our opinion the Legislature needs no elaborate defense. A fair statement of what it has done is sufficient for the present while the future will entirely vindicate [prove right] the annual session of 1868–'9."

3. Which of the following statements best describes the political views of the *Raleigh Daily Standard*?
   a. The *Standard*'s editors are probably northerners.
   b. The *Standard*'s editors are members of the Ku Klux Klan.
   c. The *Standard*'s editors are probably Conservatives.
   d. The *Standard*'s editors are Republicans.

4. How did the editors of the *Raleigh Daily Standard* believe the actions of the legislature would be judged in the future?

Alternative Assessment

Building Your Portfolio

Linking to Your Community
Research your local community or a nearby city to learn how its residents experienced Reconstruction. Using the local library, read old newspapers and other primary and secondary sources to create a picture of life during this period. Make sure you address the topics of political change, economic change, and social change (including race relations). Then present your findings to the class in an oral report.

internet connect

Internet Activity: go.hrw.com
keyword: SN3 NC12

Choose a topic on Reconstruction in North Carolina to:
- Create a chart about those involved in the state and national Reconstruction plans.
- Write a story about African Americans and Reconstruction.
- Write an essay about the end of Reconstruction in the South.

UNIT 5 Modern Times
(1870–Present)

CHAPTER 13 North Carolina in the Industrial Age (1870–1930)

CHAPTER 14 Depression and War (1929–1945)

CHAPTER 15 A Changing State (1945–1970)

CHAPTER 16 A Modern State (1970–Present)

Young People
IN HISTORY

From Farms and Factories to Schoolhouses

In the late 1800s, most North Carolinians still lived on farms. Young people still helped their families year-round with the planting and harvesting. Tobacco had to be tended by hand and then carried to the tobacco shed for curing. Cotton had to be weeded constantly. Corn had to be shucked. Young people helped with all these farm chores. They made do with relatively little, but they also had a wealth of family and community ties. They enjoyed nighttime stories by the fireplace, church socials and county fairs, and "frolics" with dancing and music at neighbors' homes.

As the state began to change in the years following the Civil War, so, too, did the lives of young North Carolinians. More children moved with their families to live in mill villages and work in textile mills. Most mill children began part-time work at age 10 and left school to work full-time at age 12. Mill children labored 11 or 12 hours a day. They might be allowed to play outside for 20 minutes—if they were not behind in their work. The mills were hot, humid, and deafeningly noisy. Cotton dust and lint could fill the air like a fog. For their work, children earned about 12 cents a day. Yet mill villages also gave young people a sense of family and belonging. Some even offered libraries, baseball fields, flower gardens, and auditoriums for entertainment.

Another change in the state greatly affected young people—the improvement of schools. Many rural schools joined together in order to offer students more resources, such as courses in chemistry and foreign languages. The invention of the internal combustion engine improved school transportation. By the 1920s, North Carolina's school transportation system was the nation's leader.

For many young North Carolinians, lifestyles and working conditions changed drastically as the state became an industrial power.

If You Were There *Would you have preferred to work on a family farm or in a mill? Why?*

LEFT PAGE: *Downtown Raleigh symbolizes North Carolina's growth as a financial, technological, and manufacturing leader in the 21st century.*

243

CHAPTER 13
North Carolina in the Industrial Age
(1870–1930)

Steam engines, celebrated as symbols of the Industrial Revolution

Build on What You Know

The Civil War left its mark on North Carolina—politically and economically. Agriculture was still the main economic activity, but over the following decades, the industrial age would arrive in North Carolina. In this chapter you will learn how the state became the South's industrial leader.

What's Your Opinion?

Do you **agree** or **disagree** with the following statements? Support your point of view in your journal.

- **Geography** Natural resources play a role in the kinds of industry a state develops.
- **Citizenship** All citizens of a certain age should be allowed to vote.
- **Science, Technology & Society** Advancements in technology improve society.

Section 1

The Rise of North Carolina Industries

Read to Discover
1. How and why did cities grow and railroads expand in North Carolina?
2. How did the tobacco, textile, and furniture industries develop in North Carolina?

Define
- mill villages

Identify
- R. J. Reynolds
- Washington Duke
- James Buchanan (Buck) Duke

The Story Continues

At the end of the Civil War, North Carolina was still an agricultural, rural state. Over the next decades, however, it would steadily change. In 1870, one out of every 25 North Carolinians lived in a town. In 1900, one in ten lived in a town. By 1930, that number had grown dramatically, to one in four. Some urban centers remained sleepy villages with "little animation in man or beasts. The very dogs look lazy," according to writer Walter Hines Page. Other cities, however, were busy centers of business.

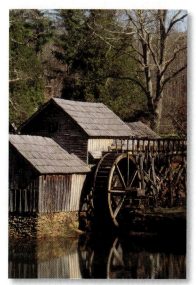

Water-powered mills like this one helped to power the Industrial Revolution in North Carolina.

 ### The Rise of Cities and Railroads

The Industrial Revolution had taken hold in the North by the early 1800s. Prior to 1865, however, most of the southern states—including North Carolina—remained largely agricultural and rural. The North's victory in the Civil War made many North Carolinians take notice. They realized that an economy that included manufacturing was, in some ways, superior to their agricultural economy.

North Carolina in the Industrial Age 245

Cities Mills and factories began to be built in and near towns that had good water sources. The chance to work in them lured people away from the farms. Urban areas grew rapidly. From 1870 to 1900, the number of North Carolina towns with more than 10,000 people grew from one—Wilmington—to six. These included Wilmington, Charlotte, Asheville, Winston, Raleigh, and Greensboro. Four of these cities lay in the Piedmont Crescent. Leadership in the state began to shift from the east to a new urban middle class of businesspeople in the Piedmont and the west.

Railroads As North Carolina cities grew, so did the state's rail system. By 1900, about 3,800 miles of railroad moved people and goods in the state. Three major north-south systems emerged: the Southern Railway Company served the Piedmont and west; the Atlantic Coastline Railroad ran through the eastern coastal plain; and the Seaboard Airline Railway served the area between. These statewide routes tied into a national rail network that carried North Carolina goods—particularly tobacco, textiles, and furniture—to the country.

✔ **READING CHECK** **Identifying Cause and Effect** How were industrialization, cities, and railroads related?

★ The Tobacco Industry

Perhaps no other industry is more associated with North Carolina than tobacco. By 1880 there were 126 tobacco factories in the state.

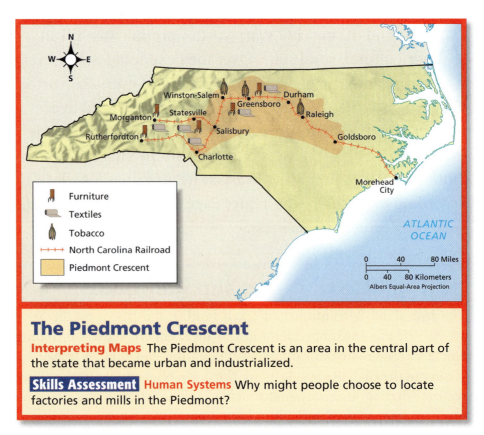

The Piedmont Crescent
Interpreting Maps The Piedmont Crescent is an area in the central part of the state that became urban and industrialized.
Skills Assessment **Human Systems** Why might people choose to locate factories and mills in the Piedmont?

Winston and Durham In 1875 <u>R. J. Reynolds</u> founded his R. J. Reynolds Tobacco Company in the young town of Winston. It became a leader in tobacco products. Other Winston tobacco manufacturers were Hamilton Scales, Pleasant H. Hanes, and T. L. Vaughn.

North Carolina's growing tobacco industry was centered in the towns of Winston and Durham. The industry's development was spectacular. In 1868, for example, Durham had one tobacco factory; by 1872 it had twelve. Durham produced North Carolina's most famous tobacco product at the time—the W. T. Blackwell Company's Bull Durham smoking tobacco. Posters and signs advertised Bull Durham around the world. In 1874 <u>Washington Duke</u> moved his family tobacco business from his farm to the town of Durham. From there he and his three sons, Brodie, Benjamin, and Buck, would build a tobacco empire.

The American Tobacco Company Under the business leadership of <u>James Buchanan (Buck) Duke</u>, the Dukes began to produce cigarettes. To advertise, they used celebrity endorsements and promotions such as trading cards and gift coupons. Demand increased so much that the Dukes replaced the employees who rolled cigarettes by hand with cigarette-rolling machines. In 1890 the Dukes' company was incorporated as the American Tobacco Company. By the 1900s it was earning about $275 million a year and controlled 75 percent of the tobacco industry in the country.

✔ **READING CHECK** Analyzing Information What role did key industrialists play in the rise of the tobacco industry?

⭐ The Textile Industry

Small North Carolina mills had produced textiles before the Civil War, but the number and size of textile mills grew greatly after 1880. Almost all were located in the Piedmont and made use of the waterpower there to drive the machinery. In addition to more cloth, the variety of cloth—plaids, stripes, shirting, sheeting, and hosiery—greatly increased.

By the early 1900s, about 200,000 North Carolinians had left the farms to seek work in textile mills. Often entire families went to work in the same factory. In 1900 the average annual wage was $216 for a man, $157 for a woman, and $103 for a child.

Many textile mills were at the center of ==mill villages== built by the textile companies. Workers paid low rent to live in houses owned by the company. They shopped in company-owned stores and attended the company-built church on Sundays. Some companies even provided schools, libraries, baseball fields, and lodge halls for their employees.

In each mill village, many of the workers were related to one another. Even among those who were not related by blood, a sense of family developed. Despite some of the benefits of living in mill villages,

BIOGRAPHY

R. J. Reynolds
(1850–1918)

Richard Joshua Reynolds worked in the tobacco company his father owned in Virginia until 1874. Then the young Reynolds struck out on his own, founding the R.J. Reynolds Tobacco Company in Winston, North Carolina. His shrewd business and advertising skills turned the company into one of the leading manufacturers of tobacco products in the country and made Reynolds a millionaire many times over. **How was R. J. Reynolds an example of a key North Carolina industrialist?**

Did You KNOW?

The modern city of Winston-Salem was created in 1913 when the two towns of Winston and Salem merged.

North Carolina-made organ, c. 1910

Analyzing Primary Sources

Making Generalizations and Predictions Based on Wrenn's comment, what would future furniture makers need to do?

mill work remained difficult. Mill employees—including children—worked long hours for low pay. The mills were hot and humid, and the roar of the machines was often deafening.

✔ **READING CHECK** Summarizing How did the textile industry grow in North Carolina in the late 1800s?

★ Furniture

The first furniture factory in North Carolina was the High Point Furniture Company, established in 1888. High Point was a good location for the new factory. It had easy access to rail transportation; it was in the middle of a vast hardwood forest; and it attracted poor rural workers eager to find employment. The "factory" itself was little more than a two-story shed. Yet it made so much furniture its first year that one of its owners, Thomas F. Wrenn, said:

"I thought surely the whole world soon would be supplied ... and from the amount of lumber we used I was positive that the forests of North Carolina were completely destroyed."
—Thomas Wrenn, quoted in *North Carolina Through Four Centuries* by William S. Powell

Soon other furniture factories were sprouting up, in High Point and throughout the Piedmont. Furniture makers began producing higher quality goods and marketing their products to the rest of the nation. By the early 1900s North Carolina was on its way to becoming the country's leading producer of fine furniture.

✔ **READING CHECK** Identifying Cause and Effect How did North Carolina's natural resources help the furniture-making business?

Section 1 Review

keyword: SN3 HP13

❶ Define and explain:
- mill villages

❷ Identify and explain:
- R. J. Reynolds
- Washington Duke
- James Buchanan (Buck) Duke

❸ Summarizing Copy the concept web below. Use it to record key information about the three main industries in North Carolina in the industrial age.

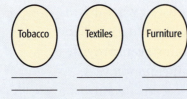

❹ Finding the Main Idea
a. Where and why did North Carolina cities and railroads grow?

b. What ways did tobacco, textile, and furniture makers use to increase their sales?

❺ Writing and Critical Thinking
Decision Making Write an editorial expressing your view on whether and how North Carolina should have industrialized in the last part of the 1800s.

Consider:
- the success of the North
- the needs of the people
- the resources of the state

Section 2

Life in the New South

Read to Discover
1. What problems did North Carolina's farmers confront in the late 1800s?
2. What institutions did African Americans create to improve their lives?
3. How did education in North Carolina change with the coming of industrialization?

Define
- sharecroppers

Identify
- Leonidas L. Polk
- John Merrick
- Walter Hines Page
- Mummies

The Story Continues

Industrialization had come to North Carolina. Towns grew in size and number. Even so, the majority of North Carolinians still lived in rural areas, and most still farmed for a living. North Carolina farmers had problems, however. One group reported: "The boasted progress and wealth in North Carolina is not shared by the farmers. They are gradually but steadily becoming poorer every year."

Even in the best of years, most tenant farmers found it difficult to make a living. They worked long, backbreaking hours to raise food for their families and to earn the cash needed for rent.

 ### Agriculture

After the war, many plantations and large farms were broken up. Original owners often kept part of their land to farm themselves. The other plots were sold to new owners or rented. Tenant farmers paid cash to rent the land, tended it, and kept the harvest. **Sharecroppers** tended the land and paid rent with a portion of the harvest. In 1880 more than one third of North Carolina's farms operated in this way. Many former slaves became tenant farmers or sharecroppers. Many poor whites eked out a living this way too.

Farm production did recover after the war. As much cotton was being produced by 1870 and as much tobacco by 1880 as had been

North Carolina in the Industrial Age **249**

produced before the war. In fact, North Carolina farms started producing more than they had before the war.

Overproduction became a problem in North Carolina and elsewhere in rural America. Farmers produced too much and got too little cash for their crops as prices fell in a glutted market. In addition, farmers paid high interest on loans and high prices for supplies. Farmers were generally in debt. To improve their situation, many began to organize.

In the 1870s many North Carolina farmers joined local units of the Grange. This national group sought to help farmers socially and economically, but it was largely ineffective.

A more successful farm organization was the Farmers' Alliance. The North Carolina branch of this group organized in 1887, and by the end of that year about 30,000 members had joined. The leader of the Farmers' Alliance in the state was **Leonidas L. Polk**, a farmer who became the state's commissioner of agriculture. Polk also published the *Progressive Farmer*, a magazine that both educated farmers and spoke out for them.

✔ **READING CHECK** **Identifying Cause and Effect** Why did many farmers in North Carolina have problems in the late 1800s?

CONNECTING TO ECONOMICS

The North Carolina Mutual Life Insurance Company

In 1900, 28 life insurance companies were doing business in North Carolina. All were out-of-state companies but one—the North Carolina Mutual Life Insurance Company. The company was organized in Durham in October 1898 by a group of African Americans headed by businessman **John Merrick**. It offered health and life insurance policies. The company and its skyscraper headquarters became a symbol of African American achievement. Its slogan—"with a Soul and a Service"—marked its commitment to the black community. Today it remains the country's oldest and largest African American-founded insurance company. **How did the North Carolina Mutual Life Insurance Company represent black achievement?**

African American Institutions

Many former slaves left the rural areas and migrated to towns and cities. There most found work as unskilled laborers and domestic workers. Some, however, worked in skilled trades as barbers, brickmakers, carpenters, masons, printers, or dockworkers. In fact, in 1900 half the skilled workers in the cities were African American.

Churches After emancipation, many black churchgoers withdrew from their former congregations. They founded their own congregations, often affiliated with black denominations, like the African Methodist Episcopal (A.M.E.) church. Sometimes black churches were the site of political meetings. More often, though, they were centers of the spiritual and social life of black communities.

Schools After the war, the Freedmen's Bureau built more than 400 schools for more than 20,000 black students in North Carolina. The state also saw the founding of nearly a dozen black colleges. Shaw University in Raleigh was one, Livingstone College in Salisbury another. At these and other

John Merrick, North Carolina business leader and co-founder of the North Carolina Mutual Life Insurance Company, came to symbolize black achievement during the early 1900s.

institutions, black students could receive an industrial education, liberal arts instruction, or training for the professions, such as teaching, law, and medicine. In 1891 the state formed the first teacher-training school for African Americans in the South, what is now North Carolina Agricultural and Technical State University in Greensboro.

✔ **READING CHECK** **Finding the Main Idea** How did African Americans move to help themselves in the last part of the 1800s?

⭐ Education

The move to industrialize North Carolina also led to calls to improve public education. An editorial in the *Raleigh News and Observer* of November 1880 proclaimed:

"We must make money—it is a power in this practical business age. Teach the boys and girls to work and teach them to be proud of it. Demand a better and more liberal system of public education and if need be, demand increased taxation to obtain it. Infuse [introduce] into that system practical, industrial education."

"Our Refuge and Our Strength," *Raleigh News and Observer*, November 9, 1880

The "Mummies" The state system of public schools had collapsed after the war. In 1880 only one third of school-age children attended school, for an average of nine weeks a year. Illiteracy was extremely high. This problem prompted one critic, **Walter Hines Page**, to call the state's leaders "**Mummies**." He claimed they were stuck in the past, longing "for the good old days instead of looking to the promise of the future." At first, poverty and North Carolinians' dislike for taxes to support schools were roadblocks to the progressive change favored by Page and other reformers in the state. Yet even when public support grew, little was done to improve education before 1900.

This beautiful building on the Duke University campus symbolizes the educational progress made in North Carolina during the Industrial Revolution.

Higher education The need for colleges and universities was not as neglected as lower levels of schooling. Colleges that had closed during or after the war reopened one by one: Wake Forest and Trinity in 1866, the University of North Carolina in 1875. In addition, the state legislature chartered several new public colleges, including the North Carolina College of Agriculture and Mechanic Arts in 1887 (now North Carolina State University in Raleigh). In 1892 the state's first public college for women opened, the State Normal and Industrial School (now the University of North Carolina at Greensboro). Two more church-sponsored colleges also opened their doors during this period, Meredith in 1899 and Elon in 1900.

✔ **READING CHECK** **Summarizing** What was the general state of public education in North Carolina in the late 1800s?

That's Interesting!

Trinity and Duke Trinity was a Methodist College in Randolph County. In 1892 it moved to Durham. Washington, Benjamin, and Buck Duke supported it financially. In 1924 Buck Duke made a generous endowment. The name of the institution was changed to Duke University, and it has become a leading institution of higher learning in the nation.

North Carolina in the Industrial Age **251**

★ Growing Class Divisions

The "Mummies" that Walter Hines Page complained about were the Democratic leaders of the state. In general, they represented the interests of the industrialists and the railroads. The interests of farmers, laborers, and the general public were not considered. Farmers lived mainly on credit and often were in debt, which got worse each year as crop prices fell. Laborers worked long hours in harsh working conditions for relatively little pay. African Americans saw their newly won political rights taken from them. Industrialization brought wealth to some North Carolinians, but that wealth was not shared by the majority of the state's citizens.

✔ **READING CHECK** Making Generalizations and Predictions What might result from the growing differences between the industrialist class and other North Carolinians?

Interpreting the Visual Record

The Biltmore House
Industrialist G. W. Vanderbilt's Biltmore House, constructed near Asheville between 1890 and 1895, is still the largest private residence in the United States. **What kind of residence does the Biltmore House resemble?**

Section 2 Review

keyword: SN3 HP13

1 Define and explain:
- sharecroppers

2 Identify and explain:
- Leonidas L. Polk
- John Merrick
- Walter Hines Page
- Mummies

3 Analyzing Information Copy the diagram below. Use it to explain the problems farmers faced in the late 1800s.

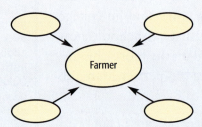

4 Finding the Main Idea
a. How did both white and African American farmers in the late 1800s try to strengthen themselves?

b. Why was the quality of education so poor in North Carolina in the late 1800s?

5 Writing and Critical Thinking
Supporting a Point of View Imagine you are Walter Hines Page. Write a column defending your description of state leaders and your call to improve education.

Consider:
- the state of the schools
- the need for education in an industrial age
- the cost of education

Section 3

A Changing Society

Read to Discover
1. What technological advances occurred from 1870 to 1920, and how did they affect life in North Carolina?
2. What political changes occurred in the 1890s, and how did they ultimately affect African Americans?
3. What changes did the Progressive Era bring?

Define
- labor tax
- white supremacy
- disenfranchise

Identify
- Wright brothers
- Furnifold M. Simmons
- Fusionists
- Red Shirts
- George H. White
- Charles B. Aycock

The Story Continues

The industrial age brought great changes to North Carolinians—economically, culturally, politically, and socially. As the 20th century approached, the state was ready to face a new world.

This struggling family of poor migrants was probably searching for opportunity and a better way of life.

Immigrants, Migrants, and the Middle Class

The late 1880s through 1920 saw a great wave of immigration to the United States. North Carolina wanted to encourage immigration to the state as a way of adding skilled labor that would lure industry. In 1874 the legislature set up a Board of Immigration staffed by immigration agents. Few immigrants came to the Tar Heel State, however. By 1890 the state ended its efforts to bring in immigrants. Later, some European immigrants established farm colonies in North Carolina: St. Helena (by Italian immigrants), Castle Hayne and Van Eden (by Dutch), and New Berlin (by Germans).

Meanwhile, some native North Carolinians were moving out of the state. In the mid-1880s many young people left to attend business and

North Carolina in the Industrial Age **253**

CONNECTING TO SCIENCE AND TECHNOLOGY

The Wright Brothers' Airplane

Orville and Wilbur Wright, of Dayton, Ohio, studied the flights of birds, recorded air pressure and winds, and designed gliders and kites—all with the hope of one day designing an airplane in which a person could fly. At Kitty Hawk, North Carolina, they found the right conditions to test their gliders and conducted several successful manned glider flights. Back in Dayton, they designed a larger machine with two propellers powered by a 12-horsepower engine—the Wright airplane. Returning to Kitty Hawk, they tested the plane on December 17 and watched it fly for 12 seconds over a distance of 100 feet. **What steps did the Wright Brothers take to design and test their airplane?**

professional schools and never returned. After 1900 many African Americans moved north to seek better lives and escape the segregation that was typical by the turn of the century.

Slowly the strict divide between rich and poor in the state began to weaken as the middle class grew in strength and number. In the towns they operated stores and banks and provided professional services. Many lived in Victorian-style houses on quiet city streets away from the business districts or even in new suburban developments.

✔ **READING CHECK** Making Generalizations and Predictions What effect might a loss of young people and workers have on a state?

Science and Technology

The industrial age also became the electric age in North Carolina in the 1880s. In that decade electricity began to be used for lights and power.

Inventions and daily life North Carolina's first telephone exchange was constructed in Raleigh in the spring of 1882. Later in 1882 telephones were installed in Wilmington, in 1886 in Asheville, and in 1890 in Winston and Salem. Electric lights lit up Raleigh in 1885, Wilmington in 1886, and Winston in 1887. Soon electricity was powering factories and mills as well as household lighting and appliances—refrigerators, sewing machines, irons, and the like. Still, many rural regions of the state did not obtain electricity until the 1930s.

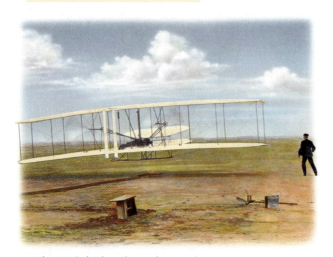

The Wright brothers changed the future on December 17, 1903, as they made the first successful powered flight.

Transportation Improved transportation was both a cause and an effect of industrialization in North Carolina. The rail system expanded greatly before 1900, but growth slowed after that. Roads and highways were not built quickly. As late as 1900, counties were responsible for road building and repair. Many, however, had no resources for roadwork except convict labor or the "labor tax"—six days a year of work from able-bodied male citizens. Some towns did improve their roads and sidewalks.

Horse-drawn streetcars began operating in Wilmington and Raleigh in 1887. In 1889, Asheville became the first North Carolina town to have an electric street railway. Fayetteville, Salisbury, Charlotte, and other North Carolina towns soon followed.

One of the greatest achievements ever in transportation occurred in North Carolina on December 17, 1903. On that date the **Wright brothers** staged the first successful manned flight of an airplane.

✔ **READING CHECK** Identifying Cause and Effect How did technological advances affect life in North Carolina?

Political Turmoil in the 1890s

Even with advances in technology and growing wealth for some, the problems of farmers remained. Their requests for help fell on deaf ears. Railroad and business interests controlled the Democrats in office.

The Populists organize In North Carolina and elsewhere, farmers and other reformers decided to start their own political party. The Populist—or People's—Party supported changes in the money system and tax and election reforms. They favored the ten-hour workday for laborers. When the Farmers' Alliance split, some members, like Leonidas Polk, became Populists.

In the election of 1892, North Carolina Democrats followed their party chairman, **Furnifold M. Simmons**. Simmons led a racist campaign that played on the fears of whites. He warned of a return of Republican and black rule. The Democrats won the governor's race and the legislature, but Republican and Populist candidates together actually won more votes.

The Fusionists In 1894 the Republicans and Populists joined forces—or "fused." They supported one ticket that had either a Republican or a Populist for each office. These **Fusionists** won a sweeping victory. In 1896 Fusion candidates ran for some offices, but their power was weakening. Republican Daniel Russell won the governor's race. From 1897 to 1899, Fusionists were in control of the state. They began to reform education and local government.

The election of 1898 In 1898 the Democrats once more followed the strategy of Furnifold Simmons. They campaigned to maintain "white supremacy," or rule by whites. A group known as the **Red Shirts** intimidated African Americans.

Furnifold Simmons, North Carolina's Democratic Party chairman in 1892, led an election campaign based on scare tactics and racial fear.

 "Men wore flaming red shirts, rode horses, carried rifles, paraded through Negro communities, and appeared at political rallies, especially Republican rallies."

Quoted in *North Carolina: The History of a Southern State*
by Hugh Talmage Lefler and Albert Ray Newsome

With the theme of white supremacy and the support of business, the Democrats won the legislature back. Many African Americans were prevented from voting. Two days after the November 8 election, a race riot erupted in Wilmington. A group of white men destroyed the printing press of a black newspaper. Eleven African Americans were reported killed, though the number may have been higher. The black mayor of Wilmington fled.

That's Interesting!

George H. White In 1896 **George H. White** of Tarboro was elected to the U.S. House of Representatives. He was the only African American in Congress during that time. After completing his second term in 1901, he and his family moved away from North Carolina due to racial prejudice in the state.

Disenfranchisement and segregation The Democrats now took steps to **disenfranchise** African Americans, or take away their right to vote. They proposed an amendment that would require a voter to pay a poll tax and be able to read and write. To avoid disenfranchising whites, they inserted a grandfather clause in the law. No one who could vote on or before January 1, 1867, or any descendant of such a person, could be denied the right to vote. In effect, that would disenfranchise most blacks but not illiterate whites.

The voting amendment was passed in 1900. Also in that election the Democratic candidate, **Charles B. Aycock**, ran on a campaign of white supremacy and improving education. He won handily. In addition, new laws were passed that required segregation of the races in schools, restaurants, railroad cars, and other public facilities.

✔ **READING CHECK** **Summarizing** What political events occurred in the 1890s, and what was their result?

★ The Progressive Era in North Carolina

The turn of the century marked the beginning of the Progressive Era—a time of attempted reform throughout the nation. Many North Carolina leaders spoke of the new century as the "Dawn of a New Day."

Education In 1900 only two thirds of the state's children were enrolled in school. Less than half attended regularly. Governor Aycock claimed all children, white and black, deserved an education. He convinced wealthy residents that local taxes for schools were an investment in the future of North Carolina. In 1901 the legislature doubled the money set aside for education. In 1907 it passed a rural high school act. Within a year 160 new high schools were opened. However, state spending for black students remained far behind that for white students.

Prohibition In 1908 the General Assembly called for a statewide referendum, or vote, on banning the sale of alcohol. The ban passed by a landslide, and North Carolina became the first state to approve prohibition. In 1919 prohibition became national law with the passage of the 18th Amendment to the U.S. Constitution.

Prisons In the 1800s private employers could lease prisoners to use as workers. Prisoners dug rocks and built railroads. In 1901 this system was reformed. Prisoners still worked for private

Interpreting the Visual Record

Prohibition Authorities destroyed huge quantities of illegal alcohol during the years of prohibition. **Why might government authorities have published photographs such as this during prohibition?**

business, but under prison guards. Chain gangs worked on the state roads. In 1910 inmates began to be paid for their work. They earned up to 15 cents a day, paid when they were released. In 1925 all prisons came under state control.

Labor For mill workers, hours were long, wages were low, and conditions were unsafe. Almost one fourth of the workers were children. The government and factory owners opposed labor unions, however. In some cases the opposition to unions turned violent.

Slowly, support for labor reform, especially for children, began to gain support. In 1903 the state passed a weak child labor law. Stronger laws were passed in 1907 and 1913 that said that no one under 16 could work nights or over 66 hours a week. A Child Labor Committee was established to inspect mills. Not until 1933 did the U.S. government outlaw child labor.

Reform laws aimed at workplace health hazards, long hours and low pay, and other problems helped to improve working conditions for young workers such as these.

Politics The Democrats dominated North Carolina after 1900. Aycock was the first Democratic governor in a line of Democratic governors that lasted until 1973. Within the Democratic Party, however, conservatives and liberals fought for control. An important political reform was the passage of direct primary election laws in 1907 and 1915. Candidates for office would now be chosen directly by the voters, rather than by political committees.

✔ **READING CHECK Summarizing** How did life improve for children during the Progressive Era?

Section 3 Review

1 Define and explain:
- labor tax
- white supremacy
- disenfranchise

2 Identify and explain:
- Wright brothers
- Furnifold M. Simmons
- Fusionists
- Red Shirts
- George H. White
- Charles B. Aycock

3 Sequencing Copy the time line below. Use it to sequence the major political events of the 1890s.

1890 1892 1894 1896 1898 1900

4 Finding the Main Idea
a. Why did some African Americans leave North Carolina after 1900?
b. How did technology change North Carolina lifestyles in the industrial age?
c. What were some major reforms accomplished during the Progressive Era?

5 Writing and Critical Thinking
Summarizing Imagine you are a historian. Write a paragraph that sums up the events of the 1890s and their impact on North Carolina.
Consider:
- the Republican-Populist political alliance
- the campaign strategy of the Democrats

go.hrw.com **Homework Practice Online** keyword: SN3 HP13

North Carolina in the Industrial Age 257

Section 4
World War I and Its Aftermath

Read to Discover
1. How did North Carolina's people respond to the war?
2. How did the war affect North Carolinians?
3. What major political change occurred following the war?

Define
- fundamentalist movement

Identify
- Thomas Wolfe
- Cameron Morrison
- Carrie L. Broughton
- Harriet Morehead Berry
- Lillian Exum Clement

The sinking of the luxury liner Lusitania *by a German U-boat in 1915 moved the United States closer to war. Among the victims of the attack were 128 American citizens.*

The Story Continues

After the turmoil of the 1890s, the early 1900s were relatively quiet. In fact, in 1916 North Carolina elected Thomas W. Bickett governor in what has been called "the quiet election." The shadow of war in Europe, however, already hung over the United States. Soon many North Carolinians would leave home in an experience that would change their lives forever.

★ North Carolina and National Politics

War broke out in Europe in 1914. The United States tried to remain neutral. In 1915 a British ocean liner, the *Lusitania*, was sunk by a German submarine. Among the victims were 128 U.S. citizens. At the time North Carolinian Walter Hines Page was the U.S. ambassador to Great Britain. Hines called for the United States to get involved, but President Woodrow Wilson, like many Americans, favored remaining neutral. In a 1916 speech, Wilson maintained the following statement.

History Makers Speak "One cool judgment is worth a thousand hasty counsels. The thing to do is to supply light and not heat."

Woodrow Wilson, Speech, January 29, 1916, in
The Columbia World of Quotations

Analyzing Primary Sources
Drawing Conclusions Why do you think Wilson and Page had opposing views about the need to go to war?

It took one more year, and the loss of several more ships, before Congress declared war.

Several North Carolina politicians played important roles during the war. Claude Kitchin was the Democratic minority leader of the House of Representatives. He also served as chairman of the Ways and Means Committee. Kitchin worked tirelessly to fund U.S. troops overseas. His counterpart, the chairman of the Senate Finance Committee, was Furnifold Simmons, who had been elected senator in 1901. Josephus Daniels served as secretary of the navy during the war. He had the responsibility of transporting more than 2 million U.S. soldiers to Europe.

✔ **READING CHECK** **Finding the Main Idea** What role did North Carolina politicians play in the war effort by the United States?

North Carolina and the War

North Carolinians were actively involved in the war effort. The war even came close to home in 1918. In August the Diamond Shoals Lightship and a British tanker just off Rodanthe, in the Atlantic, were both sunk by German submarines.

The state sent many young men and women to Europe. Most of the women served in medical units. More than 85,000 men, nearly a quarter of them black, went overseas. Nearly 2,500 died. The 30th Division and the 81st "Wildcat" Division fought bravely in France. One major general, three brigadier generals, and three rear admirals also came from North Carolina.

With so many men away from home, much of the work in the state fell to women. They worked with the Red Cross, YMCA, and other organizations to provide clothes and supplies for the troops. They also took on jobs in offices, factories, and shops. War in Europe meant tightening the belt at home. Citizens cut back to allow food and supplies to be sent overseas. North Carolinians spent $10 million more on war bonds than the government asked.

Training camps were established in Charlotte and Raleigh, and Camp Bragg was built near Fayetteville. These camps provided a boost to the local economy. Civilians found work in the shipyards at Wilmington and in an ammunitions factory in Raleigh.

✔ **READING CHECK** **Summarizing** How did North Carolina support the war?

Throughout World War I, the Red Cross stood as a symbol of care, mercy, and humanity in the midst of conflict on a scale never before seen.

North Carolina in the Industrial Age **259**

⭐ Postwar Changes

The war ended in 1918. Young men and women who served in the war came home changed by their experiences. Some began to challenge what they saw as old ways of thinking and acting.

Jazz music became popular at dance clubs and on the radio. In fact, the 1920s are sometimes called the Jazz Age. Motion pictures were especially popular during and after the war years. D. W. Griffith's silent film epic, *Birth of a Nation*, was based on North Carolina author Thomas Dixon's novel *The Clansman*, which romanticized the Ku Klux Klan.

The **fundamentalist movement** arose as a reaction to the changes of the time. Christian fundamentalists believe in a literal interpretation of the Bible. Their greatest concern was with the teaching of evolution, especially the idea that all living creatures descended from common origins. Bills were introduced into the General Assembly to prohibit teaching evolution. Educators were criticized for discussing the scientific theory in classes.

North Carolina literature blossomed in the new century. Samuel A. Ashe wrote the first comprehensive history of the state. William Sydney

CONNECTING TO Literature

Look Homeward, Angel
Thomas Wolfe

North Carolina novelist Thomas Wolfe

North Carolinian Thomas Wolfe is best known for his first novel, Look Homeward, Angel, *published in 1929. The novel tells the story of Eugene Gant, a young man who leaves home to find his fortune in Boston. Eugene's hometown of Altamont is a thinly veiled portrait of Wolfe's hometown, Asheville. Eugene's father in the novel, Oliver, and mother, Eliza, are based on Wolfe's real parents. The following scene is from the first meeting between Oliver and Eliza.*

[Eliza said] "If I were you, I'd pitch right in and take an interest in the town's progress. We've got everything here it takes to make a big town . . . Do you see this corner here—the one you're on? It'll double in value in the next few years. . . . They're going to run a street through here some day as sure as you live. And when they do—" she pursed her lips reflectively, "that property is going to be worth money."

She continued to talk about property with a strange meditative hunger. The town seemed to be an enormous blueprint to her: her head was stuffed uncannily with figures and estimates—who owned a lot, who sold it, the sale-price, the real value, the future value, first and second mortgages, and so on. When she had finished, Oliver said with the emphasis of strong aversion . . . "I hope I never own another piece of property as long as I live—save a house to live in. It is nothing but a curse and a care, and the tax-collector gets it all in the end."

Eliza looked at him with a startled expression, as if he had uttered a . . . heresy.

Understanding Literature

1. What is the difference between how Oliver and Eliza feel about property? What does this say about their relationship?
2. How might this conversation between Oliver and Eliza reflect popular opinions about development in North Carolina during the industrial age?

Porter published short stories in national magazines under the pen name O. Henry. Charles W. Chestnutt wrote stories and novels describing the experiences of African Americans in the state. **Thomas Wolfe** became one of North Carolina's most famous writers.

✓ **READING CHECK** Identifying Cause and Effect How did popular culture influence the rise of fundamentalism?

⭐ Changes in Government

In 1920 North Carolina elected **Cameron Morrison** governor, ushering in an era of great economic growth. Morrison is known as the "Good Roads Governor." Under his leadership, the state built and improved 6,000 miles of roads, connecting every county seat and major town. Morrison also worked to improve the universities and public schools.

In 1884 Margaret Richardson was the first woman in North Carolina to publicly support women's suffrage, the right of women to vote. By 1914, 16 towns in the state had suffrage organizations. In 1919 an amendment giving women the right to vote passed Congress. The next year it became the 19th Amendment to the Constitution.

Women gradually took their place beside men in state government. When **Carrie L. Broughton** became state librarian in 1918, she was the first woman to head a state department. **Harriet Morehead Berry** was called the best woman politician in the state. In 1920 **Lillian Exum Clement** became the first woman elected to the North Carolina General Assembly.

✓ **READING CHECK** Drawing Conclusions How did government in North Carolina improve following World War I?

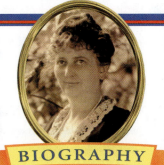

BIOGRAPHY

Harriet Morehead Berry
(1877–1940)

Harriet Berry entered public life as the secretary of the North Carolina Geological and Economic Survey. This agency worked with the Good Roads Association to construct better roads. Berry took control of the agency in 1917. She became known as the "Mother of Good Roads." She continued to work for better schools and increased industry and tourism. **How did Harriet Morehead Berry help improve the state?**

Section 4 Review

keyword: SN3 HP13

1. Define and explain:
- fundamentalist movement

2. Identify and explain:
- Thomas Wolfe
- Cameron Morrison
- Carrie L. Broughton
- Harriet Morehead Berry
- Lillian Exum Clement

3. Analyzing Information Copy the web diagram below. Use it to record changes in women's roles and women's achievements before, during, and after World War I.

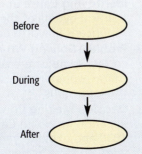

4. Finding the Main Idea
a. How did North Carolina respond to World War I?
b. How did North Carolina change after the war?

5. Writing and Critical Thinking
Supporting a Point of View Imagine you are a woman living in North Carolina in 1918. Write an essay explaining why you deserve the right to vote.

Consider:
- women during World War I
- women in state government

North Carolina in the Industrial Age **261**

Chapter 13 Review

Chapter Summary

Section 1
- North Carolina cities and transportation networks—especially railroads—grew rapidly as a result of post–Civil War industrialization.
- Economic expansion in North Carolina in the years between 1870 and 1930 was driven, in part, by the tobacco, textile, and furniture industries.

Section 2
- Farmers in North Carolina faced growing challenges in the years following Reconstruction.
- North Carolina's African American community developed social, economic, and cultural institutions in the face of continuing prejudice and segregation.
- Education in North Carolina became more progressive, and educational opportunities expanded as a result of industrial growth.

Section 3
- North Carolina became the scene of important technological, as well as industrial, advances.
- Political and social development in North Carolina was strongly affected by a new sense of progressivism after about 1900.

Section 4
- North Carolinians did much to support their nation's war effort during World War I, both at home and abroad.
- The changing American culture of the postwar years gave rise to new religious and artistic movements in North Carolina.

Identifying People and Ideas
Use the following terms or people in complete sentences.

1. mill villages
2. James Buchanan (Buck) Duke
3. sharecroppers
4. Leonidas L. Polk
5. Walter Hines Page
6. disenfranchise
7. Furnifold M. Simmons
8. Fusionists
9. fundamentalist movement
10. Harriet Morehead Berry

Understanding Main Ideas

Section 1 (Pages 245–248)
1. In what ways did industrialization come to North Carolina?

Section 2 (Pages 249–252)
2. What problems did farmers in North Carolina face?
3. What was the state of education in the late 1800s, and why?

Section 3 (Pages 253–257)
4. What scientific and technological advances affected life in the industrial age?
5. What political turmoil occurred in the 1890s in North Carolina?

Section 4 (Pages 258–261)
6. How did life change in North Carolina after World War I?

What Did You Find Out?

1. **Geography** What role did natural resources play in the industries that developed in North Carolina?
2. **Citizenship** How did poll taxes and literacy tests affect people's ability to vote in North Carolina?
3. **Science, Technology & Society** How did new inventions affect life in North Carolina in the years between 1870 and 1930?

Thinking Critically

1. **Identifying Cause and Effect** What effect did the political events of the 1890s have on African Americans in North Carolina?
2. **Problem Solving** What could have been done to correct some of the problems tenant farmers, sharecroppers, and even farm owners faced in the late 1800s?
3. **Decision Making** Consider the effects of industrialization on North Carolina between 1870 and 1930 and explain whether you think overall they were positive or negative.

Building Social Studies Skills

Interpreting a Graph
Study the graph below. Then use the information on the table to answer the questions that follow.

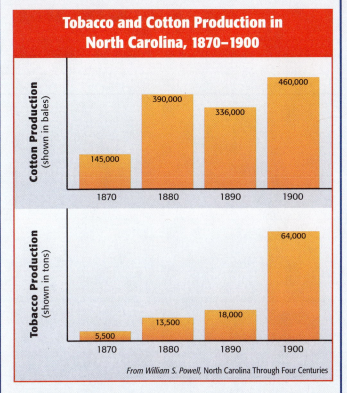

1. Both cotton and tobacco showed an increase in production in every decade except
   a. 1870–1880
   b. 1880–1890
   c. 1890–1900

2. Which farm product—cotton or tobacco—showed the greater increase in production between 1870 and 1900?

Understanding Frames of Reference
Read this quotation describing a student's experience in North Carolina in the late 1800s. This student attended what was called a subscription school, where parents paid a small amount per month for their children's education. Then answer the questions.

"I remember it was just a little bit of a log cabin, and you could stick your fingers down through the cracks in the floor. There was one single row of windows by the workbench. That was all the light we had, don't you know. But they were all broken out and it was open through there.... We went just three months during the cold winter-time. We had a big old fire-place, and the teacher and children would go out to the woods and bring in brush to make a fire.... If we wanted a drink of water, we went to the spring.... We had six lessons a day: Blue Back spelling, arithmetic, reading.... Then we had history and geography, and... I can't remember what the other one was called.... Grammar? I guess that's what it was—grammar."

3. Which of the following statements best describes this quotation?
   a. The quotation is a primary source.
   b. The quotation is a secondary source.
   c. The quotation is from both a primary source and a secondary source.
   d. The quotation is not a reliable source.

4. Why do you think this child went to school for just the three winter months?

Alternative Assessment

Building Your Portfolio

Cooperative Learning
Work in small groups to discover what life was like for a 13-year-old mill worker in the late 1800s in North Carolina. How many hours was a young mill worker on the job? What was the work like? What was life like in a mill village? Would such a worker have received an education? Draw a picture showing such a worker, write a poem expressing his or her feelings, or write a short report detailing his or her life.

internet connect

Internet Activity: go.hrw.com
keyword: SN3 NC13

Choose a topic on North Carolina in the Industrial Age to:

- Write a report on the rise of the tobacco giants in North Carolina.
- Build a model of one of the Wright brothers' airplanes.
- Create a World War I recruitment poster for North Carolina.

CHAPTER 14
Depression and War
(1929–1945)

An agricultural day laborer and his family, 1929

Build on What You Know

The years after World War I were generally years of economic growth in North Carolina. Most workers, except farmers, had steady and reliable incomes. Transportation and public schools were being improved. Many North Carolinians were feeling generous and optimistic about the future.

 Themes Journal

What's Your Opinion?

Do you **agree** or **disagree** with the following statements? Support your point of view in your journal.

- **Economics** In times of economic crisis, a government is responsible for the welfare of its citizens.
- **Global Relations** Allied nations should support each other in times of war.
- **Culture** During an economic crisis or a war, everyone in a country suffers equally.

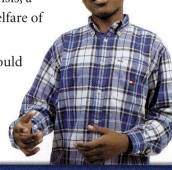

Section 1

The Great Depression

Read to Discover
1. What were the effects of the Great Depression in North Carolina?
2. What was the New Deal and how did it affect North Carolina?
3. What social changes resulted from the New Deal in North Carolina?

Identify
- O. Max Gardner
- Live-at-Home program
- Jane Simpson McKimmon
- Unemployment Compensation Commission
- General Strike
- Civilian Conservation Corps
- Rural Electrification Administration

The Story Continues

In the late 1920s, most Americans believed economic prosperity would go on for years. Based on that belief, many people relied heavily on credit. Some people bought new consumer goods through installment plans. Others invested their money in the stock market, often taking out loans to do so.

The Great Depression

America's economic prosperity came to an end starting in October of 1929. Stock prices had been falling since late September, and on October 24, a large number of nervous investors sold their stock. The sale of so much stock caused stock prices to plunge. By October 29, prices were in a free fall. In New York City, investors on Wall Street panicked. Thousands sold their stocks at huge losses. Many investors were wiped out. The worldwide economic crisis known as the Great Depression had begun.

The stock market crash started a major banking crisis. People could not pay back the money they had borrowed. When worried depositors tried to withdraw their savings, banks did not have enough money to cover the withdrawals. More than 5,000 banks failed.

Interpreting the Visual Record

Children protesting the high rate of unemployment In 1932, almost one quarter of America's workforce was unemployed. *What effect do you think unemployment had on children such as those pictured?*

Depression and War **265**

Businesses also suffered. In 1930 and 1931, more than 54,000 businesses went bankrupt. In 1932, the unemployment rate in the country was 23.6 percent.

✓ **READING CHECK** Summarizing How did reliance on credit influence the Great Depression?

Effects of the Great Depression on North Carolina

From 1929 to 1933, the Great Depression spread throughout the nation. North Carolinians, along with everyone else, were affected.

Deflation and loss of jobs When the Great Depression hit North Carolina, prices dropped sharply. The furniture, textile, and tobacco industries were hurt. Cotton dropped to five cents a pound. Other crop prices fell as well. Mills and factories cut wages, laid off workers, or ran only part time. Many businesses closed. Thousands of people were out of work.

Between 1930 and 1933, hundreds of banks and savings and loan associations in North Carolina failed. Thousands of depositors lost their life savings. Townspeople lost their homes, and many farmers lost their farms. Large numbers of rural people moved into towns looking for work, but there was none. Conditions were worse than they had been since the Civil War.

Limited government aid President Herbert Hoover and the federal government were slow to recognize the seriousness of the depression. Finally in 1932, Congress made some funds available to the states. All the money North Carolina received was used for wages. Workers built and maintained roads, public buildings, and water and sewer lines. Federal funding, however, did not solve the state's problems.

Governor **O. Max Gardner** led North Carolina's own relief efforts. Gardner tried to help people without spending state money. He started the **Live-at-Home program**. The program encouraged farmers to grow their own food and preserve it, instead of buying it at the store. Home demonstration agents showed women how to plant gardens, can food, and sew family clothing. One of the most successful of these agents was **Jane Simpson McKimmon** of Raleigh.

Local agencies gave what help they could. The Red Cross and the Salvation Army provided services. Hospitals gave the needy free health care. Schools provided free lunches. Communities gave men hot meals and places to sleep in exchange for work. Even so, these relief efforts were not enough. Much more had to be done.

✓ **READING CHECK** Identifying Cause and Effect What effect did the Great Depression have on the people of North Carolina?

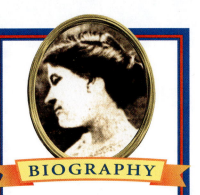

BIOGRAPHY

Jane Simpson McKimmon
(1867-1957)

Jane Simpson McKimmon was one of the pioneers of state home demonstration in America. She achieved such outstanding results in North Carolina that her methods became models for many other states and countries. In 1911, McKimmon became North Carolina's first State Home Demonstration Agent. From then on through the depression and World War II, she had a great effect on rural life in the state. Her emphasis on gardening and canning helped women improve their families' lives. **How would gardening and canning improve a family's standard of living?**

That's Interesting!

Hoover carts During the Great Depression, many people in North Carolina could not afford to operate their cars. Some people used car axles and wheels to make carts. People called these "Hoover carts," because they blamed President Hoover for the depression.

The New Deal in North Carolina

In 1932, Franklin D. Roosevelt was elected president. The nation was still in the grips of the Great Depression. In his inaugural speech Roosevelt promised to tackle the economic crisis as if going to war.

 "The only thing we have to fear is fear itself.... I shall ask the Congress for... broad Executive power to wage a war against the emergency, as great as the power that would be given to me if we were in fact invaded by a foreign foe."

Franklin D. Roosevelt, inaugural address, March 1933

Analyzing Primary Sources
Analyzing Information Why did Roosevelt compare the depression to a war?

Congress gave Roosevelt the support he requested. He began the social and economic reforms and programs known as the New Deal.

Aid to farmers One of the first goals of the New Deal was to help farmers. The government made loans to farmers to save farms and finance crops. Through the Agricultural Adjustment Acts of 1933 and 1938, the government paid farmers to cut production and provided price supports to stabilize markets. Under this program, crop prices rose. By 1936, the total income of North Carolina farmers had more than doubled. Tobacco farmers benefited from these programs more than cotton farmers did.

Industrial reforms Under the New Deal, government reforms protected the rights of workers. Laborers were given the right to form unions. Congress also passed the National Industrial Recovery Act and the Fair Labor Standards Act. They both set minimum wages and maximum hours to protect workers. North Carolina created its own <u>Unemployment Compensation Commission</u> in 1936. The agency provided temporary funds for people who were out of work.

Even with these reforms, however, workers were not always treated fairly. Textile workers, in particular, faced continuing layoffs or had to work harder for no more pay. On September 1, 1934, textile workers across North Carolina and throughout the South walked off their jobs in protest. This <u>General Strike</u> was, up to that time, the largest labor action in American history. State officials called out the National Guard, and a number of workers were killed in clashes along the picket lines. The General Strike collapsed within three weeks. Afterwards, employers refused to hire many of the workers back. Thousands lost their jobs and their homes in the mill villages.

The Civilian Conservation Corps built many temporary camps, like this one in the Nantahala National Forest of North Carolina, seen here in 1935.

Relief and recovery programs Some New Deal programs were meant to get money to desperate people as soon as possible. One of these, the <u>Civilian Conservation Corps</u> (CCC), provided jobs for single young men. They lived in temporary camps and worked at a variety of land conservation jobs, including the construction of hiking trails and park facilities.

Depression and War **267**

Another program, the Works Progress Administration (WPA), created thousands more jobs in North Carolina. Workers built schools, parks, roads, and public utilities. A WPA program called the Federal Writers' Project used oral history interviews to record the lives of ordinary men and women. Similar initiatives, the Federal Theater Project and the Federal Arts Project, brought theatrical performances to small communities and decorated public buildings with murals depicting local history.

✔ **READING CHECK** Finding the Main Idea How did the New Deal help North Carolina recover from the Great Depression?

★ Social Changes from the New Deal

The government also hoped to improve living standards. One agency that had a huge effect was the **Rural Electrification Administration** (REA), started in 1935. Its purpose was to bring electricity to rural areas. The REA made low-interest loans to farm cooperatives. They in turn built power plants and power lines in rural areas. A large part of rural North Carolina gained electricity this way.

The largest New Deal improvement agency was the Tennessee Valley Authority (TVA). Its purpose was to improve the lives of rural people in the Tennessee River basin. The basin covers parts of seven states, including North Carolina. The region flooded often and the soil was eroded. Starting in 1933, the TVA built a number of dams and power stations. These provided flood control, low-cost electricity, and recreation. Today, the TVA is still a major producer of electrical power for the region.

North Carolina's Fontana Dam is the highest dam in the Tennessee Valley Authority system.

✔ **READING CHECK** Making Generalizations How did the New Deal improve living standards in rural areas?

Section 1 Review

keyword: SN3 HP14

❶ Identify and explain:
- O. Max Gardner
- Live-at-Home program
- Jane Simpson McKimmon
- Unemployment Compensation Commission
- General Strike
- Civilian Conservation Corps
- Rural Electrification Administration

❷ Categorizing
Copy the organizer below. Use it to show the New Deal reforms and programs concerned with farms, industry, unemployment, and rural areas.

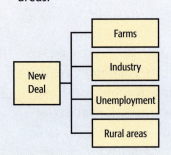

❸ Finding the Main Idea
a. How did the Great Depression affect North Carolina?

b. How did the New Deal help North Carolinians?

c. How did the New Deal affect the standard of living of farmers and other rural people?

❹ Writing and Critical Thinking
Supporting a Point of View Imagine you are a North Carolina farmer during the depression. Write a paragraph describing why you do or do not support the Live-at-Home program.
Consider:
- the effects of the depression on farms
- growing and preserving your own food

Section 2

World War II

Read to Discover
1. What was North Carolina's military involvement in World War II?
2. How did World War II affect the economy of North Carolina?
3. How did prisoners of war help North Carolina's farmers?

Define
- sabotage
- blackout
- defense work

Identify
- Pearl Harbor
- Fort Bragg
- Camp Lejeune
- "Torpedo Junction"

The Story Continues

The Great Depression was not in the United States alone. It was worldwide. In Europe, economic problems led to political unrest that would change the lives of most North Carolinians.

★ The Coming of War

During the 1930s, Adolf Hitler seized power in Germany. Another dictator, Benito Mussolini, had already taken control of Italy. People hoped these dictators would improve conditions in their countries. At the same time, Japan's aggressive military started to expand into Asia.

Americans were worried about what was happening in Europe and Asia. However, many people supported isolationism. This meant they wanted the United States to stay out of the affairs of other countries. Events in Europe began to change people's minds. On September 1, 1939, Germany invaded Poland. Two days later, Britain and France declared war on Germany. World War II had begun.

As the war in Europe raged, Japan continued its expansion. Then on December 7, 1941, Japanese planes bombed the U.S. naval base at **Pearl Harbor** in the Hawaiian Islands. Many warships and aircraft were

Interpreting the Visual Record

Pearl Harbor *The USS Shaw explodes as Japanese planes bomb Pearl Harbor.* **What does this image tell you about the damage done by the Japanese attack?**

Depression and War **269**

destroyed. Some 2,400 Americans were killed. The bombing shocked and united Americans. The next day, the United States entered the war.

✔ **READING CHECK** Sequencing What series of events caused the United States to go to war?

⭐ North Carolina in World War II

When the United States declared war, Americans gave the decision broad support. Jonathan Daniels was editor of the *Raleigh News and Observer* at the time. Thirteen days after the attack on Pearl Harbor, he wrote an article that reflected how many people felt.

Analyzing Primary Sources
Finding the Main Idea
According to this passage, why does Daniels think it is right for America to go to war?

> **History Makers Speak**
> "The American dream for people is still what underlies the irresistible power of our arms. That American dream is a world force now, the force of men whose whole history has been a movement toward the chance of freedom. . . . Aroused now, we can show a strength which will not only mean terrible war but the possibility of a splendid peace."
>
> Jonathan Daniels, in an article published in *The Nation*, December 20, 1941

Enlistment More than 350,000 North Carolinians served in the military during World War II. Of these, about 7,000 were women. Some 258,000 people served in the Army. About 90,000 were in the Navy, and 13,000 were Marines.

Bases North Carolina was the site of important military bases during World War II. **Fort Bragg**, near Fayetteville, had been an Army post since World War I. It was greatly enlarged, and could house almost 100,000 troops. **Camp Lejeune** was the second-largest Marine base in the country. Camp Butner and other training camps also opened around the state.

Thousands of troops were trained at military bases in North Carolina during World War II. Shown here is Camp Davis.

There were also several aircraft-related bases. Cherry Point, one of the largest Marine air bases, opened in 1942. Camp Mackall was the second-largest airborne training center in the country. Greensboro and Goldsboro both housed air units. Camp Davis was an antiaircraft training base. By the time the war ended, more troops had been trained in North Carolina than in any other state.

Fear of sabotage North Carolinians helped the military with the state's defense during World War II. There was a fear that important places might face **sabotage**, or destruction by the enemy. Civilian home guard units were organized, particularly in the coastal region. They stood guard over sites that the enemy might try to destroy. The civilian population along the coast was also required to observe a **blackout** on many nights. A blackout was when all lights had to be hidden or turned off. This was to prevent U-boats from seeing lights at night.

"Torpedo Junction" North Carolina became involved in the war almost immediately because of German submarine activity in the Atlantic Ocean off Cape Hatteras. There was so much activity that the

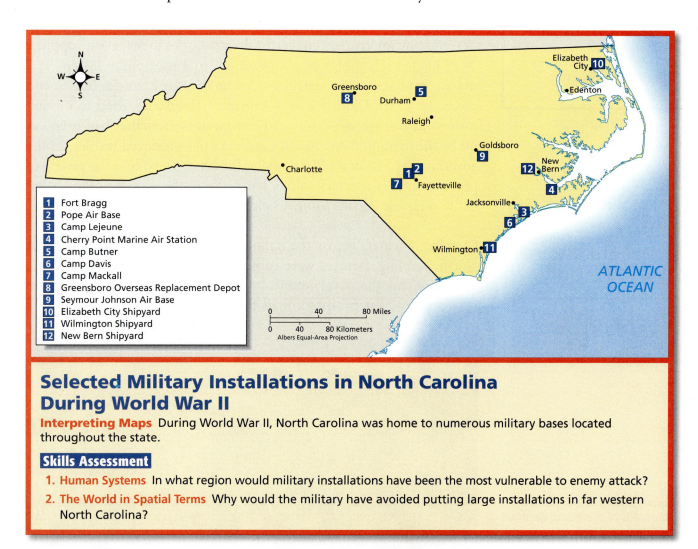

Selected Military Installations in North Carolina During World War II

Interpreting Maps During World War II, North Carolina was home to numerous military bases located throughout the state.

Skills Assessment

1. **Human Systems** In what region would military installations have been the most vulnerable to enemy attack?
2. **The World in Spatial Terms** Why would the military have avoided putting large installations in far western North Carolina?

Depression and War 271

area became known as **"Torpedo Junction."** The submarines targeted oil tankers. Burning oil slicks became a common sight in the area. Local hospitals treated large numbers of badly injured and burned sailors. The bodies of many dead sailors washed ashore. Some British sailors who washed ashore are buried in Ocracoke.

✔ **READING CHECK** Summarizing In what ways did North Carolinians participate in World War II?

★ Mobilizing the Economy

World War II brought an end to the Great Depression in the United States. Unemployment fell sharply as factories hired workers to produce military supplies ordered by the government. By the end of the war, federal contracts had reached $10 billion.

Factories About $2 billion worth of government contracts came to North Carolina. Nearly one million men and women in the state did **defense work**, making military weapons and supplies. There were shipyards in Wilmington, Elizabeth City, and New Bern. They built submarine chasers, minesweepers, and merchant ships.

Other manufacturers converted their factories to make war supplies. They made such things as ammunition, rockets, bomb clusters, and radar components. The state provided lumber for barracks, bunks, and boxes. In Vance County a new source of tungsten—used to harden steel—was discovered. It replaced European sources that had been cut off by the fighting there. North Carolina mills produced textiles for the government. A federal official said at the time, "so wide is the variety of production . . . that every soldier and sailor in the service of the Nation either wears or carries some article manufactured in North Carolina."

Farming Farmers across the nation contributed to the war effort. In North Carolina, farmers were commended for providing "food, feed, and fibre" for the government. Peanut, hay, and potato production increased. Wheat production in the state doubled. North Carolina

That's Interesting!

The Rose Bowl In January 1942, Americans were still reeling from the Japanese attack on Pearl Harbor. Many people were afraid the Japanese would attack California. To be safe, the Rose Bowl—for the only time in its history—was not played in Pasadena. The January 1, 1942, Rose Bowl was played in Durham. In that game, the Duke Blue Devils lost to Oregon State 20-16.

Ships under construction at the shipyards of the North Carolina SB Company, 1942

ranked in the top five states in the nation in the volume of agricultural crops it produced for the war effort. Farmers accomplished this even though they faced a labor shortage, since many farm workers had enlisted in the military.

✔ **READING CHECK** **Contrasting** How did the economy in North Carolina during World War II contrast with the economy before the war?

★ Prisoners of War in North Carolina

During World War II, thousands of prisoners of war (POWs) were taken on both sides. More than 400,000 captured enemy soldiers were brought to the United States. There were 511 U.S. POW camps located in 44 states. POWs in America were very well treated. By treating prisoners well, the United States hoped Americans in enemy hands also would be well treated.

There were several POW camps in North Carolina. Most of the prisoners were German or Italian. Because farmers in the state were short of workers, the military allowed some of the POWs to work on farms. They helped farmers by doing such work as picking cotton and harvesting peanuts. The prisoners were even paid a small amount for their work.

After the war, thousands of POWs chose to come back to the United States and become citizens. Many years later a number of former POWs returned to North Carolina to visit the farm families they had worked for during the war.

✔ **READING CHECK** **Drawing Inferences** Why might many POWs choose to come back to America and become U.S. citizens?

Interpreting the Visual Record

Prisoners of war in North Carolina These German prisoners of war were photographed at Fort Bragg in May 1942. From this image, what can you tell about the way these prisoners were treated?

Section 2 Review

keyword: SN3 HP14

1 Define and explain:
- sabotage
- blackout
- defense work

2 Identify and explain:
- Pearl Harbor
- Fort Bragg
- Camp Lejeune
- "Torpedo Junction"

3 Categorizing Copy the following chart. Use it to organize developments in North Carolina during World War II.

	North Carolina during World War II
Military enlistment	
Military bases	
Civil defense	
Economy	

4 Finding the Main Idea
a. What was North Carolina's military involvement in World War II?
b. How did World War II affect North Carolina's economy?

5 Writing and Critical Thinking
Decision Making Some Americans thought the POWs in the United States were treated too well. Decide whether you think the prisoners should have received the treatment they did. Then write an explanation of your position.
Consider:
- why the government treated the POWs well
- why people might have resented how the POWs were treated

Depression and War **273**

Section 3
Life during Hard Times

Read to Discover
1. How did the Great Depression and the New Deal affect everyday life in North Carolina?
2. What contributions did North Carolinians in the armed forces make during World War II?
3. What was life like in North Carolina during World War II?
4. What were the effects of World War II on North Carolina?

Define
- rationing
- victory gardens

Identify
- Margaret O. Craighill
- Henry F. Warner
- Ray E. Eubanks
- Rufus G. Herring
- William David Halyburton Jr.

The Story Continues

The Great Depression and World War II reshaped the lives of most Americans, and North Carolinians were no exception. Hardship and suffering affected almost every family in the state.

★ Growing Up during the Great Depression

During the early years of the depression, thousands of North Carolina families struggled just to feed and clothe themselves. By 1935, New Deal programs had provided many with relief and employment.

Hunger was widespread in North Carolina during the early depression. Often families survived on one or two meals a day. Sometimes only one type of food would be available, so that many children suffered from malnutrition. Desperate men stole to feed and clothe their families. Some broke into smokehouses and raided orchards. Others stole firewood and clothes off clotheslines to keep their children warm.

Like people in the rest of the country, North Carolina families soon felt the effects of the New Deal programs. Loans helped farmers save their farms. Agencies such as the CCC and the WPA provided

The hopelessness and despair felt by many Americans during the Great Depression was strongly portrayed in this New Deal poster.

thousands of jobs. By the late 1930s, most people were able to return to their normal lives.

✓ **READING CHECK** **Contrasting** How was life after the New Deal different from life before the New Deal?

Did You KNOW?

The board game *Monopoly,* introduced in 1934, uses themes from the Great Depression.

Veterans of World War II

During World War II, North Carolinians served in many different military units around the world. Those in the Army and the Marines saw action in Europe and the Pacific. Some also were sent to North Africa, India, Burma, and China. North Carolinians in the Navy also served around the globe, on troopships, submarines, battleships, and aircraft carriers. Still others served in the Army and Navy air corps.

Women served in auxiliary services of the Army, Navy, and Marines. They served as aircraft mechanics, doctors, drivers, parachute riggers, nurses, and telephone operators. Dr. **Margaret O. Craighill** of Southport was the first female doctor in the Army Medical Corps.

The war in Europe North Carolinians were often sent first to England. From there, many took part in the Allied invasion of Europe on D-Day, June 6, 1944. Others joined the Allied forces in Italy, Germany, and elsewhere in Europe. In December 1944 Corporal **Henry F. Warner** of Troy was serving as a gunner in a battle with German forces near Dom Butgenbach, Belgium. During two days of battle Warner destroyed several enemy tanks before being killed. He was awarded the Congressional Medal of Honor after his death.

The Pacific The war in the Pacific produced several Medal of Honor winners from North Carolina. In July 1944 Sgt. **Ray E. Eubanks** of Snow Hill was with a company that was hit heavily by enemy fire on an island in Dutch New Guinea. Eubanks and a small group of soldiers went ahead to try to knock out the enemy and let the American company advance. Eubanks took out several Japanese fighters himself before being killed. His attack helped the larger company to advance. In February 1945 Navy Lt. **Rufus G. Herring** distinguished himself in fighting at the Battle of Iwo Jima. This was one of the most important battles for the United States in securing the Pacific front.

Not every hero was a fighter, however. **William David Halyburton Jr.** of Canton aided wounded soldiers as a pharmacist's mate in the Naval Reserves. In May 1945 he was helping a Marine unit during heavy fighting on Okinawa. Halyburton rushed onto the battlefield to treat a wounded Marine. Halyburton was killed trying to help the man, who lived, thanks to Halyburton's efforts.

✓ **READING CHECK** **Summarizing** Where did North Carolina's military personnel serve during World War II?

BIOGRAPHY

Rufus G. Herring

(1921-1996)

Rufus G. Herring was born in Roseboro, North Carolina. In February 1945, Herring was commanding a landing craft gunboat at the Pacific island of Iwo Jima. As the gunboat approached shore, it was hit by Japanese mortar fire. Those navigating the gunboat were killed and Herring was critically wounded. Even so, he encouraged his men to aid the wounded and piloted his crippled ship to safety. **How did Rufus G. Herring distinguish himself during World War II?**

Depression and War **275**

Those on the Home Front

Daily life changed dramatically for those at home during the war. A major problem was finding workers to replace departing soldiers.

Women and work Before World War II many women, particularly married women, had not worked away from home. With the coming of war, that changed. In North Carolina, women now worked alongside men. They worked in manufacturing, construction, and other jobs that formerly had been limited to men. In 1944, a writer for the Women's Bureau commented on women in shipyards:

Analyzing Primary Sources
Critical Thinking From this passage, what do you think was the reason the Women's Bureau had an interest in shipyards?

> **History Makers Speak**
> "By late 1943, thousands of women . . . were actively engaged in almost every phase of ship building and repair work. . . . Organized training programs had to be set up . . . for the thousands of workers, men as well as women, who had never held tools before, much less seen a ship under construction."
>
> Dorothy K. Newman, from the 1944 Bulletin of the Women's Bureau, Washington, D.C.

Women learned new skills in order to manufacture and construct goods needed for the war.

Rationing Another of the wartime changes in daily life was **rationing**. This restricted people to limited amounts of food and other items that were in short supply. Foods such as coffee, sugar, butter, and meat were rationed. So were gasoline and shoes. People were issued books of coupons—ration books—to make sure goods were distributed equally. Recycling centers collected rubber, tin, paper, and other scarce material.

Many North Carolinians helped the war effort by growing their own vegetables and other produce in their backyards. These **victory gardens** helped make more food available to Allied soldiers. Others helped by buying war bonds. Money raised by a special sale of bonds in North Carolina bought 14 ambulance planes. This was more than any other state.

✓ **READING CHECK** *Identifying Cause and Effect* How did World War II lead to labor shortages and rationing in the United States?

Effects of World War II on North Carolina

Over 350,000 North Carolinians had served in the war. Nearly one million had done defense work. Many had also been unusually generous buying war bonds.

Farmers had met all of the demands made on them by the federal government, in spite of labor shortages and inadequate machinery. North Carolina also provided valuable minerals to the war effort. With government help, more than four hundred mines of various kinds had been opened.

Toward the end of the war, North Carolina's state and local governments began to make plans for peacetime. They knew that when the war ended, many of the military installations would be closed. There would be surplus equipment and buildings available. Communities made plans to buy these items. The state made plans as well to start up projects that had been put on hold. These projects included building highways, rural electrification, and telephone lines.

By 1944, North Carolina was preparing for thousands of returning veterans. Many would be attending school under the new GI Bill of Rights. The GI Bill provided tuition and living expenses for veterans who wanted to attend college. Many of those veterans would be the first in their families to pursue higher education. The GI Bill opened new opportunities to an entire generation of North Carolinians. It helped produce well-educated citizens who would build a dynamic postwar economy.

Almost 8 million veterans attended college or vocational school on the GI Bill.

✔ **READING CHECK** **Making Predictions** What long-term effects do you think World War II had on North Carolina?

Section 3 Review

Homework Practice Online keyword: SN3 HP14

1. **Define** and explain:
   - rationing
   - victory gardens

2. **Identify** and explain:
   - Margaret O. Craighill
   - Henry F. Warner
   - Ray E. Eubanks
   - Rufus G. Herring
   - William David Halyburton, Jr.

3. **Identifying Cause and Effect** Copy the organizing web that follows. Use it to identify the effects the Great Depression, the New Deal, and World War II had on life in North Carolina.

4. **Finding the Main Idea**
   a. How was daily life in North Carolina affected by the Great Depression and the New Deal?
   b. Where and in what ways did North Carolinians serve in the military during World War II?
   c. What were the overall effects of World War II on North Carolina?

5. **Writing and Critical Thinking**
   Comparing and Contrasting Write a short paper describing the similarities and differences between your daily life and the life of a 1940s student.
   Consider:
   - rationing and victory gardens
   - military bases and blackouts

Depression and War 277

Chapter 14 Review

Chapter Summary

Section 1
- The effects of the Great Depression in North Carolina were deflation, bank failures, business and farm failures, and high unemployment.
- The New Deal brought North Carolina farmers assistance, industrial reforms that helped workers, and significant relief and recovery programs. The Rural Electrification Administration and the Tennessee Valley Authority improved living standards in rural areas.

Section 2
- World War II brought an end to the Great Depression when industry and agriculture geared up to support the war effort.
- North Carolina's involvement in World War II included thousands enlisting in the military, numerous large military bases located in the state, and direct assistance to casualties from German submarine activity off the coast.
- Thousands of prisoners of war were brought to POW camps in the United States, including several camps in North Carolina.

Section 3
- Many families in North Carolina struggled to survive during the depression, but New Deal programs and reforms helped them return to normal lives.
- North Carolinians served in various military units during World War II. Millions of women worked to fill in for departing soldiers, and food and other goods were rationed.
- North Carolinians met all the demands made of them by the government and the military and tried to prepare for the changes that would come at the end of the war.

Identifying People and Ideas
Use the following terms or people in complete sentences.

1. Live-at-Home program
2. Jane Simpson McKimmon
3. Civilian Conservation Corps
4. sabotage
5. defense work
6. Camp Lejeune
7. "Torpedo Junction"
8. Margaret O. Craighill
9. Rufus G. Herring
10. rationing

Understanding Main Ideas

Section 1 *(Pages 265–268)*
1. What sparked the Great Depression and how did it affect North Carolina?
2. What was the effect of the New Deal on North Carolina?

Section 2 *(Pages 269–273)*
3. What military involvement did North Carolina have during World War II?
4. What effect did World War II have on North Carolina's economy?

Section 3 *(Pages 274–277)*
5. How did the depression and World War II affect the lives of North Carolinians?
6. Where and in what ways did North Carolinians in the military participate in World War II?

What Did You Find Out?

1. **Economics** What actions did the United States government take to help the citizens of North Carolina during the Great Depression?
2. **Global Relations** Why were troops from North Carolina fighting in Europe during World War II?
3. **Culture** Which groups in North Carolina were hardest hit by the Great Depression?

Think Critically

1. **Supporting a Point of View** One cause of the Great Depression was that people could not keep up their credit payments. For this reason, many who lived through the depression refuse to use modern credit cards. Do you agree or disagree with their position? Support your point of view.
2. **Evaluating** Of the New Deal programs and reforms, which do you think benefited North Carolina the most, and why?
3. **Drawing Conclusions** During World War II, there were a large number of military installations in North Carolina. What effect do you think this had on the development of the state after the war?

Building Social Studies Skills

Interpreting Visual Evidence

Study the photograph below. Then answer the questions that follow.

The members of this farm family were evicted from their land during the Great Depression.

1. Which statement correctly describes what you can infer from the photograph?
   a. The family is moving to a new home they have purchased.
   b. Some farm families had very little money, even before the Great Depression.
   c. Only African American farmers were evicted from their land.
   d. The family owns the truck they are using to move their belongings.

2. What do you think happened to this family after they were evicted from their land?

Understanding Frames of Reference

Read this quote from John Steinbeck's introduction to his book *Once There Was a War*. Steinbeck was a war correspondent during World War II. Then answer the questions.

> "I attended a part of that war, you might say visited it, since I went in the costume of a war correspondent and certainly did not fight, and it is interesting to me that I do not remember very much about it. Reading these old reports sent in with excitement at the time brings back images and emotions completely lost.
>
> Perhaps it is right or even necessary to forget accidents, and wars are surely accidents to which our species seems prone. If we could learn from our accidents it might be well to keep the memories alive, but we do not learn. In ancient Greece it was said that there had to be a war at least every twenty years because every generation of men had to know what it was like. With us, we must forget, or we could never indulge in the murderous nonsense again."

3. Which of the statements below describes how John Steinbeck felt about war?
   a. War is necessary every twenty years.
   b. It is good that people forget about the wars of the past.
   c. If people remembered what war was really like there would be no more wars.
   d. War is a good way to solve conflicts between groups of people.

4. In what way does Steinbeck's view of war agree with that of the ancient Greeks?

Alternative Assessment

Building Your Portfolio

N.C. History

Linking to the Community
Many North Carolinians served in the military in World War II. Local communities created memorials to honor those who had served their country. Prepare an oral report or a poster about World War II veterans in your community and how they have been honored. Try to include information about how many veterans came from your area, what branches of the military they served in, and where they were stationed during the war.

internet connect

Internet Activity: go.hrw.com
keyword: SN3 NC14

Choose a topic on depression and war to:

- Build a chart that explains several New Deal programs.
- Create an annotated map of North Carolina that shows World War II activity in the state.
- Write diary entries detailing life in North Carolina during World War II.

CHAPTER 15
A Changing State
(1945–1970)

Wood-processing plant, Elkin, North Carolina

Build on What You Know

The Great Depression and World War II brought major changes to North Carolina and its people. The pace of change continued and quickened after the war. In this chapter you will learn about important social, political, economic, and geographic changes that occurred in the state in the decades following the war.

 What's Your Opinion?

Do you **agree** or **disagree** with the following statements? Support your point of view in your journal.

- **Science, Technology & Society** Television expands people's knowledge about the world.
- **Citizenship** Strong-willed and courageous people who are committed to their goals can achieve major changes in their society.
- **Government** Government can do very little to improve people's quality of life and standard of living.

280 Chapter 15

Section 1

A Postwar Economy

Read to Discover
1. How did North Carolina's economy change after World War II?
2. What population trends developed in the state?

Define
- right-to-work law

Identify
- W. Kerr Scott
- Luther Hodges
- Research Triangle Park

The Story Continues

A number of factors combined to bring great changes to North Carolina's economy after World War II. As governors worked to lure out-of-state companies to North Carolina, a decline in farming provided the workers that these and other companies needed. New state laws and programs assured companies that those local workers would be well trained.

Aerial view of the Research Triangle Park area

The Postwar Economy

North Carolina continued to be the nation's leading manufacturer of textiles, tobacco products, and wood furniture between 1945 and 1970. However, leaders worried that the state was too dependent on these industries and a few others. Therefore, they made efforts to attract new and different industries to the state.

In 1949 the legislature approved what Governor **W. Kerr Scott** called his "Go Forward" program for the state. It provided millions of dollars to build and improve roads, schools, and port facilities. By the end of Scott's term, leaders were talking about also creating a place where research and industry could come together to benefit the state.

A Changing State **281**

Did You KNOW?

By 2000, more than 100 companies operating in Research Triangle Park employed some 45,000 North Carolinians. Their wages pump more than $1.2 billion per year into the state economy.

A few years later, Governor **Luther Hodges** turned this talk into action. He proposed that an industrial "park" be built in the triangle-shaped region between Durham, Chapel Hill, and Raleigh. Research labs built in the park would hire young scientists who graduated from nearby North Carolina universities. Hodges convinced business leaders to help raise money for the project. By 1961 the first two research centers, owned by the Chemstrand Corporation and the U.S. Forestry Service, opened in what is known as **Research Triangle Park**.

✓ **READING CHECK** **Finding the Main Idea** What was the main economic goal of state leaders in the years after World War II?

★ New Technology and Industry

Some 21 companies had located in Research Triangle Park by 1969. They represented the very kinds of industries that state officials had hoped to attract.

New industries and technology Another early arrival in Research Triangle Park was International Business Machines (IBM), one of the nation's leading computer makers. Other companies that made electrical or electronic products operated elsewhere in the state. These included General Electric, Westinghouse, and Sylvania. In 1970, Burroughs Wellcome, then one of the world's leading drug research and manufacturing companies, moved its New York operations to North Carolina. To make North Carolina even more attractive to businesses, officials launched one of the nation's first state-sponsored job training programs in 1957. This program paid the costs of teaching workers the skills they needed for the state's new industries. In 1947, only 28 percent of workers were employed in manufacturing. By 1970, that figure had risen to 40 percent.

The decline of agriculture At the same time, the number of North Carolinians involved in farming was falling dramatically—from 42 percent of the population in 1947 to just 8 percent in 1970. One reason for this trend was a decline in demand for cotton. The decline occurred after artificial materials such as rayon and nylon began replacing cotton in clothing. State cotton production dropped from 550,000 bales in 1951 to 160,000 bales in 1970. Many people gave up farming and moved to cities. Others remained on their land but took manufacturing jobs nearby.

The rise of organized labor Membership in labor unions grew rapidly after 1935, when a new federal law supported the rights of union members. A labor union is an organization formed by workers to improve their conditions. In 1947, however, North Carolina

Cotton farmers like this one became rarer as cotton production decreased dramatically in the state between 1950 and 1970.

282 Chapter 15

became one of the first U.S. states to pass a **right-to-work law**. Such laws make it illegal to require a worker to join a union in order to work at a company. They make states that have the laws more attractive to business. This is because workers' wages tend to be lower than in states without right-to-work laws. Still, unions continued to have an effect on labor.

The longest labor strike in North Carolina until the 1970s occurred at the Harriet-Henderson Mill. The strike began in November 1958 over management attempts to oust the union. It continued for more than a year and a half, becoming increasingly violent as time wore on. Finally, in the summer of 1960 the governor called in the National Guard to help break the strike.

✔ **READING CHECK** Identifying Cause and Effect Why did cotton production fall, and what effect did this have?

Interpreting the Visual Record

The Harriet-Henderson Mill Strike A group of striking workers confronts a law enforcement officer in this 1959 photo of the Harriet-Henderson cotton mill strike. *What does this photo reveal about tensions during the strike?*

★ The Growth of Cities

State leaders encouraged new companies to operate in rural areas. However, many of these businesses chose to locate in urban areas instead. This resulted in tremendous growth for North Carolina's cities. In 1950 only Charlotte had a population of more than 100,000. By 1970, Winston-Salem, Greensboro, and Raleigh did too, and Charlotte's population had grown to nearly 250,000. At the same time, populations decreased in 34 rural counties in the 1950s, and in 38 counties in the 1960s. By 1970, some 45 percent of North Carolinians lived in urban areas.

✔ **READING CHECK** Summarizing How did the urban-rural population ratio shift?

Section 1 Review

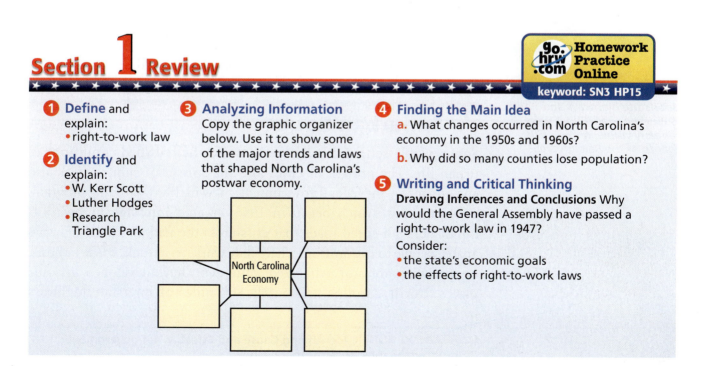

1 Define and explain:
- right-to-work law

2 Identify and explain:
- W. Kerr Scott
- Luther Hodges
- Research Triangle Park

3 Analyzing Information Copy the graphic organizer below. Use it to show some of the major trends and laws that shaped North Carolina's postwar economy.

4 Finding the Main Idea
a. What changes occurred in North Carolina's economy in the 1950s and 1960s?
b. Why did so many counties lose population?

5 Writing and Critical Thinking
Drawing Inferences and Conclusions Why would the General Assembly have passed a right-to-work law in 1947?
Consider:
- the state's economic goals
- the effects of right-to-work laws

A Changing State

Section 2

Social Shifts

Read to Discover

1. In what ways did the road-building program of the 1950s and 1960s affect North Carolina?
2. What changes occurred in public and higher education?
3. How did government promote the arts and culture in the state?

Define

- interstate highways
- conurbations
- community colleges

Identify

- School Machinery Act
- Terry Sanford
- Dan K. Moore
- Fred Chappell
- Dean Smith
- Andy Griffith
- Edward R. Murrow
- NASCAR
- Petty family

Interstate highways and suburban subdivisions were already visible in this 1950s photo of the Raleigh area.

The Story Continues

Only about one third of all North Carolinians live in or around Charlotte, Winston-Salem, Greensboro, Durham, and Raleigh. However, these areas have had a great influence on life in the state. Business and educational leaders from these cities have worked with the state's political leaders to shape North Carolina's development.

Suburban Society

Some people settled in suburbs to avoid the crowded conditions of urban life. The growth of cities and the spread of suburbs was also encouraged by the federal government's new highway-building program. This program, which began in 1956, created **interstate highways**—multilane, high-speed roads that criss-cross the nation. These highways enable people to live far from where they work. As a result, **conurbations**, or sprawling areas of urbanized settlement, have developed in some places. North Carolina had nearly 800 miles of interstate highways by 1966.

✓ **READING CHECK** Identifying Cause and Effect What government program enabled suburbs to develop?

284 Chapter 15

Advances in Education

Article I of the North Carolina constitution states that "the people have a right to the privilege of education and it is the duty of the State to guard and maintain that right." During the postwar period, state leaders built on earlier efforts to strengthen North Carolina schools.

Public schools In 1931 the General Assembly passed the **School Machinery Act**. This law and others passed in the 1930s established the basic system of education that exists in North Carolina today. In 1933 the school year was lengthened from six months to eight. Most importantly, the state began paying for a large part of the costs of schools. This was a revolutionary change from the reliance on local sources of support that had been common before the 1930s. Not until the 1970s did most other states follow North Carolina's lead in this area.

In the 1940s the present nine-month school year became law. Other reforms during that decade included raising the required attendance age from 14 to 16, adding a twelfth grade, and creating the school lunch program. Another major reform after World War II was an effort to combine small schools into larger ones that could offer more and better programs, such as music, art, and special education. The total number of schools fell from some 3,500 in 1951 to about 2,000 by 1971.

Two governors of the 1960s, **Terry Sanford** and **Dan K. Moore**, were behind many of the state's educational reforms. Sanford became known as the "Education Governor" for his commitment to quality education

That's Interesting!

Textbooks Through most of the state's history, public school students had to purchase their textbooks. In 1935 the General Assembly created a plan that allowed students to rent their books for a charge equal to 20 percent of the book's cost. Two years later this plan was changed to provide free textbooks to students in grades one through seven. Not until 1967, however, were free textbooks available to all high school students in North Carolina.

Interstate Highways in North Carolina

Interpreting Maps The interstate highway system in North Carolina began construction in the 1950s. Today it provides major transportation routes across the state from both north to south and east to west.

Skills Assessment **Human Systems** How did the distribution of the population of North Carolina in 1970 correspond to the interstate highway system as it existed in 1966?

A Changing State 285

in North Carolina. The important reforms of the 1970s included creation of statewide testing and kindergarten programs.

Higher education Important changes also took place in higher education under Sanford and Moore. In 1957 the legislature passed a law to create community colleges in the state. A community college is a school that offers the first two years of a college education as well as technical and career-training programs. By 1963, six of these colleges were operating. Just nine years later the number had grown to 56 community and technical colleges, giving North Carolina one of the largest community college systems in the nation.

The 1950s and 1960s were a time of great change for the state's four-year colleges and universities as well. Wake Forest College moved to a new and larger site in Winston-Salem in 1956. The college became a university in 1967. Meanwhile, Duke University grew in size and reputation too. The University of North Carolina at Chapel Hill was recognized as one of the nation's finest state universities by 1970.

The University of North Carolina system also expanded in the 1960s, and the UNC branch at Raleigh became North Carolina State University. Another important reform during this period was the creation of nine regional universities around the state. In 1971 the legislature placed all 15 state universities and the North Carolina School of the Arts in Winston-Salem under the control of a single board of governors.

✔ **READING CHECK Identifying Cause and Effect** What changes made education in North Carolina more efficient?

★ Popular Culture

The economic, educational, and population changes that swept North Carolina after World War II also affected popular culture in the state. The growth of cities and suburbs encouraged developments in the arts as well as in communications and sports.

Literature and the arts Neither of the best-known North Carolina writers of the postwar period were native Tar Heels. Carl Sandburg was already a famous writer when he moved to a farm near Flat Rock in 1945. There he completed the novel *Remembrance Rock*. Then, in 1950, he published *Complete Poems*, for which he won a Pulitzer Prize. Charlotte newspaper editor Harry Golden wrote several best-sellers. Two of them, *Only in America* and *For 2¢ Plain*, were best-sellers in the 1950s.

North Carolina's urban growth encouraged symphony orchestras to develop. In the 1940s the North Carolina Symphony became the first American orchestra to receive continuous state funding. Although it is located in Raleigh, the symphony performs all over the state as North Carolina's "official" orchestra.

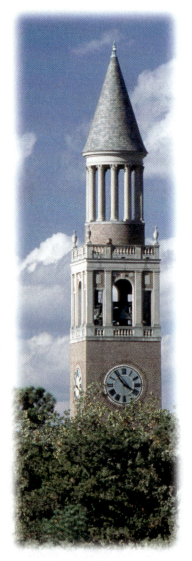

The University Bell Tower of the University of North Carolina at Chapel Hill

CONNECTING TO Literature

I Am One of You Forever
Fred Chappell

A native of Canton, **Fred Chappell** is one of the state's leading authors. Among his many awards, he was named North Carolina Poet Laureate in 1997. Besides 14 books of poetry, Chappell has written two collections of short stories and eight novels. His 1985 novel I Am One of You Forever tells of a boy growing up on a western North Carolina farm in the 1940s and 1950s. In addition to his writing, Chappell teaches at the University of North Carolina at Greensboro.

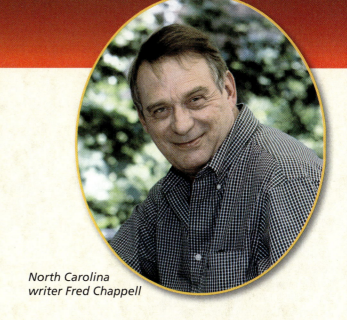

North Carolina writer Fred Chappell

Word of Uncle Luden's visit came in the form of a postcard from Reno, Nevada, with his loose purple scrawl: *Make plenty that good cornbread, Il'e be there soon.* He signed both names, *Luden Sorrells.* . . .

My father nudged Johnson's elbow. "We're going to eat fine now. Uncle Luden is the prodigal son. Any fatted calf in the neighborhood, his days are numbered."

"Prodigal son how?" Johnson asked.

"Just like in the Bible," my father said. . . .

The farm work that had got the best of us until Johnson showed up to help had disgusted Uncle Luden early in his career. My mother's brother had little of her sunny but long-suffering patience. In the back alfalfa fields he had found a dilapidated old hay wagon and had worked it over until it looked sturdy and bright and something like new. On his sixteenth birthday he sold the wagon to a gullible [easily fooled] neighbor, bought a second-hand motorcycle, and sped off to California in a cloud of gravel and a hail of loose bolts.

In the golden land of opportunity he hauled down a job that paid actual cash money, greenback dollars that were as scarce as kangaroos to us on our scratchankle mountain farm. Now and again he would send my grandmother a check representing some of those fabled entities, and he sent other presents too. I once got a nifty cap pistol, for instance, and my grandmother had received that box of fancy candies which had been the occasion of what she called "a lavish of tomfool." . . .

A week passed before he arrived, and not on a motorcycle, but in a tall red panel truck. . . . I was let down he hadn't roared in on the motorcycle. I wanted to learn that machine so that when it was my turn to escape to California, I'd have no difficulty. Just crank her up and boil away into the sunset. . . .

My father had prophesied that we would eat well while Uncle Luden was home to visit, and so we did. We got not only an unusual hearty tonnage, but saw for the first time since Easter my grandmother's chow-chow and precious pickled peaches, and she even made a lopsided tar-colored chocolate cake.

"I believe this Prodigal Son business must be a handsome racket," my father said. "We ought to try it sometime, you and me."

Understanding What You Read

1. What trend in North Carolina farming during this period does this excerpt illustrate?
2. How would you describe this family's quality of life? What information does the writer give you that creates this impression?

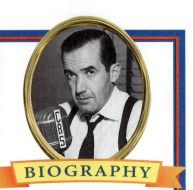

BIOGRAPHY

Edward R. Murrow
(1908–1965)

Edward R. Murrow was America's best-known news broadcaster of the 1940s and 1950s. Murrow was born in Polecat Creek, near Greensboro. Although he spent most of his life outside North Carolina, he never lost the speech patterns of his Quaker mother. Inverted phrases such as "This I believe" contributed to a distinctive style of delivering information that appealed to a wide audience of Americans. **To what did Murrow owe his broadcasting style?**

The North Carolina Museum of Art, which opened in Raleigh in 1956, was one of the nation's first state-funded museums. It holds about 200 works by Rubens, Rembrandt, and other famous artists. The North Carolina School of the Arts was the nation's first state-supported residential school for the performing arts. Today more than 1,000 students enroll there each year, many from other states and foreign countries.

Popular entertainment In 1957 North Carolinians watched on their black-and-white television sets as UNC–Chapel Hill's basketball team won its first national championship. The event sparked a passion for college basketball that continued as North Carolina, North Carolina State, and Duke became powerhouses in the sport from the 1970s through the 1990s. UNC coach **Dean Smith** became the winningest coach in college basketball history. During the 1960s, *The Andy Griffith Show* reached number one in the ratings. The show's setting in the fictional town of Mayberry was based on Mt. Airy, the hometown of actor/producer **Andy Griffith**. The show celebrated the simplicity of small-town life in North Carolina in a humorous manner.

Another form of entertainment for which North Carolina became well known during this period was auto racing. The sport gained national attention after the National Association for Stock Car Racing (**NASCAR**) was formed in 1949. The premiere of what is now the Lowe's Motor Speedway in 1960 secured North Carolina's position as a leading state in stock car racing. North Carolina has produced some of the biggest stars in racing, including the **Petty family** of Level Cross, which has produced four generations of NASCAR drivers.

✔ **READING CHECK** **Finding the Main Idea** What spectator sports became wildly popular in North Carolina?

Section 2 Review

❶ **Define** and explain:
- interstate highways
- conurbations
- community colleges

❷ **Identify** and explain:
- School Machinery Act
- Terry Sanford
- Dan K. Moore
- Fred Chappell
- Dean Smith
- Andy Griffith
- Edward R. Murrow
- NASCAR
- Petty family

❸ **Analyzing Information**
Copy the graphic organizer below. Use it to illustrate the types and levels of schools that make up the state's public education program.

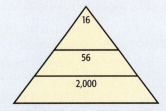

❹ **Finding the Main Idea**
a. What change in the state's geography encouraged suburban growth?

b. In what ways did state government support the arts in North Carolina?

❺ **Writing and Critical Thinking**
Identifying Cause and Effect How was the quality and availability of education in North Carolina improved?
Consider:
- changes in public schools
- changes in higher education

288 Chapter 15

Section 3

Political Changes

Read to Discover

1. How was North Carolina affected by national and world events?
2. In what ways was discrimination addressed?
3. What changes occurred in state government?

Identify

- Pearsall Plan
- *Swann v. Charlotte-Mecklenburg Board of Education*
- Ezell Blair Jr.
- Franklin McCain
- Joseph McNeil
- David Richmond
- Greensboro sit-in
- Henry E. Frye
- Howard N. Lee
- Jesse Jackson
- North Carolina Fund
- Constitution of 1971

The Story Continues

Events in the rest of the nation and the world had a great influence in North Carolina in the 25 years following World War II. Powerful forces of social change brought both unrest and reform to the state. Many people realized that North Carolina would never again return to the attitudes and ways of the past.

Communist activist Junius Scales is seen here being arrested for his political activities.

 ## National Politics in North Carolina

Most North Carolinians in the 1950s were politically conservative. They supported the Cold War and opposed communism. In the 1940s and 1950s a great fear of communism swept the nation. In North Carolina, Junius Scales was tried in 1955 for directing communist activities in the state. He was sentenced to six years in prison. In 1963 the North Carolina State General Assembly passed a law banning Communists from speaking on college campuses. Although the law specifically referred to Communists, it was used to more broadly silence growing civil rights protests, in which large numbers of college students participated. In 1968 a federal court ruled that the ban violated the U.S. Constitution's protection of free speech.

A Changing State **289**

Another national issue that divided North Carolinians in the 1960s was the Vietnam War. In North Carolina most antiwar protests occurred on a few college campuses. After some war protesters were killed at Kent State University in Ohio in May 1970, antiwar demonstrators disrupted classes at some 700 colleges around the country. Thousands of students tried to close UNC–Chapel Hill. However, a compromise was reached. The school term continued and ended peacefully.

✓ **READING CHECK** Identifying Points of View Why might some people oppose the legislature's ban on Communist speakers?

The Civil Rights Movement in North Carolina

One of the greatest challenges the nation confronted after World War II was the issue of civil rights. African Americans across the country had long been denied the rights and freedoms of citizenship.

Interpreting the Visual Record

School integration Josephine Boyd (center) is seen here in 1957 in a classroom at Greensboro Senior High School. Boyd was the first African American student to attend the formerly all-white school. **What seems to be the reaction of the white students in the classroom?**

School integration Separate schools for black and white students had existed for decades. In 1954 the U.S. Supreme Court ruled that this arrangement denied black students an equal education.

Violent resistance to desegregation erupted in some southern states. In North Carolina, the General Assembly responded with the **Pearsall Plan**. It required the state to pay for private school for children whose parents did not want them attending an integrated, or racially mixed, school. In 1966, however, the federal courts declared the Pearsall Plan to be unconstitutional.

School integration proceeded very slowly. By 1961 only about 200 black students were enrolled in integrated schools. In Charlotte, black parents sued the school system for its lack of progress. In the 1971 case **Swann v. Charlotte-Mecklenburg Board of Education**, the U.S. Supreme Court ordered the school system to bus students to end segregation. This North Carolina case established busing as a way of integrating schools throughout the nation.

The Greensboro sit-ins As efforts to integrate schools were continuing, African Americans began to seek an end to segregation in all public facilities. In Greensboro, four black college students—**Ezell Blair Jr., Franklin McCain, Joseph McNeil**, and **David Richmond**—sat at a "whites only" lunch counter on February 1, 1960, and ordered coffee. When service was refused, they would not give up their seats. The students remained committed to their policy of nonviolent resistance. Franklin McCain explained:

290 Chapter 15

"[W]e wanted to make that very clear to everybody, that it was a movement that was seeking justice more than anything else and not a movement to start a war.... We knew that probably the most powerful and potent weapon that people have literally no defense for is love, kindness. That is, whip the enemy with something that he doesn't understand."

—Franklin McCain, quoted in *My Soul Is Rested: Movement Days in the Deep South Remembered* by Howell Raines

The next day the students returned, with the same result. Other black students soon joined the protest. In a few days, 63 of the 65 seats were occupied by protesters. Large crowds of demonstrators both for and against segregation gathered, and the **Greensboro sit-in** spread to other food-service businesses in the city and across the state. The sit-in ended in July, when food-service businesses agreed to serve customers regardless of race. The strategy was later used to end segregation in other public facilities in North Carolina and elsewhere. For this reason, the Greensboro sit-in has been called the "Boston Tea Party" of the civil rights movement. In 1964 Congress passed the Civil Rights Act, which outlawed discrimination in schools, businesses, and other public places.

Four African American college students sit in protest at a whites-only lunch counter at a Woolworth's in Greensboro. In the foreground are Joseph McNeil (far left) and Franklin McCain (second from the left).

Black political gains Political equality for black North Carolinians proved especially difficult to achieve. A federal study of voting in North Carolina discovered that in 1960 only about 31 percent of black adults were registered to vote, compared with about 76 percent of white adults. Black political participation increased dramatically after Congress passed the Voting Rights Act of 1965. This act outlawed the literacy tests and other barriers to voter registration that had been in place since the turn of the century. In 1968 **Henry E. Frye** became the first African American in the North Carolina House of Representatives in the 20th century. A year later, **Howard N. Lee** of Chapel Hill became the century's first black mayor elected in a mainly white southern city. In 1973 Raleigh voters also elected a black mayor.

Other civil rights issues Women and Native Americans made gains in the 1970s. North Carolina Indians were sometimes denied voting rights and treated poorly in restaurants, schools, and other public places in the 1950s and 1960s. In 1971 the state created a new government office, the Commission of Indian Affairs, to promote Native Americans' rights. North Carolina was one of several states that blocked the ratification of the Equal Rights Amendment (ERA) to the U.S. Constitution. Despite opposition to the ERA, several women gained important positions in North Carolina government in the 1970s.

✓ **READING CHECK** **Finding the Main Idea** What groups made gains in rights and power in North Carolina in the 1960s and 1970s?

That's Interesting!

Jesse Jackson Jesse Jackson, student-body president at North Carolina A&T University, played a major role in the Greensboro sit-in. From this beginning, Jackson went on to become one of America's foremost civil rights leaders. In Raleigh, sit-in leaders from across the South formed the Student Non-Violent Coordinating Committee (SNCC) to carry out their activities. Like Jackson, SNCC also became an important force in the national civil rights movement.

A Changing State **291**

Historical Document

1960

ACCOUNT OF THE GREENSBORO SIT-IN

William A. Thomas Jr. was a high school student who took part in the Greensboro sit-ins. At first, the protesters did not want to involve someone that young in the demonstrations. However, after many of the college students went home for the summer, his role in the protests increased. In 1981, Thomas recalled the events of 1960.

"What really triggered the massive demonstrations was an inability on the part of the political and business structure to take the . . . thing seriously. Because we didn't have the violent outbreaks and disturbances that characterized demonstrations that existed in other parts of the country, they thought that the thing would just go away. They attempted to ignore us. In fact, at one point, the mayor did not even want to negotiate with the students. He suggested that we send some "reasonable, mature" adults down to negotiate. . . . We quickly informed him . . . that it was not the mature adults that were out in the street and that if he wanted to get us out of the street, he would sit down and talk to us, which he eventually did, and that's when the problems were worked out.

Once students knew what was going on, it had a snowballing effect. We utilized the media, we utilized leaflets. The local churches were very cooperative in letting us use their churches for mass meetings. You had to have some central place where instructions could be given as to exactly what tactic would be used that particular evening, exactly what strategies we would be using, where we were going, etc. . . .

Things, in terms of action, went pretty much according to plan. The basic form of action was

As the Woolworth's sit-in continued it attracted increasing numbers of demonstrators.

through economic withdrawal, another name for boycotting, and through street demonstrations. Very little litigation [legal action] went on at that time, other than defending those people who were arrested.

After they started to arrest people, we literally adopted the slogan that we were going to fill up the jails. Again, that was an economic thing. It cost the city of Greensboro and the state of North Carolina a considerable amount of money to house these people, to feed them and to guard them, for no reason. The jails were literally filled. They were overflowing."

Analyzing Primary Sources

1. Why does Thomas think the authorities did not take the sit-ins seriously at first?
2. How did the demonstrators use economics to achieve their goals?

Reforming State Government

Major changes occurred in state government during the 1960s and 1970s. These helped state leaders keep up with civil rights and other social changes that were sweeping North Carolina and the nation. In 1963 Governor Sanford created the **North Carolina Fund**. This organization was supported by private contributions and federal funds rather than state money. It worked with local business, religious, and political leaders to help people overcome poverty. Programs taught poor adults to read and write, exposed children to art and literature, and encouraged traditional crafts in many areas of the state.

An even greater reform was the adoption of a revised state constitution. A commission appointed by Governor Moore concluded that the 1868 constitution was outdated and needed changes in wording and content. For example, some references to race violated federal civil rights laws. These references and the poll tax were eliminated.

The voters approved the revised constitution in 1970, and it took effect the following year. The **Constitution of 1971** also authorized the General Assembly to streamline state government. The legislature responded by combining more than 350 state agencies into fewer than 20 government departments.

Shown here is the General Assembly in Raleigh, where the North Carolina legislature holds session.

✔ **READING CHECK** Summarizing Why did state leaders make broad changes in North Carolina government during the 1960s and 1970s?

Section 3 Review

1. **Identify** and explain:
   - Pearsall Plan
   - *Swann v. Charlotte-Mecklenburg Board of Education*
   - Ezell Blair Jr.
   - Franklin McCain
   - Joseph McNeil
   - David Richmond
   - Greensboro sit-in
   - Henry E. Frye
   - Howard N. Lee
   - Jesse Jackson
   - North Carolina Fund
   - Constitution of 1971

2. **Sequencing** Copy the time line below. Place events on it to trace the progress of ending racial discrimination.

3. **Finding the Main Idea**
   a. How did the nation's fight against communism in the Cold War affect North Carolina?
   b. Why did North Carolina adopt a new constitution in 1971?

4. **Writing and Critical Thinking**
   Analyzing Information What factors explain why Chapel Hill and Raleigh elected black mayors in the 1970s?
   - racial attitudes in the state
   - changes in voting patterns

Homework Practice Online
keyword: SN3 HP15

1950 — 1975

A Changing State 293

Chapter 15 Review

Chapter Summary

Section 1
- Farming declined and manufacturing became more important as state leaders worked to lure more industry to locate in North Carolina.
- As new industries located in urban areas more than in rural ones, North Carolina cities experienced rapid growth.

Section 2
- The state's road-building program and the interstate highway system encouraged the development of suburbs and the spread of urban regions.
- State leaders improved educational opportunities by combining small public schools into larger ones, creating a large community college system, creating new state universities, and opening more UNC branches.
- State government encouraged growth of the arts by funding the North Carolina Symphony, the North Carolina Museum of Art, and the North Carolina School of the Arts.

Section 3
- In the 1950s and 1960s the Cold War and anticommunism and then the Vietnam War affected the state and sometimes divided North Carolinians.
- State and local leaders confronted racial segregation in schools and other public facilities, but not until forced to do so by court action and widespread protests.
- In 1970 North Carolina adopted a revised state constitution that replaced outmoded and illegal provisions and streamlined state government.

Identifying People and Ideas
Use the following terms in complete sentences.
1. Luther Hodges
2. right-to-work law
3. conurbations
4. community colleges
5. School Machinery Act
6. Terry Sanford
7. Dan K. Moore
8. Pearsall Plan
9. *Swann v. Charlotte-Mecklenburg Board of Education*
10. Constitution of 1971

Understanding Main Ideas

Section 1 (Pages 281–283)
1. What economic and population trends existed in the state in the decades after World War II?
2. What three actions did North Carolina leaders take in the 1940s and 1950s to lure outside industries to the state?

Section 2 (Pages 284–288)
3. How did better roads encourage the growth of suburbs?
4. What improvements in public schools took place between 1930 and 1970?

Section 3 (Pages 289–293)
5. What national issues divided North Carolinians?
6. How did the Supreme Court decision in the *Brown* case affect North Carolina?
7. What changes did the Constitution of 1971 make?

What Did You Find Out?
1. **Science, Technology & Society** In what ways did television increase the nation's awareness of North Carolina?
2. **Citizenship** What actions by North Carolina citizens not only weakened racial segregation in the state, but across the nation as well?
3. **Government** How did the actions of government increase cultural, economic, and educational opportunities in North Carolina?

Thinking Critically
1. **Identifying Cause and Effect** What short- and long-term effects did the creation of Research Triangle Park have for North Carolina?
2. **Drawing Inferences and Conclusions** How did the construction of interstate highways affect the daily lives of North Carolinians?
3. **Supporting a Point of View** Do you think "Boston Tea Party of the civil rights movement" is an appropriate label for the Greensboro sit-in? Explain why or why not.

Building Social Studies Skills

Interpreting Photographs

This 1957 photograph records the enrollment of the first black students at a high school in Charlotte. Study the photo and answer the questions that follow.

Fifteen-year-old Dorothy Counts is seen here on her way to school in September of 1957. Counts was the first African American student to attend Harding High School in Charlotte.

1. What term best describes the white students in the photo?
   a. happy
   b. violent
   c. celebrating
   d. taunting

2. Historical accounts of school integration in North Carolina often describe the process as a fairly peaceful one. Does this photo support that interpretation? Explain why or why not.

Analyzing Primary Sources

Read the following excerpt written in 1949 by well-known political scientist V. O. Key. Then answer the questions.

> "Industrialization has created a financial and business elite whose influence prevails in [controls] the state's political and economic life. An aggressive aristocracy of manufacturing and banking . . . has had a tremendous stake in state policy and has not been remiss [neglectful] in protecting and advancing what it visualizes [sees] as its interests. Consequently a sympathetic respect for the problems of . . . large employers permeates [spreads throughout] the state's politics and government."

3. With which of the following statements would Key have most likely agreed, based on this analysis?
   a. Agricultural interests have long held too much power in the state.
   b. Much of the money the legislature has spent to promote the arts has been donated by the state's largest businesses.
   c. The right-to-work law shows that in 1947 the legislature was controlled by and sympathetic to big business.
   d. State government has actually done very little to attract out-of-state companies to relocate in North Carolina.

4. Based on what you have learned about North Carolina's economic and political development, do you agree or disagree with Key's point of view. Explain.

Alternative Assessment

Building Your Portfolio

Linking to Your Community
Interview relatives, family friends, or other adults who lived in your community during the 1950s and 1960s. Ask them what they remember about the integration of schools and other public facilities in your community. Then imagine that you were a middle school student during that time and create a fictional journal of your observations and experiences. Base your journal entries on information gained from your interviews.

internet connect

Internet Activity: go.hrw.com
keyword: SN3 NC15

Choose a topic on a changing state to:
- Write a newspaper article on education in the post–World War II era.
- Write an essay on the Red Scare/Cold War in North Carolina.
- Create a time line of the civil rights struggle in North Carolina.

A Changing State

CHAPTER 16
A Modern State
(1970–Present)

The skyline of the city of Charlotte shows the prosperity of contemporary North Carolina.

Build on What You Know

How do governments and citizens prepare for the future? How does a state respond to changing social and economic trends? During the late 1900s and early 2000s, North Carolina's government and its citizens were determined to meet these challenges and build a better state for the future.

 Themes Journal Do you **agree** or **disagree** with the following statements? Support your point of view in your journal.

- **Culture** State governments and citizens should encourage immigration and settlement.
- **Economics** State governments should protect traditional industries even if those businesses are declining.
- **Citizenship** State governments and citizens should make concrete plans for the future.

What's Your Opinion?

Section 1

A Diverse State

Read to Discover
1. How did the political climate of North Carolina change in the late 1900s?
2. What effect did religious changes have on North Carolina?
3. How did the population of North Carolina change in the late twentieth century?

Define
- televangelism
- refugees

Identify
- Executive Organization Act of 1971
- James E. Holshouser Jr.
- Jesse Helms
- Grace J. Rohrer
- Susie Sharp
- Jim and Tammy Faye Bakker
- Christian right
- Moral Majority
- Hmong

The Story Continues

The last half of the twentieth century brought enormous changes to North Carolina. African Americans and other minorities gained new access to political and social opportunities. Women became increasingly involved in public life. The organization of the state government changed as well. One observer defined these transformations as "turning toward the mainstream."

Political Diversity

North Carolina entered a period of dramatic political change during the 1970s. State residents even approved a new constitution. The Constitution of 1971 eliminated outdated references to race. It also abandoned the poll tax, a tax levied on people as a requirement for voting. This tax had been used to discourage African American voters. Another law, the **Executive Organization Act of 1971**, reduced government agencies from more than 350 to less than 20. It also created the position of secretary, to be named by the governor, to act as the head of each of these new departments.

African Americans in North Carolina have exercised growing political power in recent decades.

A Modern State **297**

BIOGRAPHY

Jesse Helms
(1921–)

Jesse Helms grew up in Monroe. He served in the U.S. Navy during World War II. After the war ended, Helms became an editor at *The Raleigh Times*. Helms became involved in national politics in the early 1950s, when he served as an assistant to a U.S. senator. Helms later won his own seat in the U.S. Senate. He served five terms in office, making him North Carolina's longest-serving Senator. In 2000, Senator Helms supported an effort to gain religious freedom in China before approving normal trade relations with the country. Helms commented, "... we must insist that progress on religious freedom precede [come before] China's entry into the World Trade Organization." **Why might Jesse Helms have made religious freedom an issue in trade negotiations with China?**

One of the most important political shifts in the state was the reemergence of a true two-party political system. For years the Democratic Party had dominated politics in the state. However, issues such as the civil rights movement and expansion of the welfare state led some white North Carolinians to crossover to the Republican Party. As a result, many Republicans began to win statewide offices. In 1972 **James E. Holshouser Jr.** won the governorship. He was the first Republican to do so since 1896. That same year, conservative **Jesse Helms** became North Carolina's first Republican U.S. senator since 1895.

Along with the revival of competitive two-party politics came a new diversity in the state's political life. African Americans, for example, gained new participation in state and local government. Henry E. Frye won a seat in the state House of Representatives in 1968. Frye later won election to the state senate. In the early 1980s he became a justice in the North Carolina Supreme Court, and in 1999 was elected Chief Justice.

Women took new government roles as well. **Grace J. Rohrer** served as the Secretary of the Department of Art, Culture, and History. She was the first woman to head a cabinet-level agency in state government. **Susie Sharp** joined the North Carolina Supreme Court in 1962, and was elected Chief Justice in 1974. She was the first woman in the United States to serve as Chief Justice of a state supreme court.

✔ **READING CHECK** Finding the Main Idea How did the political climate in North Carolina change in the 1970s?

★ Religious Changes

Religious diversity affected North Carolina culture, as well as politics. In the last decades of the twentieth century, religious denominations and practices became increasingly diverse.

Christian denominations and other faiths The vast majority of North Carolinians remain members of Protestant denominations. The Southern Baptist denomination is the largest in the state, accounting for almost 22 percent of the state population. The African Methodist Episcopal Zion Church, made up mainly of African Americans, is also a sizable denomination. In recent years, immigration has somewhat increased the size and number of other religious groups, including Catholics, Muslims, Jews, Hindus, and Buddhists. Many Catholics have come to North Carolina from other states or from Latin America. Most Hindus and Buddhists have been Asian immigrants attracted by North Carolina's universities and high-tech industries.

Televangelism One of the biggest changes to religious worship in North Carolina has been the rise of **televangelism**, the use of television to spread a religious message. Two of the most successful televangelists of the 1970s and 1980s were **Jim and Tammy Faye Bakker**, who achieved a national following through their *Praise the Lord* (PTL) television network, based in Charlotte. The Bakkers raised millions of dollars towards the creation of a Christian-themed amusement park near Charlotte. In the late 1980s some PTL contributors to the project complained that the Bakkers had cheated them out of their money to support a lavish lifestyle. The ministry soon fell apart and in 1989 Jim Bakker was convicted of fraud.

The Christian right Other religious leaders used the power of the media to shape politics. In the mid-1970s many Christian fundamentalists joined together. Using the power of television and mass mailings, they started an effort to apply their morals and beliefs to national issues and politics. The movement was known as the **Christian right**, led by Reverend Jerry Falwell's group, the **Moral Majority**, among others. The Christian right wanted political leaders to support policies that reflected fundamentalist Christian beliefs. This effort was popular in North Carolina. Senator Jesse Helms helped to lead the Christian right's efforts in the U.S. Capitol. He once explained:

"The paramount thing is whether a man believes in the principles of America and whether he is willing to stand up for them, win or lose."

Jesse Helms, as quoted by *ABC News.com*, August 22, 2001

✔ **READING CHECK** Summarizing How did religion change in North Carolina?

Analyzing Primary Sources
Critical Thinking What might Senator Helms mean by the phrase "principles of America"?

Interior of an Episcopal church in Bald Head Island, North Carolina

The Ethnic Population of North Carolina in 2000

[Bar graph showing:
- Caucasian Americans 72%
- African Americans 22%
- Hispanic Americans or Hispanic Immigrants* 5%
- People of another race or ethnic group 2%
- People of two or more races 1%
- Asian Americans or Asian Immigrants 1%
- American Indians 1%

X-axis: Percent of Total Population (0, 25, 50, 75)
Y-axis: North Carolina Ethnic Groups]

*Hispanic people may be of any race. Thus, numbers may add up to more than 100 percent.
Source: U.S. Census Bureau

Interpreting the Graph The population of North Carolina became increasingly diverse during the late 1900s. **Which racial or ethnic groups made up at least five percent or more of the state's population?**

Ethnic Diversity

North Carolina's population became more diverse in the late 1900s. Several factors contributed to this new diversity. International political events forced many people to seek shelter in the United States. Some **refugees** settled in North Carolina, attracted by the economy and the geography. A refugee is a person who flees his or her home country due to political persecution. In the mid-1980s a number of **Hmong** people from the Southeast Asian nation of Laos immigrated to North Carolina. The Hmong had been driven from their homes by the aftermath of the war in Vietnam. Other refugees from Eastern Europe and Asia immigrated to North Carolina after the Soviet Union collapsed in the late 1980s.

Many immigrants relocated to North Carolina to find better lives. Among the fastest-growing of these groups were Hispanic immigrants. The Hispanic population in North Carolina, for example, increased by about 400 percent from 1990 to 2000. These immigrants came mainly from Mexico and the countries of Central America. Many found work on farms in eastern North Carolina and in the construction and service industries of the urban Piedmont.

North Carolina's new immigrants offer both challenges and opportunities for the state. Many people argue that refugees and immigrants help fuel the economy by providing labor and starting up businesses. Others worry that rapid population growth strains state-provided services such as schools and hospitals.

✓ **READING CHECK** Identifying Cause and Effect Why did many refugees and immigrants settle in North Carolina during the late twentieth century?

Section 1 Review

keyword: SN3 HP16

1 Define and explain:
- televangelism
- refugees

2 Identify and explain:
- Executive Organization Act of 1971
- James E. Holshouser Jr.
- Jesse Helms
- Grace J. Rohrer
- Susie Sharp
- Jim and Tammy Faye Bakker
- Christian right
- Moral Majority
- Hmong

3 Analyzing Information Copy the web diagram below. Use it to identify changes that took place in state politics in the 1970s.

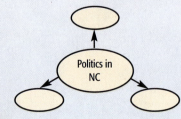

4 Finding the Main Idea
a. How did religion change in North Carolina?
b. What changes took place in North Carolina's population during the late twentieth century?

5 Writing and Critical Thinking
Finding the Main Idea Imagine that you are an immigrant moving to the United States. Write a letter to your family in your native country explaining why you are going to move to North Carolina.

Consider:
- educational opportunities in the state
- economic opportunities in the state

Section 2

The New Economy

Read to Discover
1. How did North Carolina's traditional industries fare in the last part of the twentieth century?
2. How did growth of high-tech industries help and potentially harm North Carolina?
3. How did North Carolina's business and political leaders attempt to diversify the state's economy and prepare it for the future?

Identify
- Hugh McColl Jr.
- Michael Jordan
- Dale Earnhardt
- North Carolina Progress Board

The Story Continues

North Carolina's economy experienced important changes during the late twentieth century. The once-agricultural state developed new industries based on high-tech products. In the late 1900s both nonfarm employment and nonfarm wages rose dramatically. The shifts indicated the presence of a new economy for North Carolina.

Traditional Industries in Recent Years

During the late 1990s, North Carolina's overall economy experienced strong growth. One magazine called the state's business economy the best in the country.

Tobacco Tobacco is still a crucial part of North Carolina's economy. In 1999 North Carolina produced about 450 million pounds of tobacco. The tobacco business employs about 114,000 people in the state. Related businesses employ an additional 255,000 in the state. In recent years, many people have wondered about the future of the tobacco industry in North Carolina. People question how anti-smoking efforts and anti-tobacco lawsuits will affect the industry and the state.

A North Carolinian holds leaves of harvested tobacco.

A Modern State **301**

Interpreting the Visual Record

Furniture workers Chairmaker Arval Woody is seen here at work in Spruce Pine, North Carolina. *What does this photo reveal about the traditional furniture industry?*

North Carolina and the Global Economy

North Carolina exports goods such as industrial machines, chemical products, electrical appliances, stone products, and tobacco items to many different countries. In 2000 the state's businesses exported more than $5 billion in goods to Canada and $382 million in goods to Belgium. International corporations and investors also form a crucial part of North Carolina's economy. In 1999 foreign companies invested almost $911 million in North Carolina. The majority of the money came from German and British firms. Taken together, all of the investments created some 4,280 jobs in the state. **Why is it important for North Carolina to play a significant role in the global economy?**

Textiles Like tobacco, textiles form an essential part of the state's economy. Textile exports from North Carolina amounted to about $3 billion in 2000. The textile industry has experienced difficulties in recent years, however. New machines have reduced the need for human workers. Foreign companies have introduced their products at competitive prices. Overall employment in the textile industry declined by about 80,000 workers from 1988 to 1998.

Furniture The furniture and fixtures industry shows similar changes. Many furniture businesses are located in the Piedmont region. Towns such as Hickory, Morganton, Greensboro, Winston-Salem, and High Point have large furniture manufacturing businesses. During the late 1990s, total employment in the furniture industry declined, leading some people to worry about the future of furniture workers.

✔ **READING CHECK Categorizing** What difficulties did North Carolina's traditional industries experience during the late twentieth century?

 ## The Boom of the 1990s

The high-tech regions of the state, such as the Research Triangle Park area, experienced a boom in the 1990s. The park itself grew to include 150 operations employing some 45,000 people. Tenants have included GlaxoSmithKline, Inc.; Underwriters Laboratories, Inc.; and Union Carbide's Agricultural Products Technical Center, among others. The area of Greensboro-High Point-Winston-Salem also experienced a huge growth in high-tech business during this period. Much of this growth was fueled by the larger growth of high-tech industries throughout the country in the 1990s. When the high-tech industry started to experience a slump around 2000, however, many North Carolina leaders worried about the effects of relying too much on a high-tech economy.

✔ **READING CHECK Identifying Cause and Effect** What were the advantages and disadvantages to high-tech growth in North Carolina during the 1990s?

 ## Diversifying the Economy

State leaders have worked to develop new businesses and industries in North Carolina. Economic diversity protects the state and its workers from sudden downturns in one or two areas of the economy.

One area of the nation's economy in which North Carolina has taken a lead is in the field of banking. Charlotte is the headquarters of the largest bank in the United States. Much of this domination in banking has come from the efforts of **Hugh McColl Jr.**, a Bennettsville native. McColl became president of the North Carolina National Bank in 1982. Over the next several years he enlarged the bank enormously through a series of over 100 mergers with other banks, including NationsBank. His biggest coup was the merger with Bank of America in 1998.

Machinery and electronics are two expanding fields of industry. The machinery industry produces goods such as engines, turbines, and tractors. The electronics industry is growing as well. In 1996 electronics manufacturers produced $13.9 billion worth of goods such as household appliances, telephones, televisions, computers, and more.

More than 40 million people visit North Carolina each year. These tourists add $12 billion to the state's economy, making tourism one of the most important industries in North Carolina. In recent years, the film industry, too, has become increasingly important. In 2000 alone producers filmed about 80 major productions in the state. Between 1980 and 2000, filmmaking contributed about $5 billion to the state economy.

Sports also contribute to the state's economy. Avid golfers flock to the state's many golf courses. The popularity of college sports continues to pump millions of dollars into the state. In recent years the presence of professional sports teams has grown. North Carolina is the current home of one professional hockey team, one professional basketball team, a National Football League team, and several arena football teams and minor-league baseball teams. The increased national

That's Interesting!

Michael Jordan The most famous professional basketball player ever, **Michael Jordan**, grew up in Wilmington and played for the University of North Carolina at Chapel Hill. As a freshman, he led his team to the national championship in 1982 by making the winning shot just as the game's final buzzer sounded.

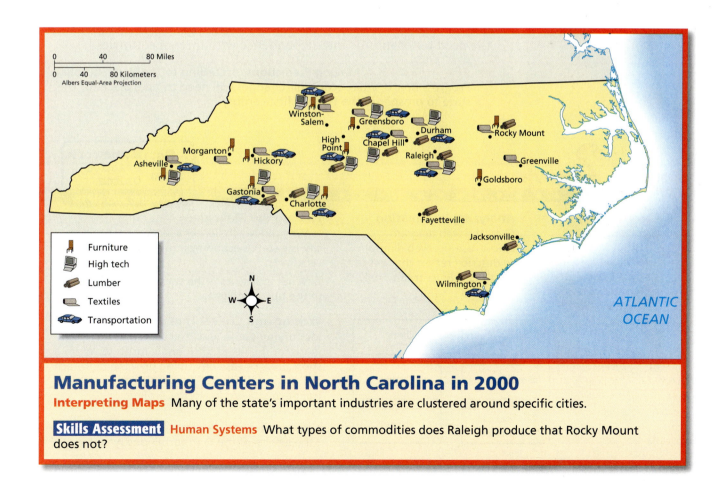

Manufacturing Centers in North Carolina in 2000

Interpreting Maps Many of the state's important industries are clustered around specific cities.

Skills Assessment **Human Systems** What types of commodities does Raleigh produce that Rocky Mount does not?

A Modern State **303**

Racing at Lowe's Motor Speedway in Charlotte

Analyzing Primary Sources
Drawing Conclusions What was one of the economic changes that the state progress board wanted to make?

fan-base of NASCAR racing has also helped the state. The enormous popularity of racing was evident in the national outpouring of grief following the death of North Carolina race-car driver <u>Dale Earnhardt</u> in February 2001.

✔ **READING CHECK** Finding the Main Idea Why do state and business leaders want to continue diversifying North Carolina's economy?

The Economy in 2000 and Beyond

The <u>North Carolina Progress Board</u> is designed to help formulate plans for the future. One North Carolina Progress Board document described an ideal vision of the state's economy in 2020.

> **History Makers Speak**
> "North Carolina's growing, dynamic economy is competitive in the global marketplace. It is diversified. High-quality jobs are plentiful. . . . 'Knowledge workers' dominate the workforce and citizens take advantage of modern communications and technology to create new economic opportunities."
>
> The North Carolina Progress Board, "North Carolina 20/20"

The Board makes recommendations to help its vision become a reality. It stresses the importance of economic growth in new fields and the need for economic interdependence with foreign countries.

✔ **READING CHECK** Making Predictions According to the North Carolina Progress Board, what economic changes will need to take place for the state to prosper in the twenty-first century?

Section 2 Review

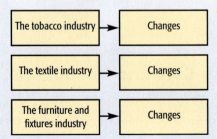
keyword: SN3 HP16

1 Identify and explain:
• Hugh McColl Jr.
• Michael Jordan
• Dale Earnhardt
• North Carolina Progress Board

2 Analyzing Information Copy the web diagram below. Use the web diagram to describe recent changes in North Carolina's traditional industries.

The tobacco industry → Changes
The textile industry → Changes
The furniture and fixtures industry → Changes

3 Finding the Main Idea
a. Why did North Carolina leaders try to diversify the state's economy in the late twentieth century?
b. What industries is the state trying to develop in the upcoming years?

4 Writing and Critical Thinking
Identifying Cause and Effect Imagine that you work for the Research Triangle Institute. Write a short press release describing how the high-tech industry has furthered economic and technological development in North Carolina.
Consider:
• advantages and disadvantages of high tech
• the effects of the high-tech industry

304 Chapter 16

Section 3

North Carolina Today

Read to Discover
1. What issues concerned North Carolinians in the early years of the twenty-first century?
2. What issues affected the North Carolina government in 2000?
3. How did national issues affect the economic climate of North Carolina in the twenty-first century?

Define
- redistricting

Identify
- Michael F. Easley
- John Edwards
- Elizabeth Dole
- James B. Hunt Jr.
- NC 2000

The Story Continues

The chancellor of North Carolina State University described the progress the state had made during the 1990s. "The American people have just enjoyed a decade of unprecedented prosperity of a magnitude beyond all reasonable expectation," she said. "It is our special good fortune to live in the Research Triangle of North Carolina, which has produced many of the innovative technologies that drove this phenomenal economic expansion." The chancellor also pointed to alarming economic and educational trends, however. How would North Carolina meet the challenges of the future?

Interpreting the Visual Record

Education for the future Fifth-grade students work on computers at the Claxton Elementary School in Asheville. *How might a class such as this help students prepare for future conditions in North Carolina?*

Challenges in the New Century

The twenty-first century has brought many new opportunities for North Carolina. Innovative technologies in areas such as communications, electronics, chemical engineering, transportation, and manufacturing

A Modern State **305**

promise to revolutionize daily life for many residents. Yet the new century brings many challenges to North Carolina as well.

Education The economic changes in North Carolina carry important consequences for education in the state. In the past decades, traditional industries such as textiles and tobacco have declined, while new technical industries have emerged. North Carolina's schools must produce graduates who have the technical training and advanced skills needed to work in these fields. The need for strong science and math skills, as well as for language and communications know-how, is particularly important.

Other educational issues pose challenges as well. Many North Carolinians feel that the government should provide additional funds for the state's schools. Among the most critical needs, according to many, are smaller class size, more classrooms and equipment, additional reading and language programs, and more in-service training for teachers. Concerned citizens have also called for improvements in the day-care system, as well as for increased adult education opportunities.

Crime The issue of crime also concerns many North Carolinians. Although the state crime rate has decreased somewhat, it is still higher than the national crime rate. Many residents feel unsafe in their own homes. The issues of alcohol misuse and drug addiction complicate the matter even further. Many residents feel that North Carolina must somehow find a way to address both the causes and effects of crime.

The environment Environmental issues also create challenges for North Carolina in the coming century. During the late 1900s, North Carolinians saw alarming signs of environmental damage in the state. Many local wastewater plants failed to meet quality standards, leading to dangerous water pollution.

Air quality was a problem as well. During the 1980s, for example, many fir trees in mountains lost their color and then their needles. Scientists eventually determined that air pollution and acid rain had caused the problem. Many North Carolinians have called for stricter standards and monitoring to protect the environment in the coming years.

These trees on Mount Mitchell, in Yancey County, show the effects that acid rain can have on North Carolina forests.

✔ **READING CHECK** Summarizing What factor makes educational improvement so important for North Carolinians?

North Carolina's Government in 2000

In 2000 the North Carolina state government responded to a wide variety of national events that affected the state. The government also worked to ensure continued prosperity as North Carolina entered the twenty-first century.

State and local government In 2000 Democrat <u>Michael F. Easley</u> was elected governor of North Carolina. Easley was born in Nash County, just outside Rocky Mount, and grew up on a tobacco farm. He attended the University of North Carolina. Before becoming governor Easley served as North Carolina's Attorney General.

One of the most pressing questions facing the state government in 2000 was the issue of **redistricting**. This has become an important issue in North Carolina as the state's population has increased rapidly. The act of redistricting occurs when public officials redraw the boundaries of districts from which officials are elected. Many North Carolina officials, such as U.S. representatives and state senators and representatives, are elected by voters in districts. Certain local officials, such as county commissioners, school board members, and city council members are elected by district as well.

The law requires that citizens in different districts have an equal right to representation. Given different population patterns, district size changes over time. In order to reflect these changes, districts must be redrawn after every census. The U.S. Constitution mandates that a new census must be taken every ten years. Redistricting often takes a long time. Many North Carolinians carefully followed the redistricting process as politicians considered potential districts.

The North Carolina State Legislative Building in Raleigh is one of the state's important centers of government activity.

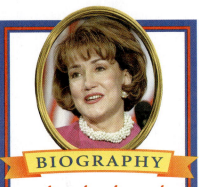

BIOGRAPHY

Elizabeth Dole
(1936–)

Elizabeth Dole was born and raised in Salisbury. She earned a degree in law and government from Harvard University. Dole then entered politics, working for President Lyndon Johnson. In the early 1980s President Ronald Reagan appointed her as secretary of transportation for his administration. Dole was the first woman to serve in this role. She continued her government work under President George H. W. Bush, acting as secretary of labor. Later, she headed the American Red Cross, a private charity.

Dole entered the race for the Republican presidential nomination in the 2000 election. Although she did not receive the nomination, her campaign reflected the growing national role of women in the Republican Party. **What national political roles did Elizabeth Dole serve?**

Religion and politics One important trend in North Carolina politics continued in 2000. The movement started by the Christian right years earlier affected politics in the twenty-first century as more political leaders emphasized the role of religion in the government. Some senators and representatives discuss their religious affiliations on their Web sites and in their official campaign literature. Others have applied their religious beliefs to their political decisions. While some North Carolinians applaud the trend of mixing politics and religion, others do not. They worry that the increasing influence of religion in politics will weaken or violate the separation of church and state established in the U.S. Constitution.

✓ **READING CHECK Finding the Main Idea** Why did North Carolina begin a redistricting effort in the early 2000s?

North Carolina in National Government

North Carolinians continue to represent their state and its people in the national government. In 2000 **John Edwards** and Jesse Helms represented North Carolina in the U.S. Senate. Edwards grew up in the Piedmont region. The son of a textile worker and a furniture refinisher, he was the first person in his family to go to college. Jesse Helms served in the Senate for five terms. In August of 2001 Helms announced that he would not seek a sixth term in office. This announcement sparked a heated race in 2002 for his seat.

North Carolina's U.S. Representatives also work for the state in the national government. In 2002 there were 12 U.S. Representatives from North Carolina in the 107th U.S. Congress, representing both major political parties. Five were Democrats: Eva Clayton, Bob Etheridge, Mike McIntyre, David Price, and Melvin L. Watt. Seven were Republicans: Cass Ballenger, Richard Burr, Howard Coble, Robert (Robin) Hayes, Walter B. Jones Jr., Sue Myrick, and Charles H. Taylor.

✓ **READING CHECK Finding the Main Idea** How do North Carolinians serve their state in the national government?

The Future of North Carolina

In the early years of the 2000s, an economic slowdown hit North Carolina and the rest of the nation. High-tech industries in particular were affected. This high-tech recession carried particularly important consequences for North Carolina. Less money was available for research and development. One magazine called for government action to help support continued economic and educational growth. Other observers pointed out that the Research Triangle Park area, with its skilled high-tech work force, plays an important role in not just the North Carolina economy but that of the nation as a whole.

Just as important a challenge is making sure all North Carolinians benefit from economic growth. While the overall economy of the state is still strong, there are pockets of the state that continue to suffer from inequity.

One thing remains clear: North Carolinians must continue to participate in the government of their state and work for a better future. In 1981 then governor **James B. Hunt Jr.** headed a commission on the future of North Carolina. This effort was known as **Clean NC 2000**. Also working with this group was at least one representative from each of the state's one hundred counties. Moreover, the commission took into account the responses of some 113,000 North Carolinians to a long questionnaire. This gave citizens a chance to express their concerns and desires. In a speech, Hunt described the importance of planning for the future.

A skilled laborer builds the circuitry of a laptop computer at an IBM facility in the Research Triangle Park area.

 "Our task today is to anticipate and prepare for the North Carolina our children will encounter tomorrow. . . . We must take responsibility for making the world what we want it to be, for ourselves and for our children. And that requires looking into the future *now*. Looking at the future can help us anticipate changes and make decisions."

James B. Hunt Jr., quoted in *North Carolina through Four Centuries*

Analyzing Primary Sources

Drawing Inferences Why do you think Hunt placed such strong importance on planning for the future?

Hunt's words remain true today. The people of North Carolina have the responsibility and the power to create a better state.

✓ **READING CHECK** Identifying Points of View How did some North Carolinians want to protect the future of the state?

Section 3 Review

Homework Practice Online
keyword: SN3 HP16

1. **Define** and explain:
   - redistricting

2. **Identify** and explain:
   - Michael F. Easley
   - John Edwards
   - Elizabeth Dole
   - James B. Hunt Jr.
   - Clean NC 2000

3. **Analyzing Information** Copy the chart below. Use it to identify and describe the issues that concerned many North Carolinians in the twenty-first century.

Education	Crime	The environment

4. **Finding the Main Idea**
   a. What recommendations did some North Carolinians make to improve the educational system of the state for the twenty-first century?
   b. Why did North Carolina begin a redistricting process in the first years of the 2000s?

5. **Writing and Critical Thinking**
   Supporting a Point of View Imagine that you are a newspaper reporter. Write a short editorial on the issue of religion and politics. Make sure to support your point of view.
   Consider:
   - the effects of the Christian right
   - the ideas supporting and opposing the involvement of religion in politics

A Modern State

Chapter 16 Review

Chapter Summary

Section 1
- Political thinking in North Carolina was strongly influenced by national events and issues during the late 1900s and the early 2000s.
- Immigration and the media began to change religious practices in the state.
- North Carolina's population has steadily grown and become more racially and ethnically diverse in recent years.

Section 2
- North Carolina worked to become more industrially and economically progressive during the late 1900s and the early years of the 2000s.
- Business and political leaders in North Carolina have successfully promoted economic planning and development across the state.

Section 3
- Issues such as crime, education, and the environment have strongly affected North Carolina's political and social scene in recent years.
- Conservatism and tradition continue to shape North Carolina's political development in the early 2000s.
- North Carolina's modern economy is closely tied to national and global economic trends and markets.

Identifying People and Ideas
Describe the historical significance of the following.
1. refugees
2. Hmong
3. Executive Organization Act of 1971
4. Christian right
5. Jesse Helms
6. Hugh McColl Jr.
7. Michael F. Easley
8. redistricting
9. James B. Hunt Jr.
10. Elizabeth Dole

Understanding Main Ideas
Section 1 *(Pages 297–300)*
1. What developments and issues affected the political climate of North Carolina in the late 1900s?
2. How did religious practices change in North Carolina?

Section 2 *(Pages 301–304)*
3. How did the high-tech industry affect economic conditions in North Carolina?
4. What industrial trends occurred in North Carolina during the late 1900s and the early years of the 2000s?

Section 3 *(Pages 305–309)*
5. How did the national economic downturn with regard to high-tech industries affect the future of North Carolina?
6. What issues concerned North Carolinians about the future of the state?

What Did You Find Out?
1. **Culture** How did the population of North Carolina become more ethnically and culturally diverse in the late 1900s?
2. **Economics** What efforts did leaders in North Carolina make to lessen the effects of declining traditional industries?
3. **Citizenship** What plans did the North Carolina government make to develop the state in the twenty-first century?

Thinking Critically
1. **Synthesizing** What were some of the political trends that affected North Carolina during the late 1900s?
2. **Decision Making** What measures could North Carolina take in order to increase its economic interdependence?
3. **Supporting a Point of View** How might North Carolina best meet the challenges of the twenty-first century?

Building Social Studies Skills

Interpreting Graphs

Study the graph below. Then use the information on the graph to answer the questions that follow.

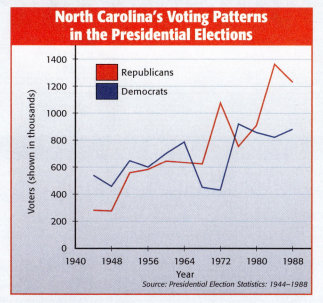

North Carolina's Voting Patterns in the Presidential Elections

Source: Presidential Election Statistics: 1944–1988

1. Which of the following statements best describes the trend in North Carolina's voting records in the presidential elections?
   a. The majority of North Carolina voters chose the Republican candidate in the 1964 election.
   b. In 1972 and in the 1980s, North Carolinians voted overwhelmingly Republican in presidential elections.
   c. Starting with the election of 1948, North Carolina voters favored the Democratic Party in presidential elections.
   d. The majority of North Carolina voters chose the Democratic candidate in the 1972 election.

2. What information does the graph provide? What is the purpose of this information?

Analyzing Information

The excerpt below is from a report entitled *First in America Special Report: Designing a High Quality Pre-Kindergarten Program*, by the North Carolina Education Research Council. Read the excerpt and then answer the questions that follow.

> ❝... [B]oth North Carolina and the federal government have made dramatic increases in funding for early childhood services, but two problems remain—high quality early childhood programs are difficult to find and even more difficult to afford. Parents continue to bear the largest share of the considerable costs of child care ... And while all families may struggle to find high quality programs, low- to moderate-income families are at an even greater disadvantage.❞
>
> Richard M. Clifford and James J. Gallagher, *First in America Special Report: Designing a High Quality Pre-Kindergarten Program*, North Carolina Education Research Council

3. Which of the following statements best summarizes the excerpt above?
   a. Parents bear only a very small share of child-care costs in North Carolina.
   b. Most families find it difficult to afford high quality early childhood programs.
   c. State programs make it easy for low-income families to afford high quality child care.
   d. North Carolina has done little to support early childhood services in recent years.

4. What two problems continue to challenge efforts by North Carolina's leaders to secure high quality early childhood services for all families?

Alternative Assessment

Building Your Portfolio

N.C. History

Cooperative Learning
Imagine that you are a member of the North Carolina Progress Board. Working with your group, create a detailed plan to improve the quality and impact of public education in North Carolina by 2020. Determine the educational goals you think are most important to the state's progress. Create a presentation supported by graphic and visual information to deliver to the class as an oral report.

internet connect

Internet Activity: go.hrw.com
keyword: SN3 NC16

Choose a topic on a modern state to:
- Create a political poster for Jesse Helms.
- Research the Hmong people of Laos.
- Write an essay on the Research Triangle Park.

A Modern State

TIME LINE OF NORTH CAROLINA

North Carolina 1200–1800s

1200 // **1500** | **1600**

c. A.D. 1200
The Arts
Native Americans build the Town Creek Indian Mound.

Clay container crafted by Iroquois potter in around A.D. 1500

1524
World Events
Giovanni da Verrazano explores the coast of North Carolina.

1585
World Events
Sir Walter Raleigh helps establish England's first New World colony on Roanoke Island.

1629
Business and Finance
Sir Robert Heath is granted the Carolina patent.

Reconstruction of the ship that carried English colonists to Roanoke Island, 1587

Orville Wright pilots the first successful flight of a heavier-than-air craft at Kill Devil Hills, near Kitty Hawk.

1903
Science and Technology
The Wright brothers complete the first airplane flight near Kitty Hawk.

1918
Daily Life
Fort Bragg is built during World War I.

1929
The Arts
Asheville native Thomas Wolfe publishes *Look Homeward, Angel*.

1945
World Events
More than 362,000 North Carolina soldiers take part in World War II.

1900 | **1920** | **1940**

North Carolina 1900–Present

Part of the scenic Appalachian Trail as it crosses through the highlands of western North Carolina

1937
Politics
New Deal programs help build the Appalachian Trail and the Blue Ridge Parkway.

1950–1953
World Events
More than 1,000 North Carolina soldiers die in the Korean War.

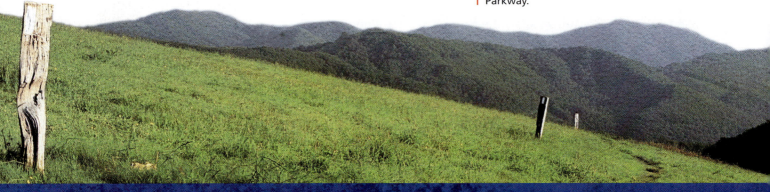

312 *Almanac*

North Carolina's state capitol at Raleigh

1706
Daily Life
Bath, the first official city in North Carolina, is founded.

1712
Daily Life
The Carolina lands are renamed North Carolina and South Carolina.

1789
Politics
North Carolina becomes the 12th state to ratify the United States Constitution.

1792
Daily Life
Raleigh becomes the state capital.

1840
Daily Life
The first North Carolina public school opens in Rockingham County.

1881
Science and Technology
The White Furniture Store uses mass production to make furniture.

1700 — **1800**

1776
Politics
The Halifax Resolves support North Carolinian independence.

1861
Politics
North Carolina secedes from the Union and joins the Confederate States of America.

1956
The Arts
The nation's first state museum of art, the North Carolina Museum of Art, opens.

1959
Science and Technology
Research Triangle Park opens.

1964
World Events
The Vietnam War, in which 1,500 North Carolinians are killed, begins.

Vietnam memorial on the grounds of North Carolina's capitol at Raleigh

1999
Daily Life
Hurricane Floyd causes massive flooding and destruction in North Carolina.

2001
World Events
In response to the terrorist attacks of 9/11, the General Assembly passes a bill to create a registry for companies dealing with toxic agents.

1960 — **1980** — **2000**

1960
Politics
America's first civil rights sit-in is held in Greensboro.

1971
Politics
North Carolina enacts a new state constitution.

1987
Daily Life
Construction of the Blue Ridge Parkway is completed.

2001
Daily Life
The General Assembly funds Governor Michael F. Easley's "More at Four" Pre-kindergarten program.

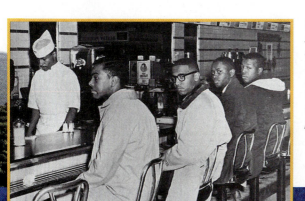

Four black students sit at a "whites only" lunch counter during the Greensboro civil rights protest of 1960.

North Carolina's "More at Four" program encourages pre-schoolers to build reading skills.

Almanac **313**

NORTH CAROLINA
SELECTED STATE SYMBOLS

Motto:
Esse Quam Videri
(To Be Rather Than To Seem)
Adopted 1893

Nickname:
"The Old North State" or **"The Tar Heel State"**

Song:
"The Old North State"
Adopted 1927

Tree: **Pine**
Adopted 1963

Insect: **Honey Bee**
Adopted 1973

Mammal: **Gray Squirrel**
Adopted 1969

Reptile:
Eastern Box Turtle
Adopted 1979

Dog: **Plott Hound**
Adopted 1989

Rock: **Granite**
Adopted 1979

Beverage: **Milk**
Adopted 1987

Fruit:
Scuppernong grape
Adopted 2001

Colors: **Red** and **Blue**
Adopted 1945

★★★★★★★★★★
That's Interesting!
★★★★★★★★★★

The sweet potato became the official State Vegetable in 1995 after students at a Wilson County school sent a petition to the North Carolina General Assembly.

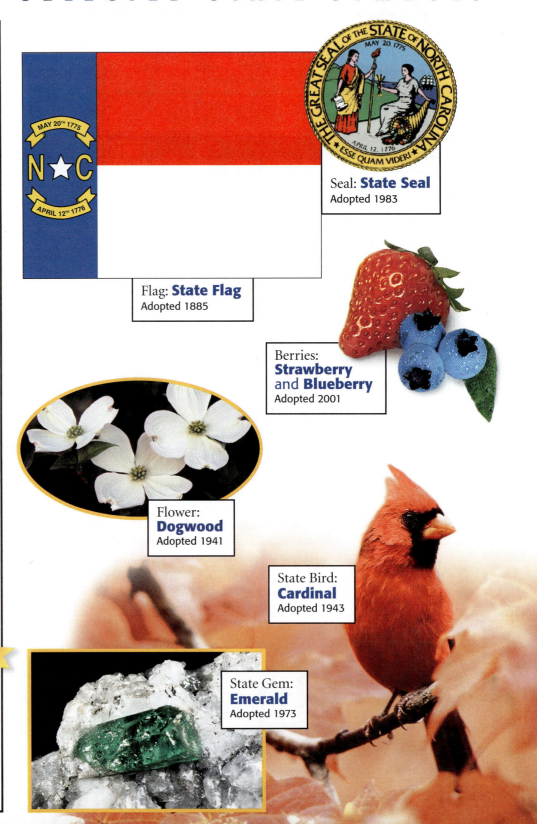

Seal: **State Seal**
Adopted 1983

Flag: **State Flag**
Adopted 1885

Berries:
Strawberry and **Blueberry**
Adopted 2001

Flower: **Dogwood**
Adopted 1941

State Bird: **Cardinal**
Adopted 1943

State Gem: **Emerald**
Adopted 1973

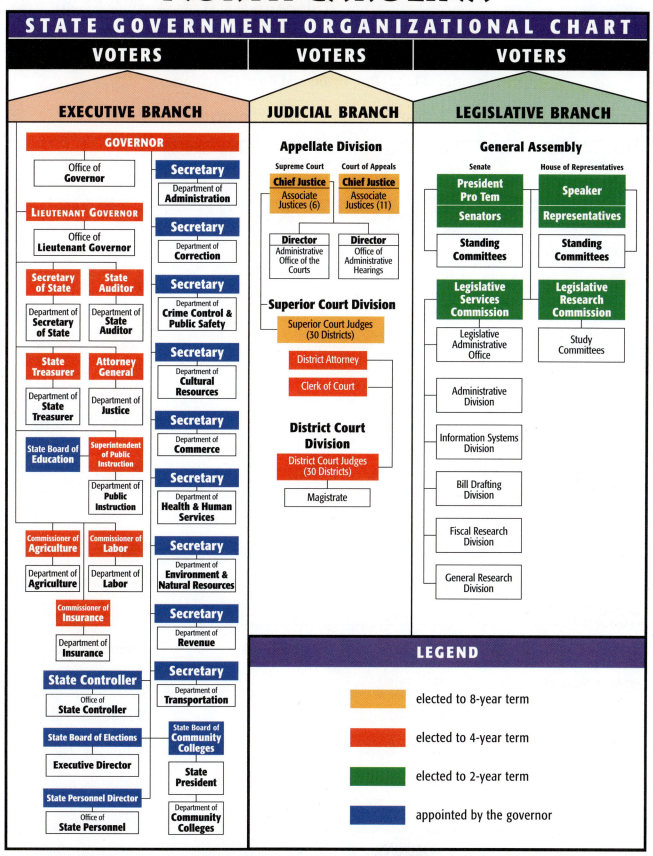

NORTH CAROLINA GOVERNORS

From 1664 to 1775, prior to declaring independence, North Carolina was governed by a series of Lords Proprietors and Royal Governors.

Governor	Term of Office	Home County	Party
Richard Caswell	1777–1780	Lenoir (then Dobbs)	None
Abner Nash	1780–1781	Craven	None
Thomas Burke	1781–1782	Orange	None
Alexander Martin	1782–1784	Guilford	None
Richard Caswell	1784–1787	Lenoir (then Dobbs)	None
Samuel Johnston	1787–1789	Chowan	Federalist
Alexander Martin	1789–1792	Guilford	None
Richard Dobbs Spaight Sr.	1792–1795	Craven	Federalist, switched to Democratic-Republican
Samuel Ashe	1795–1798	New Hanover	Democratic-Republican
William Richardson Davie	1798–1799	Halifax	Federalist
Benjamin Williams	1799–1802	Moore	Democratic-Republican
James Turner	1802–1805	Warren	Democratic-Republican
Nathaniel Alexander	1805–1807	Mecklenburg	Democratic-Republican
Benjamin Williams	1807–1808	Moore	Democratic-Republican
David Stone	1808–1810	Bertie	Democratic-Republican
Benjamin Smith	1810–1811	Brunswick	Democratic-Republican
William Hawkins	1811–1814	Warren	Democratic-Republican
William Miller	1814–1817	Warren	Democratic-Republican
John Branch	1817–1820	Halifax	Democratic-Republican
Jesse Franklin	1820–1821	Surry	Democratic-Republican
Gabriel Holmes	1821–1824	Sampson	None

Governor	Term of Office	Home County	Party
Hutchins Gordon Burton	1824–1827	Halifax	Federalist
James Iredell Jr.	1827–1828	Chowan	Democratic-Republican
John Owen	1828–1830	Bladen	None
Montfort Stokes	1830–1832	Wilkes	Democrat
David Lowry Swain	1832–1835	Buncombe	Whig
Richard Dobbs Spaight Jr.	1835–1836	Craven	Democrat
Edward Bishop Dudley	1837–1841	New Hanover	Whig
John Motley Morehead	1841–1845	Guilford	Whig
William Alexander Graham	1845–1849	Orange	Whig
Charles Manly	1849–1851	Wake	Whig
David Settle Reid	1851–1854	Rockingham	Democrat
Warren Winslow	1854–1855	Cumberland	Democrat
Thomas Bragg	1855–1859	Warren	Democrat
John Willis Ellis	1859–1861	Rowan	Democrat
Henry Toole Clark	1861–1862	Edgecombe	Democrat
Zebulon Baird Vance	1862–1865	Buncombe	Democrat
William Woods Holden	1865	Wake	Republican
Jonathan Worth	1865–1868	Randolph	Democrat
William Woods Holden	1868–1871	Wake	Republican
Tod Robinson Caldwell	1871–1874	Burke	Republican
Curtis Hooks Brogden	1874–1877	Wayne	Republican
Zebulon Baird Vance	1877–1879	Buncombe	Democrat
Thomas Jordan Jarvis	1879–1885	Pitt	Democrat
Alfred Moore Scales	1885–1889	Rockingham	Democrat
Daniel Gould Fowle	1889–1891	Wake	Democrat

Governor	Term of Office	Home County	Party
Thomas Michael Holt	1891–1893	Alamance	Democrat
Elias Carr	1893–1897	Edgecombe	Democrat
Daniel Lindsay Russell	1897–1901	Brunswick	Republican
Charles Brantley Aycock	1901–1905	Wayne	Democrat
Robert Broadnax Glenn	1905–1909	Forsyth	Democrat
William Walton Kitchin	1909–1913	Person	Democrat
Locke Craig	1913–1917	Buncombe	Democrat
Thomas Walter Bickett	1917–1921	Franklin	Democrat
Cameron Morrison	1921–1925	Mecklenburg	Democrat
Angus Wilton McLean	1925–1929	Robeson	Democrat
Oliver Max Gardner	1929–1933	Cleveland	Democrat
John Christoph Blucher Ehringhaus	1933–1937	Pasquotank	Democrat
Clyde Roark Hoey	1937–1941	Cleveland	Democrat
Joseph Melville Broughton	1941–1945	Wake	Democrat
Robert Gregg Cherry	1945–1949	Gaston	Democrat
William Kerr Scott	1949–1953	Alamance	Democrat
William Bradley Umstead	1953–1954	Durham	Democrat
Luther Hartwell Hodges	1954–1961	Rockingham	Democrat
Terry Sanford	1961–1965	Cumberland	Democrat
Daniel Killian Moore	1965–1969	Jackson	Democrat
Robert Walter Scott	1969–1973	Alamance	Democrat
James Eubert Holshouser Jr.	1973–1977	Watauga	Republican
James Baxter Hunt Jr.	1977–1985	Wilson	Democrat
James Grubbs Martin	1985–1993	Iredell	Republican
James Baxter Hunt Jr.	1993–2001	Wilson	Democrat
Michael F. Easley	2001–	Nash	Democrat

NORTH CAROLINA COUNTIES

County	Date of Formation	County Seat	Area in Sq. Miles*	Population	Named For
Alamance	1849	Graham	431	130,800	Indian word meaning "blue clay"
Alexander	1847	Taylorsville	261	33,603	William J. Alexander
Alleghany	1859	Sparta	233	10,677	Delaware Indian word meaning "a fine stream"
Anson	1750	Wadesboro	531	25,275	George, Lord Anson
Ashe	1799	Jefferson	427	24,384	Samuel Ashe
Avery	1911	Newland	247	17,167	Colonel Waightstill Avery
Beaufort	1712	Washington	827	44,958	Henry Somerset, Duke of Beaufort
Bertie	1722	Windsor	699	19,773	James Bertie
Bladen	1734	Elizabethtown	876	32,278	Martin Bladen
Brunswick	1764	Bolivia	857	73,143	Town of Brunswick
Buncombe	1791	Asheville	657	206,330	Colonel Edward Buncombe
Burke	1777	Morganton	505	89,148	Dr. Thomas Burke
Cabarrus	1792	Concord	364	131,063	Stephen Cabarrus
Caldwell	1841	Lenoir	472	77,415	Joseph Caldwell
Camden	1777	Camden	240	6,885	Charles Pratt, Earl Camden
Carteret	1722	Beaufort	524	59,383	John Carteret, Earl Granville
Caswell	1777	Yanceyville	426	23,501	Richard Caswell
Catawba	1842	Newton	400	141,685	Catawba Indian tribe
Chatham	1771	Pittsboro	683	49,329	William Pitt, Earl of Chatham
Cherokee	1839	Murphy	455	24,298	Cherokee Indian tribe
Chowan	1670	Edenton	173	14,526	Chowanoc Indian tribe
Clay	1861	Hayesville	214	8,775	Henry Clay
Cleveland	1841	Shelby	464	96,287	Colonel Benjamin Cleveland
Columbus	1808	Whiteville	937	54,749	Christopher Columbus
Craven	1705	New Bern	695	91,436	William, Lord Craven

*Areas have been rounded to the nearest whole number.

County	Date of Formation	County Seat	Area in Sq. Miles*	Population	Named For
Cumberland	1754	Fayetteville	652	302,963	William Augustus, Duke of Cumberland
Currituck	1668	Currituck	261	18,190	Indian word meaning "wild geese"
Dare	1870	Manteo	384	29,967	Virginia Dare
Davidson	1822	Lexington	552	147,246	William Lee Davidson
Davie	1836	Mocksville	265	34,835	William Richardson Davie
Duplin	1750	Kenansville	818	49,063	Thomas Hay, Lord Duplin
Durham	1881	Durham	290	223,314	Town of Durham and Bartlett Snipes Durham
Edgecombe	1741	Tarboro	505	55,606	Baron Richard Edgecombe
Forsyth	1849	Winston–Salem	409	306,067	Benjamin Forsyth
Franklin	1779	Louisburg	492	47,260	Benjamin Franklin
Gaston	1846	Gastonia	356	190,365	William Gaston
Gates	1779	Gatesville	341	10,516	Horatio Gates
Graham	1872	Robbinsville	292	7,993	William A. Graham
Granville	1746	Oxford	530	48,498	John Carteret, Earl Granville
Greene	1799	Snow Hill	266	18,974	Nathanael Greene
Guilford	1771	Greensboro	649	421,048	Francis North, Earl of Guilford
Halifax	1759	Halifax	726	57,370	George Montague, Second Earl of Halifax
Harnett	1855	Lillington	595	91,025	Cornelius Harnett
Haywood	1808	Waynesville	553	54,033	John Haywood
Henderson	1838	Hendersonville	374	89,173	Leonard Henderson
Hertford	1760	Winton	354	22,601	Francis Seymour Conway, Earl of Hertford
Hoke	1911	Raeford	391	33,646	Robert F. Hoke
Hyde	1705	Swan Quarter	612	5,826	Edward Hyde
Iredell	1788	Statesville	574	122,660	James Iredell
Jackson	1851	Sylva	491	33,121	Andrew Jackson

*Areas have been rounded to the nearest whole number.

County	Date of Formation	County Seat	Area in Sq. Miles*	Population	Named For
Johnston	1746	Smithfield	792	121,965	Gabriel Johnston
Jones	1779	Trenton	472	10,381	Willie Jones
Lee	1907	Sanford	257	49,040	Robert E. Lee
Lenoir	1791	Kinston	399	59,648	William Lenoir
Lincoln	1779	Lincolnton	299	63,780	Benjamin Lincoln
Macon	1828	Franklin	516	29,811	Nathaniel Macon
Madison	1851	Marshall	448	19,635	James Madison
Martin	1774	Williamston	462	25,593	Josiah Martin
McDowell	1842	Marion	444	42,151	Joseph McDowell
Mecklenburg	1763	Charlotte	531	695,454	Princess Charlotte Sophia of Mecklenburg–Strelitz, Queen of England
Mitchell	1861	Bakersville	220	15,687	Elisha Mitchell
Montgomery	1779	Troy	491	26,822	Richard Montgomery
Moore	1784	Carthage	699	74,769	Alfred Moore
Nash	1777	Nashville	540	87,420	Francis Nash
New Hanover	1729	Wilmington	198	160,307	House of Hanover
Northampton	1741	Jackson	533	22,086	James Crompton, Earl of Northampton
Onslow	1731	Jacksonville	767	150,355	Arthur Onslow
Orange	1752	Hillsborough	400	118,227	William V of Orange
Pamlico	1872	Bayboro	337	12,934	Pamlico Indians
Pasquotank	1668	Elizabeth City	227	34,897	Indian word meaning "where the current of the stream forks"
Pender	1875	Burgaw	871	41,082	William D. Pender
Perquimans	1668	Hertford	247	11,368	Perquimans Indian tribe
Person	1792	Roxboro	391	35,623	Thomas Person
Pitt	1761	Greenville	652	133,798	William Pitt
Polk	1855	Columbus	237	18,324	William Polk

*Areas have been rounded to the nearest whole number.

County	Date of Formation	County Seat	Area in Sq. Miles*	Population	Named For
Randolph	1779	Asheboro	787	130,454	Peyton Randolph
Richmond	1779	Rockingham	473	46,564	Charles Lennox, Duke of Richmond
Robeson	1787	Lumberton	948	123,339	Thomas Robeson
Rockingham	1785	Wentworth	565	91,928	Charles Watson–Wentworth, Second Marquis of Rockingham
Rowan	1753	Salisbury	511	130,340	Matthew Rowan
Rutherford	1779	Rutherfordton	563	62,899	Griffith Rutherford
Sampson	1784	Clinton	945	60,161	John Sampson
Scotland	1899	Laurinburg	319	35,998	Scotland
Stanly	1841	Albemarle	395	58,100	John Stanly
Stokes	1789	Danbury	450	44,711	John Stokes
Surry	1771	Dobson	535	71,219	English county of Surrey
Swain	1871	Bryson City	526	12,968	David L. Swain
Transylvania	1861	Brevard	378	29,334	Latin words meaning "across woods"
Tyrrell	1729	Columbia	392	4,149	John Tyrrell
Union	1842	Monroe	637	123,677	The compromise of creating a new county from parts of two others
Vance	1881	Henderson	245	42,954	Zebulon Baird Vance
Wake	1771	Raleigh	844	627,846	Margaret Wake
Warren	1779	Warrenton	429	19,972	Joseph Warren
Washington	1799	Plymouth	346	13,723	George Washington
Watauga	1849	Boone	312	42,695	Watauga River
Wayne	1779	Goldsboro	554	113,329	Anthony Wayne
Wilkes	1778	Wilkesboro	754	65,632	John Wilkes
Wilson	1855	Wilson	371	73,814	Louis D. Wilson
Yadkin	1850	Yadkinville	336	36,348	Yadkin River
Yancey	1833	Burnsville	312	17,774	Bartlett Yancey

*Areas have been rounded to the nearest whole number.

NORTH CAROLINA
POPULATION DATA

North Carolina Population: 1660-2025*

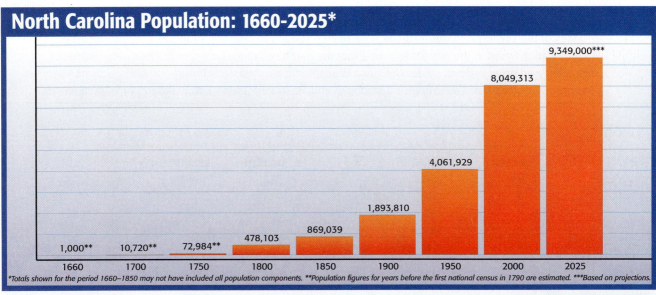

Year	Population
1660	1,000**
1700	10,720**
1750	72,984**
1800	478,103
1850	869,039
1900	1,893,810
1950	4,061,929
2000	8,049,313
2025	9,349,000***

*Totals shown for the period 1660–1850 may not have included all population components. **Population figures for years before the first national census in 1790 are estimated. ***Based on projections.

Population of North Carolina's Ten Largest Cities: 1970-2000

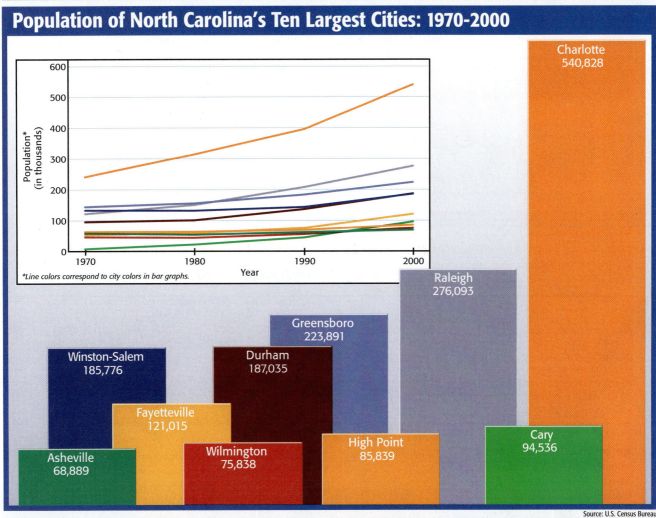

*Line colors correspond to city colors in bar graphs.

- Charlotte 540,828
- Raleigh 276,093
- Greensboro 223,891
- Durham 187,035
- Winston-Salem 185,776
- Fayetteville 121,015
- Cary 94,536
- High Point 85,839
- Wilmington 75,838
- Asheville 68,889

Source: U.S. Census Bureau

Almanac 323

Glossary

This Glossary contains terms you need to understand as you study North Carolina history. After each key term there is a brief definition or explanation of the meaning of the term as it is used in Holt *North Carolina!* The page number refers to the page on which the term is introduced in the textbook.

Phonetic Respelling and Pronunciation Guide

Many of the key terms in this textbook have been respelled to help you pronounce them. The letter combinations used in the respelling throughout the narrative are explained in the following phonetic respelling and pronunciation guide. The guide is adapted from *Webster's Tenth New College Dictionary, Merriam-Webster's New Geographical Dictionary,* and *Merriam-Webster's New Biographical Dictionary.*

MARK	AS IN	RESPELLING	EXAMPLE
a	alphabet	a	*AL-fuh-bet
ā	Asia	ay	AY-zhuh
ä	cart, top	ah	KAHRT, TAHP
e	let, ten	e	LET, TEN
ē	even, leaf	ee	EE-vuhn, LEEF
i	it, tip, British	i	IT, TIP, BRIT-ish
ī	site, buy, Ohio	y	SYT, BY, oh-HY-oh
	iris	eye	EYE-ris
k	card	k	KAHRD
ō	over, rainbow	oh	OH-vuhr, RAYN-boh
ù	book, wood	ooh	BOOHK, WOOHD
ò	all, orchid	aw	AWL, AWR-kid
òi	foil, coin	oy	FOYL, KOYN
aù	out	ow	OWT
ə	cup, butter	uh	KUHP, BUHT-uhr
ü	rule, food	oo	ROOL, FOOD
yü	few	yoo	FYOO
zh	vision	zh	VIZH-uhn

*A syllable printed in small capital letters receives heavier emphasis than the other syllable(s) in a word.

Alamance plaids Colored cloth first produced in Alamance County in the 1830s. 168
Albemarle Ironclad warship built by the Confederate Navy, equipped with a special battering ram to sink other ships. 211
almanacs Yearly publication containing information about weather, farming, and subjects of general interest. 156
altitude Height above sea level. 4
Amadas-Barlowe expedition Mission of exploration to the New World led by Philip Amadas and Arthur Barlowe in 1584. 34
amend To make changes to a written constitution. 134
amnesty Pardon. 76
anarchy Complete absence of government. 75
antebellum Era before 1860 in the southern United States. 170

anthropologists Scientists who study human beings and their cultures. 14
apprentice Young person placed under contract to an artisan to work in return for learning a trade. 71
archaeologists Scientists who study ancient peoples by examining the objects they have left behind. 10
arsenal Place where weapons and ammunition are stored. 206
artisans Skilled craftspeople. 71

backcountry The Piedmont area during colonial times. 65
barrier islands Islands that protect a mainland from an ocean. 5
Battle of Alamance Battle between Regulators and government forces that ended the Regulator movement. 77

Battle of Bentonville Battle fought in 1865 between Confederate forces and those of Union General William T. Sherman. 219

Battle of Moore's Creek Bridge American victory over British forces near Wilmington, North Carolina. 88

blackout Turning off of all lights to avoid detection by the enemy. 271

blockade-runners Confederate ships that attempted to avoid the Union naval blockade during the Civil War by sailing at night. 208

Blue Ridge The eastern part of the Appalachian mountain system. 4

bond Sum of money guaranteeing a promise and forfeited if that promise is not kept. 161

borough towns Settlements with 60 or more families, entitled to representation in the North Carolina Assembly under colonial law. 58

Camp Lejeune U.S. Marine Corps base on the North Carolina coast. 270

camp meetings Large outdoor evangelical gatherings. 150

Camp Vance Confederate training camp located near Morganton, North Carolina. 212

Carolina Charter of 1663 Royal charter authorized by Charles II granting the Eight Lords Proprietors control over the Carolina territory. 45

Carolina Charter of 1665 Royal charter issued by Charles II expanding the territory of the Eight Lords Proprietors. 46

Cary's Rebellion Attack launched by Thomas Cary against North Carolina governor Edward Hyde. 53

cash crop Any crop grown to sell for a profit. 69

cavalry Troops trained to fight on horseback. 212

census Official count of the population of an area. 160

Charlotte City that was hotbed of Patriot activity in North Carolina; occupied by the British in 1780. 92

Charlotte Mint U.S. mint built in Charlotte, North Carolina, to convert gold into coins. 169

Christian right Movement of conservative Christians to apply their beliefs to national issues and politics. 299

Civilian Conservation Corps New Deal program that provided jobs for young men at temporary camps. 267

clan A group of people descended from a common ancestor; the basic unit of American Indian society. 17

Clean NC 2000 Commission created in 1981 to establish goals and plans for the future of North Carolina. 309

Coastal Plain The easternmost of North Carolina's three regions, lying between the Piedmont and the Atlantic Ocean. 4

community colleges Schools offering the first two years of a college education along with technical and career-training programs. 286

Congress of Augusta Meeting held after the French and Indian War between colonial governors, English officials, and American Indians to reach a peace treaty and settle colonial boundaries. 82

conquistadores Spanish military leaders seeking riches in the New World. 29

Conscription Act Law passed in 1862 to allow men between the ages of 18 and 35 to be drafted into the Confederate Army; also allowed the hiring of substitutes. 215

conscripts Citizens forced to join an army. 215

Conservative Party Political party formed in North Carolina in the 1860s. 214

conservatives Group of mostly wealthy citizens in colonial North Carolina who favored trade ties with England and strong government. 99

Conservatives Conservative Democrats; political party in post–Civil War North Carolina, consisting mostly of white prewar Democrats. 226

Constitution of 1971 Revised constitution for the state of North Carolina that replaced the 1868 constitution. 293

conurbations Sprawling areas of urbanlike settlement. 284

cotton bolls That part of the cotton plant containing the cotton fibers. 170

cotton fibers Small hairs that grow on seeds inside cotton bolls. 170

Cowpens Town in South Carolina that was site of American victory over British forces in 1781. 94

Culpeper's Rebellion Attack of Carolina colonists, led by George Durant and John Culpeper, against the governor and other officials. 50

culture The set of beliefs, material characteristics, and other practices that a people share. 10

culture area A region in which all peoples share the same basic way of life. 14

defense work Making military weapons and supplies. 272

Democratic Party Political party created by President Andrew Jackson's supporters. 130

denomination A religious group. 152

deserter Soldier who leaves military service without permission. 212

disenfranchise To take away the right to vote. 256

draft resister One who refuses to join the army when drafted. 212

drivers Slaves who assisted the overseer in the supervision of other slaves. 175

economy The way in which a society uses its resources to obtain things that it wants or needs. 16

Eight Lords Proprietors (pruh•PRY•uh•tuhrs) Group of powerful English nobles who controlled the Carolina territory, all supporters of Charles II. 45

embargo A government order banning some or all trade with other nations. 116

established religion A religion supported by a government as an official church. 150

evangelism Efforts to convert people to Christianity. 150

Executive Organization Act of 1971 North Carolina law that reorganized state government agencies into departments headed by a secretary appointed by the governor. 297

expedition A trip of exploration. 22

extended family Concept of family that can include friends as well as biological relatives. 178

extortion Demands for illegal fees. 76

fiction An imagined story. 157

Fort Bragg U.S. Army base near Fayetteville, North Carolina. 270

Fort Fisher Confederate fort near the mouth of the Cape Fear River. 206

free suffrage Voting rights not tied to wealth. 143

Glossary **325**

Freedmen's Bank Federal savings and trust company created during Reconstruction to help African Americans save money. 235

freedmen's convention 1865 meeting of African Americans that called for justice and equality for former slaves in North Carolina. 227

Fundamental Constitutions of Carolina Document proposed by the Eight Lords Proprietors to attract large landowners to Carolina by guaranteeing property rights. 48

fundamentalist movement Conservative Christian religious movement that advocated a literal interpretation of the Bible and opposed the teaching of the theory of evolution. 260

Fusionists Republicans and Populists in North Carolina who in 1894 joined forces to elect candidates. 255

General Strike Three-week-long protest in which textile workers throughout the South walked off their jobs in 1934. 267

gentry Wealthy upper class of colonial North Carolina, including planters, public officials, and professionals. 71

Gibbs's Rebellion Incident in 1689 in which Captain John Gibbs claimed to be the rightful governor of Carolina. 51

ginning Process of separating cotton fibers from cotton seeds. 170

Granville District Tract of land owned by John Carteret along the northern border of North Carolina. 61

Great Dismal Swamp Swamp located between North Carolina and Virginia often used as a hiding place by runaway slaves. 180

Great Revival Wave of evangelism that began in the 1790s. 150

Great Wagon Road 800-mile-long trail that served as the principal road for the Piedmont area during colonial times. 65

Greensboro sit-in Incident in which African American students occupied a "whites only" lunch counter as a means of nonviolent resistance to segregation; led to sit-ins elsewhere. 291

groundwater Water that is held within the earth. 7

Halifax Resolves Document giving North Carolina delegates the power to declare independence along with the other American colonies. 88

Highland Scots Inhabitants of northwest Scotland who faced harsh English rule following their military defeat in 1746. 66

Hillsborough Convention Meeting of the North Carolina legislature held in 1788 to vote on ratification of the U.S. Constitution. 110

Hmong Ethnic group that immigrated to North Carolina as refugees from the nation of Laos. 300

Huguenots French Protestants who faced religious persecution within Catholic France. 27

illiterate Unable to read or write. 127

immigrate To move to a new place from one's homeland. 66

Impending Crisis of the South, The Antislavery book published in 1857 by Hinton Rowan Helper. 197

impressment British practice of seizing British-born sailors serving on U.S. ships and forcing them into military service. 116

indentured servants Poor people who signed contracts to work for others for a period of years in exchange for food and shelter; an important source of labor in colonial North Carolina. 71

Indian Removal Act Law authorizing the removal of Indian tribes living east of the Mississippi River to Indian Territory in present-day Oklahoma. 130

inlets Narrow passages of water, as between two islands. 5

interstate highways Multilane, high-speed roads crossing the United States. 284

Jack Tales Body of folk stories about a young hero named Jack, who used his wits and good luck to overcome difficult times. 154

James City Settlement for free African Americans established near New Bern by the Freedmen's Bureau. 227

Kings Mountain Site of 1780 battle between Loyalist forces and Over-Mountain men. 93

Kirk-Holden War Incident during Reconstruction in which Governor William Holden jailed Ku Klux Klan members. 237

labor tax Six days per year of work required of all able-bodied male citizens in North Carolina during the Industrial Age. 254

literature Written works. 157

Live-at-Home program State program in North Carolina begun during the Great Depression to encourage farmers to grow their own food and preserve it. 266

maize Corn, the most important crop grown by American Indians in North America. 30

manumission The act of legally freeing someone from servitude. 177

maroons Free communities established by runaway slaves. 180

Mecklenburg Resolves Declaration made in Mecklenburg County in 1775 that British laws would no longer be in force. 86

militia Civilian fighting force of colonial North Carolina. 71

mill villages Small settlements built by textile companies that provided rented housing and other facilities for workers. 247

mission A settlement designed to convert people to a particular religion. 28

Mississippian Culture The culture shared by American Indian groups throughout the Lower South and the central regions of North America. 11

Mississippians American Indians who practiced the Mississippian Culture way of life. 11

monoculture Growing method in agriculture in which the same crop is grown year after year on the same field. 127

Moral Majority Conservative Christian organization led by Reverend Jerry Falwell. 299

Moravians The United Brethren, a German Protestant group. 67

Mountains The mountainous region of western North Carolina. 4

Mummies Critical term for North Carolina leaders accused of not doing enough to improve education during industrialization. 251

NASCAR National Association for Stock Car Racing, formed in 1949. 288

Nashville Convention Conference organized to address the concerns of southern states in response to the Compromise of 1850. 195

naval stores Non-lumber products made from trees, such as tar, pitch, and turpentine, used by sailors. 70

nomads People who move from place to place in small groups, usually hunting and gathering. 10

Non-Importation Association Group formed by American colonies as an agreement not to buy British goods. 84

North Carolina Fund Organization created by Governor Terry Sanford in 1963 to relieve poverty and provide educational and cultural opportunities. 293

North Carolina Gold Rush Mining industry of the early 1800s in North Carolina. 169

North Carolina Progress Board State government organization created to plan for the future of North Carolina. 304

North Carolina Railroad Company Rail line running from Goldsboro through Raleigh to Charlotte. 138

North-Carolina Reader Book by Calvin H. Wiley relating to the history and geography of North Carolina, published in 1851. 157

novels Book-length works of fiction. 157

Outer Banks A chain of low, narrow islands that make up the eastern limit of North Carolina's Coastal Plain. 5

Over-Mountain men Patriot militia group based in the Appalachian region of North Carolina. 93

overseer Supervisor of field hands on a plantation under the system of slavery. 175

pacifists People who refuse to fight due to a belief that violence is wrong. 150

patent Granting of land from the King of England to an individual. 38

Pearl Harbor U.S. naval base in Hawaii; its bombing by the Japanese in 1941 led the U.S. to enter World War II. 269

Pearsall Plan North Carolina law requiring the state to pay for private school for children whose parents did not want them to attend an integrated school; declared unconstitutional in 1966. 290

Pennsylvania Dutch German-speaking immigrants to the New World. 66

Piedmont Huge plateau in central North Carolina, covering about 45 percent of the state. 4

Plantation Duty Act of 1673 Act issued by the English Parliament taxing certain goods shipped within the North American colonies. 49

plateau Raised, generally level area of land. 4

poll tax Tax levied on all adults, rich and poor alike. 75

popular party Political party made up of Carolina colonists opposed to the Eight Lords Proprietors and the governor. 47

prerogative (pri•RAH•guh•tiv) **party** Political party made up of Carolina colonists who supported the Eight Lords Proprietors and the English monarchy. 47

privateers Smugglers who transported goods during times of blockades or harsh shipping laws. 57

Prometheus The first steamboat in North Carolina, completed in 1818. 189

Provincial Congress Governing body formed in North Carolina in 1774 to manage the colony's affairs in place of a royal governor. 86

Qualla Boundary Cherokee reservation in western North Carolina. 131

quitrent Land tax imposed on early settlers in Carolina by the Eight Lords Proprietors. 47

radicals Citizens in colonial North Carolina who opposed the conservatives and wanted few government controls. 99

Raleigh The capital of North Carolina; named in honor of Sir Walter Raleigh. 99

Raleigh and Gaston Railroad Rail line running from Raleigh to Gaston. 138

rationing Practice during wartime of restricting people to limited amounts of food or other goods that are in short supply. 276

reader Collection of literary works. 157

reconnaissance A fact-finding expedition. 34

Red Shirts Group of white supremacists in North Carolina who threatened and terrorized African Americans and Republicans during the election of 1898. 255

redistricting The drawing of new boundaries for districts from which government officials are elected. 307

referendum Procedure allowing citizens to vote on a proposed public measure. 134

refugee Someone who flees his or her home country to escape violence or political persecution. 300

regions Areas of land in which places have the same basic characteristics. 4

Regulators Group formed in North Carolina in the 1760s in opposition to the colonial government. 76

repudiate To reject or refuse. 226

Research Triangle Park Region of North Carolina between Durham, Chapel Hill, and Raleigh, known for industry. 282

restoration Giving control of government back to a monarch who has lost power. 39

Restoration, The The period of rule of Charles II in England, beginning in 1660. 45

right-to-work law Law making it illegal to require a worker to join a union in order to obtain a certain job. 283

Rip Van Winkle state Nickname given to North Carolina in the early 1800s as a result of the state's general condition of isolation and underdevelopment. 125

rituals Ceremonies. 16

Rural Electrification Administration Government agency that brought electricity to many rural areas beginning in 1935. 268

Glossary **327**

sabotage Destruction of property by an enemy during war. 271
School Machinery Act One of a series of laws passed in the 1930s creating the North Carolina system of education. 285
Scots-Irish Descendants of Scottish settlers sent to Ireland by English monarchs in the early 1600s. 66
sea dogs English sailors encouraged by Queen Elizabeth I to raid Spanish ships in the late 1500s. 34
secessionists Those in the antebellum South who supported withdrawal from the United States. 200
sectionalism Strong loyalty to the region, or section, in which one lives. 73
shaman Healer and holy person in American Indian society. 16
sharecroppers Agricultural workers who tended farms and paid part of the harvest as rent. 249
Shoffner Act Law passed by the North Carolina General Assembly to allow the governor to use military force to restore order in areas of Ku Klux Klan activity. 236
stagnation Situation in which economic conditions do not change over a long period of time. 126
Stamp Act Law passed by the British Parliament placing a tax on legal papers and other documents. 83
State of Franklin Territory to the west of the Blue Ridge Mountains originally claimed by North Carolina; tried to form own state, but failed. 107
suffrage The right to vote. 135
survey An official measurement of land. 60
Swann v. Charlotte-Mecklenburg Board of Education U.S. Supreme Court case ordering the state of North Carolina to bus students as a way of ending segregation. 290

Tar Heel State Nickname given to North Carolina because of its naval stores industry. 168
televangelism Use of television to spread a religious message. 298
tenant farmers Farmers who lived and worked on small rented plots of land. 153
terrain The physical features of an area of land. 4
Tidewater Low-lying area of the Coastal Plain extending inland 30 to 80 miles. 5
"Torpedo Junction" Area of the Atlantic Ocean near Cape Hatteras, North Carolina, known for heavy German submarine activity during World War II. 272
Tory War Conflict in which Loyalists, or Tories, on one side and Patriots on the other raided towns in North Carolina. 96
Trail of Tears 800-mile march of Cherokee west as a result of the Indian Removal Act, during which about 4,000 died. 131
Tuscarora War Armed conflict between North Carolina settlers and Tuscarora Indians that took place from 1711–1712. 54

Unemployment Compensation Commission North Carolina agency created during the Great Depression to provide temporary funds for people out of work. 267
Union League Organization that worked to maintain northern morale in the Union during the War. 230
Unionists Those in antebellum North Carolina who wanted to remain part of the United States. 200

Vestry Act Law passed by Governor Henderson Walker in 1701 ordering the creation of Anglican churches in Carolina and establishing new taxes to support Anglican clergy. 52
victory gardens Gardens of produce grown during World War II by citizens for their use at home in order to make more food available to soldiers. 276

Walton War Armed conflict between North Carolina and Georgia, fought over ownership of land in the Blue Ridge Mountains. 192
War on Sugar Creek Conflict between North Carolina squatters and surveyors in 1765. 76
Whig Party National political party formed in 1834 to oppose President Andrew Jackson's policies. 132
white supremacy Doctrine of rule by whites. 255
Wilmington and Weldon Railroad North Carolina rail line completed in 1840; the longest railroad in the world at the time. 138
Woodland Period Era following the development of farming in North America, beginning about 1000 B.C. and lasting until about A.D. 1200. 10

yeomen Small farmers in colonial North Carolina who generally raised only enough to provide for their own families. 71

Index

Key to Index:
c = chart
f = feature
m = map
p = photo

Abbott, Joseph C., 233
abolitionists, 196, 198, 199
acid rain, 306, *p306*
Act of Pardon and Oblivion, 98
Act to Provide for the More Efficient Government of the Rebel States, An, 228
Adams, John Quincy, 129
Africa: slaves from, 172
African Americans, 252, *p297*; Black Codes and, 227; after Civil War, 227; as Civil War soldiers, 213, *p213*; at constitutional convention, 232; disenfranchisement of, 256; *Dred Scott case* and, 197; 1835 constitution and, 135; free blacks, 160–63; Freedmen's Bureau for, 235; migration of, 254; North Carolina Mutual Life Insurance Company and, *p250, f250*; Revolution and, 88, 97; as slaves, 153; social institutions of, 250–51; in state and local government, 298; voting rights of, 232; wedding of, 148, 178; white supremacists and, 255. *See also* Africans; slavery; specific persons
African Methodist Episcopal (A.M.E.) church, 250
African Methodist Episcopal Zion Church, 298
Africans: in North Carolina, 29, 66, 68, *c68*. *See also* African Americans
age of exploration, 21
agriculture, 69–70, *f188*; antebellum, 170–71; after Civil War, 221; decline of, 282; innovation in, *p188*; laborer in, *p264*; monoculture and, 127, *f127*; in New South, 249–50; overproduction in, 250. *See also* farms and farming
airplanes: Wright brothers and, 254, *f254*
air pollution, 306
Alamance: Battle of, 77
Alamance (Wiley), 159
Alamance plaids, 168, *f168*
Alaska: land bridge to Asia, 9
Albany Plan of Union, *f82*
Albemarle, 46; Bertie County and, 58; conflict in, 50–51; governor of, 47; revolt in, 75; Tuscarora Indians and, *f54*
Albemarle (ship), 211
Albemarle Sound, 23, 28, *f28*, 38, 207
Albright, William R., 230

alcohol and alcoholism. *See* prohibition
Alexander, Nathaniel, 192–93
Algonquian peoples, 14, 15
almanacs, 156–57
altitude, 6; of peaks, 4
Amadas, Philip, 34
Amadas-Barlowe expedition, 34–35
amend (process), 134
amendments: Bill of Rights as, 110; Eighteenth, 256; Fifth, *f238*; Fourteenth, 228; guidelines for, 136; to state constitution, 134, 238–39
America: naming of, 22
American Indians, 9–10; beliefs and practices of, 16–17; civil rights of, 291; Columbian Exchange and, 22, 31–32; Constitution of 1835 and, 135; conversion to Catholicism, 28, 29, 31; Eastern Woodland cultures, 14; English and, 35; enslavement of, 53; as equipment carriers, 28; by 1500, 13–17, *m14*; French and Indian War and, 81–82; geography and, 8; legacy of, 17; mound building peoples and, 11–12; in North Carolina (1830), 131; North Carolina Indians, 15; place names and, *f17*; population decline among, 32, *c32*; removal/resettlement of, 130–31; settlers and, 53–54; slave codes for, 174; social status of, 72; Tecumseh and, 117, 119; trade with, 30–31; Trail of Tears and, 131; after Tuscarora War, 56; vessel of, *p15*; Woodland Indians and, 10–11. *See also* Columbian Exchange; disease; specific groups and persons
American Revolution, 81–86, 92–93; battles in, *m93*; Bicentennial of, *f84*; end of, 95; financing of, *f94*; ideals of, 103–4; immigrant culture and language during, 67; independence declared in, 90; Loyalists vs. Tories in, 88; in North, 91–92; North Carolina after, 96–99; opening of, 86
American Tobacco Company, 247
Americas: early people in, 9
amnesty: after War on Sugar Creek, 76
anarchy: Albemarle revolt and, 75
ancient people, 9, *f10*
Andy Griffith Show, The, 288
Anglican Church, 37, 51–52, *p52*, 149; Presbyterian immigrants and, 66; schools and, 98
animals, 22, 70. *See also* wildlife
antebellum period, 166–83, 170–71
anthropologists, 14
Antifederalists, 109–10, 113
antislavery movement, 181
antiwar protests, 290
Appalachian mountain system, 4
Appeal to the Colored Citizens of the World (Walker), *f174*

apprentice, 71
archaeologists, 10, *p10, f10*
arsenal: at Fayetteville, 206
Articles of Confederation, 105–6, 108
artisans, 71
arts and artifacts, 11, *p165*, 286–88. *See also* literature; poetry
Ashe, John B., 83, 111
Asheville: Garden Creek Mound near, 12
Asia: land bridge from Alaska, 9
Assembly, 84; Anglicans in, 52; dissolution of, 86; North vs. South and, 74–75; of 1746, 75. *See also* General Assembly
Atalanta (ship), 118
Atlantic Ocean: climate and, 6
Attucks, Crispus, 84
Autobiography of Asa Biggs, 147
automobiles: as "Hoover carts," *f266*
auto racing, 288, 303–4, *p304*
Aycock, Charles B., 256
Ayllón, Lucas Vázquez de, 25, 26

backcountry, 65, 76
Bahamas, 22
Bakker, Jim and Tammy Faye, 298–99
bank failures, 265
Bank of America, 303
Bank of the United States, 130
banks: Freedmen's Bank, 235, *p235*; Great Depression and, 265–66; North Carolina National, 302–3
Baptists, 150, 152, 179
Barker, Penelope, 86, *f86*
Barlowe, Arthur, 34, *f35*
Barnwell, John, 54
barrier islands, 5, 8
bases: World War II military, *p270*, 270–71, *m271*
Bath, 51, *p51*; St. Thomas Church in, *p63*; Tuscarora War in, 54; Van Der Veer house in, *p58*
Bath County, 58
battles. *See* specific battles and wars
Bear River Indians, 54
Beaufort, 58
Bell, John, 200
Bentonville, Battle of, 219
Beringia, *f9*
Bering Strait, *f9*
Berkeley, John Lord, *c46*
Berkeley, William, 45, *c46*
Berry, Harriet Morehead, 261, *f261*
Bertie County, 58, 179
Bickett, Thomas W., 258

Big Bethel, battle at, 206
Biggs, Asa, 147
Bill of Rights, 110
Biltmore House, p252
Birth of a Nation (movie), 260
Blackbeard. *See* Teach, Edward "Blackbeard"
Blackbeard (Sawyer), 159
Black Codes, 227
Black Mountains, 4
blackout: in World War II, 271
blacks. *See* African Americans; free blacks
Bladen County, 180
Blair, Ezell, Jr., 290
Blakeley, Johnston, 117–18
Blalock, Sarah Pritchard, 216
Bleeding Kansas, 196, 198
blockade running: in Civil War, 208
blockades: in Civil War, 208, 209
Bloodworth, Timothy, 110, 111
Blount, William, 109
Blue Ridge Mountains, p3, 4, 28
Blunt, Tom, f54
Board of Immigration, 253
Board of Trade (England), 59, 60
bolls (cotton), 170
bond: from free blacks, 161
Bonnet, Stede, 57
Bonny, Anne, f56
Boone, Daniel, 106
borough towns, 58
Boston Massacre, 84
Boston Tea Party, 86
Boyano, Hernando, 28
Boyd, Josephine, p290
Bragg, Braxton, 219
Branch, John, 130
Brandywine, Battle of, 92
Breckinridge, John C., 199–200
bright-leaf tobacco, 170
Britain. *See* England (Britain)
Broad River, 8
Broughton, Carrie L., 261
Brown, John, 198, 203
Brunswick, 58
Buddhists, 298
Bull Durham smoking tobacco, 247
Bunting, John, 159
burial mounds, 11–12
Burke, Thomas, 96
Burns, Otway, 118
Burnside, Ambrose E., 207
Burroughs Wellcome, 282
business: bankruptcies of, 266. *See also* commerce; trade
Butler, Benjamin F., 206, 218
Byrd, William, 54
Byrd, William, II, 60

Cabot, John, 23, 33
Caldwell, Tod, 238, p238
calendars, f34
California, 194
Campbell, John, 236
Camp Butner, 270
Camp Davis, p270, 271
Camp Lejeune, 270
Camp Mackall, 271
camp meetings, 150, f151, f152
Camp Vance, battle at, 212
Canby, E. R. S., 230, 233
Cape Fear region, 57, 58, f58, 75
Cape Fear River, 25, 220
Cape Fear Valley, 46
Cape Hatteras, p4
capital (city). *See* state capital
capitol (building). *See* state capitol
Caribbean region, 24
Carolina: division of, 52–53; establishment of, 38; naming of, 38
Carolina Charter: of 1663, 45–46, p46, f46; of 1665, 46
carpetbaggers, 231, 239
Carteret, George (Earl Granville), f46
Carteret, John (Earl Granville), 61, c61, 74
Carteret County, 58
Cary, Thomas, 52
Cary's Rebellion, 53
cash crops, 69–70
casualties: in Civil War, 205, 221, 224; in World War I, 259
Caswell, Richard, 86, 90, p90, p104, 107; on state constitution, 112
Catawba Indians, 15, 82
Catawba River, 8
Catholicism, 298; Indian conversion to, 28, 29, 31; in Maryland, 37; missions and, 28
cavalry, 212
census, 160
Central America: diseases brought to, 32
Chappell, Fred, f287, p287
Charles I (England), 38, 39
Charles II (England), 39, 45–46, 51
Charleston, 37, 92
Charleston harbor, 204, 205
Charleston Mercury, p200
Charles Town. *See* Charleston
Charlotte, 92–93, p224, p296
Charlotte Mint, 169
charters: *See* Carolina Charter
Chavis, John, 88, f163
Cherokee Indians, 15, 26; in Civil War, 212; Eastern Band of, 131; legends of, 11, 19; lifestyle of, 72; mound-building ancestors of, 12; myth of, 16; Trail of Tears and, 130, 131; treaty with, 82; weaving by, p131

Cherry Point, 271
Chesapeake Bay, m20, 37
Chickasaw Indians, 82
child labor, 247–48, 257, p257
Child Labor Committee, 257
children: family life of, 72
Chimney Rock, p2
Choctaw Indians, 82
Chowanoc Indians, 15; attack by, 49
Christ, Rudolf, p155
Christianity: denominations of, 298; European spread of, 21; Indian conversion to, 28, 29, 31; among slaves, 179. *See also* specific groups
Christian right, 299, 308
churches: African American, 250. *See also* religion; specific religions
Church of England. *See* Anglican Church
cigarettes. *See* tobacco industry
"Circular Letter of 1768," 84
cities and towns, 58; industrialization and, 245–46; in Piedmont, 8; postwar growth of, 283; by 1740, m57. *See also* specific cities and towns
citizenship: active, 277; for African Americans, 197; for freedpeople, 239
civic participation. *See* elections; General Assembly; voting; voting rights
Civilian Conservation Corps (CCC), 267, p267
civil rights: during Civil War, 215–16, 217
Civil Rights Act (1964), 291
civil rights movement, 289, 290–92; Greensboro sit-in during, 290–91, f291, p291, f292, p292; Indians and, 291; women and, 291
civil war (England), 39
Civil War (U.S.), 204–23; African-American soldiers in, 213; blockade-runners during, 208; civil rights during, 215–16, 217; coastal protecting during, 206–7; in eastern North Carolina, 209–11; effects of, 221; end of, 218–21; fighting in North Carolina, 209–13, m210, 218–221; home front in, 214–17; mobilization during, 205–6; peace movement during, 217; Union support in mountains, 212; in western North Carolina, 212; women in, 216–17. *See also* Confederate States of America; Reconstruction
clan (Indian), 17
Clansman, The (Dixon), 260
Clarendon County, 46
Clark, William, 192
Clarke, Mary Bayard, f158
class (social and economic): 70–72, 295; in antebellum period, 171; in New South, 252; *See also* specific classes
Clayton, Eva M., 308
Clean NC 2000, 309
Clement, Lillian Exum, 261
climate, 6
Clinton, Henry, 88, 92

clothing: Moravian, 67; Native American, 16; Quaker, 149; slave, 176
Coastal Plain, 4, 5, m5; Algonquian peoples of, 14; European settlement on, 8; groundwater in, 7; temperatures of, 6
Coble, Howard, 308
Coffin, Levi, f181
coins: gold, 169
Colleton, John, c46
Collins, Josiah, f176
colonies: cooperation among, 85–88; English, 36–38; establishment of Carolina, 38; Rio Jordán, 25–26; sectionalism in, 73; slave codes in, 174; thirteen, 37
Columbian Exchange, 22, 31–32
Columbus, Christopher, 22
"Coming of Corn, The," 11
commerce: between Virginia and England, 37. See also trade
Commission of Indian Affairs, 291
Committee of Correspondence, 85–86
Commonwealth (England), 39, 45
communication, 73. See also transportation
Communists, 289, p289
communities: formation of early, 10; Moravian, p44; after World War II, 277. See also society
community colleges, 286
Complete Poems (Sandburg), 286
Compromise of 1850, 194
computers, 302, p305, 308, p309
Concord, 86
Confederate States of America, 200, 201; flag of, p215. See also Civil War (U.S.)
conflicts: with Confederate States of America, 215–16; internal, 74–77; sectional, 73; over slavery, 195–98. See also specific wars
Congress (U.S.), 109, 228, 230, 308
congressmen, 111
Congress of Augusta, 82
Connecticut, 37
conquistadores, 29
Conscription Act (1862), 215
conscripts, 215
conservatism: political, 289
Conservative Party, 214; after Civil War, 226, 228, 230, 231, 236–39
conservatives, 99, 104; as Federalists, 109–10
constitutional convention: in 1868, 232–33; in 1875, 238–39
Constitutional Convention (U.S.), 108–9
Constitutional Union Party, 200
Constitution of North Carolina (1776), 90, 104, f105, 112–113, 121
Constitution of North Carolina (1835), 133–36
Constitution of North Carolina (1868), 232–33; amendments to, 238–39
Constitution of North Carolina (1971), 285, 293
Constitution of the United States, 108–10, 115

Continental Army, 91
Continental Congress, 90, 105
conurbations, 284
Convention of 1865, 226
conversion: of Indians, 28, 29, 31
Cooke, James W., 211
Cooper, Anthony Ashley, c46
Coree Indians, 53
corn, 170
Cornwallis, Charles, 88, 92, 93, 94–95
Coronas, Pedro de, 28
corporate colonies: conversion to royal colonies, 60
cotton and cotton industry, p126, 127, p127, 166, 168, f168, 170–71, 249–50, 282, p282; bolls, 170; fibers, 170; innovation in, 188
cotton gin, 170, p170
council, 47
Council of Safety, 90
counties: creation of, 46–47, 58
Coweeta Creek Mound, 12
Cowpens, battle at, 94
crafts: folk arts and, 155
Craighill, Margaret O., 275
Craven, William, c46
Craven County, 46–47
Creek Indians: peace treaty with, 82
crime, 306
criminal law, 140
Croatoan, 36
Cromwell, Oliver, 39, 45
crops: in antebellum period, 170–71; cash, 69–70; Native American, 17; slave labor for, 175; yields of, 189. See also cotton industry; tobacco industry; specific crops
Cuba, 24, f117
Culloden, Battle of, 66
Culpeper, John, 50
Culpeper's Rebellion, 50
culture, 10; Eastern Woodland, 14; Mississippian, 11; in postwar period, 286–88; between 1663–1770, 64–79; of slaves, 178–79; in Woodland Period, 10–11
culture area, 14
Currituck Inlet, 28
customs, 153–55

daily life: in colonies, 72–73; in Great Depression, 274–75; inventions and, 254; in 19th century, 153–54; technology and, 190
dams. See Tennessee Valley Authority (TVA)
Daniels, Jonathan, 270
Daniels, Josephus, 259
Dare, Virginia, 36
dark-leaf tobacco, 170
Davidson County School, p144
Davie, William R., 108, 109, 110, 114

Davis, James, f73
Davis, Jefferson, 200, 216, 217
day-care system, 306
day labor, p264
debt: in Civil War, 226; after Revolution, 99; of states, 113–14
Declaration of Independence, 90, 103, 118
declaration of rights, 104
defense work, 272, p272
deflation, 266
Delaware, 37, 60
democracy: lack of, 126
Democratic Party, 130, 132, 136, 143, 214, 252, 255, 257, 298; election of 1860 and, 199–200
Democratic-Republicans, 111. See also Democratic Party
denominations, 152
depopulation: disease and, 32
depression. See Great Depression
deserters: in Civil War, 212
development: geography and, 8
diet, 154. See also foods
direct primary election laws, 257
Disciples of Christ, 152
disease: in Columbian Exchange, 22, 31–32; among slaves, 176
disenfranchisement, 256
diversity: economic, 302–4; ethnic, m67, 300; political, p297, 297–98; regional, m67; religious, 51–52, 298–99
Dix, Dorothea, 140
Dixon, Thomas, 260
Dobbs, Arthur, 74, 75, 82
documents. See specific documents and sources
Dole, Elizabeth: f308
domestic servants, 175, f175, 176
Dominican Republic, 24
Dominion of New England, 60
Douglas, Stephen A., 196, 199
draft: in Civil War, 215
draft resister: in Civil War, 212
Drake, Francis, 36
Dred Scott case, 197
driver (slave), 175
Dudley, Edward B., 137
Duke, James Buchanan (Buck), 247
Duke, Washington, 247
Duke University, p251, 286
Durant, George, 50
Durham, 247
Dutch, 37
duties (taxes), 49–50

Earnhardt, Dale, 304
Easley, Michael F., 307
Eastchurch, Thomas, 50, f50
Eastern Band of Cherokee, 131
eastern counties: vs. west, 75–76

Index **331**

INDEX

Eastern Hemisphere: Columbian Exchange and, 22
Eastern North Carolina: Civil War in, 209–11
Eastern Woodland cultures, 14
economy, 16, 69–72; Alamance plaids and, f168; cash crops and, 69–70; after Civil War, 221; before Civil War, 167–72; during Civil War, 216; diversification of, 302–4; exports and, 70, c70; financing of Revolution and, f94; global, f302; Great Depression and, 265–68; Indians and, 16–17; industry and, 187–90; monoculture and, 127, f127; 1970–present, 301–4; 1990s boom in, 302; North Carolina Mutual Life Insurance Company and, f250; recession in, 308–9; after Revolution, 97–98; stagnation in, 125–27; in 2000 and beyond, 304; after World War I, 264, 265–68; after World War II, 281–83; in World War II, 272–73
Edenton, 58
Edenton Tea Party, f86
education: advances in, 285–86; computers and, p305; of free blacks, 162; for freedpeople, 235; future of, 306; under GI Bill, 277; higher, 140, 286; pre-kindergarten program, 311; literacy and, 127; in New South, 251; in Progressive Era, 256; reforms in, 139–40, 144–45; textbooks and, 157; of women, 72. See also schools
Edwards, John, 308
Eighteenth Amendment, 256
elections: of 1824, 129–30; of 1828, 129; of 1836, 137; of 1844, 193; of 1848, 143; of 1850, 143; of 1860, 199–200; of 1862, 214–15; of 1864, 217; of 1865, 226; of 1867, 231; of 1916, 258; of 1920, 261; for Assembly, 47; after Civil War, 226
electricity: Rural Electrification Administration and, 268
electronics industry, 282, 303
Elizabeth I (England), p33, 33–34, 35
Ellis, John W., 205–6, 214
emancipation. See manumission; slavery
embargo, f117; War of 1812 and, 116
Emerson, Ralph Waldo, 198
employment. See unemployment
England (Britain): arrival in Chesapeake, m20; civil war in, 39; colonization by, 36–38; commonwealth in, 45; Declaration of Independence and, 90; exploration and settlement by, 33–39; French and Indian War and, 81–83; Navigation Acts and, 49–50; restoration in, 39; war debt of, 83; War of 1812 with, 116–19; in World War II, 269
entertainment: popular, 288
environment, 306, p306
Ephraim Bales Place, p72
Episcopal Church, 152, p299
equality: for African Americans, 291. See also civil rights movement
Equal Rights Amendment (ERA), 291
established religion, 150

ethnic groups: diversity of, 300, c300; 1685–1765, m67. See also immigrants and immigration; specific groups
Eubanks, Ray E., 275
Europe: as Old World, 22; World War II veterans and, 275
Europeans, 20–41; exploration by, 21–24; geography and settlement by, 8; Indians and, 17, 53–54
evangelism, 150, 152
executive, 109
Executive Organization Act (1971), 297
expansion, 58; beyond Appalachians, 83; Mexican territory and, 145, 193; Mexican War and, 193; westward, in 1800s, 191–94
expeditions: of Columbus, 22; English, 35
exploration, m26; effects of, 30–32; English, 33–39; European, 21–24; French, 23; geography, settlement, and, 8; Portuguese, 21–22; Spanish, 24, 25–29. See also geography; specific explorers
exports, 70, c70
extended family: slave, 178
extortion, 76

factories, 141
Falwell, Jerry, 299
families: in colony, 72; of slaves, 178
Fanning, David, 96–97
Fanning, Edmund, 76, 79
Farmers' Alliance, 250
Farmers' Almanac, 156
Farmer's and Planter's Almanac, 156
farms and farming: beginning of, 10; after Civil War, c234; classes and, 71; in 1840s and 1850s, 168; family farm, 70; free blacks in, 161; innovation in, 188–89, 190; Moravian, 67; New Deal and, 267, 268; railroads and, 139; tenant farmers and, 153–54; Virginia tobacco crops and, 69–70; whiskey tax and, 114; in World War II, 272–73. See also agriculture; tenant farmers
Federal Arts Project, 268
Federalists, 109–10, 111, 113, 115, 119
Federal Theater Project, 268
Federal Writers' Project, 268
Ferdinand and Isabella (Spain), 22, 24
Ferguson, Patrick, 93
Fifth Amendment, f238
Fifth Provincial Congress, 90
First Continental Congress (1774), 86
First in America Special Report: Designing a High Quality Pre-Kindergarten Program, 311
"First in Freedom" (slogan), f84
First North Carolina Continentals, 91
Fisher's River (North Carolina) Scenes and Characters (Taliaferro), 159
flag: U.S., f118; Confederate, f215

Florida, 24, 26, 27, 29
folkways, 153–55
Fontana Dam, p268
foods, 30; in Columbian Exchange, 22; Native American, 16; slave, 176; of tenant farmers and yeomen, 153–54. See also crops
Fool's Errand, A: By One of the Fools (Tourgée), f231
foreign business. See economy; world affairs
foreigners, 76
forest products, 70
forests, 7
Forsyth, Benjamin, 118
Fort Bragg, 270, p273
Fort Caroline, Florida, 27
Fort Duquesne, 81, 82
Fort Fisher, 206, 218–19
fortress: design of, f27
forts, 28, 206. See also specific forts
Fort Sumter, 201, 204
For 2¢ Plain (Golden), 286
Fourteenth Amendment, 228
Fourth Provincial Congress (North Carolina), 88
France: exploration by, 23; Huguenots and, 27; Spanish competition with, 29; in World War II, 269
Francis I (France), 23
Franklin, Benjamin, f82
Franklin, State of, 106–7
free blacks, 160–63, 171, f177, 225, 234–35, 239
Freedmen's Bank, 235, f235
Freedmen's Bureau, 235, p235
freedmen's convention, 227
freedom: of free blacks, 161; of religion, 37; for slaves, 177
Freedom's Journal, f174
freedpeople. See free blacks
freemen, 48
free soilers, 196, p196
free states, 192, 194
free suffrage, 143
French and Indian War, 81–83
French Broad River, p6
Frobisher, Martin, 33
Frolic (ship), 102
frontiers, 81–82, 83
Frye, Henry E., 291
fugitive slave law, 194
Fundamental Constitutions of Carolina, 48
fundamentalist movement, 260
furnaces, 187
furniture and furniture industry, 248, p248, 302, p302
Fusionists, 255

Gaelic language, 66
Gales, Joseph, 115

332 Index

Gales' North-Carolina Almanack, 156
Galloway, A. H., 227, 232
Gama, Vasco da, 22
Garden Creek Mound, 12
Gardner, O. Max, 266
Garfield, James A., 234
Gaston, William, 117, 134, 135, *f158*
Gatling, Richard Jordan, *f211*
Gatling gun, *f211*
General Assembly, 90, 98, 238; Black Codes and, 227; 1835 constitution and, 135; organization of, *c315*; petition to (1831), 165; representation in, 133–35; state government and, *p293*
General Orders, 230
General Strike (1934), 267
gentry, 71, 171
geographic regions, 4–5, *m5*
geography, 3–7; early cultures and, 10–11; effect of, 8; hurricanes, *f6*; James City, *f227*; Qualla Boundary, *f131*; settlement and, 48
George II (England), 37, 75
Georgia, 37, 82, 192–93
German Reformed Church, 152
Germans. *See* Pennsylvania Dutch
Germantown, Battle of, 92
Germany: settlers from, 51, 65, 66–67
Gettysburg Address, 205
Gibbs, John, 51
Gibbs's Rebellion, 51
GI Bill of Rights, 277, *p277*
Gilbert, Humphrey, 34
ginning (process), 170
GlaxoSmithKline, 302
Glover, William, 52
gold, 29, 169
Golden, Harry, 286
Gold Rush (California), 194
Gold Rush (North Carolina), 169
golf, 303
government: changes in, 261; after Civil War, 232; creation of, 47; Executive Organization Act (1971) and, 297; of independent North Carolina, 90; instability of, 48; lack of democracy in, 126; under Lords Proprietor, 45–48; of Mississippians, 11; of Native Americans, 16–17; of North Carolina, 307–8; reforming state, 293; after Revolution, 98–99; revolutionary ideals about, 103–4; as royal colony, 61; after separation from South Carolina, 56; stability in, 51; after Tuscarora War, 56; after World War II, 277. *See also* national government; state government
government departments, 297
governor, 47; election of, 135, 136; political party of, 114–15; after Revolution, 99
Graffenried, Christopher von, 51, 63
Graham, William, 138
Grange, 250
Grant, James, 82
Grant, Ulysses S., 220, 237, *f239*

Granville, Earl. *See* Carteret, John (Earl Granville)
Granville District, 61, 74–75
"graveyard of the Atlantic," 48
Great Alamance Creek, 77
Great Britain. *See* England (Britain)
Great Compromise, 109
Great Depression, 265–68, 274–75
Great Dismal Swamp, 180, *f180*
Great Revival, 150, *f151*
Great Smoky Mountains, 4
Great Trading Path, 70
Great Wagon Road, 65, *m65*
Greene, Nathanael, 94, 95
Greenhow, Rose O'Neal, *f216*, 216–17
Greensboro sit-in, 290–92, *f291*, *p291*, *f292*, *p292*
Gregorian calendar, *f34*
Grenville, Richard, 34
Griffith, Andy, 288
Griffith, D. W., 260
groundwater, 7
Guilford Courthouse, Battle at, 94–95
Guinea: slaves from, *f176*
gunpowder, *f220*
gun trade, 31
Gwynn, Walter, 206

Haiti, 24
Halifax Resolves (1776), 88, *p89*, *f89*
Hall, James, *f151*
Halyburton, William David, Jr., 275
Hamilton, Alexander, 111, 113
Hampton, Wade, 220
Hanes, Pleasant H., 247
Harpers Ferry: Brown's raid on, 198, 203
Harper's Monthly Magazine, 159
Harriet-Henderson Mill, 283, *p283*
Harriot, Thomas, 31, 36
Harris, James H., 232
Harvey, John, 84
Hatteras Indians, 15
Hawaii: Pearl Harbor bombing and, 269–70
Hawkins, Benjamin, 111
Hayes, Rutherford B., 239
Heath, Robert, 38
Helms, Jesse, 298, *f298*, 299, 308
Helper, Hinton Rowan, 197
Henry, O. *See* Porter, William Sydney
Henry the Navigator (Portugal), 21–22
Herring, Rufus G., 275, *f275*
Hewes, Joseph, 90
higher education, 140, 251, 286
Highland Scots, 66, 88, 90
High Point Furniture Company, 248
high-tech industries, 302, 308
highways: interstate, 284, *p284*, *m285*
Hill, Daniel Harvey, 206, *f206*, 210
Hillsborough, *f61*

Hillsborough Convention, 110
Hindus, 298
Hispanics: as immigrants, 300
Hispaniola, 24, *m24*
historical documents. *See* specific documents and sources
historical fiction, 159
Historical Sketches of North Carolina to 1851 (Wheeler), 157
History of North Carolina (Williamson), 157
Hitler, Adolf, 269
Hmong, 300
hockey, 303
Hodges, Luther, 282
Hoke, Robert F., 211
Holden, William W., 142–43, 214, 217, 226, 230, 232, 237; impeachment of, 238
Holshouser, James E., Jr., 298
Holt, Edwin M., 168, *f168*
home front: in World War II, 276
honey, 171
Hood, James W., 232
Hooper, William, 90
Hoover, Herbert, 266
"Hoover carts": cars as, *f266*
Hope of Liberty, The (Horton), 159
horses, 73
Horton, George Moses, 159, *f162*
House of Representatives (U.S.), 111, 308
houses of Congress, 109
housing: colonial, 72–73; log cabin, 124; pioneer farmstead and, *p72*; slave, 176–77; of tenant farmers and yeomen, 154
Howard, Henry (Lord Maltravers), 38
Howard University, 232
Howe, Robert, 91, 92, *f92*
Howell, Rednap, 76, 79
Huger, Isaac, 94
Huguenots, 27, 51
human rights: slavery and, 181
humor writing, 159
hunger: in Great Depression, 274
Hunt, James B., Jr., 309
hunting, 10
hurricanes, 6, *f6*
Husband, Herman, 76
Hyde, Edward, *c46*, 53, 54

I Am One of You Forever (Chappell), *f287*
Ibn Said, Omar, 68
Ice Age, 9, *f9*, 10
illiteracy, 127
immigrants and immigration, 65–68, 253–54; Africans and, 66, 68; Hispanics and, 300; refugees and Southeast Asians as, 300; from Virginia, 51
impeachment: of Holden, 238
Impending Crisis of the South, The (Helper), 197, *f197*

Index **333**

imports: tariffs on, 130
impressment, 116
Incidents in the Life of a Slave Girl (Jacobs), 180
indentured servants, 71
independence, 90, 103–4
independence movement, 85–90
Indian Removal Act (1830), 130–31
Indians. *See* American Indians
Indian Territory: removal to, 130–31
Indian Woods, f54
industrialization, 245–52, 295
industrial park. *See* Research Triangle Park
Industrial Revolution, f187, 187–90, 244
industry: in Civil War, 209; growth of, 303; inventions and, 188; lack of, 127; mining, 169; naval stores, 168; New Deal aid to, 267; in Piedmont, 8; recovery of, 301–2; textile, 168; training for, 306; after World War II, 281–83; in World War II, 272. *See also* cotton industry; economy; factories; Industrial Revolution; manufacturing; mills; tobacco industry
inlets, 5
innovation, 187–88. *See also* inventions
institutions: African American, 250–51; education and, 251, 256; higher education and, 140, 251; prisons, 256–57. *See also* class (social and economic); education; schools; specific churches, religions, and schools
integration: of schools, 290, p290
internal improvements: Jackson and, 129, 130. *See also* roads; transportation
international affairs. *See* world affairs
International Business Machines (IBM), 282
interstate highways, 284, p284, m285
inventions, 188–89, 254. *See also* technology; specific inventions
Iraq, f117
Iredell, James, 110, f110, 111
Ireland: immigrants from, 66
ironclads (warships), 208
iron industry, 169, 188, 189, 190
Iroquoian Indians, 15
Isabella (Spain). *See* Ferdinand and Isabella (Spain)
Islam: slaves and, 68, 179. *See also* Muslims

"Jack and the Beanstalk" (fairy tale), f154
Jackson, Andrew, 118–19, f129, 129–32, f132
Jackson, Jesse, f291
Jack Tales, 154, f154
Jacobs, Harriet, 180
James I (England), f36, 37
James City, m227, f227
Jamestown, 37
Japan: World War II and, 269–71, f272

Jazz Age, 260
Jefferson, Thomas, 111, 115, 192
Jenkins, John, 50
Jews, 298
job training programs, 282
Johnson, Andrew, 225–26, 228, 229, 230, 235
Johnson, Charles, 56
Johnston, Gabriel, 66, 74, 75
Johnston, Joseph E., 219–20
Johnston, Samuel, 111
Johnston, William, 214–15
Jones, Hamilton C., 159
Jones, Walter B., Jr., 308
Jones, Willie, 110
Julian calendar, f34

Kansas: slavery and, 196
Kansas-Nebraska Act (1854), 196
Kansas Territory, p196
Keith, James A., 216–17
Kent State University, 290
Key, Francis Scott, f118
Key, V. O., 295
king. *See* specific kings
King Andrew. *See* Jackson, Andrew
Kings Mountain, Battle of, 93, 107
Kirk, George W., 212
Kirk-Holden War, 237, f237
kitchen cabinet (Jackson), f129
Kitchin, Claude, 259
Ku Klux Klan, 236–37, 238, 260

labor: agricultural, p264; immigrants as, 253; occupations among free workers, c171; organized, 282–83; reforms in, 257; slave, 127, 173–74, 174–76, f176. *See also* child labor; strikes
labor organization: farmers and, 250
labor tax, 254
labor unions, 282–83
Lafayette (Marquis de), 91
Lamb, William, 206
land: cession of, 106–7; disputes with Virginia, 60; Indian vs. European attitudes toward, 53
land bridge: between Alaska and Asia, 9
land grant, 38
landless poor, 171
Lane, Lunsford, 177, f177
Lane, Ralph, 36
language: German, 67
language families: of Native Americans, 13
Laudonnière, René de, 27
law(s), 56
law enforcement, 236

leaders: diversity of, 227; World War II veterans, 275. *See also* Military leaders; specific individuals
leadership, 48; after Civil War, 232
Lee, Howard N., 291
Lee, Robert E., f169, 207, 210, 211, 219–20
legends: Cherokee, 11
legislature, 112, 126, 241; General Assembly, p293; North Carolina Legislative Building, p307; organization of, c315; political parties in, 113. *See also* General Assembly
Lewis, Meriwether, 192
Lewis and Clark expedition, 192, p192
Lexington, 86
Life as It Is, or the Writings of Our Mose (Bunting), 159
lifestyle. *See* daily life
lighthouse: at Cape Hatteras, p4
Lincoln, Abraham, 197, 199–200, 201, 205, 225
literacy, 127, 141, 235. *See also* literature
literature, 156–59, 260–61, 286, p287, f158, f162, f180, f231, f287. *See also* specific works
Littlefield, Milton, 236
Live-at-Home program, 266
livestock, 70
Livingstone College, 250
local government, 277, 307
log cabin, 124
Longfellow, Henry Wadsworth, f180
Longstreet, James, 210, 212
Look Homeward, Angel (Wolfe), f260
Lords Proprietors, 45–47, c46, 48; departure of, 61; listing of, c46; power taken from, 59–60; Quaker protests to, 52–53
Lost Colony (Roanoke Island), p10, 36
Louisiana, 160, 191–192
Louisiana Purchase (1803), 191–92
Lower Cape Fear area, 58
Loyalists, 88, 90, 92, 93, 96–97, p97, 98
Ludwell, Philip, 51
lumber. *See* forest products
Lusitania (ship), 258
Lutherans, 152

Macdonald, Flora, f66
Macedonian (ship), 116
Machapunga Indians, 53
machine age, f187
machinery industry, 303
Macon, Nathaniel, 115, f115
Macon County: mounds in, 12
Madison, Dolley, 118, f118
Madison, James, 118
maize, 30
Maltravers, Lord. *See* Howard, Henry (Lord Maltravers)
Manhattan Island, 37

INDEX

Manly, Charles, 138, 143
Manteo, 35, *f35*, 36
manufacturing, 167; centers of, *m303*; in 1840s and 1850s, 168; lack of, 127; revolution in, 188; in World War II, 272
manumission, 177
maps. *See* specific topics
Marco Polo, 21
markets, 126; for tobacco, 70; transportation to, 167
maroons, 180
marriage, 72, 148, 178
martial law: in Kirk-Holden War, 237, 238
Martin, Alexander, 108
Martin, François Xavier, 157
Martin, James G., 210
Martin, Josiah, 86, 88, 92
Maryland, 37; free blacks in, 160
Massachusetts, 37
McCain, Franklin, 290–91, *p291*
McClellan, George B., 207
McColl, Hugh, Jr., 302–3
McKimmon, Jane Simpson, 266, *f266*
McNeil, Joseph, 290, *p291*
Mecklenburg Resolves, 86, *f87*
meeting house: of mound builders, 12
Meherrin Indians, 53
Mendenhall, Judith, 181
Menéndez de Avilés, Pedro, 27
mental illness: reforms and, 140
Merrick, John, *f250*, *p250*
Merrimac (ship), 208
metal products, 187
Methodists, 152, 179
Mexican Cession (1848), 193, 194
Mexican War, 193
Mexico, 145; independence of, 193
Michel, Franz Louis, 51
middle class, 171, 254
migration, 128, 253–54; by African Americans, 161; to Louisiana Purchase lands, 192; of nomadic people, 10; westward, 191–94. *See also* immigrants and immigration
military: in Civil War, 207; quartering of British, 83; rule by, 229–30; in World War II, 270. *See also* training camps; specific battles and wars
military leaders, 259; in Civil War, 206–7, 210, 211, 212, 213, 216; conquistadores, 29
militia, 71, 91
Miller, Thomas, 50
mills, 141, 167, 188, *p245*, 245–46
mill villages, 247–48
minerals, 6–8, *p8*, 29
mining industry, 169
minorities. *See* ethnic groups; specific groups
minting, 169
missions and missionaries, 28, *p31*. *See also* Catholicism; conversion
Mississippian Culture, 11

Mississippi River: western land claims and, 106
Missouri Compromise, 192, 194, 196
mobilization: in Civil War, 205–6
monarchy. *See* specific monarchs
Monck, George, *c46*
Monitor (ship), 208
monoculture, 127, *f127*
Montgomery County: Town Creek Mound in, 12
Moore, Dan K., 285
Moore, James, 54, 88, 91
Moore's Creek Bridge, Battle of, 88
Moral Majority, 299
Moravians, *p44*, 65, 67, 152, 155
Morehead, John Motley, 125, 138
Morgan, Daniel, 94
Morrison, Cameron, 261
motion pictures, 260
mound building, 11–12, *p12*
mountains, 4, *m5*; railroads and, 167; roads through, *p125*; settlement of, 8; soil of, 7; streams and rivers in, 7; temperatures of, 6
Mount Gilead: Town Creek Mound near, 12
Mount Mitchell, *f4*
"Mummies," 251, 252
Murphey, Archibald D., *p133*, 133–34, *f134*
Murrow, Edward R., *f288*
music, 155; of slaves, 179
Muslims, 298. *See also* Islam
Mussolini, Benito, 269

NASCAR (National Association for Stock Car Racing), 288, 303–4
Nash, Abner, 112–13
Nash, Francis, 92
Nashville (ship), 209
Nashville Convention, 195
national government: Articles of Confederation and, 105–6; after Civil War, 228; Constitution and, 108–10; Great Depression aid from, 266; North Carolina in, 308; politics in 1950s and, 289; post-World War II, 308
Native Americans. *See* American Indians
Nat Turner's Rebellion, 177, 179
natural resources, 6–7, *p8*, 167
nature: Indian beliefs and, 16
naval blockade: in Civil War, 208
naval stores, 70, *c70*, 168
Navigation Acts, 49–50
navy. *See* specific ships
Neeley, Mary, 234
Neuse River, 51; Tuscarora War and, 54, 55
neutrality policy: in World War I, 258
New Bern, *f51*, 75, 186; battle of, 207; capital at, 98; in Civil War, 207, 210–11
New Deal, 267–68, 274–75
New England, Dominion of, 60

Newfoundland, 23
New Hampshire, 37
New Hanover County, 58
New Jersey, 37, 60
New Mexico Territory, 194
New Orleans, Battle of, 118–19
New South: lifestyle in, 249–52
newspapers, *f73*
New World: Columbian Exchange and, 22
New York (colony), 37, 60
nickname: Tar Heel State, 168, *f169*
Nikwasi Mound, 12
nomads, 10
Non-Importation Association, 84
North: Revolution in, 91–92
North Carolina: American Revolution in, 92–93; boundary survey of, 60; coast of, *m21*; as colony, 37; establishment of, 53; explorations of, *m26*; future of, 308–9; geographic regions, 4–5, *m5*; Gold Rush in, 169; government of, 56; internal conflicts within, 74–77; invasion of, 219; map of coast, *m21*; Native Americans by 1500, *m14*; new challenges in, 305–9; occupations among free workers (1860), *c171*; rejoining of Union by, 233; settlement of boundary disputes, 82; towns by 1740, *m57*; war with Georgia, 192–93. *See also* state government
North Carolina Constitution. *See* entries under Constitution of North Carolina
North Carolina Education Research Council: report by, 311
North Carolina Fund, 293
North Carolina Gazette, *f73*
North Carolina Legislative Building, *p307*
North Carolina Museum of Art, 288
North Carolina Mutual Life Insurance Company, *f250*
North Carolina National Bank, 302–3
North Carolina Progress Board, 304
North Carolina Railroad Company, 138–39
North-Carolina Reader (Wiley), 157, f157
North Carolina School of the Arts, 288
North Carolina Standard (newspaper), 142, 214
North Carolina State University, 251, 286, 305
North Carolina Symphony, 286
Northeast Culture Area, 14
Northwest Passage, 23
novels, 157

oath of loyalty, 226
occupations, 161, *c171*
Oglethorpe, James, 37
"Old North State, The" (Gaston), *f158*
Old World: Columbian Exchange and, 22
Once There Was a War (Steinbeck), 279
Only in America (Golden), 286

Index **335**

Index

oral tradition: of slaves, 179
Orange County, 76
organized labor, 250, 282–83
Otway Burns, 118
Outer Banks, 5, 28; English in, 34–35; Hatteras Indians of, 15; Verrazano on, 23, 30
Outlaw, Wyatt, 230, 236–37
"Over-Mountain men," 93
overseer, 175

Pacific Ocean, 192, 275
pacifists, 150
Page, Walter Hines, 251, 252, 258
Pamlico Indians, 53
Pamlico River, 51, 54, 55
Pamlico Sound, 23, 35
pamphlets, 156–57
paper money, f94, 98
Pardo, Juan, 28
pardons: after Civil War, 226
Paris, Treaty of (1783), 95
Parliament (England), 39, 49–50
parties. See political parties
party system, 111
patent (land grant), 38
Patriots, 88, 91, 92; "Over-Mountain men," 93; Tory War and, 96–97
peace movement: in Civil War, 217
peaks: altitudes of, 4
Pearl Harbor: attack on, p269, 269–70
Pearsall Plan, 290
Pee Dee River region, 8, 12
Penn, John, 90
Pennsylvania, 37, 60, 114
Pennsylvania Dutch, 66
people. See specific groups
performing arts: school for, 288
persecution: religious, 27
Person, Thomas, 110
Petty family (NASCAR drivers), 288
Philadelphia, 37
physical features. See geography
Pickett, George, 210
Piedmont, 4, m5; cities in, 8, 246; furniture factories in, 248; settlement of, 8; slaves and, 68; soil of, 7, 8; streams and rivers in, 7; temperatures of, 6
Piedmont Crescent, m246
pioneers: farmstead of, p72
pirates, f56, 56–57
Pisgah National Forest, p6
place names, f17
plank road, 189
Plantation Duty Act of 1673, 49–50
plantations, 71, p126, 166, f176. See also cotton industry; slavery
planters, 38, 126, 130, 132
plants, 7, 22, 30

plateau, 4
plows, 190
Plymouth: in Civil War, 211
poetry, 157, f158, 159, f162
Poland, 269
political organizing: by women, f86
political parties, 47–48, 111, 113, 136. See also specific parties
political system, 136, 298. See also Politics
politics: black gains in, 291; Christian right and, 299, 308; Civil War and, 199–201, 214–15, 217; conflicts and, 61; in 1890s, 255–56; in New Deal, 267; after 1900, 257; during Reconstruction, 225–28, 230–33; after Revolution, 99; "Rip Van Winkle" state and, 125–28; since 1970s, 296–311; in World War I, 258; after World War II, 289–90. See also civil rights movement; diversity; political parties; Progressive Era
Polk, James K., 145, 193, f194
Polk, Leonidas L., 250
Pollock, Thomas, 54
poll tax, 75
pollution, 306, p306
Ponce de León, Juan, 24, 25
Pool, John, 233
poor, 171, 254. See also poverty
poorhouses, 140
popular culture, 286–88
popular party, 47, 48, 50
population: Cherokee (1500s), 15; disease and, 32; diversity of, 300, c300; of Eastern Woodland region, 14; ethnic (2000), c300; of free blacks, 160; growth nationally, 191–92; native (after 1500), c32; redistricting and, 307; rural and urban, 153, 283; slave, 153, 160, 173–74, m175
Populist (People's) Party, 255
Porter, David D., 218
Porter, William Sydney, 260–261
Port Royal, South Carolina, 27
Portugal: exploration by, 21–22
Pory, John, 38
pottery, 155, p155
poverty: after Revolution, 98. See also poor
POW camps: in World War II, 273
Praise the Lord (television network), 299
prerogative party, 47, 48, 50
Presbyterians, 66, 150, 152
president: as executive, 109
Price, David E., 308
primary elections, 257
printing press, f73
prisoners of war: in World War II, 273, p273
prisons, 256–57
privateers, 57
Proclamation of 1763, 83
production: overproduction and, 250
Progressive Era, 256–57
Progressive Farmer, The, 250
prohibition, 256, p256

Prometheus (steamboat), f189
property, 67, 197
proprietary colonies, 44–61. See also royal colony
Protestants, 298; Huguenots as, 27; in Maryland, 37; settlement by, 51
Provincial Congress, 86
PTL. See Praise the Lord.
public schools, 139–40, 235, 251. See also education; schools
Puerto Rico, 24
Puritans, 39
puzzle jug, p165

Quakers, 52–53, 56, 68, 97, 149–50, 181
Qualla Boundary, 131, f131
quarries, p7
Quartering Act, 83
Queen's College (Liberty Hall Academy), 98
Quillo (slave), 97
quill pen, p103
quilts, 155
quitrent (tax), 47

R. J. Reynolds Tobacco Company, 247, f247
race: school integration and, 290. See also African Americans; civil rights movement; slavery
race riots, 255
racing. See auto racing
Rackham, Jack, f56
radicals, 99, 104, 109–10
raids: by pirates, 56–57
railroads, 138–39, m139, 167, 246; bond scandal and, 236; Civil War and, 207, 212, 221; steam engines and, 244
rainfall, 6
Raleigh (city), 98–99, 227
Raleigh, Walter, 34, f34, 35, 36, f36, 99
Raleigh and Gaston Railroad, 138
Raleigh Daily Sentinel, 236, f237, p237
Raleigh Daily Standard, 241
Raleigh News and Observer, 251, 270
Raleigh Register, 115, 179, 203, 214
Raleigh State Journal, 214
Randolph, John, 117
Randolph, Peter, 183
ratification: of Articles of Confederation, 105; of Constitution of 1868, 232–33
rationing, 276
readers, 157
rebellions: Cary's Rebellion, 53; Culpeper's Rebellion, 49–50; Gibbs's Rebellion, 51; Nat Turner's Rebellion, 177; slave, 88, 177, 179, p179
recession: in 2000s, 308–9
reconnaissance, 34

336 Index

Reconstruction, 224–41; end of, 239; military rule during, 229–30; resistance to, f239. See also Civil War (U.S.)
Red Cross: in World War I, 259
redistricting, 307
Red Shirts, 255
referendum(s): Constitution of 1835 and, 134
reform, p133; Constitution of 1835 and, 133–36; educational, 139–40, 144, 285–86; industrial, 267; social, 140; of state government, 293; in transportation, 138–39; voting rights, 143, 144; workplace, 257, p257
refugees, 300
regional diversity: sectional conflicts and, 73
regions, 4–5, m5. See also diversity; regional diversity; specific regions
Regulators, 76, f76, 77
Reid, David S., 143, f143, 188
Reindeer (ship), 117–18
religion, 149–52; in colonies, 37; conflict over, 51–52; denominations, 152; diversity of, 298–99; 1835 constitution and, 134, 135; established, 150; of free blacks, 162–63; fundamentalist movement and, 260; missions for, 28; of Native Americans, 16; organized, 52; persecution for, 27; of Scots-Irish, 66; Separatists and, 37; slave, 179; trends in, 308. See also churches; conversion; specific religions
Remembrance Rock (Sandburg), 286
removal and resettlement policy: for Indians, 130–31
Report of General William T. Sherman on the Campaign in the Carolinas, 223
representation, 113; in General Assembly, 126, 133–35; redistricting for, 307
Representatives: in U.S. Congress, 308
republic, 104
Republican Party, 196–97, 230–31, 232–33, 238, 298
Republicans, 111, 114–15
repudiation: of Confederate war debt, 226
Research Triangle Park, p281, 282, 302, 309, p309
reservations: Qualla Boundary, 131
resistance: to slavery, 177, 178–81
resources. See natural resources
Restoration (England), 39, 45; new proprietary colonies after, 59–60
revivals, 150, f151, f152
revolts. See rebellions; slavery; specific revolts
Revolutionary War. See American Revolution
Reynolds, R. J., 247, f247
Rhode Island, 37, 105
Ribault, Jean, 27, 41
rice, 170
Richardson, Margaret, 261
Richmond, David, 290
rights: of free blacks, 161
right-to-work law, 283
Rio Grande, 193
Rio Jordán colony, 25–26
riots: Regulators and, 76. See also race riots

"Rip Van Winkle" state, 125–28
rituals: of Native Americans, 16
rivers: navigable, 126; in Piedmont, 8; as trade routes, 73; transportation on, 189
roads, 70, 125, 126, m139, 189; Great Wagon Road, 65, m65; improvements in, 128; interstate, 284, p284, m285
Roanoke (Wiley), 159
Roanoke Island, p10, f35; in Civil War, 207, 209–10
Roberts, Frank, 213
Robeson County, 180
rocks, 6–7
Rohrer, Grace J., 298
Roman Catholicism. See Catholicism
Rose Bowl, f272
royal colony, 59–61, 74
Ruffin, Thomas, 134
runaway slaves, 163, 180
rural areas, 153; after World War II, 283
Rural Electrification Administration (REA), 268
Rush, Benjamin, 103

sabotage: in World War II, 271
Sacagawea, p192
St. Augustine, Florida, 27
St. Thomas Church (Bath), p52
Salisbury: quarry in, p7
Sandburg, Carl, 286
Sanford, Terry, 285, 293
Saunders, William L., f238
Sawyer, Lemuel, 157–59
scalawags, 231
Scales, Hamilton, 247
Scales, Junius, 289, p289
Schaw, Janet, 72
Schenck, Michael, 168
School Machinery Act (1931), 285
schools, p144, p145; African American, 250; funding of, 306; integration of, 290, p290; need for, 127; reform of, 139–40; after Revolution, 98; subscription, 263; textbooks in, f285. See also Education
science and technology, f73, f211, p211, 254, f254. See also technology
Scotland: immigrants from, 64, 65–66. See also Highland Scots
Scots-Irish immigrants, 66
Scott, W. Kerr, 281
sea dogs, 34
secession, 200, p200, 201, 205
secessionists, 200, 214
Second Great Awakening, 150
Second North Carolina Continentals, 91
sectionalism, 73, 196–97
segregation: integration and, 290–91
Senate (U.S.), 308
Senators, 111
Separatists, 37

servants: domestic, f175; indentured, 71; slaves as, 175. See also Slavery
settlement(s), m41; beyond Appalachians, 83; of English colonies, 36, 37–38; Fundamental Constitutions of Carolina and, 48; geography and, 8
settlers: from Scotland, 64; tensions with Indians, 53–54; in West, f106, 106–7
Sevier, John, 107, 111
shaman, 16
sharecroppers, 249
Sharp, Susie, 298
Shaw University, 250
Shelby, Evan, 107
shelter: Native American, 16
Sherman, William T., p219, 219–20, 223
ships and shipping: pirate raids and, 56
Shoffner Act, 236–37, 238
Sickles, Daniel, p229, 229–30
Sierra Leone: African Americans in, 97
silver, 29
Simmons, Furnifold M., 255, p255, 259
Siouan Indians: Catawba as, 15
Siouan language, 13
sit-ins, 290–91, p291, f292, p292
slave codes, 174
slaveholders: blacks as, 163
"Slave in the Dismal Swamp, The" (Longfellow), f180
slavery: Africans and, 29; antislavery movement and, 181; Compromise of 1850 and, 194; conditions of, 176–77; conflict over, 195–98; counting as citizens, 109; culture and, 178–79; economy and, 127; election of 1860 and, 199–200; freedom and, 225; freedpeople and, 227; insurrection and, 97; Kansas-Nebraska Act and, 196; manumission and, 177; marriage and, 178; in new territories, 192; population in 1860, m175; proportion of population, 153; Quakers and, 97; religion and, 68, 179; resistance and, 88, 101, 177, 178–81, p179; secession and, 200–201; social status of, 71; in Texas, 193; Whig Party and, 145; work and, 174–76. See also free blacks; population
"Slave's Complaint, The" (Horton), f162
slave states, 192, 193, 194
slave trade, 22, 53, 68, 172
smallpox, 22
smoking. See tobacco industry
Snap Dragon (ship), 118
snow, 6
social reforms, 140
society: civil rights and, 290–91, 292; folkways and customs in, 153–55; immigrants in, 253–54; Indian, m14, 17; New Deal and, 268; in New South, 249–252; during Reconstruction, 234–35; since 1970s, 296–300, 305–6, 308–9; social classes in, 70–72; suburban, 284–87; World War I and, 259–61; after World War II, 282–83, 284–88; World War II and, 270–72, 273, 276–77. See also industrialization; religion

Index **337**

soil, 6–7; in Piedmont, 8
soldiers: African American, 213, *p213*. *See also* military
Somerset Place, *f176*
Sothel, Seth, 50–51
Soto, Hernando de, 26, *f26*
South: Confederate States of America and, 200, 201; North Carolina's economy and, 167–83. *See also* New South
South America, 22, 29
South Carolina: boundaries of, 82; establishment of, 53; Ribault in, 27; as royal colony, 60; settlement of, 37; Spanish exploration of, 26, 28
Southeast Asians: as immigrants, 300
Southeast Culture Area, 14
southern Democrats, 199–200
Southern Plantation area, 38
southern region: vs. north, 74–75
Spaight, Richard Dobbs, 108, 109, 114
Spain: exploration by, 22, 24, 25–28; France and, 29; Mexican independence from, 193; missionaries and, *p31*
Spangenberg, August, 65, 67
Spanish Armada, 34
Spencer, Samuel, 110
spices: search for, 21–22
spinning machine, 188
sports, 303–4
stagnation (economic), 125–27
Stamp Act (1765), 83, 85
standard of living, 139
Stanly, Edward, 225, *p225*
Stanly, John, 163
"Star-Spangled Banner, The," *f118*
state(s): debts of, 113–14; federal government and, 105–6; Franklin as, 106–7; slave vs. free, 192; trade among, 190. *See also* Sectionalism
State Agricultural and Mechanical College. *See* North Carolina State University (Raleigh)
state capital (city), 74, 98–99
state capitol (building), 75, *p76, f98, f137*, 141
state constitution. *See* entries under Constitution of North Carolina
state government, 307–8; early period of, 112–13; formation of, 104; national government and, 108–11, 228, 266, 267–68, 289, 308; qualifications for office in, 121; reform of, 293; voting for, 232–33; after World War II, 277
state histories, 157
statehood, 110, 111; free vs. slave states and, 194
State of Franklin, 106–7
states' rights, 106, *f110*, 115
steamboats, 167, 189, *f189*
steam engine, 187, 244
Steele, John, 111
Steinbeck, John, 279
Stephens, Samuel, 38
stock market crash, 265

Stoneman, George H., 220
strikes: at Harriet-Henderson Mill, 283, *p283*
Stuart, John, 82
Student Non-Violent Coordinating Committee (SNCC), *f291*
subscription school, 263
suburbs, 284–87
suffrage, 143, 232. *See also* voting rights
Sugar Act (1764), 83
Supreme Court of the United States, 111; *Dred Scott* case and, 197; *Swann v. Charlotte-Mecklenburg Board of Education* and, 290
survey, 60
Swain, David L., 134–136
Swann v. Charlotte-Mecklenburg Board of Education, 290
Swepson, George, 236
Switzerland: settlers from, 51

Taliaferro, H. E., 159
Tar Heel State, 168, *f169*
tariffs, 130
Tarleton, Banastre, 94
taxation, 75, 115; Culpeper's Rebellion and, 49–51; for governor's palace, 76; labor, 254; North Carolina opposition to, 83–84; poll tax, 75; quitrent as, 47; rates of, 48; to support Anglicans, 52; Whiskey Rebellion and, 113–14
Tea Act (1773), 86
Teach, Edward "Blackbeard," 56–57, *f57*
tea parties: in Boston and North Carolina, 86
technology, 254; daily life and, 190; innovation in, 305–6; post-World War II, 282–83; printing press and, *f73*; in transportation, 189; Wright brothers airplane and, *f254*
Tecumseh, 117, 119
televangelism, 298–99
temperatures, 6; in Ice Age, 9
tenant farmers, 153–54, *p249*
Tennessee, 107
Tennessee Valley Authority (TVA), 268, *p268*
terrain, 4
Texas, 193
textbooks, 157, *f285*
textile industry, 168, 188; in industrial age, 247–48; innovation in, 190; decline of, 302
thirteen colonies, 37
Thomas, William A., Jr., *f292*
Thomas, William H., 212
Thomson, Mortimer, 172
three-fifths compromise, 109
Tidewater region, 5, 68
tobacco industry, 37, *p38*, 127, 170, 249–50, *p301*; as cash crop, 69–70; duties and, 50; in industrial age, 246–47; innovation in, 188; land for, 38; decline of, 301–2

Tories. *See* Loyalists
"Torpedo Junction," 271–72
Tory War, 96–97
Tourgée, Albion, *f230*, 231, *f231*, 232
tourism, 303
Town Creek Mound, 12, *p12*
towns. *See* cities and towns
Townshend Acts (1767), 84
trade: in Civil War, 208; Indians and, 17, 30–31, 35, 53; Moravian, 67; with other states, 190; profits from, 60; along rivers, 73; routes for, 70; spice, 21–22; between Virginia and England, 37; War of 1812 and, 116–17. *See also* transportation
Trail of Tears, 130, 131
training camps, *m271*; in World War I, 259; in World War II, *p270*, 270–71
trains. *See* railroads
transportation, 73, 187; in 1840s and 1850s, 167; improvements in, 125, 128, 138–39, 254; innovation in, 189; plans for, 56; steamboats, 167, 189, *f189*; trade routes and, 70. *See also* railroads; roads
travel, 70. *See also* roads; transportation; specific forms
Treasury: Hamilton and, 113–14
treaties: with Cherokee (1761), 82
Treaty of Paris (1783), 95
trees. *See* forests
Trent River, 51
Trent River settlement, 160
Trinity College, 251
Tryon, William, 74, 75, *f75*, 76, 77; Assembly dissolved by, 84; palace of, 75, *p76*; Stamp Act and, 83
Tsali (Cherokee), 131
Turner, Josiah, Jr., 236
Turner, Nat, 179. *See also* Nat Turner's Rebellion
Tuscarora Indians, 15; Albemarle region and, *f54*
Tuscarora War, 53–54, 55–56
two-party system, 136, 298

U-boats: in World War I, 258
Underground Railroad, 181
unemployment: in Great Depression, *p265*, 266
Unemployment Compensation Commission, 267
Union: North Carolina in, 233; southern secessions from, *p200*, 201; support in North Carolina mountains, 212. *See also* Civil War (U.S.)
Unionists, 200, 214; civil rights of, 215, 216
Union League, 230, 232
unions. *See* labor unions
United States: North Carolina in, 110, 111. *See also* world affairs
United States (ship), 116
United States Constitution. *See* Constitution of the United States

United States government. *See* national government

universities and colleges. *See* higher education; specific schools

University of North Carolina, 98, 251, 286, *p286*, 290

urban areas, 153, 283

urbanization, 187, 245–46

Utah Territory, 194

Valley Forge, 91

Vance, Robert B., 212

Vance, Zebulon B., 214–15, 239

Vanderbilt, G. W.: Biltmore House and, *p252*

Van Der Veer house (Bath), *p58*

Vaughn, T. L., 247

Venice: spice trade and, 21

Verrazano, Giovanni da, 23, *p23*, 30; report by, *f23*

Vespucci, Amerigo, 22

Vestry Act (1701), 52

veterans. *See* GI Bill of Rights; World War II

victory gardens, 276

Vietnam War, 290

villages, 10

Virginia, 37; boundaries with, 60, 82; Carolina colony and, 38; on federal government, 105; Granville District and, 61; immigrants from, 51; land disputes in, 60; naming of, 35; in Revolution, 95; tobacco in, 69–70

Virginia Company, 37

Virgin Mary: medallion of, *p31*

voting: for assembly, 47; for constitution of 1868, 232–33

voting rights, 143, 144; for African Americans, 291; after Civil War, 232, *f232*; disenfranchisement of African Americans and, 256

Voting Rights Act (1965), 291

Wachovia, 67

Wake Forest College, 251, 286

Walker, David, *f174*

Walker, Henderson, 52

Walker's Appeal, *f174*

Walton War, 192–93

Wanchese, 35, *f35*, 36

war hawks: in Congress, 117

Warner, Henry F., 275

War of 1812: cause of, 116–17; impact of, 119; North Carolina and, 117–19

War on Sugar Creek, 76

wars and warfare. *See* conflicts; specific wars

warships: in Civil War, 208

Washington, D.C.: slave trade banned in, 194

Washington, George, 109, 111, *p111*; in French and Indian War, 81; as president, 111; in Revolution, 91, 92, 94

Wasp (ship), 102, 117–18

water, 7; in Ice Age, 9

water pollution, 306

waterpower: in Piedmont, 8

wealthy: vs. poor, 254

weapons: cannon, *p221*; of explorers, *p25*; Gatling Gun, *f211*

weather, 6

weddings. *See* Marriage

west, *f106*, 106–7

West Africa: slaves from, 172

western counties: vs. east, 75–76

Western Hemisphere: Columbian Exchange and, 22

westward migration, 191–94

wheat, 170

Wheeler, John, 157

When Fanning First to Orange Came (Howell), 79

Whig Party, 136, 200; Constitution of 1835 and, 134; decline of, 142–43, 145; Mexican War and, 193; reforms under, 137–41

Whiskey Rebellion, 113–14

White, John, 36

whites, 228, 231, 233, 239

white supremacy, 255

Whitney, Eli, 170, *p170*

wildlife, 7

Wiley, Calvin H., 144, 157, *f157*, 159

Williamson, Hugh, 108, 109, 110, 111, 157

Wilmington, 58

Wilmington and Weldon Railroad, 138

Wilson, Woodrow, 258–59

winds, 6

Winston, 247

Winston-Salem, *f247*

Wolfe, Thomas, *f260*, 261

women: civil rights of, 291; Civil War and, 216–17; education of, 72; in government, 261, 298; in military, 270; patriotic, 86; political organizing by, *f86*; role of Elizabeth Dole and, *f308*; status of, 140; in World War II, 276, *p276*

Woodland Indians, 10–11, 13, 14

Woodland Period, 10

Wood Notes (Clarke), *f158*

wood-processing plant, *p280*

Woolworth's: sit-in at, *p291*, *p292*

work. *See* labor

workers, 71, *c171*

Works Progress Administration (WPA), 268

world affairs: in Civil War, 208; coming of World War II and, 269–70; demand for slave labor, *f176*; embargoes in, *f117*; global economy, *f302*; neutrality policy in World War I, 259. *See also* specific countries and wars

World War I, 258–61; North Carolina in, 259; postwar changes, 260

World War II, 269–73; coming of war, 269–70; economy after, 281–83; effects on North Carolina, 277; home front during, 276; North Carolina in, 270–72; popular culture after, 286–88; veterans of, 275

Worth, Daniel, 199

Worth, Jonathan, 226, *p226*, 235

Wrenn, Thomas, 248

Wright brothers, 254, *f254*

writing. *See* literature

Yadkin River, 8

Yamasee Indians, 54

yeomen farmers, 71, *p153*, 154, 171

Yorktown, battle at, 80, 95

Acknowledgments

For permission to reprint copyrighted material, grateful acknowledgment is made to the following sources:

Marye Ann Fox: From "Keeping North Carolina Competitive and Prosperous" by Dr. Marye Ann Fox from *The News and Observer*, May 14, 2001. Copyright © 2001 by Marye Ann Fox.

Louisiana State University Press: From *I Am One of You Forever* by Fred Chappell. Copyright © 1985 by Fred Chappell.

Eugene Pfaff: From "Greensboro Sit-ins" by Eugene Pfaff from *Southern Exposure®*, vol. IX, no. 1, Spring 1981. Copyright © 1981 by Eugene Pfaff.

Scribner, an imprint of Simon & Schuster Adult Publishing Group: From *Look Homeward, Angel* by Thomas Wolfe. Copyright © 1929 by Charles Scribner's Sons; copyright renewed © 1957 by Edward C. Ashwell, Administrator, C.T.A. and/or Fred W. Wolfe.

University of North Carolina Press: From *Rough Weather Makes Good Timber* by Patsy Moore Ginns. Copyright © 1977 by the University of North Carolina Press.

Viking Penguin, a division of Penguin Putnam Inc.: From *Once There Was a War* by John Steinbeck. Copyright © 1943, 1958 by John Steinbeck; copyright renewed © 1971 by Elaine Steinbeck, John Steinbeck IV, and Thomas Steinbeck.

Sources Cited:

From *Hakluyt's Voyages*, selected and edited by Richard David. Published by Houghton Mifflin Company, Boston, 1981.

Quote by Franklin McCain from *My Soul Is Rested: Movement Days in the Deep South Remembered* by Howell Raines. Published by G. P. Putnam's Sons, a division of Penguin Putnam Inc., New York, 1977.

Photography Credits:

iv (cr) ©The Art Archive/Album/Joseph Martin, (b) Stone, (inset) North Carolina Office of Archives and History; v (b) ©Bettmann/Corbis; vi (tr) ©Christie's Images/SuperStock, (bl) North Carolina Collection Photo Archive; vii (tr) North Carolina Division of Archives & History, (cl) ©North Wind Picture Archives, (br) Courtesy Royal Artillery Historical Trust/ ©DK Images; viii (cl) ©Underwood & Underwood/Corbis, (cr) Minnesota Historical Society, (br) ©Jane Faircloth/Transparencies Inc., (bottom inset) HRW Photo; xii ©Steven McBride/ Picturesque/PictureQuest; 1 Eugene and Claire Thaw Collection, Fenimore Art Museum, Cooperstown, NY, U.S.A./Photo ©John Bigelow Taylor/Art Resource, NY; 2 (t) ©Franz-MarcFrei/Corbis, (b) Sam Dudgeon/HRW Photo; 3 ©William A. Bake/ Picturesque/ PictureQuest; 4 ©David Muench/Corbis; 6 ©Randy Berger/Picturesque/ PictureQuest; 7 Courtesy Rowan Granite Quarry, Salisbury, N.C.; 8 ©C. D. Winters/Photo Researchers, Inc.; 9 ©British Library, London, UK/Bridgeman Art Library; 10 ©National Geographic Society; 11 ©Giraudon/Art Resource, NY; 12 ©Jim Hargan Photography; 13 ©Giraudon/ Art Resource, NY; 15 Head Effigy Vessel, 1300/1500. Founders Society Purchase with funds from the Mary G. and Robert H. Flint Foundation. Photograph © 1997 The Detroit Institute of Arts; 16 ©Giraudon/Art Resource, NY; 17 ©Werner Forman/Art Resource, NY; 18 Sam Dudgeon/HRW Photo; 19 ©The Mariners' Museum/Corbis; 20 (t) ©Giraudon/ Art Resource, NY, (b) ©PhotoDisc, Inc.; 21 ©Stapleton Collection, UK/Bridgeman Art Library; 22 ©Archivo Iconografico,S.A./Corbis; 23 ©New-York Historical Society, New York, USA/ Bridgeman Art Library; 24 ©Eileen Tweedy/The Art Archive; 25 ©The Art Archive/ Album/ Joseph Martin, 27 ©New York Public Library/Harper Collins Publishers/The Art Archive; 28 ©New York Public Library/Harper Collins Publishers/ The Art Archive, (frame) ©Comstock, Inc.; 29 ©Stock Montage; 30 ©Library of Congress, Washington D.C., USA/ Bridgeman Art Library; 31 Courtesy St. Catherine's Island Foundation, Inc./Photo supplied by the American Museum of Natural History, Division of Anthropology; 33 ©Victoria & Albert Museum, London/The Art Archive; 34 ©Michael Nicholson/Corbis; 35 Courtesy National Agriculture Library, USDA; 36 ©Bettmann/Corbis; 38 ©Stone; 39 ©Leeds Museums and Galleries (City Art Gallery) U.K./Bridgeman Art Library; 40 ©PhotoDisc, Inc.; 42 ©Reynolds Museum, Winston Salem, North Carolina, USA/ Bridgeman Art Library; 43 ©Christie's Images/ SuperStock; 44 (t) ©Scott Taylor Photography, Inc., (b) Sam Dudgeon/HRW Photo; 45 ©National Gallery of Art, Washington, D.C./ SuperStock; 46 North Carolina Office of Archives and History; 47 Courtesy University of North Carolina, Chapel Hill, Wilson Library, Carolina Collection.; 48 ©North Wind Picture Archives; 49 ©Getty Images; 50 ©North Wind Picture Archives; 51 ©Raymond Gehman/ Corbis; 52 ©Scott Taylor Photography, Inc.; 53 Used with permission from THROUGH INDIAN EYES, copyright © 1995 by The Reader's Digest Association, Inc., Pleasantville, NY, www.rd.com. Illustration by Craig Nelson.; 55 ©North Wind Picture Archives; 56 ©Bettmann/ Corbis; 58 © Lee Snider/Corbis; 59 ©Private Collection/Bridgeman Art Library; 60 Guildhall Art Gallery, Corporation of London, UK/ Bridgeman Art Library.; 61 ©UK/Bridgeman Art Library; 62 Sam Dudgeon/ HRW Photo; 63 ©Scott Taylor Photography,Inc.; 64 (t) ©Haworth Art Gallery, Accrington, Lancashire, UK/Bridgeman Art Library, (b) Sam Dudgeon/HRW Photo; 66 ©Allan Ramsay/ Bridgeman Art Library; 67 ©Austrian Archives/Corbis; 68 ©Corbis; 69 ©Getty Images; 70 ©Corbis; 71 ©SuperStock, Inc.; 72 ©David Muench/ Corbis; 74 Courtesy University of North Carolina, Chapel Hill, Wilson Library, Carolina Collection.; 75 ©North Wind Picture Archives; 76 ©Lee Snider/Corbis; 77 ©North Wind Picture Archives; 78 Sam Dudgeon/ HRW Photo; 80 (t) ©Réunion des Musées Nationaux/ Art Resource, NY, (b) Sam Dudgeon/ HRW Photo; 81 ©Stock Montage; 82 ©The Corcoran Gallery of Art/Corbis; 83 Courtesy University of North Carolina, Chapel Hill, Wilson Library, Carolina Collection.; 84 ©Bettmann/ Corbis; 85 ©Stock Montage; 86 Courtesy University of North Carolina, Chapel Hill, Wilson Library, Carolina Collection.; 87 North Carolina Office of Archives and History; 88 Courtesy Moore's Creek National Battlefield, Currie, NC; 89, 90 North Carolina Office of Archives and History; 91 ©Bettmann/ Corbis; 92 Courtesy University of North Carolina, Chapel Hill, Wilson Library, Carolina Collection.; 94 ©Brown Brothers; 95 ©North Wind Picture Archives; 96 North Carolina Office of Archives and History; 97 ©Ted Spiegel/ Corbis; 98 North Carolina Office of Archives and History; 100 Sam Dudgeon/HRW Photo; 101 North Carolina Office of Archives and History; 102 Sam Dudgeon/HRW Photo; 102 (t) ©North Wind Picture Archives, (b) Sam Dudgeon/HRW Photo; 103 Index Stock Imagery, Inc.; 104, 105 North Carolina Office of Archives and History; 106, 107 ©North Wind Picture Archives; 108 Courtesy University of North Carolina, Chapel Hill, Wilson Library, Carolina Collection.; 109 ©North Wind Picture Archives; 110 ©Bettmann/Corbis; 111, 112 North Carolina Office of Archives and History; 113 ©Bettmann/Corbis; 114 ©North Wind Picture Archives; 115 North Carolina Office of Archives and History; 116 ©Smithsonian American Art Museum, Washington,DC/Art Resource, NY; 117 ©North Wind Picture Archives; 118, 119 ©Stock Montage; 122, 123 ©Christie's Images/SuperStock; 124 (t) ©North Wind Picture Archives, (b) Sam Dudgeon/HRW Photo; 125 ©Keith Longiotti/Picturesque/ PictureQuest; 126 PRC Archive; 127 ©Arthur C. Smith III/Grant Heilman Photography, Inc; 128 Courtesy Maryland Historical Society, Baltimore, MD; 129 Courtesy Museum of American Political Life, University of West Hartford, West Hartford, CT; 130 Courtesy Woolaroc Museum, Bartlesville, OK; 131 Mint Museum of Art, Charlotte, North Carolina. Gift of Mr. and Mrs. David N. Spainhour in memory of Lottie Hart.; 132 ©Bettmann/Corbis; 133 Picturesque, Inc./Murray & Associates, Inc; 134 North Carolina Office of Archives and History; 135, 136 North Carolina Collection Photo Archive; 137 ©North Wind Picture Archives; 138 North Carolina Office of Archives and History; 140 ©Corbis; 141 ©North Wind Picture Archives; 142 North Carolina Collection Photo Archive; 143 North Carolina Office of Archives and History; 144 North Carolina Collection Photo Archive; 145 ©Jim Hargan Photography; 146 Sam Dudgeon/HRW Photo; 148 ©North Wind Picture Archives; 148 ©PhotoDisc, Inc.; 149 ©Gianni Dagli Orti/Corbis; 150, 151 ©North Wind Picture Archives; 152 North Carolina Office of Archives and History; 153 ©Peter Harholdt/Corbis; 154 ©North Wind Picture Archives; 155 Mint Museum of Art, Charlotte, North Carolina. Museum Purchase: Delhom Service League and Museum Purchase Fund.; 156 ©Corbis; 157, 158, 159 North Carolina Office of Archives and History; 160, 161 ©Corbis; 162, 163 North Carolina Office of Archives and History; 164 ©PhotoDisc, Inc.; 165 Mint Museum of Art, Charlotte, North Carolina. Gift of the Mint Museum Auxiliary and Daisy Wade Bridges from the Collection of Walter and Dorothy Auman.; 166 (t) ©Mary Evans Picture Library, (b) Sam Dudgeon/HRW Photo; 167 ©Stock Montage, Inc; 168 (t) ©Burlington/Alamance County Convention & Visitors Bureau, (b) North Carolina Office of Archives and History; 169 ©North Wind Picture Archives; 170 ©Bettmann/Corbis; 172 ©Mary Evans Picture Library; 173 ©American Christie's Images New York/ SuperStock, Inc.; 174 North Carolina Office of Archives and History; 175, 176 ©North Wind Picture Archives; 177 Courtesy University of North Carolina, Chapel Hill, Wilson Library, Carolina Collection.; 178 ©Getty Images; 179 North Carolina Office of Archives and History; 180 ©David Muench/Corbis; 181 ©North Wind Picture Archives; 182 Sam Dudgeon/HRW Photo; 184 ©Hulton Archive; 185 Library of Congress/Copy print courtesy Museum of the Confederacy.; 186 Courtesy University of North Carolina, Chapel Hill, Wilson Library, Carolina Collection, (b) ©PhotoDisc, Inc.; 187 ©Getty Images; 188 ©Jim Hargan Photography; 189 ©Smithsonian American Art Museum, Washington, DC /Art Resource, NY; 190, 191 ©North Wind Picture Archives; 192 ©N. Carter/North Wind Picture Archives; 193 ©Corbis; 194 ©Getty Images; 195 ©North Wind Picture Archives; 196 ©Getty Images; 197, 198, 199 ©Northwind Picture Archives; 200, 201 ©Getty Images; 202 ©PhotoDisc, Inc.; 204 The Museum of the Confederacy, Richmond, Virginia/ Katherine Weitzel Photography; 204 ©PhotoDisc, Inc.; 205 Bettmann/ Corbis; 206 Courtesy Valentine Museum and Historical Center, Richmond, Virginia.; 207 Courtesy University of North Carolina, Chapel Hill, Wilson Library, Carolina Collection.; 208 Francis G. Mayer/Corbis; 209 Courtesy University of North Carolina, Chapel Hill, Wilson Library, Carolina Collection.; 210 ©Corbis; 211 Courtesy Royal Artillery Historical Trust/Image ©DK Images, London; 212, 213 Bettmann/Corbis; 214 The Museum of the Confederacy, Richmond, Virginia; 215 The Museum of the Confederacy, Richmond, Virginia/Katherine Wetzel Photography; 216 The Museum of the Confederacy, Richmond, Virginia; 217 The Museum of the Confederacy, Richmond Virginia/Katherine Wetzel Photography; 218 Courtesy University of North Carolina, Chapel Hill, Wilson Library, Carolina Collection.; 219 ©SEF/Art Resource, NY; 220 Courtesy University of North Carolina, Chapel Hill, Wilson Library, Carolina Collection.; 221 ©Kevin Fleming/Corbis; 222 ©PhotoDisc, Inc.; 224 (t) ©Corbis, (b) Sam Dudgeon/HRW Photo; 225, 226 North Carolina Division of Archives & History; 227 ©New South Associates; 228 ©North Wind Picture Archives; 229 ©Bettmann/Corbis; 230 North Carolina Division of Archives & History; 231 Rare Book Collection, University of North Carolina at Chapel Hill; 232 ©Bettmann/Corbis; 233 North Carolina Division of Archives & History; 235 ©Corbis; 236 ©Mary Evans Picture Library; 237, 238 North Carolina Division of Archives & History; 239 ©Corbis; 240 Sam Dudgeon/HRW Photo; 242 ©Joseph Sohm; ChromoSohm Inc./ Corbis; 243 ©Hulton Archive; 244 (t) ©Private Collection/Bridgeman Art Library, (b) Sam Dudgeon/HRW Photo; 245 ©Peter Finger/Corbis; 247 Courtesy Reynolda House, Museum of American Art, Winston-Salem, NC; 248 Courtesy The High Point Museum, High Point, North Carolina; 249 ©Underwood & Underwood/Corbis; 250 Courtesy North Carolina Mutual Life Insurance Company, Durham, NC; 251 ©Mark E. Gibson/Corbis; 252 ©David Muench/Corbis; 253, 254 ©Bettmann/Corbis; 255 North Carolina Collection Photographic Archives; 256 ©Underwood & Underwood/Corbis; 257 ©Lewis W. Hine/ Corbis; 258 ©Bettmann/Corbis; 259 ©Getty Images; 260 ©Bettmann/Corbis; 261 ©North Carolina Collection Photographic Archives; 262 Sam Dudgeon/HRW Photo; 264 (t) ©Russell Lee/Corbis, (b) Sam Dudgeon/HRW Photo; 265 Minnesota Historical Society; 266 North Carolina Office of Archives and History; 267 ©C.R. Hursh/Corbis; 268 ©Jim Hargan Photography; 269 ©Bettmann/ Corbis; 270 North Carolina Office of Archives and History; 272 ©Corbis; 273 North Carolina Office of Archives and History; 274 Franklin D. Roosevelt Library; 275 U.S. Naval Historical Center Photograph; 276 ©Bettmann/Corbis; 277 Margaret Bourke-White/ TimePix; 278 Sam Dudgeon/HRW Photo; 279 ©National Archives/PRC Archive; 280 (t) ©Getty Images, (b) Sam Dudgeon/ HRW Photo; 281 ©Greg Plachta/ Picturesque; 282 ©Jane Faircloth/Transparencies Inc.; 283 AP/Wide World Photo; 284 North Carolina Office of Archives and History; 286 ©SuperStock, Inc.; 287 ©Bob Cavin/ University of North Carolina Greensboro Publications; 288, 289 ©Bettmann/Corbis; 290 The News & Record/Dave Nicholson, Greensboro, NC; 291 ©Bettmann/Corbis; 292 The News & Record/©John "Jack" Moebes, Greensboro, NC; 293 ©Donna Jernigan/ Transparencies Inc.; 294 Sam Dudgeon/HRW Photo; 295 ©AP/Wide World Photo; 296 (t) ©Jane Faircloth/Transparencies Inc., (b) ©PhotoDisc, Inc.; 297 ©Charles Gupton/Stock, Boston Inc./PictureQuest; 298 ©Bettmann/Corbis; 299 ©Ron Chapple/ Getty Images; 301 ©Owen Franken/Corbis; 302 ©Richard A. Cooke/Corbis; 304 ©Jane Faircloth/ Transparencies Inc.; 305 ©Owen Franken/Corbis; 306 ©Getty Images; 307 ©Jim Hargan Photography; 308 ©Mario Tama, AFP/Corbis; 309 ©Charles Gupton/Stock, Boston Inc./PictureQuest; 310 ©PhotoDisc, Inc.; 312 (tl) ©Werner Forman/Art Resource, NY, (tr, b) ©Jim Hargan Photography, (c) ©Bettmann/ Corbis; 313 (t, c) ©Jim Hargan Photography, (bl) ©Bettmann/Corbis, (br) ©Jeffry Myers/ Index Stock Imagery/PictureQuest; 314 (State Flag, State Seal) State Library of North Carolina,(cl) ©Adam Jones/Photo Researchers, Inc., (strawberry) Comstock, Inc., (blueberries) ©Rod Planck/ Photo Researchers, Inc, (bl) ©Biophoto Associates/Photo Researchers, Inc., (b) ©Steve Maslowski/ Photo Researchers, Inc.

Feature Border:

Young People in History: Pages 1, 43, 123, 185, 243, (cap) Image copyright ©2003 PhotoDisc, Inc., (cameo, umbrella) Sam Dudgeon/HRW Photo

Section Openers: Dogwood flowers for all section opener pages, John White/ The Neis Group.